Becoming an Addictions Counselor
A Comprehensive Text
Third Edition

Peter L. Myers, PhD
Professor and Director of Addiction (Retd.)
Counselor Training Program
Essex County College

Norman R. Salt, MA, CPS
Former Director of Training
Division of Addiction Services
New Jersey Department of Health

JONES & BARTLETT
LEARNING

World Headquarters
Jones & Bartlett Learning
5 Wall Street
Burlington, MA 01803
978-443-5000
info@jblearning.com
www.jblearning.com

Jones & Bartlett Learning books and products are available through most bookstores and online booksellers. To contact Jones & Bartlett Learning directly, call 800-832-0034, fax 978-443-8000, or visit our website, www.jblearning.com.

Substantial discounts on bulk quantities of Jones & Bartlett Learning publications are available to corporations, professional associations, and other qualified organizations. For details and specific discount information, contact the special sales department at Jones & Bartlett Learning via the above contact information or send an email to specialsales@jblearning.com.

Production Credits
Publisher: Cathleen Sether
Executive Editor: Shoshanna Goldberg
Editorial Assistant: Sean Coombs
Production Editor: Jessica Steele Newfell
Marketing Manager: Jody Yeskey
VP, Manufacturing and Inventory Control: Therese Connell
Composition: Cenveo Publisher Services
Cover Design: Kristin E. Parker
Cover Images: (top) © Bellemedia/Dreamstime.com; (bottom) © Kirsty Pargeter/ShutterStock, Inc.
Printing and Binding: Malloy, Inc.
Cover Printing: Malloy, Inc.

To order this product, use ISBN: 978-1-4496-7300-0

Library of Congress Cataloging-in-Publication Data
Myers, Peter L.
  Becoming an addictions counselor : a comprehensive text / authors, Peter L. Myers and Norman R. Salt.—3rd ed.
     p. ; cm.
  Includes bibliographical references and index.
  ISBN 978-1-4496-3213-7 (pbk. : alk. paper)
  I. Salt, Norman R. II. Title.
  [DNLM: 1. Counseling—methods. 2. Substance-Related Disorders—therapy. WM 270]

  362.29'186—dc23

                                                                                    2012003191

6048
Printed in the United States of America
16 15 14 13 12   10 9 8 7 6 5 4 3 2 1

Contents

CHAPTER 2
Individual Counseling Skills 40

CHAPTER 6
Family   165

CHAPTER 7
Case Management: From Screening to Discharge   198

Preface

Becoming an Addictions Counselor: A Comprehensive Text, Third Edition, is designed for undergraduate and master level courses in addictions, counseling, social work, and preparation for entry into or career enhancement in the addictions professions. Our training philosophy and goals are expressed throughout the chapters of this text.

We encourage critical thinking about assumptions underlying the models counselors habitually employ and the attitudes and feelings that counselors bring to the counseling setting (Myers 2002). We need to continually rethink why we do what we do and what the benefit is to the client. We must be open to changing our clinical practice based on new research and new paradigms about substance abuse and behavioral change (DiClemente 2006; Miller and Carroll 2006; Tucker, Donovan, and Marlatt 1999; Yalisove and Korkow 2013).

We encourage experiential understanding through exercises and participation. To this end, structured activities offer opportunities to practice individual and group counseling skills, ponder the ethical dilemmas that arise in treatment, and practice case management and treatment planning.

Training must generate ethical, competent counselors who respond to clients' unique needs with a menu of options rather than impose "cookie-cutter" routines. We encourage counselors to work with clients at whatever stage of recovery that they are, to understand that ambivalence about change is normal before and after achieving sobriety, to understand that there are many pathways to recovery, and to avoid stigmatizing, judgmental language.

Counselors must understand the broader context within which addictive behaviors and treatment occur, the historical and systems context of treatment, and the family, community, and cultural systems within which clients are embedded (Mignon et al. 2009) and have a familiarity with the latest psychopharmacological knowledge, a subject not within the scope of this text.

We support a strengths perspective that focuses on the client's internal resources and motivations for change. Traditional practice has viewed substance abusers as caught in the thrall of an inevitably progressive disease leading to denial that can only be breached by intense confrontation and/or a painful "hitting bottom." This model has been giving way to a view of motivation as an ambivalent and dynamic state, with substance abuse as a behavior that can be modified by working with the client at any stage of readiness for change. Rather than concentrating on why clients can't change (a stigmatized, deficit model), we're looking at how they can change (Miller and Rollnick 2002). An empowering, strengths perspective is standard in social work training but newer in addictions. The new paradigm of addictions counseling is to work collaboratively to facilitate the movement of clients through natural stages of change as seen in the many addicts who have "quit" on their own (Prochaska et al. 1994).

We encourage students, counselors, and educators to be active in professional networks such as INCASE (INCASE 2012) and NAADAC (NAADAC 2012) and in facilitating a community-based treatment and recovery advocacy movement.

The Tipping Point in the Second Decade of the Century

The years 2010–2012 have been a "tipping point" in crystallizing organizational efforts to broaden the scope of recovery facilitation, standardize professional training, and "mainstream" recovery facilitation.

For decades, addictions treatment was a relatively short episode, disconnected from long-term recovery processes and from mainstream medicine and psychiatry. Top addictions researcher Dr. Thomas McClellan referred to this as the "segregation" of addictions treatment (The Partnership 2011).

In recognition of the crucial nature of providing recovery support after a short, discrete, treatment episode:

1. In 2010, Treatment Professionals in Alumni Development was founded, bringing together those who specialize in working with groups of treatment "graduates" to maintain long-term recovery support (Obernauer 2011).
2. In 2011, a National Association of Recovery Residences (sober living facilities) was founded (Fischer 2001; NARR 2011) to work to develop standards for what has been a chaotic mix of post-treatment sober living facilities.
3. Credentialing for peer-to-peer recovery mentors/coaches continued to expand under the aegis of state addiction credentialing bodies.

In recognition that professional training of the addictions workforce needs standards, such as are found in other helping professions, in 2010–2011 an independent National Addiction Studies Accreditation Commission (NASAC 2012) was developed to provide accreditation of higher education addictions curricula.

In an effort to integrate addictions treatment into the medical/psychiatric mainstream:

1. The first nationally accredited addiction medicine residency programs started on July 1, 2011, under the American Board of Addiction Medicine (ABAM) Foundation, in anticipation of increased demand for addiction treatment under the new Patient Protection and Affordable Care Act. In 2011, the journal *Substance Abuse* published a special issue (Haber 2011) on international perspectives in postgraduate medical training in addiction medicine.
2. The SBIRT model (Screening, Brief Intervention, and Referral to Treatment) was increasingly implemented worldwide via networks of primary care physicians.
3. A new definition of recovery encompassing mental health and addictive disorders was released in May 2011 by the U.S. Substance Abuse and Mental Health Services Administration (SAMHSA 2011).

Although Treatment Pays Us Back, It Is Still Not Paid For

Research proves over and over that even modest cost outlays to increase treatment services have significant cost benefits to society in the reduction of crime, incarceration costs, and medical treatment (Belenko et al. 2005; Harwood et al. 2002). Yet reimbursement for addictions treatment is not on par for other medical care or even mental health care, and there is a huge gap between demand and availability of treatment. The infrastructure of addiction services, as evidenced by program closings and reimbursement for treatment, has declined in the past dozen years, making it harder to support appropriate levels of care, new technologies, family treatment, or the new long-term recovery management paradigm (McLellan et al. 2003).

A Note on "Manualization"

Several evidenced-based, empirically supported treatments are now presented in manual form with recipes, formats, and protocols for parceling out interventions. Their adoption and reception across the helping professions is growing but remains uneven (Fals-Stuart and Logsdon 2004; Gotham 2004; Simons et al. 2005). Several colleges and universities have used this text along with a cognitive-behavioral therapy manual (Carroll 1998) or a motivational enhancement therapy manual (CSAT 1999) or both. As we use these manuals, we should note that the efficacy of these treatments may or may not translate into settings and populations other than those identical to where manual research took place. We must also take care to not blunt the focus on the healing, helping relationship in the here-and-now, or fall into a "cookbook" approach without creativity, flexibility, individualized treatment, and spontaneity.

New to the *Third Edition*

- Two new chapters: "Facilitating Motivation for Recovery" presents the basic tools of Motivational Interviewing, and "Recovery" presents the Recovery Oriented Systems of Care and works with clients on all dimensions of recovery
- Information on new medications for pharmacotherapy of addictions

- More comprehensive treatment of case management, including a new section on client documentation, description of new diagnostic format for addictions in the DSM5, and use of language in writing treatment planning objectives
- Information on new sobriety-based recovery support groups
- Online teaching and learning resources available at **go.jblearning.com/myers3e**

Acknowledgments

Many members of the International Coalition for Addiction Studies Education (www.incase-edu.net) provided valuable feedback on how we should best prepare the *Third Edition* of this text. The authors wish to thank the staff at Jones & Bartlett Learning for their guidance: Shoshanna Goldberg, Executive Editor; Sean Coombs, Editorial Assistant; Jessica Newfell, Production Editor; Jody Yeskey, Marketing Manager; and Joan Flaherty, who edited the *First Edition*.

Peter Myers wishes to acknowledge the wonderful human services trainees and colleagues at Essex County College, and The New York City College of Technology, friends and colleagues in INCASE and NAADAC; the Essex County treatment consortium; Susan B. Myers, LCSW, for her loving support and clinical wisdom; and the newest member of our family, Zane Samuel Rizvi.

Norman Salt wishes to thank his wife, Margie, for her support and patience, and his daughters, Jennifer and Amanda, for their help and assistance. He also would like to express his love for his grandchildren, Kelsey and Colin, a hope and inspiration for the next generation; the late Ed Crawford, who taught him about the power and simple wisdom of self-help groups; Riley Regan, the retired director of the New Jersey Governor's Council on Alcohol and Drug Abuse; early mentors Vernon Johnson and Father Martin; and his many students.

The authors also would like to thank the following reviewers for their feedback:

Penny P. Willmering, PhD, CRC, LPC
Associate Professor Rehab Science
Arkansas Tech University

Frank Norton, PhD, ABPP
Assistant Professor
Bowie State University

References

Belenko, S., N. Patapis, and M. T. French. 2005. *Economic Benefits of Drug Treatment: A Critical Review of the Evidence for Policy Makers.* National Rural Alcohol and Drug Abuse Network. Available at http://www.jointogether.org/resources/the-economic-benefits-of-drug.html

Carroll, K. M. 1998. *A Cognitive-Behavioral Approach: Treating Cocaine Addiction. Manual 1: Therapy Manuals for Drug Addiction.* Rockville, MD: National Institute on Drug Abuse.

CSAT (Center for Substance Abuse Treatment). 1999. *Enhancing Motivation for Change in Substance Abuse Treatment.* Treatment Improvement Protocol (TIP) Series 35. Rockville, MD: Substance Abuse and Mental Health Services Administration, Center for Substance Abuse Treatment, DHHS Publication No. (SMA) 05-4081.

DiClemente, C. C. 2006. *Addiction and Change.* New York: The Guilford Press.

Fals-Stuart, W., and T. Logsdon. 2004. Diffusion of an empirically supported treatment for substance abusers: An organizational autopsy of technology transfer success and failure. *Clinical Psychology: Science and Practice, 11*, 2: 177–182.

Fischer, B. 2011. NARR and the evolution of the "halfway house" *Addiction Professional blog 6/27/11* Available at http://www.addictionpro.com/ME2/dirmod.asp?sid=440B847037BC4AFA8B377E381E9C548D&nm=&type=Blog&mod=BlogTopics&mid=67D6564029914AD3B204AD35D8F5F780&tier=7&id=E9B28D9BEFF340D684E4E1BB25ED7B28

Gotham, H. J. 2004. Diffusion of mental health and substance abuse treatments: Development, dissemination, and implementation. *Clinical Psychology: Science and Practice, 11*, 2: 160–176.

Haber, P. S. 2011. Special issue: International perspectives in postgraduate medical training in addiction medicine. *Substance Abuse 32*, 2.

Harwood, H. J., D. Malhotra, C. Villarivera, C. Liu, U. Chong, and J. Galani. 2002. *Cost Effectiveness and Cost Benefit Analysis of Substance Abuse Treatment: A Literature Review.* Rockville, MD: Substance Abuse and Mental Health Services Administration. Center for Substance Abuse Treatment. Available at http://www.healthandwelfare.idaho.gov/Portals/_Rainbow/Documents%5Catr/CSAT_HarwoodCostLitReview2002.pdf

INCASE. 2012. International Coalition for Addiction Studies Education. Available at www.incase-edu.net

McLellan, A. T., D. Carise, and H. D. Kleber. 2003. Can the national addiction treatment infrastructure support the public's demand for quality care? *Journal of Substance Abuse Treatment,* 25: 117–121.

McClellan, T. 2011. Addiction and Segregation. Available at http://www.drugfree.org/join-together/addiction/dr-tom-mclellan-addiction-and-segregation?utm_source=feedburner&utm_campaign=Feed%3A+AttcNetworkNews+%28ATTC+Network+News%29&utm_medium=feed

Mignon, S. L., M. M. Faiia, P. L. Myers, and E. Rubington. 2009. *Substance Use and Abuse: Exploring Alcohol and Drug Issues.* Boulder, CO: Lynne Rienner Publishers.

Miller, W. R., and Carroll, K. M., eds. 2006. *Rethinking Substance Abuse.* New York: The Guilford Press.

Miller, W. R., and S. Rollnick. 2002. *Motivational Interviewing: Preparing People for Change,* 2nd ed. New York: Guilford Press.

Myers, P. L. 2002. "Beware the man of one book": Processing ideology in addictions education. *Journal of Teaching in the Addictions, 1,* 1:69–90.

NAADAC. 2012. Association of Addiction Professionals. Available at www.naadac.org

NARR. 2011. National Association of Recovery Residences. Available at http://www.narronline.com/NARR_formation_website/Welcome.html

NASAC. 2012. National Addiction Studies Accreditation Commission. Available at http://www.nasacaccreditation.com

Obernauer, L. 2011 Alumni Professionals Meet Addictions Professional. 6/16/2011. Available at http://www.addictionpro.com/ME2/dirmod.asp?sid=440B847037BC4AFA8B377E381E9C548D&nm=&type=Blog&mod=BlogTopics&mid=67D6564029914AD3B204AD35D8F5F780&tier=7&id=A0B4B3B10CCE4D2E961C1460A119758D

Prochaska, J. O., J. C. Norcross, and C. C. DiClemente. 1994. *Changing for Good.* New York: William Morrow.

SAMHSA. 2011. Recovery defined: A unified working definition and set of principles. Available at http://blog.samhsa.gov/2011/05/20/recovery-defined-a-unified-working-definition-and-set-of-principles

Simons, L., R. Jacobucci, and H. Houston. 2005. Undergraduate and graduate students' attitudes towards addiction treatment manuals. *Journal of Teaching in the Addictions* 4, 2: 23–43.

Tucker, J. A., D. M. Donovan, and G. A. Marlatt, eds. 1999. *Changing Addictive Behaviors: Bridging Clinical and Public Health Strategies.* New York: Guilford Press.

Yalisove, D. L., and J. Korkow. 2013. *Introduction to Alcohol and Drug Research: Implications for Treatment, Prevention, and Policy.* Boston, MA: Allyn & Bacon.

Introduction
to Addictions
Treatment

Objectives

By the end of this chapter, students will be able to:

1. Describe the eight practice dimensions of addiction counselors according to the Center for Substance Abuse Treatment.
2. Explain the importance of the therapeutic relationship.
3. Describe the levels of care as outlined by the American Society of Addiction Medicine (ASAM).
4. Differentiate services among detoxification, inpatient, outpatient, and intensive outpatient services.
5. Describe the various approved medications used in pharmaco-therapy of addictions.

6. Describe the major influences and traditions in the addictions field including the Self-Help movement, the Minnesota Model of Treatment, and the therapeutic community model.

Basic Characteristics

Addictions treatment is an array of professional interventions, techniques, and organized services designed to initiate, facilitate, and support recovery from chemical dependency or other behaviors considered to be addictions. This section summarizes features of contemporary addictions treatment and distinguishes it from other forms of counseling and therapy.

The Focus

When an actively addicted individual enters counseling and treatment, the addiction is usually treated first. Personal growth is unlikely when an individual is chronically intoxicated or when life revolves around the acquisition and use of drugs. It is difficult to facilitate a helping process with an actively addicted individual. The saying in the treatment field is, "You're just talking to a chemical." Addiction is not treated as a symptom of other problems but as a primary condition in its own right. However, the treatment of addiction with coexisting psychiatric disorders dictates special considerations. An exception to "treat the addiction first" may occur where an individual is actively psychotic and needs to be stabilized to the point that they can participate in counseling. Although we say that the focus is to treat active addictions first, we do not mean that the client must accept the label of "addict" first! We may engage clients on any of a variety of problem issues and concerns, with the strategy of developing a discrepancy between their problematic chemical use and their life aspirations.

The Client

People referred to addictions treatment programs vary tremendously on a spectrum of addictions severity, degree to which they have remained functional, and behavior patterns typical of people using depressants, stimulants, hallucinogens, or a combination of them (*polyabuse*). Clients with severe chemical addictions are often emerging from a chemical anesthesia and are typically more mentally confused and psychosocially and medically deteriorated than nonaddicted clients. They may suffer from every sort of medical and social problem, and may resist or disavow the need for help. Some are approaching a life-threatening situation. Typically, this client needs more guidance, care, and a wider scope of services than other clients, for example, an individual seeking help for a mild depression or adjustment problem.

Practice Dimensions

Addictions treatment includes, but must go far beyond, what many people call counseling. A sufficiently ecumenical definition of *counseling* and *psychotherapy* is a supportive and empathic professional relationship that provides a framework for the exploration of emotions, behaviors, and thinking patterns, and the facilitation of healthy changes. Addictions treatment certainly provides this service and, in fact, it provides individual, group, and family counseling. However, as indicated by the clinical assessment of a client, it may involve several levels of a multiphasic treatment system, which requires professional counselors who have detailed knowledge, skills, and attitudes in a wide variety of areas. The National Steering Committee on Addiction Counseling Standards, which represents the major accreditation, counselor, and educational organizations in the addictions field, chose as its consensus document *Addiction Counseling Competencies: The Knowledge, Skills, and Attitudes of Professional Practice.* This document, authored by the Addiction Technology Transfer Center National Curriculum Committee in 1998 and updated in 2006 (CSAT 2006), details eight practice dimensions of addiction counseling, which include 100 discrete competencies. The practice dimensions are:

1. *Clinical evaluation*, which includes screening and assessment, knowledge of diagnostic criteria, assessment instruments, and treatment options
2. *Treatment planning*, in collaboration with the client, based on assessment, and including long range goals that are broken down into shorter, concrete measurable objectives
3. *Referral*, based on knowledge of resources
4. *Service coordination*, which includes implementing the treatment plan, consulting other professionals, case management, and continuing assessment and treatment
5. *Counseling* individuals and groups, including families, couples, and significant others
6. *Education* of client, family, and community
7. *Documentation*, including management of records and preparation of reports, plans, and discharge summaries
8. *Professional and ethical* responsibilities, including confidentiality of personal health records.

Benchmarks for competency in the Practice Dimensions are described in the Performance Assessment Rubrics (Gallon and Porter 2011). They describe levels of competence including awareness, understanding, applied knowledge, and mastery that may be attained by counselors and supervisors. A link to the complete rubric of competency benchmarks is provided in the bibliography. Phelps and colleagues (2011) have prepared a practical guide to the Technical Assistance Publication (TAP) 21 Practice Dimensions.

In addition to the Practice Dimensions, a competent addictions counselor must have a wide knowledge base, which the addictions consensus document (CSAT 2006) calls Transdisciplinary Foundations. These include familiarity with the categories, range and effect of legal and illegal psychoactive chemicals, risk and resiliency factors in the development of substance use disorders, models and theories of addiction and treatment, cultural competency in working with a wide variety of client populations, standards of conduct in helping relationships, diagnostic criteria, insurance and health maintenance options, and the roles of family, social network, and community in recovery.

The Counseling Relationship

The supportive, empathic counseling relationship is the glue that binds the client and counselor through assorted treatment stages, facilities, anxieties, and growing pains. The importance of the collaborative, therapeutic alliance cuts across and indeed supersedes the particular therapeutic approach or model employed. The necessity of mastering the multiplicity of administrative, or "housekeeping," tasks (in the broadest sense, case-management tasks) might seem to shift the focus away from the counseling relationship and define the addictions counselor as little more than a caseworker. But intake, assessment, and treatment planning are opportunities to engage clients and establish a collaborative relationship.

The counseling relationship in addictions treatment is fraught with emotional thunder and lightning. Emotional unresolved history ("baggage") that a client brings to counseling and the emotional response of the counselor are important in all counseling efforts. The client may approach the counselor with any of a number of newly tapped dependency needs, rage and resentment, grief and loss, evasive maneuvers, and attempts to manipulate or test the relationship. The counselor must develop skills to stay aware of his or her strong reactions to a client's behaviors and maintain a professional and helpful role.

Treatment of addicts in general is typically more directive, structured, and managed than counseling and mental-health services for nonaddicted and nonpsychotic individuals. For example, the use of a formal treatment plan is not common in counseling for adjustment, self-esteem, and relationship issues. Much addictions treatment is interfaced with criminal-justice and social-service institutions that mandate treatment. Even where counseling is initiated involuntarily, this does not mean that the counselor tells the client "what to do." It operates on the same basic principle of empathetic, collaborative planning to facilitate recovery, focusing on the client's short-term recovery and abstinence from addictive substances and trying to influence the client toward healthy behaviors and decisions. It uses simple, direct, and concrete methods and treatment concepts, which show some results in a relatively short span of time. Counseling modalities that are complementary to this approach tend to be chosen in addictions treatment.

Counseling methods for chemically dependent people are far from a standardized system. There is a strong influence of self-help groups from which formal addictions treatment emerged. As the field has become more professionalized, counselors and trainers have gravitated toward integrated, eclectic, and transtheoretical counseling models. Addictions counseling does not claim or attempt to be a comprehensive psychotherapy, yet the broad goals of psychotherapy complement those of addictions treatment. To achieve stable sobriety and avoid relapse, with professional help, the client must identify, communicate, accept, and manage emotions and learn nonchemical and assertive coping strategies, communications and interpersonal skills, self-efficacy, and responsibility. The client must unlearn catastrophizing and negative self-statements and other unhealthy thinking patterns. These dimensions of recovery are covered in this text.

Addiction specialists recognize that treatment is carried out in stages. In early treatment, deep-seated, painful, and threatening issues should not be forcibly introduced by the counselor, except as necessary to maintain the client's sobriety. Gradually, the client internalizes mechanisms to govern his or her recovery. Self-statements by clients progress from "I can't drink" to "I won't drink" and hopefully to "I don't have to drink" (Zimberg 1987, pp. 17–19). Addictions treatment most approaches or converges with generic counseling and psychotherapy in the last stage. Counselors must pay close attention to the special treatment needs of each stage. For example, when treatment includes a phase of inpatient or intensive outpatient rehabilitation, there may be a tendency to consider later outpatient counseling sessions as less critical. This would be a dangerous mistake. "Factors that emerge during aftercare, such as changes in motivation, reactions to treatment, patient–therapist interaction variables, environmental cues, may be more important determinants of continued participation than factors present at the beginning of aftercare, with the possible exception of alcohol and drug use during intensive outpatient treatment" (McCay et al. 1998, p. 160). Treatment is a fairly short episode in a lengthy process of recovery, and more and more emphasis is now devoted to long-term, post-treatment recovery support. A formal aftercare phase is only the start of building a stable recovery, as care and support, even at a reduced level, may be needed for years.

Effectiveness of Treatment

The study of the effectiveness of counseling and psychotherapy is notoriously complex and controversial. There is a plethora of competing models of the human personality, its health and dysfunction, and methods of change. Each of these could be applied to hundreds of possible diagnoses and to variable populations according to gender, ethnicity, and so on. As Garfield and Bergin (1994, p. 6) pointed out, to assess the relative value of each approach in each situation would require millions of statistical comparisons. In the addictions field, some of the difficulties in evaluating the effectiveness of treatment outcome include:

- Variety in the patient mix that influences retention, completion, and success.
- Variation in definitions of success, for example, graduation, abstinence, stabilization of social functioning, moderation of use, and reduction in harmful effects. As Miller et al. (2001, p. 211) state, "It is unclear how much imperfection constitutes a 'relapse' and how much deviation from perfect abstinence defines a treatment failure."
- Programs that winnow out all but the most motivated, resulting in "graduates" who tend to stay abstinent.
- Outcome studies or analyses of outcome studies conducted by individuals strongly associated with one point of view, whose methods tend to confirm their biases.
- Treatment-effectiveness studies conduct follow-ups of clients that may skew results due to client minimization of use when staff are used in telephone checks and due to the fact that severe relapse can result in difficulty to contact for follow up.

Most major addictions treatment modalities are associated with a significant drop in use of alcohol and other drugs (SAMHSA 1994) and in the associated health, social, and legal ramifications and costs. A major meta-analysis conducted by Miller et al. (2001) found that one-fourth of persons exposed to treatment remained totally abstinent in the year following treatment, and one-tenth drank moderately. However, the remaining clients reduced alcohol consumption by 87% on average, abstained three out of four days, and suffered 60% fewer alcohol-related health problems. If our measure of success is total abstinence, obviously treatment has pretty poor results, but from the perspectives of public health and harm reduction, it's a smashing success! Comprehensive studies by Belenko et al. (2005) and Harwood et al. (2002) provide current evidence of the tremendous cost-benefits of addictions treatment to society.

The authors discourage trying to calculate exact cost-benefits, such as the famous "one dollar spent on treatment is paid back seven times"

(Swan 1995), as it varies wildly by situation, client type, drug used, and so forth (Springer et al. 2003).

Getting into Treatment

Initiation of addictions treatment involves some mix of desperation, compulsion, and natural recovery processes.

Desperation

Addiction creates a great deal of pain, yet hopeless and helpless individuals tolerate a great deal of pain on a daily basis. In early Alcoholics Anonymous (AA) groups, it was believed that the addict had to sink lower and lower until he or she "hit bottom," that is, until the alcoholic felt misery, illness, and pain that for the moment overshadowed the pleasures or perceived benefits of an addictive lifestyle. Early members of AA epitomized the desperate "low-bottom alcoholic" as someone who was one step from "insanity or death." Later it became clear that earlier intervention was possible and preferable because it minimized medical and social damages and costs.

Addictions professionals increase an addict's desperation when they encourage relatives and peers to end their attempts to help the addict. By protecting and buffering the addict from the painful consequences of his or her behavior, these helpers enable the addiction to continue and progress. Examples of enabling include making excuses for the addict, paying debts and bills, posting bail, and dragging the addict into bed. Ending enabling is a key principle in helping to initiate recovery.

Compulsory Treatment

The need to use drugs and alcohol often leads to consequences that force clients into programs that they did not or would not choose on their own. In the vast majority of cases, initiation of treatment involves an element of involuntary or semivoluntary referral. Referral pathways may be:

- Through the courts, as alternatives to sentencing or incarceration, or as part of a child-protective action
- From an employer, through an assessment and referral program called an Employee Assistance Program (EAP)
- From an alcohol and drug counselor at an educational institution with a Student Assistance Program
- From family and friends, through an organized intervention, or from child welfare systems and welfare-to-work initiatives

This compulsory element in initiating treatment is far more common in addictions counseling than in mental-health services, and has grown even more common in recent years, with the increased clientele from criminal justice systems. This can be viewed as a disadvantage because this client does not want to be in treatment and will resist and resent attempts to help. On the other hand, the client cannot disappear easily when pressure to change builds. Involuntary, or mandated, presence and other stipulations (e.g., progress reports to a child welfare agency or to an employer) are elements of "therapeutic leverage." Some in AA call it "raising the bottom." That is, it creates initial incentive or pressure for the addict to accept treatment before he or she sinks to a more desperate level, from which there may be no recovery. Once in a drug-free environment, addicts are often engaged in treatment and may make profound changes in their lives. One of the authors worked in a therapeutic community setting where all of his supervisors were originally residents sent as an alternative to sentencing in a court-operated program.

Natural Recovery Motives

Persons with substance use problems and disorders yearn for a normal and healthy life, even if these motives are not apparent, or if they are masked by a hopeless, helpless mindset. The power to recover may lie dormant but awaits awakening in treatment. Many addicts do become abstinent or return to moderate use of psychoactive substances without treatment or after treatment has not appeared to achieve recovery. "Natural recovery" motives, processes, and dimensions are detailed elsewhere in this text.

The desire to attain normalcy is an important component of getting addicts into treatment, and it is our task to bring out, facilitate, and provide hope for such yearnings, to demonstrate that "recovery works," and to outline a roadmap that can lead to recovery.

It is normal and natural for persons to be deeply ambivalent about substance use, the benefits of continuing versus change. This ambivalence exists before and after initiating efforts for recovery. Issues of ambivalence, costs and benefits associated with change, and how to facilitate motivation for change are involved. The mixture of desperation, compulsion, and yearnings for recovery may outweigh the perceived benefits of continued use and the fear of change just long enough to create a window of opportunity to initiate treatment. This window may close if a client cannot be admitted quickly into a treatment program.

No one personality type fits the addict. A wide variety of etiological and risk factors predispose, encourage, and drive chemical abuse and its progression into addiction (Doweiko 2011). These risk factors exist on many system levels: genetic/neurological, personality and psychosocial development, peer and family influence, community, societal and cultural. Each client suffers from a unique mix of these factors; they may emerge from a hard-drinking family, college fraternity, or community; they may inherit vulnerability for depression or hyperactivity and insomnia; or childhood or adolescent trauma may play a part. Counselors need education in what drives substance abuse that goes beyond the scope of this volume. It is usually covered in a basic course on substance use and abuse that readers in a college and university program will have taken.

Uniqueness of the Field

Most individuals treated for chemical dependency do not simply "go to a counselor." In the majority of cases, they participate in an organized treatment program. Programs and self-help fellowships provide a great deal of social support, an alternative to the culture of abuse, and the therapeutic effects of the milieu. Most treatment occurs in group settings, even aside from client participation in twelve-step programs such as Alcoholics Anonymous and Narcotics Anonymous.

There is a tremendous diversity in type, intensity, and length of stay in treatment. Some addicts qualify for admission to inpatient therapeutic communities funded to treat indigent clients, with a length of stay of 18 months. Others participate in insurance plans that reimburse for only a five-day detoxification. Schuckit (1994, p. 3) remarked, "We function in a complex world where health-care providers must share scarce resources while reaching out to a pool of impaired individuals who, at least theoretically, have many more needs than we can possibly meet."

Treatment programs are part of or influenced by broader regulatory, economic, and political systems at state or national levels. Changes at these levels (e.g., legislative and funding initiatives, managed care regulations) reverberate swiftly throughout the system of treatment providers, bringing rapid change in the status of facilities and employees alike. For example, as a result of such regulatory changes, a large proportion of inpatient rehabilitation facilities closed during the 1990s.

Who are addictions counselors? Thirty years ago most addictions counselors were nondegreed, paraprofessionals with a personal recovery history. In the 1970s counselor credentialing systems emerged, and some states instituted separate certification for alcohol and drug counselors. Requirements were initially light but have continuously added education, testing, and experiential requirements. National certification is available through state affiliates of the International Certification Reciprocity Consortium (ICRC/AODA) and The Association for Addiction Professionals (NAADAC). In addition, at least 17 states have instituted addictions licensure boards on par with those that license social workers and psychologists. Today addictions counseling is a profession that requires rigorous preparation in a wide variety of areas. A tiered system has emerged in many states, ranging from paraprofessional credentials to masters level licensure. Healthcare delivery systems and reimbursement entities increasingly require professionally accountable treatment providers.

A large proportion of addictions counselors are still motivated by personal or family recovery issues but most of them now have at least a bachelor's degree in a helping profession. The occupational niche for nondegreed paraprofessionals has been contracting, and is limited more and more to counselor aide positions in some large treatment programs. In response to these changing occupational needs, more than 500 higher education programs in addictions studies have come into being. Training of addictions counselors has shifted gradually from a haphazard system of workshops and training programs into the academic mainstream. Many college addictions programs are affiliated with the International Coalition for Addiction Studies Education (INCASE). INCASE and NAADAC merged their curriculum approval processes in 2011 to found the National Addiction Studies Certification Commission, LLC with an Advisory Board representing the entire addictions field.

Treatment Settings

There is a great range and variety of addiction-specific treatment settings, such as freestanding clinics, units in hospitals, mental health centers, and other social service agencies. (Methadone maintenance programs are discussed separately later in this chapter.) There are at least three variables by which to classify an addictions treatment facility: model of treatment, level of care, and continuum of care.

Model of treatment is the treatment or recovery tradition upon which a program is based. These traditions and models, such as the therapeutic community and the Minnesota Model inpatient alcoholism program, are discussed later in this chapter.

Level of care is the intensity of treatment dictated by the severity of addiction and the degree to which the client's psychological and social functioning has deteriorated. The level of care is indicated by the number of hours per week of treatment, the degree of structure and supervision, and the scope of services. Facilities often specialize in providing a particular level of care. The evolution of a rational system of placement criteria to refer clients to an appropriate level of care is fairly new. Although use of such criteria may seem an elementary necessity, level of care had often been arbitrary, based on faith or tradition or the desire to curtail costs. The most widely accepted patient placement system is that of the American Society of Addiction Medicine (ASAM 2001).

To provide a simple example, a homeless, physically addicted, physically and mentally ill client would likely start out in a medically managed inpatient facility (level IV), whereas a full-time office worker who has a family and who has been identified as occasionally coming back from lunch in an intoxicated state would probably be referred to an outpatient treatment program (level I). Figure 1.1 shows the levels of care as outlined by the American Society of Addiction Medicine in 2001.

Continuum of care is the movement of addicts through a process of recovery. Although it may be woven out of treatment at disparate facilities, the ideal plan is to tailor a fairly seamless treatment "career." It may begin with intervention and referral from any of a variety of referring agents. Employee Assistance Programs in industry, Member Assistance Programs in organizations, and Student Assistance Programs in schools assess, intervene, and refer but do not treat addictions and substance abuse. The treatment career may include movement through several specialized facilities, such as a "detox," "rehab," and halfway house. Case management tries to ensure smooth continuity of treatment. As stated, initial referral and admission should be determined by assessment of the severity of the addiction and the client's needs, and should be to a facility that provides an appropriate level of care.

Recent Changes in Treatment Settings

The types and variety of facilities in which treatment takes place have changed in response to several factors. Three of them are cost containment, tradition, and the correctional system.

Figure 1.1 ASAM PPC-2R levels of care.

0.5	Early Intervention Services for Individuals with Problems/Risk Factors
I	Outpatient Treatment
II	Intensive Outpatient Treatment (II.1) and Partial Hospitalization (II.5)
III	Residential Inpatient Treatment
III.1	Clinically Managed Low Intensity Residential Treatment
III.3	Clinically Managed Medium Intensity Residential Treatment (Adults)
III.5	Clinically Managed Medium/High Intensity Residential Treatment
III.7	Medically Monitored Intensive Inpatient Treatment
IV	Medically Managed Intensive Inpatient Treatment (hospital/ medical center)

Note: Clinically managed refers to nonmedical treatment professionals. An overview of ASAM's Patient Placement Criteria is provided in Chapter 7.

Cost containment efforts by managed care entities have led to an overall move away from retrospective payment ("blind" reimbursement) and toward efforts to limit benefits for treatment services not considered medically crucial. Unfortunately, many mental health and substance abuse services are often seen as "not medically necessary." Some states have established parity for mental health coverage with other medical care, but even among these some exclude substance abuse services.

Because no research has demonstrated that inpatient rehabilitation is necessary for the vast majority of addicts, it has become easier for medical reimbursement and managed care entities to deny approval for inpatient care. This has quickly reverberated throughout the addiction service-provider industry. Since 1987 more than one-half of inpatient residential treatment facilities have closed or converted to shorter-term treatment settings. In addition, there has been a decrease in the reimbursability for outpatient care, regardless of the need for more intensive care as assessed by addictions or medical staff.

More funding has been available from correctional and other criminal-justice systems. Referrals for treatment of addicted offenders occur in the forms of pretrial intervention, alternatives to sentencing, serving sentence in treatment, and parole to treatment. In several states, drug courts and collaborative planning between criminal-justice personnel and addictions treatment providers have resulted in a new subfield for treatment of addicted offenders (Springer et al. 2003).

Trends in the treatment of addicted offenders vary by state. In Texas extensive initiatives were instituted, then reversed under a succeeding administration. Arizona reported extensive savings from a system to treat rather than imprison nonviolent drug offenders (Wren 1999). The Texas reversal was said to reflect a change from liberal to conservative government. Yet, as a *New York Times* editorial commented, "Arizona voters, tired of paying the exorbitant costs of imprisoning drug users and addicts who might be helped more cheaply, voted twice to provide a treatment alternative to jail. . . . Arizona is a politically conservative state. Its voters showed that they were tired of paying the costs of a bad idea. In requiring that drug offenders be treated before being freed of supervision, they may have made themselves safer" (Wren 1999, p. 12).

Types of Treatment Facilities

- Outpatient treatment. Most addictions treatment takes place in outpatient treatment programs. These are organized nonresidential treatment services in which the client visits the clinic at least once a week, up to about ten hours per week. There may be any number of activities such as individual, group, family, or didactic therapies. The multiple functions that may be served by outpatient facilities include:

- A setting in which the entire course of treatment takes place, as for the office worker in the example of level IV care, who may be stabilized and moved toward recovery without removal from the community or disruption of his or her occupational status.
- An initial point of contact for the many people who enter treatment at an outpatient treatment program, either as "walk-ins" or because that is the agency known to an employer or family member.
- Upon discharge from an inpatient program, a referral is usually made to an outpatient treatment program that may last three to six months or even longer.

- *Intensive outpatient programs (IOPs)*, or *intensive outpatient treatment programs (IOTPs)*, are more full and structured treatment settings in which the client is present from about 10 to 30 hours per week. The broad category of intensive outpatient treatment may include programs that term themselves day treatment or, in a medical setting, partial hospitalization. Since the mid 1980s IOPs have sprouted exponentially (Washton 1997). This is a result of both cost containment by third-party payers and research that indicates that the 28-day inpatient stay, formerly the mainstay of addictions treatment, is a "faith" system not based on rational criteria. The IOP fills a large service gap in the treatment system between inpatient and outpatient care. Its cost is about half that of residential care, and it allows clients to continue in work and family life, promotes bonding among clients, and allows clients to practice relapse-prevention techniques in real-life situations. In addition, assessment of clients' readiness to complete treatment, and of their problems and progress, can be made in a realistic setting.

    Clients of IOPs may be living at home, in a therapeutic or long-term residence of some sort, or in apartments as part of special programs. IOPs can even be operated in prisons. All of the components of rehabilitative treatment should be provided including counseling (individual, group, and family), treatment planning, crisis management, medication management, client education, self-help orientation, case management, discharge planning, and so forth (CSAT 1994; Gottheil 1997). IOTP is similar to "partial hospitalization." Both are ASAM PPC-2, Level II.5.

- *Inpatient rehabilitation*, or *intensive inpatient treatment*, involves a live-in setting. This category is quite diverse and includes therapeutic communities, in which the length of stay varies from four to twenty-four months, and a variety of other rehabilitation units such as those based on the AA or Minnesota Model, which usually involve four-week stays. Inpatient treatment may be medically managed, medically supervised, or nonmedical. It also may involve a number of phases, such as orientation, treatment, discharge, and re-entry. Individual, group, and family treatment may occur as well as considerable patient education and relapse-prevention training. Treatment plans are constructed collaboratively by client and counselor, who identify long-term and short-term goals that are continually reassessed and updated. Plans are made for re-entry into the community and ability to cope after discharge; they might include vocational, educational, and housing referrals as well as continuing care as an outpatient of either the rehabilitation agency itself or another agency.

- *Detoxification* (or *detox*) *units* may be freestanding facilities or inpatient medical units in which the client can be stabilized medically and can withdraw safely from drugs before entering a rehabilitation setting. Not all addicts or abusers require formal detoxification. Detoxification also can be an initial stage of inpatient rehabilitation, in the same unit. Detoxification is only the very first stage of recovery; it is not a complete or even a partial treatment process. Many addicts have detoxed repeatedly. The mistaken idea that detoxification is treatment contributes greatly to the idea that treatment is useless. Some addicts check themselves into detox units to reduce their level of tolerance, to "get their heads together" when they are homeless and cold, or to satisfy some impending legal proceeding. Others enter with the intention of recovery but retreat when the worst withdrawal symptoms have abated.

  Detoxification from alcohol traditionally has taken place in inpatient settings. During the 1990s outpatient detoxification units were set up, which appalled some addictions counselors. However, some studies (Hayashida et al. 1989) suggest that outpatient detoxification is not out of the question for a good chunk of the population in need (those with mild to moderate symptoms of alcohol withdrawal) and, in fact, it can free scarce resources to help more addicts. Nonmedical detoxification programs, sometimes called social-setting detoxification facilities or sobering-up stations, were common in the 1960s and 1970s but have fallen out of favor with regulatory and funding agencies since then, and thus have declined greatly in number.

- Intermediate steps between treatment and total re-entry into society. The *re-entry residence* or *halfway house* may be a built-in segment of the therapeutic community treatment of drug addiction. Independent halfway houses, recovery residences, or sober living facilities vary from simple cooperative and democratic living arrangements, to therapeutically structured residential settings that follow rehabilitation; they usually require that residents work or pay a fee. The term *halfway house* also is used to refer to a variety of supportive and transitional residences for psychiatric patients and offenders just released from incarceration. Oxford Houses, which arose in the Capitol District in the late 1970s (CSAT 1992), are democratically operated, financially self-supporting houses with no paid staff. These are essentially communes of alcoholics, living in buildings rented by the residents. This participatory democracy is believed to strengthen responsibility and end dependency, replacing it with self-sufficiency. The democratic operation of Oxford Houses extends to votes on admission of members and election of officers for six-month terms. The only house rule is sobriety, and use of any alcohol or other drug results in immediate expulsion. All the houses belong to the Oxford House, Inc., network. As a prerequisite to receiving federal block grants for alcohol and drug treatment, states must establish a revolving loan fund to help open new Oxford Houses. According to researchers at DePaul University (Jason and Ferrari 2010), the Oxford House model builds autonomy, community, and self-esteem, and is underused and under-recognized. A national organization of sober living facilities/recovery residences (National Association of Recovery Residences [NARR]) was founded in 2011.

- *Long-term residential care* can be arranged for clients who are not yet capable of independent living; it is provided by the Salvation Army and many other nonprofit entities. Often these are little more than a structured shelter situation, although the "Sallie," as clients call it, also has a work requirement. Salvation Army residences may refer to themselves as rehabilitation programs, but this is a misnomer by most treatment community standards.

- *Programs that serve special populations* include those set up to treat the client with a co-occurring psychiatric disorder and those for pregnant addicts or addicted mothers and their children.

Continuity of care in the treatment career is essential. A large percentage of clients are "lost" when there is a gap between intervention and detox, detox and rehab, and so forth. Referring agents or case managers spend a great deal of time and effort struggling with the timing of available beds at the right time and place. For example, if a client referred by her Human Resources Department (HRD) needs to complete a 5-day detoxification program, followed by a 21-day rehabilitation stay at a facility with a 10-day waiting list, the client would have to wait 5 days before going into the detox so that she could slide neatly into the next phase, preferably transported directly between the facilities. Figure 1.2 shows the route this client's treatment would take.

Pharmacological Treatments for Addictions

Treatment for Opiate Addiction

Methadone maintenance (MM), perhaps miscategorized when called a treatment for opiate (narcotic-analgesic) addiction, is simply the

Figure 1.2 The route of one client's treatment career, which is monitored by her case manager.

1. Meeting with EAP administrator
2. Evaluation at outpatient clinic
3. Inpatient detoxification (5 days)
4. Inpatient rehabilitation (21 days)
5. Aftercare at outpatient clinic
6. Ongoing reports to EAP

systematic dispensation of a synthetic opioid that enables the addicted client to attain social stability, abdicate the criminal career, and enter the educational or occupational world. Last but not least, it reduces the risk of contracting or spreading HIV/AIDS by reducing the number of addicts who use and re-use hypodermic needles.

Methadone maintenance is effective because:

- It is administered orally, in controlled doses.
- It can be administered only once a day.
- The rushes, highs, and lows that accompany much drug use are absent. The client can study, operate a vehicle, or file library books without nodding out or experiencing changes in mood or functioning.

There is tremendous variety among MM programs, for example, in counseling and other services offered, in the attempt to screen for alcohol and other drug use, and in attempts to taper the patient off to a truly drug-free status. Although MM programs wish it otherwise, many clients drink and use drugs, and many increase their use of alcohol and other drugs (AOD) if and when they taper off their methadone dosage. Higher dosages of methadone are associated with less illicit drug use (Hargreaves 1983).

Methadone maintenance occupies a peculiar position in addictions treatment. Although this modality serves more clients than drug-free treatment programs, MM is the shabby, outcast stepsister in the addictions field. Methadone-maintenance clients are stigmatized by the public at large, by the healthcare system, and within the addictions field itself. To many, their participation in the dispensation of an opioid substitute denies them the honorific of "recovering addict" but rather institutionalizes and ritualizes their addiction. This attitude dehumanizes clients and discourages the goal of abstinence.

Drug-free treatment models seem to make MM and treatment mutually exclusive categories. Yet methadone maintenance, whatever its shortcomings, need not be limited to a grim routine of early morning dispensation of the opioid. In fact, programs that are so limited often fail even in their mission to replace illegal opioids with a legal one.

Case in Point

Methadone Clients Supplementing Opioids

A counselor at one program in the urban Northeast confessed that the vast majority of his clients drank fairly heavily, and at least half of them also consumed benzodiazepines and marijuana. He attempted to steer new clients away from the peer-group gatherings of the client subculture for fear that the new clients would progress in their overall polyaddicted status just as they were "stabilized" in their heroin addiction. Another program in the same city tested vigorously and randomly for 15 substances and did not tolerate polyabuse.

Methadone programs vary along several axes, and so are difficult to compare. First, they may vary in the extent to which the program monitors and tolerates the use of other psychoactive substances. A philosophical paradox arises when drawing up standards for polyabuse behavior in methadone programs, which fall roughly under the rubric of the harm-reduction model. That is, as intolerance of other, non-opioid drugs increases, the number of clients decreases, as do the consequent benefits to society in terms of crime reduction and the reduced spread of HIV.

Another continuum along which MM programs fall is the degree to which there is individual, group, and family counseling. At one end of the spectrum are the programs that offer infrequent case management sessions; in the middle are various levels of intensity to which programs attempt to involve clients in counseling processes; at the most treatment-intensive end of the spectrum are a few therapeutic community (TC) day programs such as the Passages program (De Leon et al. 1993). MM violates the traditional, central community treatment tenet of abstinence from the very start of treatment. The Passages program (De Leon et al. 1993) modifies the therapeutic-community format in terms of a more flexible phased schedule, a less confrontational style, and individualized case management. Integrating treatment with opioid substitution may seem to fly in the face of basic addictions treatment philosophy, which holds that one cannot treat an individual who is influenced by psychoactive drugs. How, for example, can an anesthetized person introspectively examine or communicate emotional states? However, while not the optimal situation, it is useful for a large segment of the MM treatment population to participate in a counseling milieu or process, the more comprehensive, the better. In this light, activities and techniques described in this text are not only applicable to MM settings but are critical to enhance the ability of MM to achieve the goals of harm reduction or abstinence. Other MM program enhancements improve the retention rate and, indirectly, help reduce the spread of HIV. For example, substitution of this synthetic narcotic substance for intravenous drugs decreases associated needle sharing and participation in crime or sex industries to finance a habit (Anglin et al. 1993, pp. 3–6).

Maddux (1993, pp. 23–24) shows that a low or absent fee is associated with better retention, as is the clients' role in regulating their dosages. While some may suspect that an addict will maximize the dosage, it is unlikely because the methadone client is motivated to avoid withdrawal syndromes rather than seek a euphoric rush. The client may be re-entering the workforce and wish also to avoid excessive sedation. Maddux (1993, pp. 24–25) reports that the client-regulated dose reduces conflict with staff as well as surreptitious return to illicit drug use and that, indeed, clients do not markedly increase their doses. Rapid admission is also a must in successful maintenance programs.

A standard methadone-maintenance program protocol may include:

- Intake
- Annual medical examination
- Attainment of increasing take-home dose privileges, in stages
- Monthly testing for drug use, with refusal to submit counted as a positive test (pregnant women tested more often, perhaps weekly)
- Two one-hour counseling sessions each month, with crisis intervention sessions on request
- Disciplinary detoxification resulting from any violation of program rules

Successful program enhancements cited by Anglin and colleagues (1993) should be designed to match an individual client's needs. These may include:

- Training for counselors and case managers
- Intensive contact during the first month
- Contingency contracts, that is, provision of rewards such as food or movie coupons for the client's compliance and progress
- Enhanced program services such as bus passes, off-site psychiatric consultations, additional urinalysis (perhaps with swift on-site processing)
- High-risk counseling and support groups for HIV-infected clients, cocaine users, and women

Methadone-maintenance programs also vary in their attempts to wean the client completely from the addictive substances to this synthetic opioid. A combination of counseling and psychopharmaceutical support to methadone detoxification is most effective (Milby 1988). Although the rates of detoxification have improved gradually since the early days of MM, many clinics do not encourage the ultimate goal of abstinence, and in fact compare opioid substitution therapy with insulin treatment for diabetes.

Methadone maintenance is associated with the harm reduction model. Methadone is also increasingly popular for alleviation of pain, and its use for that purpose has tripled in recent years because it is relatively cheap and long lasting. Unfortunately, it has been the cause of many overdoses. The abuse of methadone as a prescription pain killer is a major cause of overdose fatalities.

Buprenorphine

A major innovation in the treatment of opioid addiction is the introduction of buprenorphine (colloquially known as "bupe"), which promises to be a major improvement over methadone maintenance treatment. Buprenorphine (BYOO-pre-NOR-feen), short for buprenorphine hydrochloride, is a generic name for a chemical compound ($C_{29}H_{41}NO_4$). It is a semisynthetic opioid. Subutex and Suboxone are brand (trade) names for buprenorphine-based medications. Suboxone contains four parts buprenorphine and one part naloxone. Subutex only contains buprenorphine as an active ingredient. Buprenorphine has properties of a partial opioid agonist. It is taken as a sublingual tablet.

An *opioid agonist* is a drug that causes an opioid effect, similar to if you took Vicodin, OxyContin, or heroin, because it binds to opioid receptor sites in the brain and activates them. Because the agonist is active at opiate receptor sites, clients won't get "high" if they take other opioids during the time that the agonist is functioning, and they also won't experience symptoms of opioid withdrawal.

Antagonist drugs occupy receptor sites but block them, blocking and reversing the effects of agonist drugs. They prevent the drug "high" and can prevent overdoses. Examples of opiate antagonists are Narcan and naltrexone.

Because buprenorphine is a partial and not a full agonist, it does not provide a morphine or heroin-like "high" while it blocks withdrawal and craving. Clients won't "nod out" as may be the case with methadone maintenance. In addition, buprenorphine has a ceiling effect adding to its safety. Other opioids continue to provide more effect as more is taken, eventually leading to respiratory depression and death. Buprenorphine's effects level off at a relatively low dose. That is, even if more is taken, there are no significant increased effects. Overdose risk is low.

In the United States, Suboxone is vastly preferred because of the limited potential for abuse, first because of its "ceiling" effect, and secondly because it contains one-fourth naltrexone. If a client attempts to crush the tablet and inject it, the opiate antagonist will kick in and precipitate an unpleasant withdrawal.

Buprenorphine was originally prescribed as an analgesic (pain killer). Following on experiences in other countries, The Drug Abuse Treatment Act (DATA) of 2000 allows physicians to prescribe buprenorphine at their private practice offices, or in general care settings such as hospitals, clinics, and substance abuse programs, for opioid dependence problems. The Federal Drug Administration approved Subutex and Suboxone in 2002 for office-based opioid treatment by physicians who are properly trained and certified. Thus, persons with addiction who wish to be treated need not gather in a large, institutional, stigmatized clinic, herded together with a horde of other clients but can take their dose under a physician's supervision every two days or even three times per week as opposed to the daily regimen of the methadone client. Clients therefore feel more positive about the experience.

The National Institute for Drug Abuse (NIDA) and the Center for Substance Abuse Treatment (CSAT, SAMHSA) are enthusiastic about buprenorphine as a pharmacotherapy for opioid addiction, and they are cooperating in training professionals as to its use. The New York City government sponsored a white paper (Johnson et al. 2003) advocating getting thousands of heroin addicts into buprenorphine programs. Another exciting innovation is the integration of buprenorphine with standard treatment programs, even those based on principles of AA/NA or the traditional drug-free therapeutic community. Phoenix House, one of the first therapeutic communities, has a combined opioid detoxification/ residential program utilizing buprenorphine at its First Step Program in Long Island City, New York (Horton and McMurphy 2004).

(Note: Buprenorphine sounds very similar to bupropion. The latter, however, is an antidepressant, marketed as Zyban and Wellbutrin, which has been found useful in the treatment of methamphetamine and nicotine withdrawal.) In guidelines for medication-assisted treatment, CSAT (2005, p. 227) recommends careful vetting of verbal expressions to remove stigmatizing and countertherapeutic language, such as "detox," "dirty urines," and "termination" as well as the active role of the patient in treatment plan formulation (2005, p. 96), a fairly revolutionary paradigm shift for the opiod-substitution therapy sector of the treatment field.

- In the treatment of acute alcohol withdrawal, the use of benzo-diazepine sedatives has been standard for decades. These include chlordiazepoxide (Librium), diazepam (Valium), and lorazepam (Ativan). They prevent seizures and reduce the physical and psychological effects of acute withdrawal syndromes but are not used as a treatment to reduce drinking or reduce cravings. Benzodiazepines are physically addictive although safe to use for the three to five days of alcohol detoxification.
- Naltrexone (marketed as ReVia, Depade, and Vivitrol) is an opiate antagonist, but it has been adapted for use with alco-holics, who lose the euphoric high but keep the sedative effects of alcohol. Research shows that naltrexone reduces craving for alcohol and that users have fewer relapses to heavy drinking and drink on fewer days than alcoholics who do not take the drug. Vivitrol is the injectable form of the drug, which the Food and

Drug Administration (FDA) approved for alcoholism treatment in 2006.

- Disulfiram (trade name Antabuse) has been used for decades as an alcoholism treatment. It stops the breakdown product of alcohol, acetaldehyde, which is toxic, to be broken down by an enzyme to a nontoxic metabolite. Acetaldehyde makes drinkers ill soon after drinking, with symptoms including flushing, vomiting, headache, and chest pain.
- Acamprosate (trade name Campral) affects neurotransmitter systems involved in alcohol dependence. Studies have shown some promising effects on alcohol cravings.
- Antidepressants known as selective serotonin reuptake inhibitors (SSRIs), including the most famous, fluoxetine (Prozac), have been tested for treatment of alcoholism. They show some effect in helping to reduce drinking, mainly among those who do not have severe alcohol use disorders (De Sousa 2010).
- Baclofen, a medication originally prescribed for symptoms of multiple sclerosis, has shown efficacy in reduction of cravings and of alcohol intake among alcohol-dependent people (Addolorato et al. 2002, National Institutes of Health n.d.).

A combination of medication together with support groups and cognitive-behavioral therapy is more effective than either medication or psychotherapy alone (Feeney et al. 2006). Pettinati and colleagues (2010) found that for the treatment of alcohol use disorders that occurs along with depression, an SSRI antidepressant such as sertraline (Zoloft), a Prozac-like drug, together with an anticraving medication such as naltrexone, as well as cognitive-behavioral therapy, resulted in half of the patients remaining abstinent throughout the 90-day research period.

There is no contradiction between taking medications and attending Alcoholics Anonymous (AA). The AA pamphlet entitled, "AA Member—Medications and Other Drugs," clearly states that AA members should not "play doctor" and advises others on medication provided by medical practitioners or treatment programs.

ACTIVITY 1.1 Tell me about your agency

It is important for counselors to be familiar with the treatment providers in their communities and with the relationships among those providers. It is interesting and useful to visit an agency with which you are unfamiliar. Request an opportunity to interview a staff member or administrator. Your instructor may be able to provide a letter of introduction to help you get the interview. Note: Do not use the agency at which you are employed, an intern, or a volunteer. Try to avoid using the same treatment modality. To prepare for the visit, bear in mind that there will be an in-class component of this activity. Each student will explain to another student or small group exactly what services the agency offers and how the agency can be helpful to its clients. Act like the marketing director for the agency and sell its product. Secondly, make a list of questions to elicit information about the following:

- *Agency philosophy*
- *Agency policies and procedures*
- *Administrative and clinical structure*
- *Staffing patterns*
- *Treatment philosophy*
- *Treatment methods and modalities*
- *Funding sources*
- *Eligibility requirements*
- *Length of stay*
- *Cultural, class, and ethnic makeup of staff and clientele*
- *Referral patterns*
- *Success rate*
- *Method of measuring success*

Major Influences and Traditions in Addictions Treatment

Self-Help Movements

Several movements for social and political change in the nineteenth and early twentieth centuries also had ideas about individual self-improvement. Most prominently, they attempted to influence people to be *temperate*, that is, cut down on the harmful use of alcohol. Temperance movements were linked in the second and third quarters of the nineteenth century to the Abolitionist (antislavery) movement. Temperance spokespersons included the famous abolitionist Frederick Douglass. At the same time, societies of men known as Abstentionists sprang up and encouraged men to take an oath in church foreswearing alcohol. This was known as "taking the pledge." Societies of former drinkers, such as the Washingtonians and the United Order of Ex-Boozers, also anticipated the rise of AA in the next century. Because women did not have the freedom to buy and imbibe alcohol, most of these movements revolved around men. Although 19th century women avidly consumed alcohol and narcotic-based tonics, and the average addict in the late 1800s was a middle-aged woman, the image of women as alcoholics was fairly unknown until the mid-twentieth century.

In the early twentieth century, the votes-for-women movement, or Suffragettes, went tandem with the Temperance movement. Being newly political, these women joined the movement to ban alcohol outright, and they were a key element in the Prohibitionist movement via a variety of organizations such as the Anti-Saloon League and the Women's Christian Temperance Union. Alcohol consumption declined for decades, and the United States went "dry" county by county, culminating in the passage of the Nineteenth Amendment to the United States Constitution in 1919, known as the Prohibition Amendment, which forbade the manufacture and distribution of alcoholic beverages. Paradoxically, in the 1920s a proto-feminist generation of women then helped organize the movement to gather a million signatures and abolish Prohibition. Congress acted upon this in 1933 (Blumberg 1991). The fascinating history of temperance movements was chronicled by William White (1998).

In the benchmark year of 1935, Alcoholics Anonymous (AA) was spun off by William Griffith Wilson and Dr. Robert Smith from the Oxford Movement, a religious organization. AA began to expand in 1941, when its success was widely publicized.

Alcoholics Anonymous is a peer self-help group, mutual-aid society, or, as members call it, a fellowship of alcoholics in recovery. It has a democratic, non-hierarchical, grassroots structure and is a source of what some call a "folk psychotherapy." From the 1930s through the 1950s it remained the only help for alcoholics who otherwise would find themselves in psychiatric facilities, the drunk tanks in jails, or—if they were lucky—in shelters run by the Salvation Army or another religious organization. The AA method is based on the Twelve Steps (Alcoholics Anonymous), and its basic organizational principles are based on the Twelve Traditions.

We may sum up the basic principles of AA as follows:

- Abstinence from alcohol as a requirement for recovery from addiction
- Alcoholism as a lifelong, chronic, progressive disease
- Anonymity
- Spirituality through a spiritual awakening and giving up control to a higher power
- Self-identification as a sufferer from a lifelong, chronic disease
- Staying sober one day at a time
- Group support from a fellowship of alcoholics
- Helping oneself by helping others
- Reaching out to others with the AA message

Much of the AA method and philosophy are boiled down into mottoes and slogans that are easy to retain, repeat, and focus upon by the barely "dry" alcoholic. Examples are "don't drink, and go to meetings," "easy does it," and "let go and let God." AA publishes a vast number of pamphlets and books, many focusing on the early history of the fellowship (AA 1957, 1976, 1980).

The success of AA may be explained by its comprehensive network, which supports abstinence and recovery; conversion to a sober ideology and perspective; frequent attendance at AA meetings where role modeling, confession, sharing, and support take place; and participation in the member network or sober subculture between meetings, including obtaining and relying on a senior member, or sponsor (Maxwell 1984).

Al-Anon, a fellowship for relatives and significant others of alcoholics, was founded in 1951, although it did not take off as a movement until 1962. Narcotics Anonymous (NA), the third of the three major Twelve-Step fellowships, was founded in 1953. It was relatively small throughout the 1950s and 1960s, with hardly any overlap with the therapeutic community movement. It grew during the 1970s and even more during the 1980s. Although the basic text of NA, *Narcotics Anonymous* (NA 1988), was written in 1962, its section of personal stories dates from 1981. The language is more modern, more emotional, and more in tune with modern subcultures of drug use. The atmosphere of NA meetings is more emotional and "nitty-gritty" than that of AA meetings. This is due in part to the fact that many members attended drug treatment programs that emphasize vigorous interpersonal interaction in group sessions.

A wide variety of twelve-step fellowships have spun off from AA and NA; the largest are Gamblers Anonymous and Overeaters Anonymous. Smaller fellowships include Debtors Anonymous, Sex and Love Addicts Anonymous, Sexaholics Anonymous, Obsessive-Compulsive Anonymous, and Attention-Deficit Disorder Anonymous.

Non-Twelve-Step Recovery Organizations

- SMART Recovery (Self-Management and Recovery Training) is an abstinence-based fellowship based on rational emotive behavior therapy, which had been originally developed by Albert Ellis (Trimpey 1992, Ellis et al. 1988). It was originally called Rational Recovery (RR). It is not based on spiritual principles and does not consider alcoholism as a disease but instead favors the use of appropriate medications, teaches self-empowerment, and is open to changing its approach to include such current practice as Motivational Interviewing and the Stages of Change. In the early 1990s, the founder of RR, Jack Trimpey, made the "addictive voice" concept the core of his approach to recovery, and he abandoned the entire REBT theory in favor of "Addictive Voice Recognition Training" (Bishop 1995, p. 143).

- Secular Organizations for Sobriety (SOS), also known as Save Our Selves, was started by Jim Christopher in 1985 as a secular-humanist alternative to AA. It is abstinence based and, like AA, considers alcoholism a disease but maintains a secular approach as opposed to a spiritual outlook (Christopher 1989). Most chapters are located in California, New York, and Texas. It promotes an approach to recovery comparable both to that of AA and cognitive behavioral therapy, and daily acknowledgment of the alcohol problem is emphasized. SOS also presents two concepts, a Cycle of Addiction and a Cycle of Sobriety, which are somewhat comparable to professional paradigms.

- LifeRing is an abstinence-based group spun off from SOS. While it is secular, it welcomes people of all faiths. It is democratically managed and works through a network of meetings that are non-confrontational and not focused on "war stories" about alcohol and drugs. Members need not take on the label "addict" or "alcoholic." The philosophy of LifeRing is strengths based; it also recognizes the ambivalence that people have over substance use, and denote these as the Addict Self and the Sober Self.

- Women for Sobriety (WFS) was founded by Jean Kirkpatrick in 1976 to serve the recovery needs of women. Kirkpatrick had been active in AA but believed it did not meet her needs or those of women in general. The program is founded on its Statement of Purpose and Thirteen Affirmations. While Kirkpatrick is now deceased, the program continues to operate.

- The Sixteen Step Program developed by Dr. Charlotte Kasl offers a relatively new program that has been called "spirituality lite." It dilutes the emphasis on spirituality and stresses empowerment rather than powerlessness. The Sixteen Steps also mention the position of women and other minorities in societies. The program incorporates a whiff of Buddhist (Reiki Zen) philosophy, in which Kasl has been trained. Kasl describes the influence of Zen and feminism on her perspective (Kasl 2002).

   (Although AA and NA are the gold standard of the addictions industry, as they are the most available nationwide, and are the recovery culture from which many counselors emerged, it would be the most ethical practice to give clients alternative pathways to sobriety and abstinence. LifeRing and the Sixteen Step Program, for example, are little known in the addictions field.)

- Moderation Management (MM) contrasts wildly from AA or any of its secular alternatives. It is a self-help organization supporting problem drinkers in its attempt to cut down to a so-called moderate, responsible level of consumption. Opponents of the MM program consider it a Russian roulette approach, as no one can know who will successfully moderate and who will fall back into a severe alcohol-use disorder.

ACTIVITY 1.2 What goes on in those meetings?

It is important for all addiction counselors to experience the atmosphere and process of a self-help fellowship. It is also a requirement of many certification and credentialing authorities.

Attend a self-help group with which you are not familiar, and write a two-page "reaction paper." Include a description of what took place, the format of the speeches, the customs you observed, the atmosphere before and after the formal meeting, and the feelings you had while attending.

Inpatient Rehabilitation Emerges from Self-Help

Alcoholics Anonymous steers clear of institutional affiliation. Early AA members, starting with Bill W., the founder, often filled their houses with those whom they were helping to "dry out." Eventually, inpatient rehabilitation programs based on AA principles grew out of this practice. These programs, which began in Minnesota in the 1950s, kept the AA philosophy but gradually added the professional framework of assessment-based treatment planning as well as individual and group counseling. The length of stay for clients in Minnesota was 28 days. For decades afterward, the dominant form of alcoholism treatment in the United States was based on this so-called Minnesota Model and a disease concept of treatment based on the philosophy of AA (Yalisove 1997). In the late 1970s and early 1980s a golden age of inpatient treatment was possible because of insurance reimbursement. Many expensive, private "rehabs" flourished. Unfortunately, the excesses of that era were used to invalidate the inpatient approach, and many people in need of such a level of care have been denied that option.

Therapeutic Community Model

The term *therapeutic community* (TC) originally denoted an innovative approach in the inpatient treatment of post-traumatic stress disorder (PTSD) in the immediate post–World War II period. It instituted a therapeutic milieu among patients as well as a structure that allowed patients' input into the management of the unit (Jones 1953, 1968; Rapoport 1960).

This democratic milieu is still a current mental health model in the United Kingdom and Europe. Students who set out to write a paper on therapeutic communities often are thrown off track because the term means something quite different in the United States, where it refers to a hierarchical and demanding long-term, drug-free residential program largely run by recovering addicts themselves. The therapeutic community model began in 1958 in California when Charles Dederich, a recovering alcoholic, brought drug addicts into an AA group. He then split off to found his own organization, named Synanon after a mispronunciation of "seminar." It differed from AA in that it addressed primarily drug addiction, used confrontational methods, abandoned the spiritual component of AA, and was residential. The residential addict community was run totally by recovering addicts. This has been a feature in subsequent TCs, although there may be a supervising layer of professionals who may or may not be recovering addicts. Synanon developed a variety of harsh confrontational techniques that were designed to strip addicts of their "street" images and defenses. These included confrontational groups, then called "the Synanon guns." Other important features of this modality are work therapy and a hierarchy of rewards, privileges, and statuses up until graduation, which are designed to resocialize the addict into responsible and mature behavior (Yablonsky 1965). The stratification system goes beyond graduation; the TC graduate may return as a role model and often becomes part of the staff. There is a tremendous camaraderie among members of a therapeutic community, which is often seen as a substitute family. Building on the principles of Synanon, the prototype of the modern therapeutic community was Daytop Village, developed by Daniel Casriel and David Deitch in 1964 and 1965 and founded on Staten Island, New York City (Casriel and Amen 1971). Other early therapeutic communities that developed in the late 1960s include Phoenix House in New York City, Integrity House in Newark, New Jersey, Marathon House in Exeter and Coventry, Rhode Island, Gateway House in Chicago, and Gaudenzia House in Philadelphia. There is a national organization, Therapeutic Communities of America, and, as the American model has spread, an International Federation of Therapeutic Communities.

Reactions to TCs ranged from the predictable NIMBY (not in my backyard), to awe at the recently addicted clean-cut young men and women hammering, sawing, and scrubbing the sidewalk, to comparisons of TCs with religious revivalists. The TC model became dominant in drug treatment during the 1970s. Hundreds of treatment programs more or less follow the TC model. Therapeutic Communities of America, a national organization, has more than 600 affiliate programs. Many or most of the original, rather harsh practices have been modified considerably.

The programs have seen the influence of social learning and cognitive psychology, and educational and occupational programs have been added to facilitate realistic re-entry into society. In addition, the model has been incorporated into many programs in prisons and programs designed as alternatives to sentencing, as intermediate sanctions, and as sentencing to treatment (Lockwood and Inciardi 1993). Unfortunately, the TC model is often stereotyped as an incredibly harsh and cult-like environment, as if it had not changed since the 1970s (Deitch 1991).

Counseling Approaches

Counseling approaches, sometimes called theories of counseling or counseling models, are systems of ideas concerning the ways that change can take place. They can identify major goals and strategies of treatment. Some advertise in their name that they subscribe to a particular personality model. For example, the term *cognitive behavioral therapy* indicates special attention to thinking (cognition), behavior, and the relationship between the two.

ACTIVITY (1.3) Thinking about counseling

Form small groups of no more than six people and elect a recorder and a spokesperson for each group. After a 20-minute discussion, each group should have a consensus that defines and describes (1) counseling and (2) addictions counseling.

PROCESS: Group by group, define counseling first. Then describe what happens in counseling. How does this differ from other relationships and conversations? Note differences and similarities among groups. Which group members have gone to a professional for help of any kind (e.g., counselor, physician, nurse, lawyer, accountant)? Explore these relationships.

Many theoreticians champion their schools of thought, which postulate the primary importance of affect (emotion), behavior, or cognition. Most therapists have come to acknowledge that each of these has a role in the human personality. Most therapists borrow from various clinical approaches, an approach that can be called eclectic or integrative (Garfield and Bergin 1994, p. 8; Lambert and Bergin 1994, pp. 143–144). A similar term is *holistic,* which simply means looking at and integrating all aspects of a system.

The counseling of chemically dependent people is far from a standardized system or method. Addictions counselors tend to gravitate toward counseling models that integrate or synthesize aspects of the personality and of change, not only because they are influenced by the trend toward integration of diverse techniques and concepts but also because they see the practical necessity of covering all bases in combating a syndrome characterized by various vicious cycles and pervasive deteriorating effects in behavior, management of emotions, and thinking.

Brief Interventions

Much research has indicated that any of a variety of brief interventions and brief treatments can have a salutary impact on alcohol and drug misuse. Brief interventions are focused on immediate behavioral objectives. They focus on symptoms, not underlying causes. The acronym FRAMES, based on motivational interviewing theory, provides an overview of the components (not steps) of brief interventions (CSAT 1999, pp. 18–19):

F = **Feedback** is provided to the abuser about personal risk or impairment

R = **Responsibility** for change is placed on the abuser

A = **Advice** on how to proceed with change is given

M = **Menu** of self-help and/or treatment options and strategies is offered based on the specific situation of the client

E = **Empathic** style and listening (nonpunitive, nonlabeling) is used

S = **Self-efficacy**, belief in the ability of the client to change (optimistic empowerment), is instilled in the client

Typically, the brief intervention includes these five steps (CSAT 1999, pp. 20–24):

1. Introducing the issue
2. Screening, evaluating, and assessing, as with a readiness ruler that roughly gauges readiness to change, as shown in Chapter 3
3. Providing feedback
4. Talking about change and setting goals
5. Summarizing and reaching closure

An important point about brief interventions is that they take the initiation of recovery out of the addictions treatment setting into a plethora of venues and "intervenors": clergy, lawyers, physicians, educators, peer counselors, and residence hall personnel, in addition to clinicians. Numerous studies have shown the effectiveness of brief interventions with moderate alcohol abusers (Wutzke et al. 2002). A meta-analysis conducted by Moyer et al. (2002) underscored the effectiveness of brief interventions, excluding severely addicted individuals when contacted three to six months after the intervention. The authors cautioned against generalizing about the use of any particular intervention outside of the setting and population involved. Brief intervention, like Stages of Change, is a transtheoretical concept and can be based on any of a number of treatment approaches. A federally supported model of brief intervention is Screening, Brief Intervention, and Referral to Treatment (SBIRT), pioneered in California. Preliminary data show a majority of alcohol abusers reduced their drinking following SBIRT interventions. Local government is following suit: New York City allocated $850,000 during 2005–2006 to train medical personnel at all levels in conducting brief intervention. SAMHSA further defines SBIRT as adding prevention to treatment, as the target population are those who have not progressed into true addiction.

One of the major themes of this text is the development of counseling skills that facilitate a helping, empathic, collaborative relationship between counselor and client. In adaptations to short-term treatment, though, such an approach can lose the human dimension and be reduced to a set of "cookbook" routines, formulae, tricks, or gimmicks, against which the Project MATCH Research Group (NIAAA 1995, p. 8) specially cautions. Such routines soothe the counselor more than the client, which is another reason to focus on counseling skills. Techniques that address only cognition or that address emotion only in terms of the cognition involved are sketchy psychotherapies that skirt the pain and tragedies of clients. In warning against taking cognitive psychology's cool, commonsense approach to emotion too far, Fancher and Freeman (1997, p. 195) quote a line from Emily Dickinson: "There is a pain so utter, it swallows substance up."

The Paradigm Shift in Initiating and Sustaining Recovery

Drug treatment through the 1980s was "stuck" in a template of inpatient rehab for more clients than was necessary. The shift to intensive outpatient care and other options began in that decade, both because we became progressively "unstuck" from dogma and because third-party payers were loath to cough up the costly sums that rehab generated. We are now in a second paradigm shift, where facilitation of recovery may include brief interventions in a variety of helping and medical contexts, brief therapies, long-term care, and long-term recovery support following formal treatment.

The new paradigm also takes into account natural motives to change and recover, recognizes that relapse tendencies are a normal part of an upward "spiral," and stresses the need for ongoing, long-term recovery support as crucial. Dr. Thomas McClellan, a leading researcher in addictions, summarized this view in an editorial he wrote for the journal *Addiction* (McClellan 2002). He pointed out that addictions treatment-effectiveness studies tended to conceptualize addiction as if it were an acute illness such as a streptococcal throat infection. If two-thirds of strep throat patients got sick again right after the course of antibiotics was finished, we would consider this an extremely ineffective treatment. But if we looked at addictions as a chronic, relapsing condition such as hypertension, we would come up with different results. We would expect hypertensives to have lowered blood pressure while being exposed to medical interventions, and we would expect bouts of high blood pressure to reoccur at some point following the discontinuance of medical aid. Miller et al. (2001) showed dramatic improvement in the majority of clients who did not totally abstain following treatment. In terms of total effect on the prevalence of active addiction, lifetime support counts for more than bringing a huge arsenal of treatment to bear during a short period (McLellan 2002; Moos 2003). *Support* in this context includes low-intensity recovery management and monitoring as well as the facilitation of environmental supports in terms of stable occupational, medical, social, and residential situations.

Table 1.1 Self-Help Organizations

Organization	Acronym	Information
Alcoholics Anonymous	AA	Twelve-Step Program
		http://www.aa.org/en_pdfs/smf-121_en.pdf
		Twelve Traditions
		http://www.aa.org/pdf/products/p-43_thetwelvetradiillustrated.pdf
Self-Management and Recovery Training	SMART Recovery	http://www.smartrecovery.org/resources/toolchest.htm
Secular Organizations for Sobriety (also, Save Our Selves)	SOS	http://www.sossobriety.org
LifeRing		http://LifeRing.org
Women for Sobriety	WFS	http://www.womenforsobriety.org
Sixteen Step Program		http://www.charlottekasl.com/site/16-step-program
Moderation Management	MM	http://www.moderation.org

References

AA (Alcoholics Anonymous).[1] 1957. *Alcoholics Anonymous Comes of Age.* New York: Alcoholics Anonymous World Services.

————. 1976 (orig. 1939). *Alcoholics Anonymous.* New York: Alcoholics Anonymous World Services.

————. 1980. *Dr. Bob and the Good Oldtimers.* New York: Alcoholics Anonymous World Services.

Addolorato, G. et al. 2002. Baclofen efficacy in reducing alcohol craving and intake: A preliminary double-blind randomized controlled study. *Alcohol and Alcoholism, 37*(5): 504–508

Anglin, M. et al. 1993. "Enhanced Methadone Maintenance Treatment: Limiting the Spread of HIV among High-Risk Los Angeles Narcotics Addicts," in *Innovative Approaches in the Treatment of Drug Abuse.* J. Inciardi et al., eds. Westport, CT: Greenwood Press.

ASAM (American Society of Addiction Medicine). 2001. *Patient Placement Criteria for the Treatment of Substance-Related Disorders,* 2nd ed. (PPC-2R) Chevy Chase, MD: Author.

Belenko, S., N. Patapis, and M. T. French. 2005. *Economic Benefits of Drug Treatment: A Critical Review of the Evidence for Policy Makers.* National Rural Alcohol and Drug Abuse Network. Retrieved 25 November 2011 from http://www.tresearch.org/resources/specials/2005Feb_EconomicBenefits.pdf

Bishop, F. M. 1995. "Rational-Emotive Behavior Therapy and Two Self-Help Alternatives to the 12-Step Model," in *Psychotherapy and Substance Abuse.* A. M. Washton, ed. New York: Guilford Press.

Blumberg, L. U. 1991. *Beware the First Drink: The Washington Temperance Movement and Alcoholics Anonymous.* Seattle: Glen Abbey Books.

Casriel, D., and G. Amen. 1971. *Daytop: Three Addicts and Their Cure.* New York: Hill and Wang.

Christopher, J. 1989. *Unhooked: Staying Sober and Drug-Free.* Buffalo: Prometheus Press.

CSAT (Center for Substance Abuse Treatment). 1992. *Self-Run, Self-Supported Houses for More Effective Recovery from Alcohol and Drug Addiction.* Technical Assistance Publication Series 5,

---

[1] Many excellent histories and accounts of AA have been written, starting in 1939 with Alcoholics Anonymous, the "Big Book" (AA 1976). Others are historical volumes (AA 1957, 1980) and books by writers and academics (Blumberg 1991; Kurtz 1988; Maxwell 1984; Robertson 1988; Thomsen 1975).

Rockville, MD: Department of Health and Human Services, Substance Abuse and Mental Health Services Administration.

———. 1994. *Intensive Outpatient Treatment for Alcohol and Other Drug Abuse. Treatment Improvement Protocol 8.* Rockville, MD: U.S. HHS, PHS, SAMHSA, Center for Substance Abuse Treatment. DHHS Pub. (SMA) 94B2077.

———. 1999. Enhancing *Motivation for Change in Substance Abuse Treatment.* Retrieved 28 October 2011 from http://www.ncbi.nlm.nih.gov/books/bv.fcgi?rid=hstat5.part.22441

———. 2005. *Medication-Assisted Treatment for Opioid Addiction in Opioid Treatment Programs.* Treatment Improvement Protocol (TIP) Series 43. DHHS Publication No. (SMA) 05-4048. Rockville, MD: Substance Abuse and Mental Health Services Administration.

———. 2006. *Addiction Counselor Competencies: The Knowledge, Skills, and Attitudes of Professional Practice (Revised).* CSAT Technical Assistance Publication Series 21, Rockville, MD: Substance Abuse and Mental Health Administration. Retrieved 28 October 2011 from http://kap.samhsa.gov/products/manuals/pdfs/tap21.pdf

De Sousa, A. 2010. The pharmacotherapy of alcohol dependence: A state of the art review. *Psychopharmacology Today, 8*(1): 69–82.

Deitch, D. 1991. Training drug abuse treatment personnel in therapeutic community methodologies. *Psychotherapy 30*(2): 305–315.

De Leon, G., S. Sacks, and R. Hilton. 1993. "Passages: A Modified Therapeutic Community Day Treatment Model for Methadone Clients," in *Innovative Approaches in the Treatment of Drug Abuse.* J. Inciardi et al., eds. Westport, CT: Greenwood Press.

Doweiko, H. 2011. *Concepts of Chemical Dependency*, 8th ed. Pacific Grove, CA: Brooks/Cole.

Ellis, A. et al. 1988. *Rational-Emotive Therapy with Alcoholics and Substance Abusers.* Boston: Allyn and Bacon.

Fancher, R., and J. D. Freeman. 1997. *Cultures of Healing: Correcting the Image of American Mental Health Care.* New York: W. H. Freeman & Company.

Feeney, G. F. et al. 2006. Combined acamprosate and naltrexone, with cognitive behavioural therapy is superior to either medication alone for alcohol abstinence: A single centre's experience with pharmacotherapy. *Alcohol and Alcoholism, 41*(3): 321–332.

Gallon, S., and J. Porter. 2011. *Performance Assessment Rubrics for the Addiction Counselor Competencies.* Portland, OR: Northwest Frontier Addiction Technology Transfer Center. Retrieved 28 October 2011 from http://www.attcnetwork.org/explore/priorityareas/wfd/getready/docs/addictcc_rubrics_FL.pdf

Garfield, S. L., and A. E. Bergin. 1994. "Introduction and Historical Overview," Chap. 1 in *Handbook of Psychotherapy and Behavior Change,* 4th ed. A. E. Bergin and S. L. Garfield, eds. New York: Wiley.

Gottheil, E., ed. 1997. *Intensive Outpatient Treatment for the Addictions.* New York: Haworth Press.

Hargreaves, W. A. 1983. "Methadone Dose and Duration for Methadone Treatment," in *Research on the Treatment of Narcotic Addiction: State of the Art.* NIDA Treatment Research Monograph Series, DHHS pub. no. ADM-83-1281, J. R. Cooper et al., eds. Rockville, MD: National Institute on Drug Abuse.

Harwood, H. J. et al. 2002. *Cost Effectiveness and Cost Benefit Analysis of Substance Abuse Treatment: A Literature Review.* Rockville, MD: Substance Abuse and Mental Health Services Administration (SAMSHA). Retrieved on 15 November 2011 from http://www.lewin.com/content/publications/2485.pdf

Hayashida, M. et al. 1989. "Comparative Effectiveness and Costs of Inpatient and Outpatient Detoxification of Patients with Mild-to-Moderate Alcohol Withdrawal Syndromes." *New England Journal of Medicine* 320 (9 February): 358–365.

Horton, T., and S. McMurphy. 2004. "Phoenix House, A Therapeutic Community" from *Community Treatment Programs Take Up Buprenorphine. NIDA Science and Practice Perspectives* 2(2): 27–29.

Jason, L. A., & Ferrari, J. R. 2010. Oxford House recovery homes: Characteristics and effectiveness. *Psychological Services, 7*: 92–102.

Johnson, B. D., A. Rosenblum, and H. Kleber. 2003. "Public Policy Challenges for Bringing Buprenorphine into Drug Treatment Programs and General Medicine Practice." New York City: New York City Department of Health and Mental Hygiene. Retrieved 28 October 2011 from http://www.nyc.gov/html/doh/downloads/pdf/basas/whitepaper.pdf

Jones, M. 1953. *The Therapeutic Community.* New York: Basic Books.

————. 1968. *Social Psychiatry in Practice: The Idea of the Therapeutic Community*. Baltimore, MD: Penguin Books.

Kasl, C. 2002. Zen, Feminism, and Recovery: 16 Steps for Discovery and Empowerment. *Counselor Magazine*. Retrieved 28 October 2011 from http://www.counselormagazine.com/feature-articles-mainmenu-63/32-women-specific/152-zen-feminism-and-recovery-16-steps-for-discovery-and-empowerment

Lambert, M. J., and A. E. Bergin. 1994. "The Effectiveness of Psychotherapy," Chap. 5 in *Handbook of Psychotherapy and Other Behavior Change*. A. E. Bergin and S. I. Garfield, eds. New York: Wiley.

Lockwood, D., and J. A. Inciardi. 1993. "Crest Outreach Center: A Work-Release Iteration of the Therapeutic Community Model," in *Innovative Approaches in the Treatment of Drug Addiction*. J. A. Inciardi et al., eds. Westport, CT: Greenwood Press.

Maddux, J. F. 1993. "Improving Retention on Methadone Maintenance," in *Innovative Approaches in the Treatment of Drug Abuse*. J. A. Inciardi et al., ed. Westport, CT: Greenwood Press.

Maxwell, M. A. 1984. *The AA Experience*. New York: McGraw-Hill.

McCay, J. R. et al. 1998. Predictors of participation in aftercare sessions and self-help groups following completion of intensive outpatient treatment for substance abuse. *Journal of Studies on Alcohol 59*(2): 152–162.

McClellan, A. T. 2002. Have we evaluated addiction treatment correctly? Implications from a chronic care perspective. *Addiction* 97: 249–252.

Milby, J. B. 1988. Methadone maintenance to abstinence: How many make it? *Journal of Nervous and Mental Disease* 176: 409–421.

Miller, W. R., S. T. Walters, and M. E. Bennett. 2001. How effective is alcoholism treatment in the United States? *Journal of Studies on Alcohol* 62: 211–220.

Moos, R. H. 2003. Addictive disorders in context: Principles and puzzles of effective treatment and recovery. *Psychology of Addictive Behavior 17*(1): 3–12.

Moyer, A. et al. 2002. Brief interventions for alcohol problems: A meta-analytic review of controlled investigations in treatment-seeking and non-treatment-seeking populations. *Addiction 97*(3): 279–292.

NA (Narcotics Anonymous). 1988. *Narcotics Anonymous.* Van Nuys, CA: Narcotics Anonymous World Service Office.

National Institutes of Health (n.d.). Treating Alcohol Withdrawal with Oral Baclofen. Retrieved 28 October 2011 from http://clinicaltrials.gov/ct2/show/NCT00597701

NIAAA (National Institute on Alcohol Abuse and Alcoholism). 1995. *Project MATCH Monograph Series, 3: Cognitive-Behavioral Coping Skills Therapy Manual.* NIH pub. no. 94-3724. Rockville, MD: NIAAA and U.S. Dept. of Health and Human Services.

Pettinati, H. et al. 2010. A double-blind, placebo-controlled trial combining Sertraline and Naltrexone for treating co-occurring depression and alcohol dependence. *American Journal of Psychiatry, 167*: 668–675.

Phelps, N., and California Association of Alcohol/Drug Educators. 2011. *Intervention, Treatment, and Recovery: A Practical Guide to the TAP 21 Addiction Counselor Competencies.* Dubuquee, IA: Kendall-Hunt.

Rapoport, R. 1960. *Community as Doctor.* Springfield, IL: Chas. C. Thomas.

SAMHSA (Substance Abuse and Mental Health Services Administration). 1994. *Cost of Addictive and Mental Disorders and Effectiveness of Treatment.* DHHS pub. no. 2095-94. Rockville, MD: Substance Abuse and Mental Health Administration.

Schuckit, M. 1994. "Goals of Treatment," in *The American Psychiatric Press Handbook of Substance Abuse Treatment.* M. Galanter and H. D. Kleber, eds. Washington, DC: American Psychiatric Press.

Springer, D. W., C. A. McNeece, and E. M. Arnold. 2003. *Substance Abuse Treatment for Criminal Offenders: An Evidence-Based Guide for Practitioners.* Washington, DC: APA Books.

Swan, N. 1995. "California Study Finds $1 Spent on Treatment Saves Taxpayers $7." *NIDA Notes 10*(2): 34.

Trimpey, J. 1992. *The Small Book: A Revolutionary Alternative for Overcoming Alcohol and Drug Dependence* (rev. ed.). New York: Delacorte Press.

Washton, A. M. 1997. Evolution of intensive outpatient treatment (IOP) as a legitimate treatment modality. *Journal of Addictive Diseases 16*(2): xxi–xxvii.

White, W. 1998. *Slaying the Dragon: The History of Addiction Treatment and Recovery in America.* Bloomington, IN: Chestnut Health Systems, Lighthouse Training Institute.

Wren, C. 1999. "Arizona Finds Cost Savings in Treating Drug Offenders." *New York Times,* 21 April, p. A12.

Wutzke, S. E., K. M. Konigrave, J. B. Saunders, and W. Hall. 2002. The long-term effectiveness of brief interventions for unsafe alcohol consumption: A 10-year follow-up. *Addiction* 97(6): 665–675.

Yablonsky, L. 1965. *Synanon: The Tunnel Back.* New York: Macmillan Prometheus Books.

Yalisove, D. 1997. The origins and evolution of the disease concept of treatment. *Journal of Studies on Alcohol* 59: 469–476.

Zimberg, S. 1987. "Principles of Alcoholism Psychotherapy," in *Practical Approaches to Alcoholism Psychotherapy,* 2nd ed. S. Zimberg, J. Wallace, and S. B. Blume, eds. New York: Plenum Press.

2

Individual Counseling Skills

Objectives

By the end of this chapter, students will be able to:

1. Describe at least four qualities of an effective counselor.
2. Demonstrate effective nonverbal skills.
3. Demonstrate effective reflection skills.
4. Demonstrate use of open-ended and probing responses.
5. Demonstrate summarizing skills.
6. Demonstrate self-disclosure skills.
7. Demonstrate effective use of feedback.
8. Describe the important emotional issues in the counseling relationship.

Individual Addictions Counseling Skills

Despite great effort over the years, no research has been able to demonstrate the superior efficacy of a particular school of thought or format in counseling and treatment. The specific school of thought to which a counselor subscribes and the counseling format are less important than rooting his or her practice in basic counseling skills. These can establish and maintain a good working relationship and involve the client in his or her recovery—moving from a problem-ridden and helpless state through an exploration of alternatives, gaining insights and motivation, and taking action for personal growth.

Counselors need to examine their understanding of how and why professionals support and motivate an individual to change. Psychotherapy research indicated as early as 1950 that the therapist's theoretical orientation and educational background were not crucial factors in treatment effectiveness (Fiedler 1950, 1951). However, many practitioners have been too invested in their theoretical identities to pay much attention to such studies. Hundreds of studies, summarized by the technique of meta-analysis, show that many different therapies help clients, and that a number of supportive, learning, and action factors common to many therapies are associated with a positive outcome. Many of these factors pertain to the quality of the therapeutic relationship, including the therapeutic alliance and interpersonal skills (Kazdin 1994; Lambert and Bergin 1994).

It is not within the scope of this text to summarize the numerous psychotherapy models that have evolved since Sigmund Freud developed psychoanalysis at the beginning of the twentieth century. However, addictions professionals should be familiar with the major schools and models of psychotherapy such as the psychoanalytic, neopsychoanalytic, behaviorist, reality therapy, humanist, and existential therapies via a course on models of therapy that is usually a component of a professional training curriculum. Today's addiction counseling practice tends to favor motivational interviewing (motivational enhancement therapy) and cognitive behavioral approaches.

The "client-centered-counseling" of Carl Rogers (1951, 1986) was one of the first approaches to emphasize empathy and the client's potential growth, shifting away from an attitude of therapist as high-and-mighty expert and putting a "human face" on the therapeutic process. Motivational interviewing owes a great deal to the Rogerian approach.

In the 1960s vocational and educational counselors began to develop a subfield known as *counseling psychology*. They were interested in short-term concrete changes in clients rather than long-term psychotherapy, and were among the first to emphasize counseling qualities such as respect, warmth, concreteness, empathy, and genuineness, again with a debt owed to Carl Rogers. Many students will have been exposed to a taxonomy of skills, such as the pyramid-shaped "microskills hierarchy" developed by Allen and Mary Ivey (Ivey and Ivey 2003), some of which are reviewed later in this chapter.

More than four decades ago, Carkhuff (1969a, 1969b), Ivey (2010), and Egan (1998) were principal pioneers in investigating counseling qualities from a behavioral perspective. They studied exactly what counselors did or said that demonstrated helping qualities. This research led to a skills approach to counseling. The behaviors and skills necessary for effective counseling can, in fact, be taught to a large proportion of intelligent, motivated individuals. These skills are those of communicating, not of providing perfect advice, answers, or brilliant commentary. (Another term is *process skills*.) Today, training of most mental health workers, social workers, and counselors is grounded in one of the several generic counseling approaches. This approach includes learnable skills to facilitate a counseling process that helps clients to achieve insight, feel better about themselves, and change behavior patterns in directions that get them what they need (Cournoyer 1996; Egan 1998; Corey and Corey 1998). Recent meta-analytic studies of treatment effectiveness appear to validate such an approach. Nonetheless, many addictions counselors—not to mention many other mental health professionals—have no formal training or preparation in specific counseling skills.

Counseling Formats

Individual counseling sessions may to some extent follow a certain predictable routine, which may be based on a particular counseling or self-help model. Counseling formats translate treatment plans into digestible and understandable steps for client and counselor alike, in the individual counseling setting. The format also may represent an adaptation of a favorite model to accommodate limitations of reimbursement. *Format* refers to both the sequence of sessions and the structure of the counseling session.

The sequence of sessions in cognitive-behavioral therapy, for example, may entail a long-term relationship or it may be limited to seven sessions. A seven-session sequence might be the following:

1. Introducing coping skills
2. Coping with cravings and urges to drink
3. Managing thoughts about alcohol and drinking
4. Learning to solve problems
5. Learning drink-refusal skills
6. Planning for and coping with emergencies
7. Consequences of seemingly irrelevant decisions (NIAAA 1995, p. 19)

The structure of the counseling session may or may not follow a predictable routine. Beck and colleagues (1993, p. 97) recommend the following elements as the structure of a cognitive therapy session:

1. Setting the agenda
2. Checking the mood
3. Bridging from last session
4. Discussing today's agenda
5. Using Socratic questioning
6. Offering capsule summaries
7. Assigning homework
8. Giving feedback in the therapy session

This example shares with many psychotherapies a concern for budgeting time, linking the present session to previous and future sessions, and application of insights gained in the session to the life of the client. Yet a breakdown into eight segments is an unusually complex format. Moreover, routines may exist but not be immediately apparent. Students should observe counseling with the aim of determining whether there is an unspoken routine, such as a typical lead question or cooling-off segment toward the end to provide an appropriate emotional return to the world.

Motivational interviewing and the Stages of Change Model illuminate the cyclical, fluctuating nature of motivation and the simultaneous approach and avoidance of recovery goals. Many clinicians recognize that a new model can be oversimplified into a faddish gimmick. Barber (1994, p. 44) and Nealy (1997) have warned against ignoring the broader context of change—which includes emotions, self-esteem, and dependence on large and impersonal social institutions—"the strengths and weaknesses of our interpersonal relationships, the extent of our social support networks, and the stability of basic survival needs" (Nealy 1997, p. 12).

Tailoring Counseling Skills for Addicted Clients

There are many ways of itemizing, categorizing, and defining counseling skills and subskills. Definitions of skills overlap considerably, and it is dangerous to try to isolate or memorize definitions. Such a robotlike approach neglects the actual interpersonal process that these skills should facilitate. In fact, it is possible to defeat the purpose of a skills approach by memorizing definitions and using stock phrases.

The skills discussed here roughly follow tasks and stages of addictions counseling. They also fall across a continuum from less pressure to more pressure, and from passive to active. Cutting across the various models, an addictions counselor must first engage the client and build a therapeutic alliance. This provides a safety zone within which the client can reveal feelings and find support for recovery. Then the counselor can facilitate the client's gradual self-awareness and finally self-direction.

Engagement Skills

Engagement skills are crucial to establish a positive counseling relationship. To reach treatment goals, a counselor must be able to make personal contact and develop a working alliance with a client (Meier and Davis 1993, pp. 2–3). Because the typical addict is isolated emotionally, the counseling bond can be healing; investment in this relationship is a major factor in carrying a client through the rough shoals of early recovery. Engagement can be facilitated through qualities of genuineness, immediacy, warmth, and a nonjudging attitude. These qualities are demonstrated when the counselor has developed the skill of attending. Cited in some form in almost all training protocols, attending refers to providing cues that demonstrate concern, warmth, respect, interest in, involvement in, and awareness of the client's communications. These cues can be nonverbal (such as eye contact, an involved and relaxed body posture, and interactive gestures) or verbal (such as an animated rather than a flat tone of voice, or reassuring and encouraging vocalizations such as "hmm," "aha," and "go on").

Development of a working alliance also requires the counseling tasks involved in orientation and training of clients. Orientation is one of the core functions of the International Certification Reciprocity Consortium. Although orientation is not related to particular skills, it is necessary. Part of the engagement process is explaining counseling, which Meier and Davis (1993, pp. 4–6) consider part of "role induction," or socialization into the client role. The idea of talking openly about problems and feelings with a person who is not a family member or close friend is often a new one. The client may expect to be interrogated and given answers, rather than be aided in the process of self-exploration. The interactive nature of the counseling process needs to be explored, and the client needs explanations of confidentiality, treatment goals, and therapeutic culture. The alliance is developed further and cemented by explaining the process by which the counselor and client will develop a treatment plan based on long-term and short-term goals. Even the involuntary client can see the helpful intent and possibilities inherent in this scheme. Successful engagement thus prepares the client to benefit from treatment.

ACTIVITY (2.1) **Who are you?**

This activity serves as a self-assessment of your skill level in listening, observing, and focusing. Conduct a five-minute interview of a classmate. Find out as much as possible about the other person. No notes are allowed. Reverse roles and become the interviewee. Both individuals report out to a third person (observer). Observer and interviewees provide feedback on what they heard from the interviewers.

Active Listening Skills

Using active listening skills (Egan 1998), the counselor connects to and can reflect emotions, thoughts, and attitudes of his or her clients. This cluster of skills is known as *attending skills* (Ivey and Ivey 2003) and reflective listening (Miller and Rollnick 2002). By providing a clear mirror to the addict, the counselor interjects an "observing ego" that may be lacking.

Paraphrasing or Restating

The therapeutic qualities of *empathy* (the ability to perceive another person's experience and communicate that perception back to the person) and warmth can be developed by acquiring the skill of paraphrasing. *Paraphrasing* refers to a counselor's verbal response that rephrases the essence of the client's message. It allows the client to hear what he or she has just said, either in parroted form or with added clarity. This interactive process increases trust and reduces resistance. The following interchange is an example of a counselor's clarifying a client's message and restating it:

CLIENT: I started to do the bills, but I couldn't stand it and made a phone call instead. I started again, but I decided to have a snack.
COUNSELOR: You kept finding ways to avoid doing the bills.
Simplified mirroring; rephrase the client statement neutrally.
CLIENT: "I don't plan to give up drinking."
COUNSELOR: "You don't think abstinence would work, hmm?"
Exaggerate the statement without sarcasm.
CLIENT: "I don't know why my wife is so worried."
COUNSELOR: "So your wife is worried needlessly?"
Reflecting.

When the content being restated is emotional, it is a *reflection of feeling.* The counselor captures and expresses to the client the essence of what the client is feeling. This facilitates the exploration and identification of emotional needs and states. The emotional message may have been stated directly; however, the client may not be aware of his or her own emotional output or of how his or her emotional message was understood. Reflection of feeling shows the client that the counselor has understood the message. An alert, nonjudgmental, and friendly ear also acknowledges and validates a client's feelings, allowing him or her to own and accept the feelings and claim the right to have them. The counselor should be careful not to interpret the client's feelings. When reflecting an expressed feeling, the counselor remains neutral, not offering opinions, judgments, or advice. Neither does a counselor tell a client what he or she is feeling. The following interchange shows a counselor's reflection of a client's expressed emotion:

> CLIENT: When he told me that, I just lost it. I pushed my plate away and stormed out.
> COUNSELOR: You sound very angry with him.
> CLIENT: You bet! I could have thrown it in his face!

Not only does the client become more aware of his or her emotions and the emotional content of his or her utterances, but there is also the implicit message that "it is okay to be angry" (or sad, happy, lonely). Reflection of feelings helps the client establish, maintain, and affirm the habit of communicating feelings directly and appropriately rather than resorting to unproductive responses such as violence, drinking, or drugging. Some counselors use the expression, "If you learn to talk about it, you won't have to drink about it." If the client is ready, the counselor may move to *leading* skills (discussed later in this chapter).

Reflection of feeling has a particular twist in addictions treatment. Addictions counselors must be aware of temporary physical states in withdrawal and early sobriety that should be identified to the client, rather than interpreted as personal or interpersonal issues. For example, a person may drink too much coffee or take too much decongestant medication and have a reaction that is misperceived or misinterpreted as anxiety pertaining to some real issue. During withdrawal from depressant drugs including alcohol, the central nervous system undergoes rebound activity, which also may be experienced as anxiety and apprehension.

Simplifying

Reflection and restatement also have the important benefit and function of *simplifying*. Simplification removes confusion, avoids intellectualizations and convoluted explanations, and helps the client stay focused on concrete feelings and problems in the here and now. The famous AA slogan "Keep it simple" expresses this key element in self-help and counseling systems. Steve de Shazer, founder of the short-term, solution-focused school of therapy, quipped that one should edit the motto "Simplify, simplify, simplify" down to the single word "Simplify" (Berg and Miller 1992, p. 9).

A further function for reflection of feeling and restatement of content is to show the client that the counselor understands and is following the client's stream of consciousness. Egan (1998) calls this "pacing" the client, an image borrowed from sports training that connotes a more active form of "attending." It gives a sense of teamwork and collaboration and, in general, builds a positive feeling about the counseling experience. Clients who have clarified their feelings and thoughts from their counselors' restatements and reflections, which they have listened to and absorbed, leave the sessions feeling clearer and more at peace.

Summarizing

A higher level of abstraction in restatement and reflection is summarizing, or tying together the main points, themes, and issues presented by clients during part or all of a session. An added benefit of skilled summarizing is illustrating clients' ambivalence to them, allowing them to see the "positives and negatives simultaneously, acknowledging that both are present."

An elaborate summary of the positives and negatives of using alcohol and drugs is a technique suggested in motivational enhancement therapy and Beck's cognitive therapy. To arrive at this summary, the counselor enlists the client in enumerating contradictory motives in the "decisional balance." The decisional balance sheet is also a nonthreatening, engaging, defense-reducing exercise.

Reinforcing and Providing Hope

Many counselors simply affirm, support, and even praise the client for whatever steps he or she has taken. While this is not exactly a listening skill, it is a nonthreatening form of engagement and involvement. Examples of reinforcing are:

- "I appreciate how hard it must have been for you to decide to come here. You took a big step."
- "That must have been very difficult for you."
- "You're certainly a resourceful person to have been able to live with the problem this long and not fall apart."
- "It must be difficult for you to accept a day-to-day life so full of stress."

Such praise must be genuine or it will sound patronizing, disengage the client, and reduce support.

A related concept to reinforcing is the "positive asset search," that is, drawing out strengths. This skill should be built throughout the counseling process but is also sometimes seen as a specific segment of the counseling session (Ivey and Ivey 2003, pp. 202–203).

ACTIVITY (2.2) Am I a good listener?

After reading through this activity, form groups of three. In each group, one person will play the role of the client, one the counselor, and one the monitor. The "client" will talk about a personal problem or issue or something he or she would like to change. Where possible, keep the focus on issues related to use of drugs or alcohol. The "counselor" will counsel

*the client, practicing active listening skills (approximately 8 minutes).
The "monitor" will give feedback, noting what skills were observed and
where they were or were not used appropriately (approximately
1 minute). Note that the purpose of this activity is to practice active
listening skills. It is not designed for solving problems or probing deep
emotions or secrets.*

DISCUSS: After all groups have concluded their role-plays, return to the
large group and discuss your feelings about the performances of the roles.
Identify specific listening skills.

- What other counseling skills did you observe?
- Were they used appropriately? If not, why not?
- Would the inappropriate use you observed be harmful or just inef-
  fective? Explain.
- How would you have done it differently?
- How did you feel doing the counseling? Receiving the counseling?
- What did you observe in response to specific questions?
- How hard was it not to give advice?

Reframing

Reframing is different from reflection or restatement because this
skill interprets a client's experience from a different perspective or in a
reorganized form. For example, reframing can facilitate the perception
of an event in a more positive light, or a "bad" situation can be seen as a
challenge and a potential learning experience.

Reframing is emphasized in psychotherapies that are based in cognitive techniques, such as rational emotive therapy (RET; Ellis 1985a and b;
Ellis and Dryden 1987; Ellis et al. 1988). The counselor should take care,
however, not to apply this technique in a manner that seems to trivialize
or glibly explain away a client's loss and grief in the face of tragedy or
adversity. An example of reframing, via patient education, is the client who
begins to see alcohol- and drug-related behavior not as bad or shameful
but as symptomatic of a disease. Reframing gives the client a different
perspective, and this reduces the heavy shame-based feelings with which
the client is often burdened.

Leading Skills

Categorizations of helping or counseling skills vary among human services.
The category of leading skills discussed here is much broader than the
definition found in many counseling textbooks.

Leading skills are ways of encouraging and suggesting connections
that help the client move along in self-exploration and keep the client
thinking about his or her acts, thoughts, and feelings. These skills also
help the client develop the habit of self-reflection.

By using leading skills, addictions counselors help the client gain personal insights. To do so, counselors merely facilitate steps taken by the client in exploring emotions, behavior, and cognition. Leading is effective only if the client has some self-awareness; no one can progress from point A to point B until he or she has gotten to point A. For example, it is premature to discuss the implications of angry feelings if the angry person has not identified and acknowledged those feelings! In addition, leading questions should be open-ended and begin with what, when, where, or how. Various schools of thought, including motivational enhancement therapy (MET; Miller and Rollnick 2002, pp. 71–72) and cognitive therapy of addictions (Beck et al. 1993, pp. 104–105), stress the importance of open-ended questions such as "What else?" "Anything else you can think of?" and "Such as …?" They encourage thinking, talking, contemplation, and exploration. These types of questions can (adapted from CSAT 1999):

- Lead to other examples of a behavior or feeling, which may suggest a pattern. "Do you think that you may do this in other areas of your life?" "Do you feel this way in other situations?" "Do you often feel like this?"
- Lead to elaboration of the original statement. "Tell me more about that feeling." "What was that like?"
- Lead clients to reflect on what they think and feel in particular situations. "How did you feel about that? Him? Her? Yourself?"
- Lead toward links among thoughts, feelings, and behaviors. "How do you act when you feel this way?" "Does that thought make you anxious?" "How do you feel after you do that?"
- Lead toward an understanding of consequences and implications of behavioral choices and patterns. "What would happen then?" "What would that mean?" "Is it OK to have those feelings?" "Why aren't you entitled to your feelings?"
- Return to the crucial topic, the here and now, the topic at hand, and addiction-specific concerns. "How does that relate to …?"
- Lead to discussions of plans and behaviors. "What are you going to do about it?"
- Lead to new directions. *Agree but change direction.* Client: "Why are you and my family so damn stuck on my drinking? Geez, you'd drink, too, if you were nagged so much." Counselor: "You know, you're right. We shouldn't blame you because drinking problems involve the whole family."

The "*downward arrow*" technique used in the cognitive therapy approach to addictions counseling is based on questions that lead the client through an identification of self-statements or unarticulated assumptions about "domino effects" of his or her choices. This model states that there are layers of "automatic thoughts" triggered by specific situations that can lead to, among other things, catastrophizing or all-or-nothing thinking. Using this technique, the counselor asks repeatedly about the meaning, consequences, or implications of an idea or situation to "deconstruct" the chains or layers of belief. In one example (Beck et al. 1993, pp. 140–142), a man is afraid of not drinking at an upcoming office party. By asking him a series of questions, each a variation on the question, "What does that mean to you?" (e.g., "What would the implications be?" and "What would the consequences be?"), the counselor finds that the man doesn't think he'd be fun sober, that no one would stick with him, that his sales career would suffer, and that he'd lose his house and family! The "downward arrow" technique has its counterpart in motivational interviewing. We "lead" the client to elicit motivational statements: "What would happen if you stopped drinking?"

Focusing is important due to the time-limited nature of addictions treatment, especially in the managed-care era. It may be a gentle or more active nudge, as in the probing/questioning skill discussed later. A crucial topic to attend to and focus upon is the counseling process itself. The counselor facilitates awareness of and open discussion of the client's experiences in the session and what happens between the parties. This is perhaps the most curing growth experience that is possible in counseling, far outweighing advice, answers, and therapeutic sleight-of-hand. A popularized expression is "staying in the here and now." As Meier and Davis (1993) advise, "When in doubt, focus on feelings" at a level appropriate to the stage of treatment and with full awareness of anxiety or even pain that this may necessitate. "How does that make you feel?" is a here-and-now question.

The other crucial topic to lead the client to is the relevancy to recovery and relapse of the content under discussion or the process just revealed. By asking, "Do you think this discussion can help you stay sober?" the skilled counselor lets the client make the connections.

Leading the client to discuss plans and behaviors helps him or her see the link between his or her actions and getting results. It leads to self-efficacy, the confidence that one has some power over one's life. By encouraging the client to make plans assertively, counselors facilitate movement toward the point of taking action to affect his or her recovery.

In developing skills to help clients develop self-awareness, a counselor must pay attention to the timing of questions as well as how assertively he or she pursues the point. The term *probing* carries the connotation of going underneath a surface feeling or idea into deeper, perhaps buried material. In choosing to move faster or more aggressively in leading, counselors tread the fine line between leading and confrontation. It is seldom appropriate for counselors to force clients to "spill their guts," that is, to suddenly access and ventilate intense rage and pain, especially in early treatment. Counselors may feel that the client is ready to go further, ask various questions that lead into new territory, and then sense anxiety that signals them to back off for now. Several concerns affect the decision of whether to pose potentially threatening questions:

- Stage of treatment
- Degree to which the client has become engaged and invested in treatment
- Degree of coercion involved in the client's participation in treatment
- Awareness of nonverbal cues provided by clients that indicate that the counseling process is generating anxiety

ACTIVITY (2.3) That's a leading question!

After reading through this activity, form groups of three. In each group, one person will play the client, one the counselor, and one the monitor. The "client" and the "counselor" will discuss a personal problem or issue the client would like to change (5–10 minutes). Keep the focus on issues related to drugs and alcohol. The "monitor" will then give feedback about which skills he or she observed (1–2 minutes).

Remember that the purpose of this activity is to practice leading skills, not to solve problems. Also remember that all information shared here is confidential.

Discuss: After all groups have concluded their role-plays, return to the large group and discuss your feelings and observations about the performance of the roles.

- Identify specific leading skills.
- Were they used appropriately? If not, why not?
- Would the inappropriate use you observed be harmful or just ineffective? Explain.
- How would you have done it differently?

Counselor Self-Disclosure

In the addictions field, *counselor self-disclosure* often means the counselor shares his or her recovery from addiction. In generic counseling, the term refers to a counselor's sharing his or her relevant feelings, attitudes, opinions, or experiences for the benefit of the client. Counselor self-disclosure can benefit the client because it:

- Reduces shame, guilt, and sense of isolation by showing the client he or she is not uniquely horrible
- Aids in maintaining a here-and-now focus
- Provides an example of intimacy to a client who has never experienced intimacy or who has lost a sense of how to be intimate

Counselors never use self-disclosure to impress the client, nor in response to the counselor's need to confess or ventilate. Skillful self-disclosure is relevant in content, occurs in an accurate context, and is timed effectively.

Self-disclosure of a counselor's recovery from addiction has been the subject of an ongoing debate in addictions counseling. Some see this disclosure as a crucial contribution of the recovering counselor in providing hope, inspiration, and role models. Paradoxically, some nonrecovering counselors feel that an agency milieu in which counselors disclose their recovery status puts them at a disadvantage. However, a client who is bent on devaluing the counselor will come up with a reason for each type of counselor (i.e., "You're just a drunk like me, how can you help?" or "You never went through it, how can you help?"). In either case, the counselor should respond by encouraging the client to identify and communicate his or her needs and goals, and exploring how the treatment plan and counseling process will facilitate movement in this direction.

The term *self-disclosure* can refer not only to revelation of recovery status but also to the sharing of any information or feelings by the counselor. Some of the goals of counselor self-disclosure are facilitation of intimacy and bonding, and reduction of shame or guilt about feelings. If done appropriately, it can open up people's "hidden spots." Counselors may wish to tell clients how behavior affects them in order to bring out some emotion, tension, or discrepancy. For example, a "chatterbox" client communicated tension and forced cheerfulness to the counselor, who remarked, "While you're telling me all these great things, I'm starting to feel anxious, and I wonder why that is."

ACTIVITY Do you know who I am?

Consider the surface and visual issues that make people seem different (e.g., hair color, skin tone, accent, manner of dress, size). Pair up with someone who seems very different from you. In pairs, share a significant experience that made you who you are. These experiences might include a terrible loss, an act of kindness from another person, getting or leaving a job or home, or getting married or divorced.

PROCESS: After 5 to 10 minutes regather to one larger group and discuss: Were there similarities in your experiences? Did the physical differences begin to be less or more significant? Did one person feel more comfortable than the other in divulging personal information? Did the person who went second feel easier about self-divulging after hearing the first person's story? How did you feel as you listened to your partner's story?

Influencing Skills

Simply being in a counseling relationship exerts an influence on clients. But sometimes counselors actively intervene to influence their clients. This is dangerous territory. Great skill and thoughtfulness are required to exert a positive influence that furthers the client's treatment.

Interpretation

Interpretation is a technique used by counselors to provide a new "frame of reference" or alternative ways of looking at situations. Interpreting involves seeing connections between situations, beliefs, feelings, and behavior. It involves understanding the influence of experience and the dynamics of different personalities. Of course, it is preferable for the client to develop insights and self-understanding than to be told things about himself or herself. As Meier and Davis (1993) emphasize, avoid advice and avoid premature problem solving. Counselors can cheat clients out of the wonderful therapeutic experiences of struggling with old ways of thinking, uncovering feelings, seeing new connections, and having exciting realizations if they supply pat answers—even when clients demand them and are angry when refused. Growth is liberating.

Confrontation

The term *confrontation* is a minefield. It has many meanings, depending on the treatment modality and setting. Confrontation is a deliberate use of a question or statement by the counselor to help the client face what the counselor thinks the client is trying to avoid. The technique is designed to provide an opportunity for change. Confrontation usually points out discrepancies:

- Within the client's statement or beliefs
- Between statements and behaviors
- Between strengths and weaknesses
- Between what a client states and what the counselor heard or observes

One may develop discrepancies somewhat indirectly. *Acknowledge statement but use contradictory information the client gave earlier.*

CLIENT: "You want me to stop using, but I won't."

COUNSELOR: "You can see there are some real problems, but you're not willing to consider stopping."

The process skill of confrontation involves five elements: timing, staying concrete, estimating, forcefulness, and keeping tabs on the counselor.

Effective *timing* of the confrontation occurs when the client can see the possibility of change or when resistance is causing stagnation. Poor timing for confrontation would be during the throes of major depression, suicidal ideation, when a client is anxious, and after a loss or defeat. There is no formula for timing of confrontations. Rather, it is related to the counseling skills of attending to the clients' verbal and nonverbal cues, which provide information on their emotional states, and to correctly estimating the development of a therapeutic alliance. One program summed this up in training as "you may confront as much as you have supported."

Staying concrete and *providing hope* are important in confrontation. Counselors should remember that the goal of confrontation is to facilitate change. Vagueness, lectures, and pontification can create confusion or even despair. First, it is important to make simple and concrete remarks. An example is, "Is your behavior getting you what you need?" Second, it is important to incorporate the possibility of specific change. This can move the client forward, past the discomfort of the confrontational moment and toward taking the next step. An example is "Can you think of other ways of feeling good?" or "What small thing can you do that will make you feel better about this?" Ending the confrontation with an item for a change plan is also a way of helping the client feel hopeful.

Estimating how much to confront and how forcefully is also critical. Meier and Davis (1993, p. 12) offer a rule of thumb: "You may confront as much as you've supported." In addictions treatment, the client is often a mandated involuntary participant, denial is practically universal, and the amount of time available for the treatment is limited. Although involuntary treatment certainly does not make it permissible to use harsh and unpleasant methods, it does make counselors a little less fearful of being frank with their comments. The supportive addictions counselor provides an opportunity for change without boxing the client in a corner to the point of being abusive or destroying the possibility of a therapeutic alliance. Although it is easy to confuse with rage and raised voices, confrontation can be done with the utmost gentleness.

Drug treatment in particular has been associated with extremes in confrontation. In one old-style drug treatment setting, author Myers recalled a group member screaming, "I hate you" for twenty minutes. Certainly there has been a tremendous fall-off in this top-volume, self-stimulating hysteria throughout many or most programs like that one, and hostile interactions have been declining for decades.

Monitoring the counselor's emotional state and motives is very important. Confrontation always should be motivated by a desire to help the client change. That is, counselors must confront clients out of concern rather than rage, annoyance, demonstration of power, transference of issues from their own recovery or other personal issues (countertransference), or need for self-glorification. Counselors must honestly assess their motives and feelings when initiating a confrontation. Confrontations that are forced or are the result of the counselor's frustration and anger usually result in serious damage to the therapeutic relationship. Confrontation in group settings, as we will discuss later, must be monitored by counselors to avoid scapegoating of a person who is weaker, more marginal, or different than other members in some way.

Ellis and colleagues (1988, pp. 56–57, 72–74) encourage counselors to confront irrational, unhelpful cognitions. They refer to this as *disputing,* which may include:

- Challenges to evidence produced by clients
- Identifications of distortions in thinking
- Development of more accurate explanations of events (reattribution)
- Argument in favor of irrational beliefs to bring out the lack of validity for this position
- Disputation of catastrophizing or awfulizing modes of thought, which may generate so much anxiety as to pose a threat of relapse

Figure 2.1 is an example of the disputing technique as applied to awfulizing.

Figure 2.1 An example of disputing.

IB (Irrational Belief): *It's awful when I don't drink and therefore I have to feel anxious.*
DC (Disputing Counselor): *Why is it awful?*
IB: *Because it is so uncomfortable.*
DC: *And you run the universe, right?*
IB: *No, but I should be able to control my own discomfort.*
DC: *That would be great. But, really, must you?*
Client: *No, I guess I do not have to have more comfort.*

Source: Ellis, A., J. F. McInerney, R. DiGiuseppe, and R. J. Yeager. 1988. *Rational-Emotive Therapy with Alcoholics and Substance Abusers.* Boston: Allyn and Bacon.

ACTIVITY (2.5) How do I influence people?

After reading through this activity, form groups of three. In each group, one person will play the role of the client, one the counselor, and one the observer. Role-play one of the situations listed below. The "counselor" will counsel the client, practicing active influencing skills (approximately 8 minutes). The "observer" will give feedback, noting what skills were observed and whether they were or were not used appropriately (approximately 1 minute). Remember to keep the focus on issues related to use of drugs or alcohol. The following list suggests some situations to role play.

- A court-mandated client in an intake session is denying or resisting the need for treatment.
- A client who has been sober and drug free for two months has skipped counseling sessions and stopped attending support group meetings. The client is somewhat withdrawn and shows some of the signs of impending relapse.
- A client is getting into trouble on the job, flying into rages at home, and acting sullen and brooding in the session.
- A client who has been sober and drug free for four months has not made progress on a goal in the treatment plan (e.g., finding a job, making friends, taking a vacation, repaying a debt).

Enact situations that your instructor suggests.

DISCUSS: After all groups have concluded their role-plays, return to the large group and discuss the effectiveness and impact of influencing skills.

- Identify specific influencing skills. Were they effective? Why or why not?
- Would you recommend handling the situation another way? How? Why?
- What feelings were invoked in the "counselors" and "clients"?
- What other counseling skills did you observe?
- Did the influencing skills of the counselors facilitate change in the clients? How?

Timing

The discussion of probing skills stresses being aware of the client's level of anxiety and knowing when to "advance" and "retreat." Throughout the application of all counseling skills, it is necessary to know how far to go, how to time comments well, and how to match the intensity of feelings and anxiety a counselor might arouse with the stage of treatment and the client's mood.

The "art of counseling," unlike the "science" or "technique" of counseling, depends very much on timing, which depends on the comfort level and skill of the counselor. Nevertheless, there are some ground rules. When clients come into treatment, their anxiety is usually high and they need anxiety-reducing responses (reassurance, explanation, attending, listening, and support). Later, when clients become complacent and comfortable, techniques that increase some level of anxiety (probing, confrontation) are useful to motivate a client. As Wallace points out in his classic piece, "Critical Issues in Alcoholism Psychotherapy" (1985, pp. 37–49), addictions counselors continually walk a fine line between allowing clients' denial to continue too long and pushing them prematurely toward self-disclosure.

Miscellaneous Techniques to Elicit "Change Talk"

While not exactly basic counseling skills, these techniques fit into the individual counseling toolkit:

- *Evocative questions* ask the client directly to talk about change. Examples cited by Rosengren (1999, p. 95) include, "If you decided to make a change, what makes you think you could do it?" and "How would things be better for you if you changed?"
- *Elaboration* asks the client to think and express his/herself more completely. If a client has made a statement about changing, the counselor asks them to describe such an instance. An example would be, "What was it like when you guys got along better? What went on, specifically, to help me understand."
- *Using extremes* elicits the worst and best possible outcomes if their behavior did not change. "What's the worst that can happen?" "What do you hope for the most?" This lays out a landscape or continuum that can be filled in with the less extreme elements (Rosengren 1999, p. 96).

Process Recording

Process recording is a way that counselors keep track of, look back at, reflect upon, think about, and analyze what is going on in the counseling process. It is more than a simple recording of events; it is recording and processing what is going on, leading to an evaluation of the use of techniques and the client–counselor relationship. It allows counselors to "attend to" and "pace" themselves. It is a standard training method in social work and mental health settings, but unfortunately it is often absent in the chemical dependency practicum (Myers 2003). It is an invaluable tool in the fieldwork or practicum component of counselor preparation. Process recording is quite useful in supervisory sessions. Figure 2.2 is an excerpt from a process recording.

Figure 2.2 Excerpt from a process recording.

Sandra Baskin (SB), a counselor at an outpatient addictions facility, wrote the following as part of her process recording of an individual counseling session with Michael Gerrity (MG). Her process comments are in parentheses. She uses the following abbreviations: Dx=diagnosis, Tx=treatment, ASP=antisocial personality, DA=district attorney.

MG entered the room.

> *(I was feeling burned out and irritable since this was the fourth client in a row, the last one being very hostile. I hoped that my mood didn't show.)*

MG: Hey, what's up? Mind if I duck outside on the terrace for a quick smoke?

SB: Hey, you know we can't do that!

MG: Nobody will know, come on, Ms. Baskin.

(Now I'm starting to really get annoyed at MG.)

MG (smiles broadly): Well, it could be worse! I'm alive! And with my favorite counselor!

> *(I felt disarmed by Michael's impish smile and smiled back. Now I remembered that Michael had a Dx of ASP and could be very charming and manipulative. I was mad at myself for being conned even for a moment. Got to check charts before client comes in. Maybe make red flags for important info. MG is also coming up for a court hearing . . .)*

SB: Are you feeling ready for your hearing with Judge Madsen?

MG: Only if you are. (A teasing reference to my role in preparing the agency report on MG's cooperation, participation, and progress in Tx.)

SB: Do you feel that I'm on your side here? (MG still tends to view me as another cop; my attempts at empathic engagement must be a con job like MG would pull.)

MG: Ummm (suddenly loses his glib repartee).

SB: I was in your position once. (Oh, crap. Why did I blurt that out? I'm so anxious to make a connection with Mike that I jumped over a boundary. Did NOT need to share that. There's that over-identification/codependency issue kicking in . . . my little brother MG is not . . . Now I'm feeling anxious and out of control.)

MG: Yeah? (smiles again, more authentically) Maybe we can be buddies after all. (An alliance or a con? What is the difference for him? My comment helped, but at what price later on?) Well, I'm pretty stressed about it. You know, Madsen gets into his Hanging Judge bag, get-the-dope-fiends-off-the-street thing.

SB: Maybe we should concentrate on concrete steps in your treatment plan that will help you stay clean AND out of the clutches of the DA. And an agency plan for an alternative to sentencing.

MG: I guess I can't go wrong with that. Thanks, doc. (MG calls me 'doc' when he is feeling positive about our relationship. I think I rescued the situation.)

(Looking back at this section, I realize I'm spending a lot of energy on second-guessing everything I say and do and on the client's response, micromanaging myself. So much for the here and now!)

Process recordings, progress notes, and case presentations are different things. *A process recording* is a transcript or summary of everything that went on between the participants and the emotions evoked by their interactions. *Progress notes* (or *chart notes*) document that appropriate tasks or interventions were completed, and they provide background for the next worker. The *case presentation* demonstrates the ability to muster an overview of an addict's entire treatment career and mastery of the entire scope of treatment.

The process recording should begin with a brief description of the client and where he or she is in the "client career," a brief summary of treatment goals that are being implemented, and any other information that can provide context for the listener or reader. After this, the process recording breaks down into two tracks, the content track and the process track. The content track is a transcript of the verbal and nonverbal behavior of the client (e.g., client came in ten minutes late, tapped his fingers rapidly while speaking, said "I hate you!" in a loud, high-pitched voice). The process track includes such items as the following, in the order that they occurred or were observed:

- Observations about a client's emotional state
- Broader inferences about how the client's expectations, transference issues, and transcultural issues affected the client's actions in the session

- The counselor's emotional reactions (e.g., "I felt . . . and this is probably related to a similar experience or relationship I had.")
- Itemization of the counseling skills applied at each point during the session
- Observations of how the counselor's use of particular approaches influenced the process

Process recordings can alternate paragraphs or make columns (content and process) to record the tracks. Typically, the column system results in some blank spaces in the content column because the commentaries usually run longer. Cournoyer (1996, p. 210) uses a multicolumn analysis to prepare a transcription of an audio- or videotaped session: content, skill used, counselor's gut reaction, and counselor's analysis.

The final section of the process recording contains suggestions for treatment (improvement) based on the counselor's observations. Examples of suggestions are to provide more client education on the treatment process, have further discussions of his or her expectations of treatment, focus on the here and now, avoid data and "war stories," stay with more modest session goals, remember to budget time for "patching up" the client after heavy self-disclosures, learn more about the client's ethnic background, do something about that burnout, and use attending skills more and influencing skills less.

Process recording is governed by legal and ethical guidelines. Preparation and use of the document must be done in collaboration with the agency's administrators. The agency should determine whether the sensitive document should be kept in the files because it could be subpoenaed for use in legal proceedings against the agency, its employees, or the client.

Emotional Issues of the Counseling Relationship

Clients and counselors carry emotional baggage into the counseling relationship. Experiences form elements of a lens through which people view each other in distorted images, affecting perceptions, attitudes, feelings, and expectations in treatment. Traditional *psychoanalysis*—the theory and practice of psychotherapy founded by Sigmund Freud—coined the term *transference* for the effects of emotional baggage brought by the client into the counseling relationship. *Countertransference* reflects the counselor's reactions to the client through his or her own transference.

While the phenomenon of transference was originally considered outside of the awareness or conscious mind of the client, in an "unconscious" domain, today most schools of counseling and psychotherapy use the terms to refer to a broad range of prior issues that color the counseling relationship (Brockett and Gleckman 1991; Kernberg 1975).

Clinical concern with transference phenomena is found in therapeutic approaches that have some connection, however indirect, to a psychoanalytic perspective. Addictions treatment has emerged primarily from a different historical legacy. Therefore, transference has not been a major focus of addictions treatment. In addition, the association of transference with psychoanalysis raises the fear that it is the kind of drawn-out, "talky" concern that might take the focus off the immediate, life-and-death issues of addiction and recovery. Transference is actually a powerful presence in addictions treatment and it is also very useful as a clinical tool in illuminating patterns of thinking and relating. It is unlikely that the term *transference* will be used in conversations with clients, but understanding these phenomena is important in the counseling relationship.

Positive Transference

Positive transference refers to positive feelings and emotional needs being transferred from another person or relationship to the counselor. Transference of positive feelings has the advantage of helping to keep the client in treatment, even when the counselor is confronting, challenging, or pressuring the client to an uncomfortable extent.

Positive transference can be intense in early recovery. With release from anesthesia comes awareness of formerly muted emotions and needs. The "emotional rebound" includes affiliative, intimate, and affectional needs. Recovery offers relief from a lonely, often stigmatized existence. Many addicts who are new to treatment have been estranged from family, friends, and community. The new counseling relationship in individual and group treatments also contributes to reawakening feelings and needs, both positive and negative.

Positive transference may involve unrealistic expectations of help, love, or protection, at times involving a fantasized relationship (of which the client is not altogether aware). When taken to the extreme, the counselor is idealized and invested with the powers and qualities of some sort of omnipotent, omniscient superparent.

For the counselor, there are interrelated traps in runaway positive transference: It is flattering and ego enhancing to be a rescuer. This meets a counselor's emotional needs for validation and importance. Thus, the counselor may unwittingly "leak" cues that subtly reinforce this message. Unfortunately, in doing so, the counselor is encouraging the client's unrealistic expectations and fantasies, which are bound to be dashed at some point. This often results in extreme disappointment and devaluation of the counselor, and in some cases of the entire counseling experience.

At the same time, the client may feel shame, guilt, anxiety, panic, or loss of control at having strong positive feelings and intense needs. Psychologist

Stanley Meyers, PhD, calls this an "intimacy freak-out"(personal communication). Therefore, the client may develop denial and resistance strategies (so-called *counterdependent behavior*), flee treatment entirely, or even relapse.

A skilled counselor tries to handle intense emotional needs by setting limits without appearing rejecting or wreaking emotional devastation. One counselor asked, "How do you chill them out without sending them out?" Finally, transference to a variety of individuals, a group, and to the entire program, rather than mainly to the individual counselor, should always be encouraged.

A special situation is one in which the client is flirtatious or sexual. Flirtatious behavior may be the result of transferring onto a counselor the relationship with a seductive parent or a parent who demanded appeasement. Such behavior may be the only method the client knows to achieve intimacy, to manipulate people into meeting his or her needs, or a combination. It also may indicate the client's inability to distinguish between a sexual relationship and other types of close relationships.

A crucial phase in which transference occurs is termination of treatment. As termination approaches, clients may become anxious and begin anticipatory grieving for the loss they are about to experience. Some try to avoid or negate this unbearable loss by being hostile, denigrating the formerly idealized counselor, or leaving treatment and possibly relapsing. Treatment planning should attempt to anticipate and plan for a healthy means of separating and moving on. Counselors should lead clients into an exploration of how they will feel when time in the program is up, and they should help them weave a new emotional safety net.

Negative Transference

Clients get angry, hostile, resentful, and jealous. It is wonderful in fact if clients feel free and safe enough to show these feelings. Counselors must respect the clients' rights to have any feelings without risk of repercussion. Clients must learn to communicate feelings appropriately in order to maintain sobriety and prevent relapse.

In the emotional rebound of early sobriety, the rejections, resentments, abuse, and disappointments of a lifetime may be piled onto the counselor. Many clients have a history of conflicts with authority, of misdiagnosis, or of punishments by the agents of authority, whom a counselor may represent. In addition, many have experienced trauma, loss, pain, and abandonment as children of addicts. Again, the counselor can become the target.

Of course, it is no fun to be the scapegoat. While it may be an uncomfortable situation for the counselor, it may be the first time that the client has felt safe in feeling and expressing anger or rage. In allowing this to happen, counselors provide a substitute for "drinking about it" and an opportunity to practice coping with negative feelings in a healthy way, without chemicals. Despite the discouragement, the counselor must maintain his or her professional role and not personalize the client's behavior. It is dangerous to take this anger personally and react defensively to it. It is a mistake to jump too quickly to explore, interpret, and explain the negative transference, which short-circuits the counseling process and explains away these strong feelings.

The first task is to verify that the counselor is in fact not the cause of such anger. It is appropriate for a client to be angry with a counselor who is always late, hostile when the counselor allows other clients to cut in on his or her meeting time, or resentful of a counselor who regularly answers phone calls during sessions. Having eliminated elements in the counselor–client relationship as causes, it is necessary to explore other causes of these emotions. Is a client's anger a mask for the fear that he or she cannot be helped by this human agency? This fear may convert into rage at the counselor, even if the client has fantasized an omnipotent counselor.

There are indeed powerful sources of both positive and negative transference among addicted clients, both sets of feelings being threatening to the client. The transference is not only strong but also marked by ambivalence, conflicts, and shifts (Wallace 1985, p. 16).

Countertransference (Counselor Transference)

This somewhat cumbersome term was coined by Sigmund Freud in 1910. In modern parlance *countertransference* describes those reactions to clients that stem from the counselor's own needs, relationships, or recovery issues. For the remainder of this chapter we will substitute the term "counselor transference." Counselors' skills in identifying personal reactions are imperative in ethical treatment. Counselors must keep clients' needs and welfare as the primary concern and avoid acting upon emotional reactions to clients in ways that are not helpful to the client or the counseling process. Examining counselor transference also can reveal important information as to what messages the client is sending: A counselor may be resonating to a client's powerful feelings not yet out in the open.

One of the toughest tasks facing the counselor is staying in touch with his or her feelings, especially when dealing with challenging and difficult clients. Being aware that a client is causing emotional reactions may make a counselor feel out of control, or at least feel a loss of self-control. However, that awareness is critical. When a counselor is not fully aware of these reactions, or how they influence his or her behavior, that counselor truly is not in control.

Positive Counselor Transference

Powerful positive reactions to clients may arise as a way of making amends for abuse or neglect suffered when he or she was actively addicted. Another unfortunate motive is the need to be worshipped and loved by a client, which masks low self-esteem, terror of abandonment, dependency needs, and a lack of gratifying relationships in the counselor's own life.

Sorting through counselor transference is often difficult. For example, if a counselor finds the client romantically interesting, is this:

- A normal reaction to an attractive client?
- An indication of the counselor's need for intimacy or love?
- A response to the client's idealization of, or love for, the counselor, which feeds a need for praise, validation, and flattery?
- A response to a client's need for affection and intimacy being communicated via nonverbal cues, subtle flattery, or seduction?
- A romantic rescue fantasy arising from the counselor's codependency?
- A reaction to a client's skillful manipulation?
- A combination or intermediate form of two or more of the above?

Counselors must, with the aid of individual or group supervision, sort through their own feelings and needs. Exploration and evaluation of the role in the counselor–client relationship contribute to the client's progress in treatment and can help the counselor avoid the following pitfalls:

- Encouraging inappropriate levels of transference, resulting in disappointment, rage, or relapse
- Failing to maintain appropriate boundaries
- Falling into an enabling or infantalizing role
- Holding on to clients when it is time for them to move on
- Establishing a "pet" client to the disadvantage of all

Negative Counselor Transference

Being human, counselors can have angry or hostile feelings toward clients. Having negative emotions about clients is normal. Being vigilant and rigorously honest about these reactions is an ethical imperative, so as to ensure that counselors do not unwittingly act on them or send double messages to the client. Aside from simple reactions to provocation, attack, or unpleasant characteristics of a client, a wide variety of personal issues and experiences of counselors can result in negative perceptions and emotional reactions. Signals that clients may be communicating through voice qualities or body language also can cause discomfort. Some negative reactions to clients occur when a counselor's reactions to a client are rooted in the counselor's own issues. A counselor may have a need to control or may expect a client to meet needs for validation, love, and so on. Unrealistic expectations may echo a counselor's negative experiences and prompt negative feelings toward a client who rejects help or who is resistant, critical, or provocative.

Counselors may become angry and disappointed when clients have setbacks or relapse because this seems to signal their own inadequacy. Relatively new, recovering counselors may overidentify with a client and feel anxious and out of control when things do not go as planned. If a counselor identifies with a client's undesired character trait, he or she might, as the addiction aphorism goes, "attack in others what we faintly perceive in ourselves."

A counselor might associate the client with a negative experience or relationship in the counselor's past. What if the client is a rapist or child abuser and the counselor has suffered from such individuals? What if the counselor is parenting or has parented a problem child, like the client? Negative counselor transference can be caused by reactions to body language or voice qualities. Facial expressions, gestures, postures, and voice qualities can be inconsistent with what a person is saying, which creates tension and discomfort. Counselors also may react negatively to clients' rigid or overcontrolled body language or speech qualities, talking in a monotone, lack of affect (which suggest hidden content or difficulties), and rejection of attempts at engagement. Unexpressed strong feelings in a client who is making a valiant attempt to present a cheerful or stoic face, but whose tension and strain "leaks through" in contradictory signals, can also make the counselor tense.

. . . .

Case in Point

Everything's Fine

Marge, the wife of a severe alcoholic, was enrolled in an addiction counseling training program. She maintained a controlled, cheerful, "chatterbox" persona behind which lay great tension and probably great pain. The internship/practicum course included a weekly seminar class in which the trainees aired their concerns, feelings, and problems, in reference to their fieldwork placements, as well as discussed clinical issues. The cheerfulness manifested by Marge was clearly forced. This "got on the nerves" of the other students, who found it difficult to deal with the façade. As often happens in a group learning to be counselors, the interactions among the group members became material to the process. The students gently and respectfully confronted Marge and encouraged her to talk about her life and problems. Through honest expression and exploration of feelings (positive and negative), the group resolved the situation—an excellent learning experience.

Unexplored negative feelings and counselor transference pose dangers. Especially a newly recovering counselor, prematurely thrust into a counseling role, may have intense reactions that could cause burnout and be harmful to the client by disrupting the treatment process. A counselor in recovery may make the recovery of each client his or her personal mission and responsibility. Personal emotional investment in a client ruins the counselor's perspective and his or her ability to behave in a professional way. For example, such a counselor may be too easy on a client, or push too hard!

Unrecognized and unexplored negative counselor transferential reactions may lead a counselor to:

- Subtly push away a client
- Withhold support
- Make incorrect negative interpretations
- Participate in scapegoating
- Feel guilty about hostile or negative feelings and act "nice"
- Be anxious when negative feelings threaten to surface

Before resorting to obscure or exotic interpretations of their feelings, counselors always should look at concrete things that are going on to which they may be responding. The excerpt from a student's process recording (Figure 2.3) provides a simple example of anxiety provoked by a client.

In the real world of counseling, emotional reactions are not sorted neatly into positive and negative categories. The client's reactions to the counselor are a mixture of positive and negative feelings, sometimes ambiguous and shifting. So are the counselor's reactions to the client. Ambiguity, in oneself and others, is difficult to process and often provokes

Figure 2.3 Process recording: Anxiety.

During the course of the session, the client talked loudly and was very animated. He maintained eye contact to a point that I thought he was trying to stare me down. We were seated in a closed-door, narrow, and rectangular conference room and sat across from each other. However, even though we were seated some distance apart, the client's demeanor and behavior was so overwhelming that his presence seemed to fill the entire room. Since both doors to the conference room were closed and locked from the outside, I began to experience some feelings of claustrophobia to the point that I wanted to run out of the conference room.

anxiety. Learning to work with and tolerate ambiguity is a necessary skill in the world of relationships; a counselor is his or her own most difficult client (Ellis 1985b).

Loss, Grief, and Regrets

Loss and grief are issues throughout the addiction and in the recovery process. Drinking can be initiated or drastically increased following a loss. This reaction is often linked to an inability to accept and integrate the experience because of an inability to go through the grieving process. Addiction itself brings many losses—of relationships, self-esteem, physical health, employment, and so forth. The coming of sobriety and healing paradoxically brings one face-to-face with these losses. Grieving losses of the preaddictive and addictive periods is part of the work of recovery.

Setting Limits and Boundaries

Boundary rules provide a framework for relationships, the parts that people play in groups, and the positions that they occupy. Setting limits and establishing boundaries are important issues in counseling, as they help the client to learn appropriate, mature, sober, and successful behaviors, and in establishing the appropriate relationships between counselors and clients.

These issues frequently generate problems for counselors and clients at addictions agencies. Some clients are emerging from such personal disintegration that they seem to have a "bottomless pit" of need; others are habituated only to manipulative relationships. Counselors, especially those whose experience has been limited to participation in self-help fellowships, are not always prepared to set definite boundaries and abide by them.

Counselors must think through and establish limits, expectations, guidelines, and frameworks in advance. It is important to anticipate that clients may push beyond what is possible, realistic, ethical, or appropriate for them or their counselors. Without clearly stated boundaries, counselors also can, without realizing it, go beyond acceptable limits.

If counselors are not aware of these issues and not aware of their own motives or attitudes that may contribute to inappropriate limit-setting, a wide range of consequences might occur for the client, the counselor, and the counseling process. Demands might be made or expectations created that are unrealistic, excessive, or inappropriate. This is a no-win situation. The counselor has the choice of allowing excessive demands or intimacy, or going along for a time and then shifting position to reject such demands. Aligning with a client's inappropriate or unrealistic expectations can lead to resentment or burnout for the counselor, failure to help the client learn to manage his or her needs appropriately within society, and blurred roles of counselor and client. Failure to establish and respect boundaries also can lead to the counselor being drawn into manipulation, which may include finances, sexuality, housing, and other favors. Such actions, regardless of good intentions, are dangerous and violate professional ethics. A counselor who lets a client stay at his or her house, for example, might face any number of disastrous consequences. A counselor who ignores or disregards a client's behavior that pushes or exceeds limits will eventually feel stressed or resentful. The resentment may begin to show, and the double message will confuse and disturb the client. In such situations, either alone or as a result of clinical supervision, the counselor must set new limits and boundaries, which changes the nature of the counselor–client relationship. Although this is necessary, it often leaves the client feeling disappointed, rejected, or even infuriated. Honest exploration of the client–counselor relationship must lead to renegotiation of the boundaries and rebuilding of the working alliance.

Physical Contact

In the addictions recovery setting, hugging especially brings up the question of physical boundaries. Hugging provides support, reduces isolation, has a healing quality, and can help someone learn to trust and build toward emotional intimacy. Between counselor and client, however, and even among clients at an agency, hugs can be hidden traps. They can:

- Be used as a "quick fix" that avoids looking at some painful truths or the need to make some difficult changes in entrenched behavior patterns
- Encourage clients to look within the treatment system to have essential needs met, which may cause a termination that can be very painful and possibly even be postponed
- Prematurely open up a long-repressed "Pandora's box" of emotional needs early in sobriety, which can be threatening and result in departure or even relapse; or the client can develop a "crush" on a counselor
- Result in sexual arousal, then guilt, and possible departure
- Cause jealousy in clients who receive fewer hugs

The type of program that to one extent or another has a "hugging" culture that emphasizes love and acceptance may seem like heaven on Earth to many. But some individuals abuse this and become intrusive or smothering. In such a setting, people who prefer not to hug are defined as withdrawn, unfriendly, or deviant. Also, the "lovey-dovey" technique can cover resentments or make it difficult, if not impossible, for individuals to explore anger and other uncomfortable or "negative" emotions within the group or program. In fact, it will cause them to feel conflicted or guilty when these feelings crop up. Finally, the real world is not always a loving environment. A counselor who fosters a client to be ill-equipped to cope with negative emotions and reactions sets him or her up for relapse.

Skills in Setting Limits

In reality, counselors all learn through error. They sometimes miss signals or clues that a client is developing expectations that cannot or should not be met; then the counselor must "back off" gracefully. There are all kinds of hidden traps that counselors cannot always anticipate. When boundaries are crossed, their renegotiation need not be a total disaster. The situation can be discussed honestly with the client, and the counselor's taking responsibility for the situation humanizes and explores the nature of this collaborative relationship. It can be reframed as an opportunity for growth in the area of relationship skills.

Although every scenario cannot be anticipated, counselors should keep a number of guidelines in mind in order to negotiate the reefs and shoals of the counseling relationship as it pertains to boundaries and limits:

- Identify the appropriate and realistic boundaries that are consistent with legal and ethical guidelines. Know your employer's standards and guidelines. Consult your supervisor about all unclear areas.
- Identify your attitudes and motives for not setting limits assertively. (Do you feel guilty or anxious? Are you confused about the role of fellowship member and the role of professional counselor? Do you need to protect or rescue clients?)
- Set limits in a manner that is assertive, direct, honest, and open as well as empathetic. Keep it simple and friendly, pertaining to a single, specific behavioral area rather than a comprehensive denunciation.

Examples of assertive statements that can be used to set limits include:

- "I have ten minutes for you today."
- "I know you need more time with me today, and I wish I had it, but I have other clients who also must see me. One is waiting for me now."
- "It makes me uncomfortable when you leave your coat in my office. I'd appreciate it if you could arrange for another place to put it."

References

Barber, J. G. 1994. *Social Work with Addictions.* New York: New York University Press.

Beck, A., F. W. Wright, C. F. Newman, and B. Liese. 1993. *Cognitive Therapy of Substance Abuse.* New York: Guilford Press.

Berg, I. K., and S. D. Miller. 1992. *Working with the Problem Drinker: A Solution-Focused Approach.* New York: Norton.

Brockett, D. R., and A. D. Gleckman. 1991. Countertransference with the older adult. *Journal of Mental Health Counseling* 13(3): 343–355.

Carkhuff, R. R. 1969a. *Helping and Human Relations 1: Selection and Training.* New York: Holt, Reinhart and Winston.

———. 1969b. *Helping and Human Relations 2: Practice and Research.* New York: Holt, Reinhart and Winston.

Corey M. S., and G. Corey. 1998. *Becoming a Helper,* 3rd ed. Pacific Grove, CA: Brooks/Cole.

Cournoyer, B. 1996. *The Social Work Skills Workbook.* Pacific Grove, CA: Brooks/Cole.

CSAT (Center for Substance Abuse Treatment). 1999. *Enhancing Motivation for Change in Substance Abuse Treatment.* Treatment Improvement Protocol.

———. 2001.[1] *Quick Guide for Clinicians.* Based on TIP 35, *Enhancing Motivation for Change in Substance Abuse Treatment.* DHHS Publication No. (SMA) 01-3602. Rockville, MD: Center for Substance Abuse Treatment, Substance Abuse and Mental Health Services Administration.

Egan, G. 1998. *The Skilled Helper,* 6th ed. Pacific Grove, CA: Brooks/Cole.

Ellis, A. 1985a. *Overcoming Resistance: Rational-Emotive Therapy with Difficult Clients.* New York: Springer-Verlag.

Ellis, A. 1985b. "Expanding the ABCs of Rational-Emotive Therapy," in *Cognition and Psychotherapy.* M. Mahoney and A. Freeman, eds. New York: Plenum.

Ellis, A., and W. Dryden. 1987. *The Practice of Rational-Emotive Psychotherapy.* New York: Springer-Verlag.

---

[1] As an alternative, you can obtain or download the free SAMHSA TIP "Enhancing Motivation for Change in Substance Abuse Treatment," which was prepared by a team chaired by William Miller (CSAT 1999). The document's appendices contain a variety of useful instruments for assessing readiness to change.

Ellis, A., J. F. McInerney, R. DiGiuseppe, and R. J. Yeager. 1988. *Rational-Emotive Therapy with Alcoholics and Substance Abusers.* Boston: Allyn and Bacon.

Fiedler, F. 1950. A comparison of therapeutic relationships in psychoanalytic, non-directive, and Adlerian therapy. *Journal of Consulting Psychology* 14: 436–445.

———. 1951. Factor analyses of psychoanalytic, non-directive, and Adlerian therapy. *Journal of Consulting Psychology* 15: 32–38.

Ivey, A. E., and M. B. Ivey. 2003. *International Interviewing and Counseling,* 5th ed. Pacific Grove, CA: Thompson Brooks/Cole.

Ivey, A. E., M. B. Ivey, and C. P. Zalaquett. 2010. *Intentional Interviewing and Counseling: Facilitating Client Development in a Multicultural Society (with CD-ROM),* 7th ed. Belmont, CA: Brooks/Cole.

Kazdin, A. E. 1994. "Methodology, Design, and Evaluation in Psychotherapy Research," in *Handbook of Psychotherapy and Behavior Change,* 4th ed. A. E. Bergin and S. L. Garfield, eds. New York: Wiley.

Kernberg, O. 1975. *Borderline Conditions and Pathological Narcissism.* New York: Jason Aronson.

Lambert, M. J., and A. E. Bergin. 1994. "The Effectiveness of Psychotherapy," in *Handbook of Psychotherapy and Behavior Change,* 4th ed. A. E. Bergin and S. L. Garfield, eds. New York: Wiley.

Meier, S. T., and S. R. Davis. 1993. *The Elements of Counseling,* 2nd ed. Pacific Grove, CA: Brooks/Cole.

Miller, W., and S. Rollnick. 2002. *Motivational Interviewing: Preparing People to Change,* 2nd ed. New York: The Guilford Press.

Myers, P. L. 2003. Process recording: Importing a technique from social work field instruction. *Journal of Teaching in the Addictions* 2, 1: 91–108.

Nealy, E. C. 1997. Early intervention with active drug and alcohol users in community-based settings. *Journal of Chemical Dependency Treatment 7,* 1/2: 5–20.

NIAAA (National Institute on Alcohol Abuse and Alcoholism). 1995. *Project MATCH Monograph Series, 3: Cognitive-Behavioral Coping Skills Therapy Manual.* NIH Pub. no. 94-3724. Rockville, MD: U.S. Department of Health and Human Services.

Rogers, C. 1951. *Client-Centered Therapy.* Boston: Houghton Mifflin.

————. 1986. "Client-Centered Therapy," in *Psychotherapist's Casebook: Therapy and Technique in Practice.* I. Kutash and A. Wolk, eds. San Francisco: Jossey-Bass.

Rosengren, D. B. 1999. *Building Motivational Interviewing Skills: A Practitioners Workbook.* New York: The Guilford Press.

Series (TIP) Number 35. DHHS Publication No. (SMA) 05-4081. Rockville, MD: Center for Substance Abuse Treatment, Substance Abuse and Mental Health Services Administration. Retrieved 1 November 2011 from http://www.ncbi.nlm.nih.gov/books/bv.fcgi?rid=hstat5.part.22441

Wallace, J. 1985. "Working with the Preferred Defense Structure of the Recovering Alcoholic," in *Practical Approaches to Alcoholism Psychotherapy*, 2nd ed. S. Zimberg, J. Wallace, and S. B. Blume, eds. New York: Plenum.

Wallace, J. 1985. "Critical Issues in Alcoholism Therapy," in *Practical Approaches to Alcoholism Psychotherapy*, 2nd ed. S. Zimberg, J. Wallace, and S. B. Blume, eds. New York: Plenum Press.

Facilitating Motivation for Recovery

Objectives

By the end of this chapter, students will be able to:

1. Describe the five Stages of Change.
2. Provide an example of a client's response appropriate to each Stage of Change.
3. Describe each of the ten Processes of Change.
4. Provide an example of an intervention for each Process of Change.
5. List which Process of Change is most appropriate for each Stage of Change.
6. Describe six motivational interviewing traps counselors need to avoid.

7. Demonstrate in role-plays OARS (open-ended questions, affirmations, reflections, and summaries) responses.
8. Describe the use of an Importance Ruler, Confidence Ruler, and Readiness Ruler.
9. Develop in a role-play a Decisional Balance Sheet.
10. Elicit and identify in a role-play the change statements made by a client.
11. Complete an appropriate change plan with a client.

Introduction: The Problem of Compliance

A 49-year-old man, whose liver function test indicates he is developing liver disease, is referred to you because he is not willing to stop drinking. A 29-year-old woman with who smokes heavily and is addicted to Xanax is referred to you because her physician is frustrated with her trying to manipulate medications from him and other physicians. A co-occurring client with a bipolar diagnosis and cocaine addiction refuses to take his medication and this triggers a relapse.

Persons like those described above, who are resistant to making necessary behavioral health changes, are a common challenge to the healthcare system and the addiction treatment system. In a broad range of medical problems, noncompliance ranges from 30% to 60% (Meichenbaum and Tuck 1987). Failure to comply with a treatment regimen is fairly ubiquitous throughout the medical, psychiatric, and psychological service systems in America. This is particularly true with clients who abuse and are dependent on alcohol, tobacco, and other drugs. It ranges from not showing up for appointments or dropping out of treatment, to failure to follow through with treatment recommendations. Chiauzzi (1996) points out that "delivering a treatment is not enough—*reception* of treatment is the critical element." Motivation to change is essential in any effort to reduce unhealthy behaviors and initiate and sustain healthier behaviors. Working effectively with alcohol- and drug-dependent clients requires skills in understanding the process of helping clients change as well as in eliciting motivation from clients.

The qualities and skills necessary to develop rapport with clients allow for deeper exploration of their presenting problems and influencing their thoughts, feelings, and behaviors. Although these skills in themselves can assist to help change unhealthy behavior to healthy behavior, research over the last 20 years has found that using the new motivational paradigm indeed can improve the behavioral outcomes for people needing to change unhealthy behaviors such as smoking, chronic and/or excessive drinking problems, eating disorders, and other health issues (Rollnick et al. 1999; Botelho 2004; Rosengren 2009).

The New Paradigm About Motivation

In the past, motivation for change was placed primarily on the client, and motivation was seen as a more or less permanent characteristic or trait of the client. The client who resisted change was perceived as "unmotivated." If a client did not adhere to the advice or confrontation by a health or counseling professional, it was assumed he or she was not motivated, lacked any will to change, was not ready, and/or had not "hit bottom." The new paradigm presents motivation as more about ambivalence toward change and as a product of the counselor–client's collaboration. What appears to be a lack of motivation or resistance can arise from a lack of information, fear of change, inability to see any importance in changing, concerns about how change will affect one's life, or lack of confidence about one's ability to change.

In helping clients commit to behavioral change, we need to recognize the value of respecting the client's autonomy and to be sensitive to the forces that resist change. A motivational approach must allow clients to see choices and examine their concerns and understand the forces that lead toward and away from change. Physician Rick Botello (2004, p. 27) states, "We must move beyond the idea of control, that is, beyond trying to control our patients or having them control themselves, to the idea of autonomy. Patients are more likely to adopt healthy behaviors if they want to change rather than if they ought to or have to change."

Motivation is affected by the counselor's style also. It either can be blocked or facilitated by how the counselor responds to the client. That desire to change and commitment to change can be elicited by emphatic understanding, meaningful feedback, non-judgmental examining of the pros and cons of change, examining the client's self-efficacy, and other well-timed interventions. Two models of change have arisen in the last 20 years that are invaluable in eliciting positive behavioral health outcomes. The first is Prochaska and DiClemente's (1982) Transtheoretical Model (TTM), also known as Stages of Change, and second is Miller and Rollnick's (1991; 2002) Motivational Interviewing (MI), sometimes referred to as motivational enhancement therapy (MET). These two models can work together to assist clients in committing to, preparing for, following through with, and maintaining healthy behavioral change.

Stages of Change Model

The Transtheoretical Model or Stages of Change research done by Prochaska and DiClemente (1982) indicated that, despite the major differences in theory and application of over 100 models of therapy, therapy seemed to work, whether it was psychoanalytic, humanistic, Gestalt, Reality Therapy, cognitive and behavioral therapies, or some eclectic combination of these. All of these approaches to some degree have some positive outcome (Luborsky and

Luborsky 2006). In an effort to understand this phenomena, Prochaska, Norcross, and DiClemente (1994) created a Transtheoretical Model that proposed that different therapies worked for different problems at different times as individuals went through a process of change. They proposed that when individuals make changes in lifestyle (stopping smoking, stopping or reducing drinking or overeating, getting a new job, or any other major change in behavior), they go through a set of incremental steps that are more or less effective in moving individuals through the process. This model is referred to as the Transtheoretical Model (TTM) because it borrows techniques and interventions from a wide variety of various psychotherapeutic theories and approaches, including analytical, humanistic, cognitive, behavioral, and social psychology.

In researching the process of change, Prochaska et al. (1994) noted that people make changes with or without professional help, and with or without support groups, but—either with or without help—the change process requires a successful negotiation of a set of stages. These stages are precontemplation, contemplation, preparation, action, and maintenance. Successful recovery or health change requires progressive movement through these stages. Later in this chapter we will discuss specific processes of change effective at different stages.

Precontemplation is characterized by not thinking about change, having no intention of changing or resisting any idea that there is a need to change, or not being aware of any need to change. Others around the person may be concerned or urge the person to change, but that person does not see a need for change. Some people are in the precontemplation stage because they believe they cannot change, have tried but failed to change and have given up on the idea of change and, therefore, have resigned themselves to not contemplate change. An example of a precontemplation statement is "I don't see any reason to stop drinking. I'm sure I don't drink any more than all my friends. I feel good so I don't know why my doctor is giving me a hard time about it."

When there is sufficient awareness that change might be of some concern and therefore the individual is beginning to think about change, the individual is moving into the *contemplation* stage. Contemplation does not mean the person will change, only that they see a concern about their present state and are ambivalent in their feelings. They may be unsure of what to do or whether it is worth making any changes. Contemplation is characterized by ambivalence. They are weighing the pros and cons of change, and they are struggling with, and perhaps confused about, whether to make any effort to change or not. They may consider the benefits of changing but just as well see problems or major concerns with changing. An example of contemplation statement is "I'm sure that I don't have any serious drinking problem; however, I know I've done some things that concern me when I drink."

When a person begins to decide that change may be necessary and makes some commitment to try and change, he or she is moving into the *preparation* stage. The preparation stage does not mean that the person is actually making meaningful action to initiate or modify behavior, but only is beginning to plan how to change or to consider steps to effectively change. Preparation is characterized by an individual considering plans to change, thinking about alternative actions they may take, and weighing consequences and benefits of each alternative. Preparation is characterized by planning and is in the future tense. An example of a preparation statement is "I will start attending an AA meeting. I will avoid hanging out at the bar."

When individuals begin to take steps to change in an active way, they are into the *action* stage. Action requires commitment and energy. Action is usually characterized by implementation of plans made in the preparation stage. The individual may make others aware of his or her efforts and seek support for new behaviors. An action statement should be in the present tense. It could sound like "I'm attending three AA meetings a week. On Friday nights instead of going to the bar, I'll go to the movies with the family."

When an individual sustains involvement in the action stage for some period of time (usually six months), he or she enters the *maintenance* stage. Maintenance is about sustaining healthy behaviors and managing barriers. Often maintenance is supported by learning new coping skills to manage new behaviors. Addicts must learn strategies to manage stress or resist peer pressure to avoid relapse. An individual may lapse or have a short return to previous unhealthy behaviors but become quickly aware of them and return to the new behaviors that he or she is trying to sustain. An example of a maintenance statement is "I've been doing well in my recovery for the last three months, but the holidays are coming up, and that's when I have the toughest time. I think I could use some help in finding ways to say 'no' and mean it."

These five stages are fluid and an individual may progress through them or relapse back to a prior stage at his or her own individual rate. An individual may stay (get "stuck") in any of the stages for a long time. Individuals may move into the action stage or maintenance stage and relapse and have to circle back through the stages again.

Because knowing the precise stage a client is in is important when using techniques and strategies to assist towards change, it is necessary to assess which stage the client is in at the time you are working with them. Activity 3.1 is designed to assist in recognizing the particular Stage of Change the client is in.

ACTIVITY (3.1) **Assessment of readiness to change**

For each statement below, select the most appropriate Stage of Change.

1. "I don't care what the doctor says. My drinking is not a problem and I don't drink any more than most of my friends."
   Precontemplation _____   Contemplation _____
   Preparation _____   Action _____   Maintenance _____
2. "I need to really think about how I'm going to plan my meals now that I'm going to diet."
   Precontemplation _____   Contemplation _____
   Preparation _____   Action _____   Maintenance _____
3. "I really don't know about if I really need to take the time to exercise, but I have put some pounds on and might need to consider doing something."
   Precontemplation _____   Contemplation _____
   Preparation _____   Action _____   Maintenance _____
4. "I do like to smoke to relieve stress particularly after a rough day, but I know it's making my asthma worse."
   Precontemplation _____   Contemplation _____
   Preparation _____   Action _____   Maintenance _____
5. "What do I need that medication for, it only makes me fat."
   Precontemplation _____   Contemplation _____
   Preparation _____   Action _____   Maintenance _____
6. "So the stupid cop picked on me and I got arrested for DUI, but that doesn't mean I've got a drinking problem."
   Precontemplation _____   Contemplation _____
   Preparation _____   Action _____   Maintenance _____
7. "My dad died of a heart attack; I better think about finding a way to watch what I eat."
   Precontemplation _____   Contemplation _____
   Preparation _____   Action _____   Maintenance _____
8. "I've stopped smoking and feel so much better. The patch makes a difference."
   Precontemplation _____   Contemplation _____
   Preparation _____   Action _____   Maintenance _____

Processes of Change

Once a counselor defines the stage for a client, he or she can use a variety of therapeutic strategies effective for that stage (Prochaska et al. 1994). Prochaska and DiClemente have identified 10 specific processes of change that are valuable methods of intervention.

Ten Processes of Change

1. **Consciousness raising.** This includes increasing the client's awareness of his or her behavior and its consequences; giving the client nonjudgmental feedback about his or her situation or its effects on significant others; and providing education concerning how their health issues are affecting them. These strategies are useful in both precontemplative and contemplative stages. An example is "Are you aware of how alcohol is affecting your liver? Let's discuss your medical report concerning your liver functions."

2. **Self liberation.** This involves freeing the client from "victim hood" and enabling her or him to see how not to be a passive victim of the behavior (e.g., drinking, drug use, smoking, unhealthy eating, and so on) Self liberation is accomplished by raising a client's sense of self-efficacy. *Self-efficacy* is the belief that one can do what one needs to do to change. Supporting self-efficacy, affirming the client's ability to accomplish change, and providing alternative choices for the client all lead to a feeling of self liberation. These strategies can be extremely beneficial in the preparation stage. An example is "I noticed that you were able to stay off drugs in the past when you avoided hanging out with certain friends. Can we discuss how you might be able to do this again?"

3. **Social liberation.** This concerns creating a social environment that offers opportunities to get one's needs met, such as avoiding the people, places, and things that can trigger unhealthy behavior. Social liberation is not so much a counseling response as an attempt to support a client by encouraging him or her to avoid environmental conditions that often trigger feelings and thoughts that lead toward unhealthy behaviors. Examples are avoiding bars if you are trying not to drink alcohol, or going to a halfway house if you must isolate yourself from your current culture of drug abuse. This strategy can help particularly in the action stage.

4. **Counter-conditioning.** This involves unlearning destructive behaviors that have become automatic, for example, learning new behaviors to replace unhealthy ones. When anxious or under stress, some people will try to manage the stress by drinking, using drugs, or smoking. Teaching a person to breathe deeply or to use some other relaxation or mindfulness technique can be very useful in countering these feelings. Learning assertiveness skills can be a useful strategy for individuals to resist

friends who urge them to continue to drink, smoke, or eat, which undermines their progress. Learning these skills works well in the action stage or maintenance stage.

5. **Stimulus control.** This method helps the client to quickly notice or avoid emotional states or situations that trigger undesirable behaviors, such as learning to reexamine and manage problematic emotions. Stimulus control means taking direct action to remove triggers to unhealthy behaviors and replace them with healthy ones (e.g., replacing drug and alcohol use with helping others, exercise, and so on). These techniques can be very useful in supporting the action stage.

6. **Self reevaluation.** This reassigns one's strengths and weaknesses in light of new insights. In the process of counseling, clients discover that they value healthy change and that they can change. Change occurs as they reassess values and their capacity to change. (Examples are learning one can assert oneself without drugs, finding new ways to exercise to relieve stress, or realizing that they enjoy and protect their children better by not smoking.) Within the contemplation stage, counselors are trying to help clients to reevaluate their ambivalence and work towards a new image that increases motivation to change. One technique that is often used is called *decisional balance*. This technique asks clients to examine the pros and cons of changing and not changing.

7. **Environmental reevaluation.** This method is a new look at one's social environment and examining the impact of the client's behavior on others that they care about. Exploring her or his family system, employment, and social network helps to connect the effects of the client's decision to change or not change on others. Examples of these links are the effects of smoking on children or a spouse, drinking's effect on loved ones, and loss of productivity at work as a result of drug use. This method can be very useful in the precontemplative stage as well as the preparation stage.

8. **Contingency management.** Changing the consequences of behaviors to give responsibility directly to the client for the consequences of his or her behavior comprises this method. It is particularly helpful in finding positive reenforcers (or rewards) for certain behaviors. Praising a client for positive efforts toward behavioral change and asking a client to set up his or her own reward system (e.g., putting away money that would have been used to buy cigarettes or alcohol toward a

vacation) are examples of management strategies. This approach can be useful in both the preparation and action stages.

9. **Dramatic relief.** Ventilation or catharsis allows clients to express emotions and have their feelings validated. Resistance to change often can be reduced when a client is able to express her or his fears, anxieties, anger, or relief as each is allowed to be expressed in a therapeutic relationship. This is often done in role-plays and group activities. This method can be helpful in both the precontemplation and contemplation stages.

10. **Creating a helping relationship.** Using a therapeutic bond allows for a feeling of support and encouragement. Responding to a client in a way that demonstrates and creates empathy, warmth, and respect can go a long way in supporting her or him towards positive healthy behaviors. This also can happen with use of mutual, self-help support groups. A client-centered, supportive, and empathetic posture is valuable throughout the Stages of Change.

These 10 processes describe the steps that individuals progress through as they attempt to change. A heathcare professional may engage a client at any of these stages. Clients may move into the next stage slowly, rapidly, or not at all, depending on the strength of their motivation and how they responded to therapy by a helping professional. They also may go back to a previous stage. However, relapse should not be seen as failure but instead examined as a learning experience and opportunity to try new strategies. The activity listed here is designed to provide students with the opportunity to identify the 10 processes of change.

ACTIVITY (3.2) Processes of change strategy

For each statement in the left column, choose the process of change strategy that best describes it from the list in the right column and write in the letter.

Statement	Process of Change Strategy
1. After a role-play, the client feels relieved to tell his mother not to push food on him. _____	A. Consciousness raising
	B. Self liberation
	C. Social liberation
	D. Counter conditioning

2. A client learns to relax by deep breathing to deal with stress. _____

3. A client is affirmed by the counselor saying, "I'm glad to hear you used a condom." _____

4. A client is referred to a halfway house in order to support her recovery. _____

5. The counselor states, "Your doctor mentioned that your blood pressure has risen at each visit. What do think about that?" _____

6. The counselor suggests that the client walk to the market instead of driving.

   _____

7. The counselor and client work on assessing the pros and cons of his not smoking. _____

8. The client considers how smoking effects her time spent with her grandchildren. _____

9. The counselor suggests that taking a long warm bath may be a reward for not eating dessert. _____

10. A counselor demonstrates empathy and respect for the client's HIV+ status. _____

E. Stimulus control

F. Self reevaluation

G. Environmental evaluation

H. Contingency management

I. Dramatic relief

J. Creating a helping relationship

Change Strategies Most Useful for Each Stage of Change

Use of the 10 Change Strategies depends very much on timing and where the client is on the continuum of the stage he or she is negotiating. There is a temporal dimension to the process. Precontemplation and contemplation are primarily concerned with activating intentions to change, while preparation, action, and maintenance are on the behaviors associated with planning and implementing action steps toward change. Five experimental type processes are best suited for the early stages concerning intention to change. These are consciousness raising (nonjudgmental feedback about the effects of your behavior on the client's goals and aspirations), environmental reevaluation (how your behavior affects others), self reevaluation (assessing your feelings and behavior against your values), social liberation (social and environmental conditions that support change), and dramatic relief (strong negative feelings that push for change). Four behavioral-oriented change processes are most useful during the preparation, action, and maintenance stages. These are self-liberation (having confidence in changing), counter conditioning (finding ways to do healthier activities that replace unhealthy behaviors), reinforcement management (rewarding positive healthy behaviors), and stimulus control (examining and managing triggers for unhealthy behaviors. Maintaining helping-type relationship skills is valuable throughout the stages of change process.

Motivational Interviewing

Motivational Interviewing (MI) is defined by Miller and Rollnick (2002, p. 25) in their second edition of *Motivational Counseling* "as a client-centered, directive method for enhancing intrinsic motivation to change by exploring and resolving ambivalence." It is client-centered in the sense that it focuses on what the client is concerned about by listening to the thoughts and feelings about whatever issues he or she expresses. However, in contrast to nondirective Rogerian therapy, the approach is directive in exploring, eliciting, and resolving a client's ambivalence about change. MI uses reflective listening skills and open-ended questions to help clients explore their natural ambivalence about change and to elicit change statements. The counselor works in collaboration with the client in examining change options and in supporting the client's self-efficacy in any efforts to change that the client chooses.

Although many specific techniques and counselor-specific behaviors and responses can be taught, Miller and Rollnick (2002) are clear that it is the "essential spirit" and posture of counselors that matters most in successfully using MI with clients. It is an approach to the client that deemphasizes labels, avoids confrontation, and avoids arguing and trying to convince clients that they must do something, and it is a willingness of the counselor to suspend an authoritarian expert role. This "spirit" includes specific attitudes concerning clients that demonstrate respect, acceptance, and affirmation, promote empathy, and provide an openness and willingness to listen. The counselor tries to avoid labeling, confrontation, arguing, and trying to convince a client that he or she must do something. Motivation is intrinsic and elicited from the client; it is not imposed. This is summed up nicely by Miller and Rollnick (1991, pp. 51–52): "The strategies of motivational interviewing are more persuasive than coercive, more supportive than argumentative. The motivational interviewer proceeds with a strong sense of purpose, clear strategies and skills for pursuing that purpose, and a sense of timing to intervene in particular ways at incisive moments."

As noted at the beginning of this chapter, resistance is a common concern in assisting clients. Resistance comes in many forms including interrupting the counselor, arguing, saying "yes...but," denying any problem, and ignoring, minimizing, or rationalizing the continuation of an unhealthy behavior. Sometimes a client will be compliant in words but seem not to follow through in action. There may be many reasons for such resistance, some of which include fear of change, failure to see a need to change, concerns about the ability to change, a sense of hopelessness, and concerns about how change would affect their life.

Approaching and Avoiding Treatment

A typical scenario is that the addict "cuts down" on drinking or drug use, as part of an attempt to "get his act together," or enters detox and is sober for a couple of days. In either event, this alleviates some of the worst of the physical symptoms, which weakens one of the motives to approach treatment. This minor relief, coupled with anxiety, helps an addict decide to "do it myself." As one addictions counselor remarked, "The client seemed to hit bottom, but he bounced."

The encounter with treatment personnel and institutions may, in fact, engender a defensive reaction. Moreover, the removal of chemical anesthesia itself in early treatment takes away the capstone of the system of defenses, which produces anxiety. Thus, the first step in ending addiction creates conditions for relapse. It is difficult to change and grow, and the process of dealing with addiction creates yet more discomfort. The counselor walks a fine line between the addict's denial and the premature unearthing of deep-seated, painful, and traumatic memories or problems (Wallace 1985a and b).

Counselor Traps

In meeting the resistance that health counselors often see in helping clients to change behaviors, Miller and Rollnick (1991) point out "traps" that counselors need to avoid. The first of these is the "question/answer trap." Asking numerous questions puts the client into a passive role and does not allow the client to explore deeply the issues that concern him or her. The second is the "confrontation/denial" trap. Confrontation usually leads to defensive behavior that leads to more confrontation and a lot of arguing and a "yes . . . but" cycle of futile attempts to convince the client to change. The third trap is the "expert role." Providing direction and advice at a time when the client is not highly motivated usually is counterproductive. The fourth trap is the "labeling" trap. Calling a client an addict, alcoholic, overeater, or any other label usually adds a stigma to the client and often makes him or her feel less empowered to change. The fifth trap is the "premature focus trap." Here the counselor is pushing the client to make decisions and take actions before she or he is ready, willing, or able to change. The sixth and final trap is the "blaming trap." Finding fault with others or blaming the client is not helpful in building a working relationship or exploring the nature of the client's problems and helping to resolve them.

Principles of Motivational Interviewing

The Motivational Interviewing (MI) approach is centered on four basic principles (Miller and Rollnick 2002, pp. 36–42):

1. **Express empathy.** This is a client-centered focus, which emphasizes active listening and reflection of the essence of the client's content and feelings in order to enhance the understanding of the client's experience by both the counselor and the client. It demonstrates respect for the client and develops rapport. Acceptance of the client does not mean agreement with the client, but it does validate the client's understanding and belief within her or his own framework. Through empathic responses the client is more likely to open up and explore the situation in depth. Empathy builds a therapeutic relationship and creates a sense of collaboration that reveals the innermost feelings, elicits potential thoughts and ways to change, and allows clients to feel safe in making efforts to change.

2. **Develop discrepancy.** This is done through reflecting information the client is giving that begins to increase tension to change. The counselor helps the client to identify and amplify discrepancies between the client's present situation and desired goals or values. Discrepancies that the client is free to examine and take ownership of often lead to what Festinger (1957) called *cognitive dissonance.* This concept is that individuals will be motivated to change behavior or beliefs or attitudes when there is significant contradiction between a held belief, attitude, fact, or behavior. As clients begin to explore their ambivalence and examine their values and beliefs, they create their own reasons for change as opposed to having them forced

upon them by the counselor. An example is a father who
believes that he should be a "family man " and "a good provider" and begins to realize his alcohol use is causing a financial and emotional price to these beliefs.

3. **Roll with resistance.** Resistance to change is seen as natural,
   and to argue against it is counterproductive. Resistance often
   comes in the form of anger, defensiveness, saying "yes …
   but," or disagreeing with and/or challenging the counselor.
   The counselor is allowing the client to express the resistance
   and not fighting with the client to accept another viewpoint.
   Counselors need to respond differently by siding with the
   resistance in order to defuse it and increase the client's sense
   that he or she is being understood. Rollnick and colleagues
   (1999, p.161) point out that the key to resistance "is convincing the patient that you share the same goals, namely to
   improve the client's health." This comes from reflecting the
   client's feelings, affirming the client's strengths, and acknowledging the client's concerns. A client forced to attend a drunk
   driver's program might say, "I don't need to be here. No one
   can make me do anything." It would only increase resistance to
   say, "Listen, you were arrested for drunk driving and you had
   better learn about how alcohol affects you and avoid drinking
   and driving." A more effective response would be, "You are
   right. Nobody can make you do anything. You're strong willed
   and independent. Because you have to be here, maybe we can
   work together to prevent this from happening again."

4. **Support self-efficacy.** A critical factor in supporting change
   is the client's belief that she or he can change (Bandura 1997).
   The counselor not only needs to assess the importance of
   changing behavior for the client and gently elicit his or her
   desire to change, but also must continually assess and help
   build the confidence of the client. A willingness to make
   changes in behavior without a sense of confidence is not sufficient for change to occur. The client may remain in a state of
   ambivalence, or even give up, without feeling capable of doing
   what's necessary to make changes. Many smokers are aware of
   the harm that smoking is doing to them and express a desire to
   stop smoking, but they often believe that they just can't stop
   (Rollnick et al. 1999, pp. 20–23).

To promote self-efficacy, the counselor needs to reinforce small steps
of success. The counselor must provide clients with a variety of ways to
change so that the client sees that there is hope, because there are choices.

For instance, a drug addict may never have tried to stop without medication, a support group, or counseling. Providing these alternatives often gives the extra boost of confidence the client needs.

These four principles lead into specific MI strategies and techniques. These are often expressed in acronyms. OARS skills provide a foundation for the strategies that follow. They require practice, and mastering them is not easy.

MI Core Skills: OARS

- **O**pen-ended questions. These lead toward more exploration of the client's situation and respect for the client's autonomy. An example is "How would you like your life to look in five years from now?"
- **A**ffirmations. These are empowerment responses that increase the client's sense of self-efficacy. An example is "The fact that you keep trying shows me how strongly you're committed to beating your addiction."
- **R**eflective listening. This is similar to paraphrasing and reflection of feeling. Reflective listening helps clients to verbalize their understanding of their experience and allows them to hear what they are saying. It helps to reduce resistance and avoid arguments with the client. Reflection can be at different levels:
  Simple reflection: Rephrasing the essence of the client's content and/or feelings in your own words
  CLIENT: "I don't plan to quit drinking any time soon."
  COUNSELOR: "You don't think abstinence would work for you right now."
  Amplified reflection: Exaggeration without sarcasm, which sometimes allows the client to see the implications of their statements.
  CLIENT: "I don't know why my wife is worried about this. I don't drink anymore than my friends."
  COUNSELOR: "So your wife is worrying needlessly."
  Double-sided reflection: Highlights the ambiguity of the client's statement(s)
  CLIENT: "I can't see giving up drinking now, even though the wife complains and the DWI was pretty costly."
  COUNSELOR: "You're not willing to give up drinking, but you see some problems as a result of when you did drink."
- **S**ummarizing. This response ties together the main thoughts, feelings, and experiences the client has expressed in order to link or transition. "So far we've discussed that you're not seeing a big problem with drinking at this point. You mentioned that

there have been times when you and your wife were arguing over
money you spent at the bar and the cost of your DWI. You like
going out to the bar with your friends but you know your wife
doesn't like it. Does that pretty much cover it?"

ACTIVITY (3.3) Feedback as affirmations

*Choose a partner who you do not know or someone you know least about.
Face each other and choose which will go first for this exercise.*

Student #1 will introduce him or herself and share three characteristics.
What are his or her best strengths and assets? Student #2 will provide
positive feedback and affirmations using OARS skills. When done, each will
reverse roles and repeat the exercise.

PROCESS: Discuss how it felt to receive affirmations. Ask yourself whether
the affirmations increased a sense of self-efficacy.

Merging Motivational Interviewing and Stages of Change

Precontemplation

There is a natural blending of motivational techniques and stages of
change. As noted by DiClemente and Velasquez (in Miller and Rollnick
2002, p. 202), "moving through the stages of change requires effort and
energy for thinking, planning, and doing. Motivational interviewing can
be used to assist individuals to accomplish the various tasks required to
transition from precontemplation stage through the maintenance stage."
Specific techniques are useful at each stage of change; however, many of
these techniques are useful throughout the change process.

Techniques are often best done when they appear most appropriate
in the process of change and in the context of a client-centered dialogue.
It is important to ask the client permission to engage in a technique: "Do
you mind if I ask you the following question or would you be willing to
fill out the following form?"

Importance, Confidence, and Readiness Rulers

The Stages of Change model has been incorporated into the assessment
process in addictions treatment. All innovations take decades to get into
practice, and it's not possible to gauge what percentage of agencies actually
have taken up this valuable assessment dimension. Generally, one would
wish to use a Decisional Balance Sheet to assess the ambivalence about
change in a particular area or areas. Following that, one of the "rulers"
would help determine if change is ready and able to occur. Several useful

tools to gauge readiness for change are available as appendices to the TIP 35 (DHHS 1999).

The Importance, Confidence, and Readiness Rulers are simple measures of the clients' readiness to change in particular areas. They measure clients' views of what needs to change, how they view their ability to change, and their overall estimation of their readiness to change, that is, their place on the Stages of Change. These rulers can be important components of assessment and of the treatment planning process. This can be done verbally or by using a form like the ones below.

Importance Ruler

How important is it for you to change _____ right now on a scale of 0 to10? Zero (0) would be not at all important and ten (10) would be extremely important.

0___1___2___3___4___5___6___7___8___9___10___

Because importance and confidence are two different issues, and both are necessary to elicit from the client, you can follow up with the Confidence Ruler.

Confidence Ruler

How important is it for you to change _____ right now on a scale of 0 to10? Zero (0) would be not at all important and ten (10) would be extremely important.

0___1___2___3___4___5___6___7___8___9___10___

The blank in the question should be filled in with the issue that brought the client into seeing you. It could be smoking, drinking, using cocaine, talking to their spouse about their drinking, using medication, attending a treatment program, and so on.

The Importance Ruler is a nonjudgmental way of assigning the client's stage of change. The higher the number marked, the more likely the client is in a contemplation or even preparation stage. More importantly is that it opens up dialogue concerning how the client feels about his or her health issues, fears, expectations, and/or interest about changing/ not changing, and assesses the value he or she places on changing. What is most important is not where the client marks an X but the follow-up questions, such as, "Why a 3 and not a lower number?" or, "What would need to happen for you to go from a 5 to a 6?" The ruler helps elicit the client's thinking (contemplation) about change.

The Confidence Ruler helps clients to examine concerns and issues around the confidence and self-efficacy issues of making a change. A follow-up question to the Confidence Ruler is "What would help raise your confidence from a 4 to a 6?" or, "Why did you mark a 3 and not a 2?"

There are many creative ways to use the Importance and Confidence Rulers. It may be useful to use both because sometimes it is difficult to know whether a client resists change because it is not important or because of a belief that he or she is unable to change.

ACTIVITY (3.4) The importance ruler

Think about something in your life that you are considering changing or working on. It could be going on a diet or exercising, better organizing their room, getting a job, or finding new ways to cope with a difficult roommate or significant other. Find a partner and sit together.

After completing Worksheet 3.1 (available at go.jblearning.com/myers3), each person will exchange worksheets with her or his partner. With one person taking the role of "counselor" and the other "client," the counselor will ask some of the questions stated under the appropriate marking, listen to the client's response, and then follow up with other OARS-type responses. Not all of the questions listed need to be asked. After a period of time, reverse roles and repeat the process.

PROCESS: Think about how you felt in the different roles. What responses did your partner make that seemed to help clarify or find solutions to his or her issues? Which questions were most relevant and effective?

ACTIVITY (3.5) The confidence ruler

Think about an issue in your life that you are considering changing or working on. It could be going back to school to earn an additional degree, taking up a musical instrument, or getting out of a long-term but unhealthy relationship. Anything you are willing to share. Find a partner. Face each other and choose who will role-play as "counselor" and who will be the "client." Complete the Importance Ruler Worksheet 3.5 (available at go.jblearning.com/myers3).

After completing Worksheet 3.2 (available at go.jblearning.com/myers3), exchange your worksheet with your partner's worksheet. The "counselor" will ask some of the questions stated under the appropriate marking and then follow up with other OARS type responses. You do not need to ask all the questions listed. Switch roles.

PROCESS: How did you feel in your role of counselor? In your role as client? What responses did your partner offer that helped you to examine your issue? Which questions were most relevant and effective?

Figure 3.1 Readiness ruler.

1	2	3	4	5	6	7	8	9	10
Not Ready				Unsure				Ready	

Readiness Ruler

Another simple tool is the Readiness Ruler, which asks clients to gauge their willingness to change on a scale of 1 to 10 (Figure 3.1; CSAT 1999, pp. 13–14).

Another version of the Readiness Ruler demarcates four spots on this continuum, corresponding to the Stages of Change, as follows: "not at all ready, thinking about changing, preparing to change, actively working on or maintaining a change" (Velasquez et al. 2001, p. 30).

Stage of (readiness to) Change should be noted in the client chart during the initial assessment and followed up frequently during treatment. Velasquez et al. (2001, p. 31) point out that a client may be in different stages of change for different substances. A dramatic example is the methadone client who is actively working on discarding a heroin addiction yet wants and continues to drink alcohol heavily, take benzodiazepines (Valium and similar drugs), and smoke marijuana. An interesting video on the Readiness Ruler is available at http://www.youtube.com/watch?v=j9nHS4dyhKk.

Engaging the Precontemplative Client

In the precontemplation stage it is valuable to begin with what led the client to see you. Be empathetic with the client's reasons, whether she or he came willingly or was pressured by external motivation (e.g., to please the spouse or doctor, comply with a judge or boss, and so on). If there are specific medical or psychological tests, provide the results in a nonjudgmental, matter-of-fact way without labeling or diagnosing. Ask the client how she feels about results.

To raise consciousness in the precontemplation stage, it can be helpful to ask, "What is a typical day like for you?" Sometimes the results of many health behaviors need to be seen in the light of time. For instance, chronic abuse of alcohol, drugs, or tobacco will cause changes in lifestyle and personal conditions that can be brought to light by asking questions like "What were things like for you five years ago?" Looking ahead also can stimulate concern: "How do you imagine things will be for you five years from now?" Querying about extremes can be consciousness raising:

"What is the worst thing that could happen if you quit smoking? or "What is the best thing that could happen if you stop smoking?" (Miller and Rollnick 2002).

It is often useful to examine a client's investment in his behavior. It is important to bring to light that all behavior serves some purpose. This can be done simply by asking, "What are the good things or benefits about (drug use; drinking; smoking, and so on)?" The counselor will probably find the client reluctant to talk about the good things or benefits of what he is doing because of an assumption that only the negative "should" be discussed. A client's response might be "Well, there can't be any good things. That's why I'm here." Then the counselor should press on and say something to the effect of: "You've invested a lot of time and money into doing this, so it must have some benefits." After the client has elicited the benefits, ask him, "What are the not so good things or negative consequences about (smoking, eating fried foods, drinking, and so on)?"

A major benefit of these questions is that they do not push the client to change but allow the client to explore personal concerns. This builds rapport and allows the client to take responsibility for her or his own decision making.

The Decisional Balance

A very useful technique that enables clients to examine their ambivalence is called the *Decisional Balance*. This is a matrix that asks the client to describe the pros and cons of changing and not changing. The balance sheet, which was used early in the treatment encounter, provides important assessment data for continuing treatment planning. Perhaps most importantly, it provides tips for proactive relapse prevention. For example, the client lists as a benefit of drinking alcohol that it "makes me feel better after I've been fighting with my wife" as a rational excuse to storm out of the home and go to a bar for a drink.

1. *Pros (or benefits) of not changing*
   What do you like about (drinking, drug use smoking, and so on)?
2. *Cons (or consequences) of changing*
   What concerns do you have about (drinking, drug use smoking, and so on)?
3. *Cons (or benefits) of changing*
   What concerns do you have if you tried to stop (drinking, drug use smoking, and so on)?
4. *Pros (or benefits) of not changing*
   What benefits do you see in not quitting or reducing (drinking, drug use, smoking, and so on)?

This is an example of what a Decision Matrix for cocaine would look like:

1. *Pros of continuing cocaine*
   It relieves my stress.
   I have more fun. I like to party.
   It makes me feel in control.
   I makes me feel more powerful.
2. *Pros of quitting cocaine*
   It would save me money.
   My family will approve of me.
   I might feel less depressed when I don't have it.
   I won't have to worry about getting arrested.
3. *Cons of continuing cocaine*
   My nose will burn out.
   It continues to be an expensive habit.
   I might get arrested.
   My wife might leave me.
4. *Cons of quitting cocaine*
   How else will I deal with stress?
   Will I be able to get the energy I need?
   I might lose some good partying friends.
   I might feel depressed.

Quadrant 1 and 2 focus on the client's concerns related to changing. Here the client is weighing the benefits versus costs of continuing the behavior. Quadrants 3 and 4 focus on the client's concerns about continuing the status quo. All four quadrants are important to explore. Clients continue addictive behaviors not only because they see more benefits or fail to see consequences but also because they are concerned with what will happen if they can no longer continue the behavior. The behavior provides some benefit and often acts as a coping mechanism. This is particularly true with smoking, drinking, drug abuse, and overeating.

If these unhealthy ways of coping (e.g., smoking, drinking, or drug use to deal with stress) are not addressed, then a situation or trigger (a stressful event) can easily create relapse. Learning new ways to cope (e.g., stress management techniques) becomes an important action and maintenance stage strategy.

Miller and Rollnick (2002) are clear that individuals are not always conscious of their ambiguity, nor do they necessarily contemplate the weight they give to pros and cons. It is the unforced, nonjudgmental, and open process of looking at the pros of cons of changing and not changing that can facilitate the awareness and potential eliciting of change statements. Change talk includes reflecting on the "disadvantages of the status quo, advantages of change, optimism about change, and/or intention to change (ibid 2002, p. 127).

ACTIVITY (3.6) Decisional balance

Pair off with a fellow student and complete the Decision Balance matrix, using a personal issue that you are changing or have recently changed. In turn, each person will ask questions to the other, using each quadrant of the matrix.

PROCESS: Examine your feelings when talking about your issue from each quadrant. What responses seemed to help when discussing your partner's issues? What insights did you gain from doing this exercise?

Listening for "Change Talk"

Using motivational interviewing styles and appropriate stage-based strategies, counselors need to listen for and respond to their clients' talk about personal change. Hearing clients begin to consider changing their unhealthy behaviors or establishing healthy ones is necessary when assessing readiness to change and supporting change efforts. These statements can be in various forms as described by the acronym DARN-C:

Desire: A client describes how she wants to change.

COUNSELOR: "What might you want to do to resolve your concern about your diabetes?"
CLIENT: "I want to start eating right."

Ability: A client describes specific ways to change and displays confidence in his ability to change.

COUNSELOR: "What gives you the confidence to stop drinking?"
CLIENT: "I think if I use ViVitrol with counseling, I can do it this time."

Reason: A client provides an explanation for why she needs to change.

COUNSELOR: "Why would you want to take your medications now?"
CLIENT: "Because now I know that I have to wait for the antidepressant to work."

Need: A client projects a need to change in order to achieve something or avoid an unwanted outcome.

COUNSELOR: "What makes you want to stop drinking?"
CLIENT: "I need to live long enough to enjoy my grandchildren."

Commitment: A client demonstrates a dedication to making necessary changes.

COUNSELOR: "So what are you willing to do now?"
CLIENT: "I will go to more AA meetings a week."

Preparation Stage Strategies

Once clients have begun to express that they have a desire and confidence to change, their counselor can support a transition to the preparation stage. This is *not* done by only focusing on the healthy side of change. If the counselor seems to only support the positive side of change, there is a natural inclination for the client to think of the negative side. Instead, the counselor is allowing the client to develop his own argument for change by reflecting the client's ambivalence.

As the client begins to consider changing, it is helpful to elaborate on what steps or goals the client is considering. Open questions that encourage the client to elaborate on what specific steps to take towards change will help focus her on how she might accomplish each step and confront any barriers she might encounter. The counselor simply could ask for a specific example: "Can you give me an example of what you will say to your friends when they ask you to go out drinking?" Or, she might ask for clarification: "Which medication would you use?" "What type of program are you considering?" or, "What else are you considering doing to stop drinking?"

A client who is considering the steps to changing may have concerns about the confidence to actually make the change. Providing affirmations about the strengths the counselor sees in the client can be helpful.

CLIENT: "I've had a hard time trying to stop drinking in the past. I don't know if I can do it now."
COUNSELOR: "You've kept trying and working hard. You seem determined to do it and express a real desire to be healthy. You are willing to attend more AA meetings.

The transition from contemplation to preparation involves helping the client to develop a change plan. It is important for clients to have a plan that is self-developed rather than the counselor imposing a plan on the client. Counselors can provide advice if it is solicited from the client or if the counselor has information the client is not aware of or hasn't considered. A counselor might say, "Sometimes it has been helpful for others who are trying to do (whatever the change might be) to (whatever suggestion the counselor may have); however, the decision is yours." It is important to clearly indicate to clients that responsibility for change is theirs. It is also helpful, and appears to improve commitment, if a client's behavioral change is a choice from several options. Again, the choice is the client's to make. So, if the counselor, with the client, can develop a menu of choices, then the client feels more commitment to having made the choice and the client also knows what might be best for them to undertake. "We've discussed various ways you could support your efforts to quit drinking, including various medications, continued individual counseling to discuss how you might handle triggers, getting a recovery coach or mentor, and joining a support group. What do you think might work best for you?"

Creating a Change Plan

A "Change Plan" can be a simple worksheet (Miller and Rollnick 2002, p. 137).

Change Plan Worksheet

The most important reasons why I want to make this change are:

_____

My main goals for myself making this change are:

_____

I plan these specific things in order to accomplish my goals ...
Specific action　　　　　　　　　When?

_____　　　　_____

_____　　　　_____

_____　　　　_____

These people can help me with change in these ways:
Name of person　　　　　　　　　Possible ways to help

_____　　　　_____

_____　　　　_____

_____　　　　_____

These are some possible obstacles to change, and how I might handle them:
Possible obstacles to change　　　　How to respond

_____　　　　_____

_____　　　　_____

_____　　　　_____

I will know my plan is working when I see these results:

_____

_____

_____

Action and Maintenance Stage Strategies

The action stage occurs when clients begin to implement a plan. They are actively engaging in new behaviors or quitting old behaviors. They consciously

change behaviors such as getting rid of cigarettes or removing all alcoholic beverages from their living space, or they develop a new regimen of
attending group meetings, taking medications as prescribed, checking in
with a sponsor, getting more rest, eating better, and actively learning new
skills like assertiveness or anger management, and so on.

In both the action and maintenance stages, vigilance is necessary.
Relapse to old behaviors can and often does occur. Clients will miss old
behaviors. Ambivalence about change still exists. Counselors need to be
supportive of change and help clients work through concerns, barriers,
and relapses.

Clients often see relapse as a weakness or failure, or they view themselves
as incapable of changing. They may feel frustrated and confused and may
want to give up. It is helpful for the client to view relapse as a learning experience, a natural part of the recovery and change process, and an opportunity
to re-establish a new plan that may incorporate additional methods. Clients
often benefit from group therapy or self-help support groups.

Throughout all the Stages of Change, it is important for the counselor
to continue the "spirit of motivational interviewing." This would include
being empathetic, listening carefully, using open-ended and evocative
questions, respecting the client's autonomy and abilities, supporting self-
efficacy, and being collaborative with the client by drawing out his or her
concerns, desires, and viewpoints (Manuel and Moyers n.d.).

Shortcomings of Motivational Interviewing

Motivational Interviewing is a "cool" rational approach to evaluating
motives, attitudes, and behaviors. A shortcoming of this approach,
acknowledged by Miller and Rollnick (1991, p. 24), is that many of the
forces driving addictive behavior are not enumerated easily by rational
reflection or introspection. These include community and peer influences,
enabling behaviors and sociocultural factors, as well as short-term forces
such as psychological discomforts of hangover or withdrawal, which "fall
off the chart." Also, one cannot simply measure pain, grief, love, and
other emotional associations against motives, habits, consequences, or
memories. If a person is emotionally devastated by, say, the loss of a child
or spouse, Decisional Balance Sheets or Readiness Rulers are not what he
or she would need. This does not diminish the successes of MI in eliciting
change even in the most recalcitrant clients.

Summary

Helping clients with substance use disorders begins with them making
lifestyle changes. Change for individuals is a process comprised of a series
of stages. These stages are precontemplation stage (not considering change

or seeing a need to change), contemplation stage (feeling ambivalent about change), preparation stage (planning to change), action stage (actually making changes by implementing plans to change), and maintenance stage (reinforcing efforts and continuing with the change). Assessing the point where a client is on the continuum of his or her process of change is important. Different counselor responses and interventions have been found to be more effective depending on the client's progress in the process of change.

Behavioral change, necessary to improve an individual's health, is dependent on motivation. Motivation is the engine that moves clients through the stages of change. Motivation to change depends on an individual's sense of the importance, confidence, and readiness to change. Motivation also requires that individuals work through their ambivalence concerning changing. Motivational Interviewing (MI) is an evidence-based strategy that involves both a counselor style and various techniques to assist clients through the change process.

Some of the most important elements of MI can be summed up in the acronym *FRAMES* (Rollnick and Miller 1995):

- **Feedback.** Nonjudgmental assessment of relevant client information delivered in a nonthreatening, matter-of-fact manner is essential.
- **Responsibility.** Change is the client's responsibility. The decisions and the choices the client makes are always his/hers.
- **Advice.** The counselor provides information and suggestions that the client may choose to use or not use.
- **Menu.** Developing options on change from which the client can choose gives the client ownership of each choice.
- **Empathy.** Use a counseling style that accurately reflects the feelings, thoughts, and experiences of the client from her or his frame of reference.
- **Self-Efficacy.** Promote and affirm the client's self confidence concerning the changes he or she is endeavoring to make.

References

Bandura, A. 1997. *Self-Efficacy: The Exercise of Control.* New York, NY: Freeman Press.

Botelho, R. 2004. *Motivational Practice: Promoting Healthy Habits and Self-care of Chronic Diseases.* Rochester, New York: MHH Publ.

Chiauzzi, E. 1996. *Motivational Enhancement in the Treatment of Addictions.* New York: Hatherleigh Press.

CSAT 1999. *Enhancing Motivation for Change in Substance Abuse Treatment.* Treatment Improvement Protocol Series 35. DHHS Publication No. (SMA) 05-4081. Rockville, MD: Center for Substance Abuse Treatment, Substance Abuse and Mental Health Services Administration, U.S. Dept. of HHS. Retrieved 4 November 2011 from http://www.ncbi.nlm.nih.gov/books/bv.fcgi?rid=hstat5.part.22441

DHHS (U.S. Department of Health and Human Service). 1999. Substance Abuse and Mental Health Services Administration, Center for Substance Abuse Treatment. *Enhancing Motivation for Change in Substance Abuse Treatment, TIP 35* (DHSS Publication No. SMA 01-3519).

DiClemente, C. C., and M. M. Velasquez. 2002. "Motivational interviewing and the stages of change," in *Motivational Interviewing: Preparing People to Change Addictive Behavior.* W. R. Miller, and S. Rollnick, eds. New York: Guilford Press.

Festinger, L. 1957. *A Theory of Cognitive Dissonance.* Stanford, CA: Stanford University Press.

Luborsky, L., and E. Luborsky. 2006. *Research and Psychotherapy: The Vital Link.* Lanham, MD: Rowan and Littlefield (Jason Aronson).

Manuel, J. K., and T. B. Moyers. n.d.. *Introduction to Motivational Interviewing Manual. Developed for the TEAM Project.* Retrieved 4 November 2011 from http://casaa.unm.edu/download/AF_MImanual.pdf

Meichenbaum, D., and D. C. Tuck. 1987. *Facilitating Treatment Adherence: A Practicioner Guidebook.* New York: Plenum Press.

Miller, W. R., and S. Rollnick. 1991. *Motivational Interviewing: Preparing People to Change Addictive Behavior.* New York: Guilford Press.

Miller, W. R., and S. Rollnick. 1995. What is motivational interviewing? *Behavioral and Cognitive Therapy* 23: 325–334.

Miller, W. R., and S. Rollnick. 2002. *Motivational Interviewing: Preparing People to Change Addictive Behavior,* 2nd ed. New York: Guilford Press.

Prochaska, J. O., and C. C. DiClemente. 1982. Stages and processes of self change in smoking: Toward an Integrative Model of Change. *Psychotherapy* 20: 161–173.

Prochaska, J. O., J. C. Norcross, and C. C. DiClemente. 1994. *Changing for Good.* New York: William Morrow Co.

Rollnick, S., P. Mason, and C. Butler. 1999. *Behavioral Change: A Guide for Practitioners.* New York: Churchill Livingston.

Rosengren, D. B. 2009. *Building Motivational Interviewing Skills.* New York: Guildford Press.

Velasquez, M. M., G. G. Maurer, C. Crouch, and C. C. DiClemente. 2001. *Group Treatment for Substance Abuse—A Stages of Change Therapy Manual.* New York: The Guilford Press.

Wallace, J. 1985a. "Working with the preferred defense structure of the recovering alcoholic," in *Practical Approaches to Alcoholism Psychotherapy,* 2nd ed. S. Zimberg, J. Wallace, and S. Blume, eds. New York: Plenum Press.

Wallace, J. 1985b. "Critical Issues in Alcoholism Psychotherapy," in *Practical Approaches to Alcoholism Psychotherapy,* 2nd Ed. S. Zimberg, J. Wallace, and S. Blume, eds. New York: Plenum Press.

Answer Keys

Activity 3.1 Answers

1. Precontemplation
2. Preparation
3. Contemplation
4. Contemplation
5. Precontemplation
6. Precontemplation
7. Contemplation
8. Action

Activity 3.2 Answers

1. I
2. D
3. B
4. C
5. A
6. E
7. F
8. G
9. H
10. J

4

Recovery

Objectives

By the end of this chapter, students will be able to:

1. Describe the new addiction recovery paradigms and how they differ from older approaches to addiction treatment and recovery.
2. Describe the phenomenon of "natural recovery" and its implications for treatment of addictions.
3. Describe four elements of lasting behavioral change.
4. Identify operant conditioning techniques, including (1) positive reinforcement and (2) negative reinforcement and extinction, as they apply to recovery from addiction.

5. Identify categories of erroneous automatic thoughts that clients often generate in response to certain situations, as they apply to facilitating and sustaining recovery.

6. Describe tasks in managing emotional states in order to facilitate and sustain recovery from addiction.

7. Describe cognitive behavioral therapy (CBT) concepts of functional analysis, Socratic questioning, and cognitive restructuring.

8. Describe Marlatt and Donovan's (1995) model of relapse.

9. Describe at least two methods to help clients reduce stress.

This chapter is divided into two parts: The first provides an overview of concepts pertaining to recovery, and the second goes into detail on techniques developed in recovery areas of thinking, feeling, behavior, and the interpersonal realm.

Overview of Recovery Concepts

Distinguishing Recovery from Treatment

Recovery is an ongoing process by which individuals suffering from substance abuse or other addictive disorders attain sobriety, get their lives under control, and move in the direction of health and wellness. Abstaining from alcohol, drugs, gambling, or other unwanted behaviors is necessary but not sufficient for a full recovery from an addictive disorder. Recovery also implies attaining healthy emotional, behavioral, and cognitive states, healthy relationships, and positive social involvements.

Recovery often, but not necessarily, involves episodes of professional treatment and/or involvement in mutual-aid groups. Persons who enter recovery from addiction often keep this as a major component of their identity for decades or on a lifelong basis (what sociologists call their *master status*), while others move on from that stance and define themselves more in terms of other involvements.

Treatment is a set of formal, professional, science-based interventions and services that offer skills and tools for initiating, facilitating, and maintaining recovery.

New Recovery Paradigms

Over the past decade, new recovery paradigms have caught on in the addictions field that we summarize here. Programs that emphasize these new paradigms are called *Recovery Oriented Systems of Care (ROSC)*, and, overall, they are referred to as a "new recovery movement," largely led by William L. White (2000 a and b). Linda Kaplan, a long-time leader in the addictions field, wrote a white paper overview of ROSC for the Substance Abuse and Mental Health Administration (Kaplan 2008).

The new paradigms of recovery in the twenty-first century are as follows:

1. The addictions field increasingly emphasizes strengths and resiliencies within people with substance-use disorders and how we can build upon and strengthen them. These approaches were developed in social work and counseling psychology decades before they were imported into addictions counseling. In this view, even in the depths of addiction, part of this person yearns to get better. This power and potential lies within all of us. This reverses the view of substance abusing persons as "sick," de-emphasizes pathologizing and labeling of clients, and radically changes the view of recovery as driven by external, coercive professional authorities. It also ends the taboo on discussing or recognizing "natural recovery" without treatment, but stresses harnessing and facilitating natural recovery motives and powers within us as the essence of treatment. According to the New York State Office of Alcoholism and Substance Abuse Services *2011 Interim Report* (OASAS 2011),

   > A ROSC supports person-centered and self-directed approaches to care that build on the strengths and resilience of individuals, families, and communities. The ROSC will drive the transition from an acute symptom stabilization model to one that manages chronic disorders over a lifetime, beginning with engagement and offering a continuum of self-directed recovery management approaches leading to long-term sustained recovery.

   ROSC emphasizes the development of a Personal Recovery Plan in addition to an externally directed treatment plan (Loveland and Boyle 2005).

2. Recovery Oriented Systems of Care seeks to build "recovery capital": the quantity and quality of both internal and external resources that a person can bring to bear on the initiation and maintenance of recovery (White 2009; White and Cloud 2008; Cloud and Granfield 2009).

3. Recovery Oriented Systems of Care recognizes the need for long-term recovery support through low-impact case management or peer-to-peer "recovery mentor" or "recovery coach" services. This is a long overdue implementation of treating addiction as a chronic, relapsing disease rather than as an acute

episode (White 2005). Treating addiction as an acute care disorder creates a revolving door of treatment and a crisis-oriented treatment approach that is inappropriate to the realities of substance use disorders. In fact, providing long-term support is more important than the barrage of services one may offer during a short stay in treatment. Some addictions professionals fear that nonprofessional or minimally credentialed recovery coaches will replace them as treatment funds diminish at the federal and state levels. It is important to understand the differences between the role of a sponsor in a recovery fellowship and the role of a recovery mentor. An essay on this distinction is in White (2006 and 2007).

Linkage of addictions treatment to communities of recovery is an issue that must be confronted by program administrators.

4. A new proud recovery community celebrates and advocates for recovery through such groups as Faces and Voices of Recovery, which plays a big role in reducing stigma associated with alcohol and drug disorders (http://www.facesandvoicesofrecovery.org).

There has been a cultural shift over the last few decades in that a larger proportion of people, even those in Alcoholics Anonymous (AA), now openly disclose their personal recovery status (Colman 2011). That trend was pioneered by the late Betty Ford three decades ago.

A wide variety of monographs and resources pertaining to the new recovery paradigm and recovery movement is available at http://www.facesandvoicesofrecovery.org/resources/publications_white.php.

This new recovery paradigm has begun to crystallize organizationally. Aside from Faces and Voices of Recovery, 2010–2011 saw the founding of a group of treatment professionals working with alumni groups that provide extended recovery support (Treatment Professionals in Alumni Services; TPAS) and an organization (National Association of Recovery Residences; NARR) working to credential sober living facilities.

Introducing the Dimensions of Recovery

The *whole person recovery* approach involves changes in many interconnected realms of human functioning. Important dimensions of recovery, which we describe in greater detail in the second section of this chapter, include emotions (sometimes called *affects* by clinicians) and behavior.

- *Cognition* (thinking, problem solving, processing of information), interpersonal functioning, skills, relationships, reduction of isolation

- Physiological improvements: improvement in cerebral function, nutrition, substance-related illness, exercise, moving from a culture of addiction or abuse to one of sobriety and wellness. This may incorporate spiritual awakening, development, and affiliation with sober networks, or what Granfield and Cloud (1999) call *cultural capital*, the local availability of culturally prescribed pathways to recovery, such as Alcoholics Anonymous groups in a language other than English or indigineous healing methods such as the Red Road (Coyhis and White 2006, White Bison 2002).
- Improvement in the social and economic aspects of *recovery capital*: stable employment; housing; a support network including family, peers, and colleagues; educational attainment or returning to school. A few state programs, such as one in Connecticut, have even paid for textbooks so that a recovering individual can get onto an educational and career ladder successfully.

Professionals as well as persons in personal recovery may emphasize one or more of these dimensions to the exclusion of others.

Many of these dimensions are examined in self-help as well as professional intervention. For example, Alcoholics Anonymous specifically addresses the role of resentments (cognitive distortions called "stinking thinking") in triggering relapse by actively "getting and using phone numbers and a sponsor" and studying the texts of AA that outline a coherent culture of healing.

It is interesting to compare addictions recovery concepts to those of its sibling, mental health recovery. The Substance Abuse and Mental Health Administration had presented 10 pillars of mental health recovery in 2006 (SAMHSA 2006) but then unified the definitions of mental health and substance abuse recovery in 2011 (SAMHSA 2011). The overarching definition is that "Recovery is a process of change whereby individuals work to improve their own health and wellness and to live a meaningful life in a community of their choice while striving to achieve their full potential."

The SAMHSA Principles of Recovery are identified as being:

- Person-driven
- Occurring via many pathways
- Holistic
- Supported by peers
- Supported through relationships
- Culturally based and influenced
- Supported by addressing trauma
- Involves individual, family, and community strengths and responsibility

- Based on respect
- Emerges from hope

They furthermore identify domains that support recovery as:

- *Health:* overcoming or managing one's disease(s) as well as living in a physically and emotionally healthy way
- *Home:* a stable and safe place to live that supports recovery
- *Purpose:* meaningful daily activities, such as a job, school, volunteerism, family caretaking, or creative endeavors, and the independence, income, and resources to participate in society
- *Community:* relationships and social networks that provide support, friendship, love, and hope

Stages of Recovery

Recovery is viewed by some as brought about by a dramatic conversion experience. For example, Bill Wilson, founder of AA, had a hallucinatory spiritual experience in 1935 while a patient at Towns Hospital, from which came his permanent sobriety. Handsome Lake, of the Seneca Nation, had a similar revelation in 1799, from which stemmed a cultural revitalization and sobriety movement among his tribe. More people see the path to recovery as a long struggle, marked by hard work, fits, and starts, and a gradually emerging state of wellness.

Many models attempt to describe the stages that people go through in attempting to change in the direction of health. One of the most popular approaches in the addictions field, and one that has spread to a wide variety of healthy changes, is the Stages of Change written by Prochaska and DiClemente.

In the early 1980s, James Prochaska and Carlo DiClemente (1982) posited an integrative model of change based on a study of cigarette smokers who quit without treatment, self-help groups, or other intervention. They identified six stages as common to all radical change in problem behaviors, including addictions, and applicable to any theoretical counseling approach. The stages are far more than periods of time; they represent a set of processes and tasks that must be done before moving to the next stage.

1. In the *precontemplation* stage, the individual resists change, denies the problem, and is demoralized. This individual may, however, be leveraged into treatment by environmental pressures, which may include significant others or authorities. At this point, information is helpful, particularly objective assessment data, not confrontation or advice.

2. In the *contemplation* stage, the individual is aware that he or she is "stuck" and acknowledges problems but is not ready to change, or even to prepare for change. The counselor's reflection of the client's ambivalence helps the client move toward action.

3. The *preparation* stage involves some commitment to and anticipation of action, although the client may still be so ambivalent (have conflicting motives) that he or she falls back from this position. (Prochaska and DiClemente originally called this the "determination" stage.) At this point, probing and reviewing consequences of different decisions may be helpful.

4. The *action* stage involves real behavioral change. Support of healthy decisions and positive reinforcement of healthy behaviors are useful at this stage.

5. During *maintenance* the client consolidates the gains made during the action stage and institutes measures to avoid falling back, or relapse. The tasks here involve learning how to "live in the world"; social skills such as assertiveness and communication skills are useful at this stage.

6. In the *termination* stage, the client moves past the problem-solving stage entirely. The focus here is still preventing relapse and dealing with many of the issues that surface in sobriety.

Prochaska and colleagues (1994, pp. 47–50) emphasized that growth is cyclical, best described as an upward spiral. An individual may "fall back" from a stage he or she has attained into an earlier one, before moving up and further along. Minor relapses or regressions are thus seen as a normal part of the cycle of growth. With this approach it is important to assess carefully the stage that the client is in and the pressures that may tend to keep him or her stuck in that stage or move him or her along to the next stage. Many or most addictions professionals do not think it is possible or desirable to move past a maintenance stage but think that one needs to be perpetually vigilant and "keep the memory green."

Bottoming Out

Traditionally, addictions counseling has held that substance abusers have to "hit the wall," that is, experience the consequences of their behavior in full force, whereby the need to change or do something about substance-abuse problems outweighs the perceived benefits and rationale for continued use. This need not (and indeed should not) entail hospitalization, jail, or homelessness. Many early AA members were in bad shape, so-called "low bottom" alcoholics. Many experiences can induce the bottoming-out feeling, including physical health; family abandonment; realization of something shameful one has done; and employers', family members', and friends' reactions to and confrontations regarding it, attempting to "raise the bottom." It is impossible to predict what will induce this sense of a need to change. For one client, the tipping point was being told by a cab driver that he was drunk. Bottoming-out is not necessarily an instant impetus for action. People ratchet up and down the Stages of Change from contemplation to action, or even back to precontemplation. Here the client is sitting on the fence about recovery. The past seems too painful and the future too uncertain and challenging. This is a phase of discomfort with the status quo, but it is also fear of change and the unknown and self-doubt about the ability to change. As we have commented elsewhere, ambivalence is present in active addiction, during the beginnings of change, and even in real recovery.

"Natural Recovery"

A large proportion of addicts become abstinent or return to moderate use of psychoactive substances without treatment or after treatment has not affected recovery. They are largely hidden from our view, as they don't advertise their former stigmatized lifestyle, don't appear in official statistics, and don't have their own lobby or advocacy group (Granfield and Cloud 1999, pp. 4–5, 11). Studies of "self-remitters" from substance-abuse disorders vary widely and by demographic and drug of choice. An overview of ten studies of natural recovery by Glenn Walters (2000) estimates that about half of abusers and addicts self-remit over any 10-year period, but that only a fourth remain truly stable in "natural recovery"; the other three quarters continue to use or enter treatment. According to Schutte and colleagues (2006), persons with less severe disorders are more likely to self-remit, and among these, mature women are more likely. We know that a large proportion of addicts do not recover naturally; nor do they moderate their use. Attempts to control addiction disease without some facilitation of insight, contemplation of problems, identification of triggers for relapse, learning of coping mechanisms, and adequate social support are chancy. Natural-recovery motives do often lose out to the power of addiction, inertia, and despair.

As early as 1962, Winick described how heroin addicts often "mature out" of use. Note, however, that many opiate addicts switch to alcohol, which offers a less strenuous and illicit lifestyle. Many studies of natural recovery or moderation of use were summarized in George Vaillant's landmark work, which includes his longitudinal study of "core city" (Boston) men (Vaillant 1983). Since then, many authors have examined "natural recovery" (Granfield and Cloud 1996, 1999; Stall and Biernacki 1986; Waldorf and Biernacki 1977, 1981; Waldorf et al. 1991).

Various factors may contribute to someone's move away from active addiction with or without treatment.

- In one survey of "self-remitters," Granfield and Cloud (1999, pp. 81–85) found that conversion to religion or other ideologies was the most common strategy of cessation even by those who did not partake of self-help group attendance or treatment. Innumerable individuals have ended alcohol or other drug abuse upon conversion to a religious or spiritual perspective, often when in dire straits or incarcerated.
- Addiction or abuse may be associated with membership in a drug abusing peer group or subculture, or, for women, involvement in a relationship with a drug abuser (Granfield and Cloud 1999, pp. 87–89). Once the individual loses that affiliation, there is a tendency to mature out of a chemical-using lifestyle. Many fraternity members move beyond binge drinking after graduation (although many do not). The "pothead" clique becomes less attractive when one is 25, and therefore marijuana is not used as widely in the age brackets above 30.
- Some people may tire of the effects of a drug, a status often expressed as, "I got sick and tired of being sick and tired." Young adults frequently weary of feeling "burnt" (e.g., apathetic, stupid, depressed, confused) from the effects of chronic marijuana use and recognize that it is holding them back from achieving important life goals.
- For some, new affiliations provide a stake in breaking from addiction. The birth of a child or the possibility of a job may make someone a stakeholder in society (Waldorf et al. 1991). Involvement in education not only can initiate, it can stabilize self-recovery.
- Having an intact social-support system—including employment and social relationships—to which one can return (Granfield and Cloud 1996, p. 50; Granfield and Cloud 1999, pp. 139–141) and the motive to return to it can protect from a severe decline into addiction and contribute to the ability to recover naturally from it. This is an important component of "recovery capital."

Treatment advocates are sometimes uncomfortable with phenomena such as natural recovery, which they believe will prove harmful to their cause (Weisner and Room 1978) or will encourage addicts to "go it alone." It is true that some seeking to disprove the value of treatment or self-help seize on observations of natural recovery. But a wide variety of researchers who are not involved in the addictions field are delving into this area and are consistently coming up with large percentages of self-remitters.

Measuring Recovery

Because recovery is individualized and has many possible pathways, the same set of measures cannot equally apply.

- Some people measure recovery in terms of the number of days, weeks, months, or years in sobriety. That can be tricky because we don't know anything about the emotional health or functioning of that individual with the two-year clean time token!
- For persons involved in formal treatment, a method of measuring recovery is to examine the attainment of goals and objectives on a comprehensive treatment plan. If an individual has completed formal treatment and is being monitored by a support system such as a recovery mentor or coach, determine how he or she is faring in comparison to the picture presented at discharge from treatment.

Karen Dodge and colleagues (2010) proposed a conceptual design for measuring recovery using six domains.

- *Physical dimension*, as measured by medical checkup and Addiction Severity Index (ASI):
  - ASI medical subscale, and brain imaging
  - Biomarkers indicative of recovery status
- *Chemical dependency status* as measured by ASI Alcohol/Drug Use subscale, and toxicology screen of urine or breast milk
- *Psychological status* as measured by standard inventories
- *Psychiatric status* as per the *Diagnostic and Statistical Manual of Mental Disorders, Text Revision IV* (DSM IV TR) and Global Assessment of Functioning
- *Family/social functioning status* as per ASI measures: Employment/Self-Support, Family Relations, Illegal Activity Subscales, Assessment of Family Problems
- *Spirituality* using the Self-Rating Scale and ASI-JCAHO Spirituality Scale

Detailed Exploration of Techniques Involving Behavior and Thought

Emotion (Affect) Management

When someone has lived for some time, perhaps during crucial developmental years, under the influence of an emotional anesthetic, he or she often suffers from *emotional illiteracy*. This term refers to the fact that many people are simply naïve about feelings; they do not have the tools or habit of "reading" their emotional states, no words to describe them, and little practice in describing or communicating them. It often is better to describe this as a deficit of remediable skills rather than a pathology. However, some people also are terrified or anxious about their feelings, and they feel guilty for having feelings that they believe are wrong or dangerous. Some tasks of counseling in the realm of emotion are to help the client:

- Identify and recognize emotions
- Differentiate emotions from thoughts and actions
- Accept emotions
- Communicate emotions appropriately

Becoming emotionally literate offers relief from:

- Having to spend so much energy fighting emotions
- Fearing buried or misunderstood emotions
- Getting stuck in cycles of self-stimulating anxiety
- Getting panicked by the experience of emotion
- Fearing the outcomes of having emotion
- Having panic or "self-hate" attacks when "forbidden" emotions occur

It also is important to help clients identify feeling states just prior to use of alcohol or other drugs. People often confabulate or distort how they were feeling prior to or during use, so-called *euphoric recall*. Keeping a log of feelings and substance use can uncover the fact that the individual was angry, lonely, bored, or anxious before using. This technique is often associated with adolescent treatment, where substance use is defined as a "fun" activity.

Clients should learn that emotions are not catastrophes: "If you can think about it and talk about it, you don't have to drink about it." Cummings, Gordon, and Marlatt (1980) reported that three-quarters of alcoholic relapses involved either "unpleasant" emotions, interpersonal conflict (which arouses uncomfortable emotional states), and/or social pressure. Affect management addresses at least two of these high-risk situations. Much of this work takes place in group settings. Loss and grief also are major issues that emerge in recovery, from the loss of alcohol itself and all that entails (e.g., friends, places to go, some activities, emotional numbness) to the losses sustained while actively addicted (e.g., marriage, job, self-respect; Goldberg 1985). Alcoholics Anonymous tells the newly recovering person not to get too hungry, angry, lonely, or tired (HALT); in other words, she or he must stay aware of relapse-triggering affects and physical states. Other individuals are numb to feelings due to a schizoid or antisocial personality disorder, and so it is important to have a medical history in your assessment before attempting to put emotional objectives into a treatment plan. Appropriate consultation with medical professionals should not be neglected if there is a suggestion that a psychiatric or neuropsychiatric issue is involved.

For some clients, a specialized anger management plan is necessary, or anger management sessions can be built right into a schedule of group sessions. A cognitive-behavioral therapy manual is available online (SAMHSA 2002). Whereas we are concerned with out-of-control anger and anger that triggers relapse, there also is the opposite tendency of being terrified of negativity because during active addiction these emotions are acted out in a destructive manner and are thus labeled as "bad."

Behavioral Change

Addictive behavior often is defeated, self-defeating, and disorganized. Research shows that the outcome of treatment often depends on an increased sense of *self-efficacy* (Bandura 1997), a sense that what one does will make a difference. Meaningful recovery necessitates learning modes of behavior that help meet personal needs, or in popular terms, *self-empowerment.* In the self-efficacy theory of Bandura (1987), clients change negative thinking by learning behaviors, performance, and coping responses via "homework" assignments.

Behavioral Concepts to Support Recovery

Behavioral psychology describes all behavior as learned and assumes that if a behavior is learned it can be unlearned. Understanding how we learn to initiate new healthy behaviors (e.g., nutritious eating, exercise, appropriate use of prescribed medicine, routine health checkups) and extinguish unhealthy behavior patterns or habits (e.g., excessive or addictive drinking, drug abuse, compulsive eating or gambling) can help addiction counselors assist clients in changing and maintaining new behaviors.

All college students have heard of the famous experiment done by Ivan Pavlov in 1927, in which Pavlov trained dogs to develop a learned response to a bell. He paired ringing a bell to introduction of meat, and eventually the dogs would salivate at the ringing of a bell without meat. This is known as *classical conditioning.* However, you can't keep up this effect forever; over time the association of the stimuli will lose its effect, known as *extinction.*

The importance of classical conditioning in terms of addiction counseling is that when addicts or alcoholics are using drugs and alcohol they begin to develop unconscious associations with the experiences and situations (the people, the places, the things) in which they routinely used their drug of choice. Re-experiencing these situations becomes a subliminal stimulus (sometimes referred to as an environmental *cue* or *trigger*), which then creates the cravings, the compulsions, and the desire to use. This is why in AA and Narcotics Anonymous (NA) it is often stated that it is best to avoid "people, places, and things" associated with your alcohol and/or drug use. An example is smoking while drinking morning coffee. When someone is attempting to stop smoking and they have their morning coffee, often the craving to smoke will be strongest. Specific associations need to be identified and avoided, or the client needs to find coping mechanism when they arise.

Operant Conditioning

Another model from behavioral theory is *operant conditioning*, attributed to the 1940s work of B. F. Skinner (Gilliland et al. 1989, p. 158). When a particular behavior (a *stimulus*), whether unhealthy (like smoking or over-eating) or healthy (like exercise or routinely taking a prescribed medicine), either increases pleasure or reduces pain or discomfort (the *response*), the behavior is reinforced and will most likely continue.

Operant conditioning looks at how the environment can shape behavior by four basic principles that were first observed in animals. The first of these is *positive reinforcement*, where a specific behavior is reinforced or strengthened by anything experienced as pleasurable. A pigeon will continue to push a lever to get food when it is rewarded with food. The behavior of pushing the lever is said to be reinforced and learned by the conditioned reward. Interestingly, when the reward is not provided every time for the behavior but only occurs intermittently, it actually is a stronger reinforcement.

Contingency management (*CM*) is a system of reinforcing client behaviors such as abstinence from drugs or alcohol (as monitored by blood or urine samples) or attendance at sessions at the facility. The use of blatant rewards for behaving well is, of course, the subject of much controversy. One of the major forms of contingency management is a voucher system, Voucher Based Reinforcement Therapy, whereby the clients collect tokens or vouchers that add up to an amount of money, a trip, a gift, or another reward. Despite gut feelings against contingency management on the part of recovering counselors, two major meta-analyses (Prendergast et al. 2006; Lussier et al. 2006) show that it can be of good effect, especially in early recovery, where there is not much investment in change, and in persons with low social capital to begin with. Despite the efficacy of CM, about one-third of counselors don't know about it (Bride et al. 2010).

"Behavioral Tailoring"

Many years of addiction leave a person without good grounding in stability and responsibility. The term *dry drunk* is used in AA to describe habitual, drunklike behaviors of a newly dried-out member, which might include impulsivity, moodiness, or irresponsibility.

Behavioral tailoring is a method to increase or introduce a new healthy behavior into a client's lifestyle, such as taking medications as prescribed, exercising regularly, or examining times when a client feels cravings. To help establish the client's usual routine, it will be necessary for the client to put together a schedule or log of his or her daily routine for at least a week. This could be a homework assignment of keeping an hour-by-hour journal of what is done from the time she or he wakes until bedtime. The counselor and client can go over the usual routine and inject a specific time for the desired behavior (e.g., taking medicine, exercising). As this is practiced over time by the client, it becomes associated with the client's usual routine and it becomes a conditioned behavior (Beck and Beck 2005). Behavioral approaches are also very valuable in relapse prevention. They involve identifying triggers of relapse and finding effective ways to deal with such situations. As stated earlier, AA does this very simply by telling alcoholics to avoid "people, places, and things" associated with alcohol.

Cognitive Change

Beliefs, attitudes, thoughts, categories, and self-statements act as lenses through which to view and interpret the world. Cognition plays a large role in emotional responses by determining reactions to stimuli and providing labels for psychological states. According to rational-emotive-behavioral therapy, addictive thinking includes many irrational beliefs and negative self-statements that can preclude positive action, force people to drive themselves unmercifully, and lead to chemical use.

1. *Demandingness* results from unfounded assumptions about requirements, usually expressed in terms of "should," "must," "ought to," "have to," and "need to." Typical statements are "I can't tolerate anxiety" and "I must drink to get through the day."

2. *Awfulizing* or *catastrophizing* is magnifying or exaggerating the badness of an event, "making a mountain out of a molehill." Catastrophizing, panicky thinking styles, and cognition that follows, what some professionals refer to as a *negative extrapolatory expectation pathway*, are found among a large subset of addicted persons. Catastrophizing or awfulizing can be a self-stimulating thinking cycle that creates paralyzing anxiety and easily contributes to relapse.

3. *Low frustration tolerance*, according to rational-emotive-behavioral therapy, is not a neurologically based behavior such as in attention-deficit hyperactivity disorder, nor is it a personality dynamic. It is an irrational belief that a person cannot tolerate discomfort, frustration, or other unpleasant feelings, and thus must drink or take drugs to cope or become numb.

4. *Overgeneralizing* is making broad conclusions from limited information. Persons who overgeneralize use words like "never," "always," "everybody," or "nobody." This often applies to the future: "I will always be alone." "I will always fail." Overgeneralization also can apply to the past and present: "He always hated me." "Good things never happen to me." "She never once said a decent thing." "I screw up everything." "Everyone I ever knew believed in cheating on taxes."

5. *Dichotomous thinking or polarized thinking* is an all or nothing, black or white, statement. "I have to be perfect or I'm a failure." "I had a slip. I've completely blown it. I'm weak."

6. *Mind reading or projection* is believing you know what others are thinking about you. "They're talking about how fat I am." "She's awfully quiet; she must be mad at me."

7. *Emotional reasoning and magnifying* comprises reasoning from feeling and not the reality of the situation. "Because I'm anxious the situation must be dangerous." "I feel down today; nothing is going to work out for me." Also, there is exaggeration out of proportion based on the emotions. "I couldn't go for that job interview without having a few drinks; it's impossible!"

8. *Personalization* is taking responsibility for things that are not our fault or making comparisons that are not reasonable to make. "She passed right by me on the street and said nothing. She must be very upset with me," or "He can stop smoking because he doesn't have the stress I have."

9. *Should statements*—"shoulda, coulda, wouldas"—are ways we continually feel regret and obsess over what might have been. "Shoulds" can be rigid rules about how we must behave or how others must act toward us. "I should never have started smoking." "She could have been a better mother." "I should be witty and more interesting."

10. *Selective abstractions or filtering* is seeing only a portion of personal experience to justify a belief or belief system. This involves ignoring or filtering out any information that does not support one's negative interpretation of a situation. "It's not important that I stayed sober for three weeks; the fact is I drank last night" (Freedman and Reinecke 1995, p. 192).

According to Marlatt and Gordon (1985), decisions about when and how much people drink are shaped by expected outcomes of their behavior. One type of expectation is *alcohol-efficacy expectation*, which holds that people are more likely to drink if they feel a lack of power (self-efficacy). In such a situation they attribute the power to alcohol (alcohol efficacy) and believe it can help them get their desired outcomes (e.g., making friends, being relaxed at parties, calmly delivering a speech, enjoying a vacation).

Although there are apparent divergences between twelve-step and professional approaches, there are actually examples where twelve-step and cognitive psychology have *parallel* approaches to the kind of thinking that precedes initial relapse. Cognitive psychology (Beck et al. 1993) describes anticipatory beliefs that are triggered by internal states (boredom, sadness) or external stimuli (a bar, holidays). They include self-statements like "I can't have fun without pot" and "I won't be able to make it through the day without a drink." This in turn triggers drug craving, which triggers a permission-giving belief (stinking thinking) such as "One drink won't hurt," "I'll stop after one drink this time," and "I deserve it this one time."

ACTIVITY (4.1) **Identifying thinking distortions or patterns**

Complete **Worksheet 4.1** (available at go.jblearning.com/myers3), identifying the specific type of thinking distortion for each statement.

Volunteer to answer each statement during class. Could the labels for various types of distorted or faulty thinking be somewhat arbitrary? Which of the statements fall into several categories? The important thing is to begin to pick up on how clients think in ways that sabotage their efforts at behavioral change.

It should be noted that when it comes to core beliefs, individuals who are struggling with addictions or other compulsive unhealthy lifestyle behaviors tend to hold three critical beliefs that occur before, during, and after indulging in the unhealthy behavior. These are *anticipatory beliefs* that provide powerful and almost magical quality to the drug or behavior. "It would feel great to do this (get high, engage in unprotected sex, have a few drinks at the bar, and so on)." This is followed by *relief-oriented beliefs.* " I need to have this drink, use drugs gamble, and so on" "I will feel well again." And this is followed by *permissive beliefs* that provide a rationale for continued use or engagement in the activity. "I deserve it this one time." "I can handle it." "This is a special occasion" (Beck et al. 1993).

Cognitive Restructuring

As the counselor and client begin to review situations and conditions under which certain automatic thoughts emerge, it can be helpful to develop a record. This document would record situations that the client has encountered, the automatic thoughts the situations have generated, the corresponding emotions, and the behaviors or actions that have resulted. Next to this list can be alternative and more rational ways of thinking and their subsequent emotional response and behavioral outcome. This basic process is known as *cognitive restructuring*. It allows clients to identify the thoughts that specific situations automatically engender and the negative experience such thoughts create. When these errors in thinking can be recognized by the client, they can reevaluate their meaning and respond more appropriately and with less stress and dysfunctional behavior. Cognitive restructuring as a strategy for dealing with negative emotions is to convey the message that feelings are to some extent generated by patterns of thought, that such thoughts are often inaccurate, and that people can learn to change irrational and unhelpful patterns of thinking.

A C T I V I T Y (4.2) **Cognitive-behavioral therapy model practice**

Write the following words as columns on your paper:

- Situation
- Automatic thoughts
- Emotions
- Response
- Outcome
- Rational response

Now think of a situation that might endanger the recovery of a client. Then list what automatic thoughts your client may have and what emotions he or she might be experiencing. Assign a percentage of level of intensity for each emotion. Without counseling, what do you believe the outcome would be for your client? What could be more rational ways to consider your client's situation? Write down your answer.

PROCESS: Consider your rational response to your client's situation. How might it change your client's feelings about the situation? What would be his or her behavior response?

Interpersonal Realm

Interpersonal skills allow for individuals to benefit from social support, get what they need from relationships, reduce conflict, improve a sense of self-efficacy and self-esteem, and reduce the pain of isolation. Developing skills such as active listening, interacting with groups appropriately, and coping with the ever-changing roles in families is important. Assertiveness is a foundation strategy that can prevent relapse.

Karl Albrecht (2006) and Joseph DeVito (2008) have written books on interpersonal coping styles and skills (what Albrecht calls *social intelligence*) that can supplement what is by necessity a short coverage of this area within this text.

Interpersonal Styles

Assertive behavior means communicating your needs, thoughts, and feelings in a clear, direct, and appropriate manner without disrespecting the needs and feelings of others or denying them their rights. Assertiveness builds self-esteem and self-efficacy, gets goals met, and gains the respect of others (I win—you win). Thus, assertiveness can be a component in a suite of relapse-prevention strategies for persons with substance use disorders. Assertiveness skills are important for counselors who need to set limits with needy or demanding clients.

Passive behavior (submissiveness) does not get goals or needs met, results in a negative self-image, and leads to low self-esteem, low self-efficacy, and helpless and hopeless thinking. It also lowers the respect of others towards you and will encourage them to take advantage of you. Passive people are chronically anxious, but they also eventually feel resentful and cheated, like a "doormat" (I lose—you win). Getting rid of resentments is a cornerstone of the AA recovery strategy because fuming about resentments will send someone straight down to the corner bar.

Aggressive behavior gets goals met at the expense of others, and it gains their resentment. Others will either give in resentfully or return the hostility. It either destroys relationships or creates a relationship from a superior vantage point towards a subordinate who is demeaned, based on fear (I win—you lose). Developing an assertive behavioral style also means dropping a defensive "street" persona that stands in the way of starting or maintaining healthy relationships.

Indirect (passive-aggressive) behavior is manipulative and dishonest. It creates suspiciousness and resentment.

Assertive Thinking

1. Assertion, rather than hostility, submissiveness, or manipulativeness, leads to a happier life and better relationships with others.
2. Standing up for ourselves and letting ourselves be known to others gains their respect and gains us self-respect.
3. Demeaning others demeans ourselves.
4. Personal relationships are more satisfying when we show our honest reactions to others and do not block their honest reactions to us.

5. Being assertive gives others the opportunity to change their behavior.
6. We are entitled to express ourselves and our needs, feelings, and thoughts.
7. Being assertive does not mean we deny the needs and feelings of others or violate their rights.
8. We have the right to set limits and to refuse to meet the expectations of others that are painful or difficult for us to meet.

Elements of Assertive Skills

1. **Escalating assertion.** Always start with the minimum amount of assertiveness, and then increase forcefulness gradually as needed, including leading to stipulation of consequences.
2. **Consequences.** "I need that item changed. If you won't do it, I'll have to take it up with your supervisor" (then, "with my lawyer," "with the police," and so on).
3. **Empathetic assertion.** Recognize the needs and feelings of others. "I realize you need me to help move furniture, but I absolutely must study for tomorrow's exam." "I know you are busy, but I need to ask you a favor."
4. **Discrepancy assertion.** "Bob, you say you want our departments to work together cooperatively, but you issue memos that are critical of our performance. I'd like to talk about that and work something out."
5. **Emotional assertion in behavioral context.** "When you don't help clean up, it really irritates me, so I'm asking you to make more of an effort to help clean up. This starts with hanging up your wet towels instead of dropping them outside of the shower."

Practice in role-play situations will give the client an opportunity to improve her or his skills in a safe place before using them in the real world outside of therapy. Next, the counselor needs to explore what might be a real-life situation that the client believes may arise or has happened in the past and has sabotaged her or his efforts to change. The counselor can take on the role of the person who is making it difficult for the client. Sometimes it's helpful to reverse roles, and the client can play the counselor or the other person. This role reversal often provides insight for the counselor and the client that can be useful in examining the emotional issues related to the situation. Here is a short dialogue with someone in recovery from alcohol dependency.

COUNSELOR: Tell me about a situation that might threaten your recovery.
CLIENT: Well, my uncle Bill comes by every weekend and we go bowling. He drinks quite a bit. He is always trying to buy me a

drink. If I say 'no' he gets upset and tells me that I can handle it and he'll make sure I only have few.

COUNSELOR: Does that work for you?

CLIENT: No, I always wind up getting drunk and in trouble.

COUNSELOR: What would you like to do about it?

CLIENT: I think for now I need to say 'no' to him about going bowling at all.

COUNSELOR: Have you tried that?

CLIENT: Yes, but somehow I always give in.

COUNSELOR: Let's practice trying to say 'no' to going out. First, I'll be Uncle Bill and you play yourself. (Being Uncle Bill) Hey Johnny, it's Friday night. Let's go bowling.

CLIENT: No, I can't go tonight.

COUNSELOR: Why not? You know we always have a great time. I guess you're afraid I'll beat you again.

CLIENT: I guess I just don't feel well tonight.

COUNSELOR: Oh you'll be fine soon as we get to the lanes.

CLIENT: Oh! Ah! I just don't know.

COUNSELOR: (Stepping out of character) Excuses usually don't work when you're trying to say no. What would you like to say?

CLIENT: I'd like to say, "Uncle Bill, it's just not good for me to go there."

COUNSELOR: OK, say it.

CLIENT: Uncle Bill, it's just not good for me to go there.

COUNSELOR: How did that feel?

CLIENT: Wow. It feels kind of good. OK, I think I can do it.

ACTIVITY (4.3) Behavioral rehearsal

To practice a role-play using an assertiveness skill, select a partner. Choose which one will play the role of "counselor" and which will be the "client." Using the scenarios from the list below, demonstrate aggressive, passive, and assertive responses to each situation. Pick one scenario and then develop a role-play where the "counselor" helps the "client" develop appropriate assertiveness skills to cope with that situation effectively. Switch roles and repeat this exercise.

1. Laura approaches a sales counter and should be first to be served. Another woman edges in front of her. When the salesperson asks who is first, the interloper says, "I am!"

2. Ms. Jones is a retired widow living in a senior colony in Florida. She is independent and creative and enjoys her privacy and solitary pursuits, which include painting, ceramics, and gardening. She

earns some spending money from selling her artwork at the local flea market. Another resident of the colony, Ms. Phillips, has been dropping in for tea and small talk about twice a week. Lately, however, Ms. Phillips has been arriving almost daily, spending two or more hours visiting. This is more than Ms. Jones really can stand, and she is not producing enough work to sell at the flea market.

3. You are in a physics lecture with 250 other students. The instructor speaks so softly that the people in the outer rows can't hear.

4. John borrowed $250 dollars from Ken a year ago. At the time, John was out of work and taking care of an ill parent. Now John is back at work at a good job, but he has made no effort to repay Ken or explain his behavior. Ken is getting more resentful every week.

5. You purchased an item, but when you got home you didn't want it anymore. Now you are returning the product to the store.

6. At a party, your friend lights up a doobie, inhales deeply, and holds it out to you. How do you say "no" to the offer of a hit of marijuana?

7. How do you tell a family member not to keep offering you a piece of cake?

PROCESS: How did you feel during the role-play? When was the "counselor" most effective in helping the "client" develop assertiveness skills? How did the "client" act in ways that the "counselor" knew the "client" had problems with getting needs/wants met?

The counselor needs to follow up on how the client used the skills they practiced in the behavioral rehearsal and ask if the skills are used in real-life situations. It is helpful for the client to keep a daily record and note the events when they try out a new behavior. They also should examine the consequences of the new behavior because if it is beneficial, it reinforces the new behavior.

It is important to know both the psychiatric diagnoses as well as the level of functioning as measured by the Global Assessment of Functioning (GAF) Scale in the *Diagnostic and Statistical Manual of Mental Disorders*. For example, the neurology of a person with schizophrenia generates apathy and withdrawal, which is also common in major depressive disorders.

Integration of Affect, Behavior, and Cognition

Affect, behavior, and cognition are clearly interwoven. For example, a young man meets a young woman in his college class. They sit next to each other for much of the semester. He likes her very much but avoids initiating any extracurricular recreation (i.e., dating). His thoughts (cognition) might include, "She will reject me" or "Even if she goes out with me, she won't like me." "I will feel worse when she rejects me than I would if I had never asked her out." "I cannot tolerate the horrible feelings I will have." "It is hopeless to try." "I am not good enough for her." "I am too ugly to interest her." He feels (*affect*) ashamed, depressed, sad, lonely, and helpless. He acts (*behavior*) helpless and passive, or, rather, he takes no action. The consequences of his failure to act are feeling worse, reinforced negative beliefs, lost opportunities, and so forth. This *learned helplessness* model of depression was introduced by Martin Seligman, who experimentally induced depression in animals (1972). Insights from the learned helplessness model have led to some of the keys for understanding depression (Abramson, Seligman, and Teasdale 1978; Costello 1978; Depue and Monroe 1978; Seligman and Maier 1967). The major treatments for depression are psychotherapy, medication, or a combination of both (Beck et al. 1993).

Several clinicians have formulated integrated strategies and applied them to the addictions. The best-known integrative counseling model is rational-emotive therapy (RET), now known as rational-emotive-behavioral therapy (REBT). It was expounded in the 1950s by Albert Ellis (Ellis 1962) who applied it to the addictions during the 1970s (Ellis et al. 1988). It is the basis of Smart Recovery, a self-help network founded in 1996 as Rational Recovery. The other major school is cognitive-behavioral therapy (CBT), an approach associated with the psychologists Alan Marlatt (Marlatt and Gordon 1985), Peter Monti (Monti et al. 1989), and others. It is especially applied to relapse-prevention strategies. Rational-emotive and cognitive-behavioral approaches dissect the cascade of effects involved in triggers to drinking and drugging, ways of identifying and managing triggers to relapse, and ways of coping with cravings and maladaptive beliefs. It teaches behavioral and cognitive problem-solving strategies and behavioral and cognitive skills, such as assertiveness, that counter helpless and hopeless behavior, thinking, and feeling.

Relapse Prevention Management

"Ever tried. Ever failed. No matter. Try again. Fail again. Fail better."
Samuel Beckett
Worstward Ho, 1983

Two-thirds of all participants in treatment research relapse within 90 days (Dimeff and Marlatt 1995, p. 176). Although this may seem foreboding, clients often enter stable recovery after a number of lapses; this relapse can be considered more the norm than the exception. Using the Stages of Change model, relapse is a normal, temporary recycling on the upward spiral of recovery. Rather than being considered a sign of failure, relapse should be viewed as an opportunity to learn new strategies to solidify recovery.

ACTIVITY **4.4** **Small group exercise "thinking about recovery versus abstinence"**

Write down your answers to the following questions:

1. What is the difference, if any, between being dry and drug-free and being clean and/or sober?
2. What is your definition of recovery?

Divide into small groups of four to six individuals. Share your answers with one another and come to a consensus on a single group answer to each question. Then review each group's answers. What are the differences and similarities between them?

Relapse prevention should be a proactive affair, discussed frankly and openly. Some counselors fear that talking about relapse would give permission for relapsing. Discussion about relapse is more likely to prevent it than avoiding the subject. Discussing relapse allows clients to feel less shame about their ambivalence about using and about their "slips" along the way, and it allows them to identify and examine potential roadblocks to recovery. Relapse prevention must be grounded in understanding of the process of change: deciding to change; taking the actual, initial steps to change; and then finally maintaining change. Each requires different sets of knowledge, skills, and attitudes (Velicer, Prochaska, Norman, and Reading 1998).

It is important for counselors to understand why people generally resist change. Some people lack the awareness that change is needed. People can be spectacularly ignorant of their self-defeating behaviors. Many clients are unable to decide what needs to be done. They may lack understanding of what they need to do to change, and they may lack the ability to do what is needed. They may lack a willingness to give up what they perceive as valuable. They may believe that what is offered is not any better than the status quo. Or, in terms of the Stages of Change model, clients may be in the precontemplative stage.

Often clients are willing to change, have the ability to change, and are ready to change, but as counselors we are unwilling or unable to allow the client to change in his or her own unique way. In other words, rigidity, formulaic approaches, and dogma are counselor attitudes that are impediments to change.

Before the client is stabilized, the focus needs to be on the here and now, "one day at a time." The major question is "What do you need to do to not drink/not use today?" At this point it is best to avoid all risky and stressful situations.

Once the client is stable, it is important to obtain a thorough bio-psychosocial history with specific focus on the people, places, situations, events, feelings, and thoughts that appear to have precipitated relapse in the past or that appear to be major contributing factors to using. Clients may be vague about how or why they relapsed, so it is important to note that some situation or event triggered thinking and feelings that led to the relapse. High-risk situations for relapse include:

1. **Negative emotions**—particularly anger and frustration
2. **Social pressure**—being in social situations where people are using or encouraging use
3. **Interpersonal conflict**—with parent, spouse, child, boss, friend, and so on
4. **Positive emotions**—celebration associated with use

(Note that not all risky experiences and feelings a client has are negative. One author had a recovering friend who noted that he never drank when unhappy or stressed. His relapses were always when he had success and wanted to celebrate.)

Risky Situations

Counselors need to thoroughly examine with their clients what appear to be high-risk situations for relapse. These include times, situations, people, places, and things that brought on the urge to use and set up past relapses. Knowledge of what the high-risk situations are for any specific client allows for planning strategies to avoid or cope with temptation and potential relapse. These often include being in the presence of the drug, seeing others use the drug, being in places where the client got high, experiencing both negative and positive moods, recalling memories associated with use, experiencing sounds and smells associated with use, and suddenly coming into money (Washton and Boundy 1989).

Warning Signs

Much of the literature on relapse prevention focuses on identifying warning signs that predate relapse and/or potential triggers or cues to use, looking at how clients have responded to situations and conditions in terms of how they thought about the situation, the feelings that these thoughts generated, and the subsequent behavioral response. This cognitive-behavioral model is useful in assisting clients to plan effectively for preventing relapse (Annis, Herie, and Walkin-Merek 1996; Marlatt and

Gordon 1985; Marlatt and Donovan 1995). The counselor assists clients in identification of these warning signs. Major signs (adapted from "37 Warning Symptoms," Gorski and Miller 1982) include:

- Return to denial or minimization of their problem
- Getting too lonely, hungry, or tired
- "Tunnel vision"
- Not planning or developing a strategy to deal with difficult situations
- Wishful or magical thinking about resolving problems
- Poor self-care, including lack of sleep, poor eating habits, and not exercising
- Harboring resentments about past life
- Stewing in self-pity about one's situation
- Desiring and returning to risky people, places, and things
- Becoming easily testy and angered by others
- Not having any daily structure, program, or support group (i.e., AA, NA, or RR)
- Having an "I don't give a damn" attitude.

Once a list of specific thoughts, feelings, and behaviors can be identified, the counselor needs to work with the client to develop an action plan to manage the thoughts, examine the feelings and responses, and modify the behaviors to minimize risk of relapse. This is best done before discharging a client and as part of the discharge plan. However, if a client returns because of a relapse or the fear of a relapse, it also can be an opportune time to frame the experience as a learning opportunity and to do a *postmortem* analysis of the situation, feelings, and experience that led to the relapse.

Exploring when the client is most tempted to use is quite useful in developing a plan. One way in which to do this is to have the client complete a form such as the one shown in Figure 4.1.

Creating a written plan helps reinforce commitment to assist the recovery process and assist in avoiding relapse. The plan would involve identifying situations that the client realizes put him or her at risk. In assembling such a plan, the client should complete the following statements:

- I plan to make these changes (name specifics).
- The most important reasons to make these changes are (what).
- Steps I plan to take are (what).
- People who can help me are (names of persons), and the possible ways they can help me are (what).
- I will know my plan is working if (e.g., what events occur, belief system changes).
- Some things that will interfere with my plans are (beliefs, people, places, events).

Figure 4.1 Handling urges.

➤ *I am most tempted to use when* _____ .

➤ *Negative emotions*   <u>*Some ways to avoid or alter this response.*</u>
   Examples include:
   Anger
   Depression

➤ *Physical Pain*   <u>*Some ways to avoid or alter this response*</u>

➤ *Social or positive events*   <u>*Some ways to avoid or alter this response*</u>
   Examples include:
   Parties
   When happy or excited

➤ *Withdrawal*   <u>*Some ways to avoid or alter this response*</u>
   Cravings or urges

Dealing with sudden urges to use is also important in helping a client avoid relapse. Clients need to know craving and urges will dissipate given the tincture of time. Having a strategy to delay the urge is important. Clients can be encouraged to do some of the following:

1. Things I can say to help me wait it out.
   I can tell myself the urge will go away.
   I can wait it out.
2. Think of negative results if I start to use.
   My marriage will be in trouble.
   My housing will be in trouble.
   My job will be in trouble.
   My quality of life will be zero.
3. Think of positive results if I don't start.
   My marriage will be better.
   My health would be better.
   I will increase in self-esteem and self-confidence. I will do things better.
   I will be able to continue living in the same house.

4. Eat or drink something else.
I can eat an apple rather than indulging in a café mocha or ice cream.
5. Do something else.
I can pray.
I can take a walk.
I can read.
I can call a supportive person.
I can listen to music.

Supporting recovery and preventing or responding effectively with relapse require counselors to actively and directly find personal and meaningful coping strategies. The more personal awareness about the potential triggers to relapse and coping skills to respond to those triggers, the better equipped the client will be to recover and thrive. This involves a learning process for clients as well as opportunities for them to gain health behaviors and develop new and healthier lifestyles and relationships. Even if a client relapses after learning relapse prevention skills, he or she stands a much better chance of returning to a full and healthy recovery.

Don't Pick Up the Second Drink

An often-neglected component of relapse prevention management is having a plan for minor relapses ("slips"). Again, counselors may be loath to even entertain such a possibility, but alcohol and drug abuse syndromes are chronic and relapsing conditions, and it is not realistic to avoid discussing all of the contingencies. According to Marlatt and Donovan's (1995) concept of the Abstinence Violation Effect, a "slip" or minor relapse can lead to greater relapse if the client believes that he has failed, has lost all the progress he has made, and feels that he has let significant others down. Therefore, there should be a very concrete, specific set of steps to follow in the eventuality that the client "picks up." AA tells us, "Don't pick up that first drink." Relapse prevention tells us, "If you do pick up that first drink, what are you going to do to not pick up the second drink?" Usually, this plan involves making immediate contact with a counselor, buddy, or AA/NA sponsor, going to a neutral place, or engaging in some of the strategies outlined above that were designed to prevent the initial lapse.

References

Abramson, L., M. Seligman, and M. Teasdale. 1978. Learned helplessness: Critique and reformulation. *Abnormal Psychology* 87: 49–79

Albrecht, K. 2006. *Social Intelligence: The New Science of Success.* San Francisco, CA: Jossey-Bass.

Annis, H., M. A. Herie, and L. Walkin-Merek. 1996. *Structured Relapse Prevention, An Outpatient Counseling Approach* (2nd ed.). Center for Addiction Mental Health.

Bandura. 1997. *Self-efficacy: The Exercise of Control.* New York: Freeman.

Bastable, S. B. 2008. *Nurse as Educator: Principles of Teaching and Learning for Nurse Practice.* Sudsbury, MA: Jones and Bartlett.

Beck, A. T., and J. S. Beck. 2005. *Cognitive Therapy for Challenging Problems.* New York: The Guilford Press.

Beck, A. T., F. D. Wright, C. F. Newman, B. S. Liese. 1993. *Cognitive Therapy of Substance Abuse.* New York: The Guilford Press.

Beckett, S. 1996. *Worstword Ho* (orig. 1983). New York: Grove Press.

Bride, B. E., A. J. Abraham, and P. R. Roman. 2010. Diffusion of contingency management and attitudes regarding its effectiveness and acceptability. *Substance Abuse* 31: 127–135.

Cloud, W., and W. Granfield. 2009. Conceptualising recovery capital: Expansion of a theoretical construct. *Substance Use and Misuse* 42(12/13): 1971–1986.

Colman, D. 2011. "Challenging the Second "A" in A.A. *The New York Times* Sunday Styles, 5/8/2011, p.1.

Coyhis, D., and W. White. 2006. Alcohol problems in Native America: The untold story of resistance and recovery—The truth about the lie. Colorado Springs, CO: White Bison, Inc.

Cummings, C., J. R. Gordon, and G. A. Marlatt. 1980. Relapse: Strategies of prevention and prediction. In W. R. Miller (ed.). *The Addictive Behavior.* Oxford:Pergamon Press.

Depue, R., and S. Monroe. 1978. Learned helplessness in the perspective of depressive disorders: Conceptional definitional disorders. *Journal of Abnormal Psychology* 87: 3–22.

DeVito, J. 2008. *Interpersonal Messages: Communication and Relationship Skills.* Boston: Pearson Education, Inc.

Dimeff, L. A., and G. A. Marlatt. 1998. Preventing relapse and maintaining change in addictive behaviors. *Clinical Psychology: Science and Practice* 5(4): 513–525.

Dodge, K., B. Krantz, P. J. Kenny. 2010. How do we begin to measure recovery? *Substance Abuse Treatment, Prevention, and Policy* 5: 31.

Ellis, A. 1962. *Reason and emotion in psychotherapy.* New York: Lyle Stuard. Ellis, A., J. F. McInerney, R. Digiuseppe, and R. J. Yeager. 1988. *Rational emotive therapy with alcoholics and substance abusers.* New York: Pergamon Press.

Freedman, A., and M. A. Reinecke. 1995. Cognitive Therapy. In Gurman, A. S. and S. B. Messer (eds.) *Essential Psychotherapies.* New York: Guillford Press.

Gilliland B. E., R. K. James, and J. T. Bowman. 1989. *Theories and Strategies of Counseling and Psychotherapy* (2nd ed). New York: Guilford Press.

Goldberg. M. 1985. Loss and grief: Major dynamics in the treatment of alcoholism. In *Psychological Issues in the Treatment of Alcoholism.* D. Cook ed. New York: Harworth Press.

Gorski, T. T., and M. Miller. 1982. *Counseling for relapse prevention.* Independence, MO: Herald House/Independence Press.

Granfield, R., and W. Cloud. 1996. The elephant that no one sees: Natural recovery among middle-class addicts. *Journal of Drug Issues* 26(1): 45–61.

Granfield, R., and W. Cloud. 1999. *Coming Clean: Overcoming Addiction Without Treatment.* New York: New York University Press.

Hanson, G. R., P. J. Venturelli, and A. E. Fleckenstein. 1998. *Drugs and Society.* Sudsbury, MA: Jones and Bartlett.

Kaplan, L. 2008. *The Role of Recovery Support Services in Recovery-Oriented Systems of Care.* DHHS Publication No. (SMA) 08-4315. Rockville, MD: Center for Substance Abuse Services, Substance Abuse and Mental Health Services Administration. Retrieved 8 November 2011 from http://www.facesandvoicesofrecovery.org/pdf/SAMHSARecoveryWhitePaper.pdf

Loveland, D., and M. Boyle. 2005. *Manual for Recovery Coaching and Personal Recovery Plan Development.* Peoria, IL: Fayette Companies and Illinois Department of Human Services, Department of Alcoholism and Substance Abuse. Retrieved 8 November 2011 from http://www.fayettecompanies.org/RecoveryCoach/RC%20Manual%20DASA%20edition%207-22-05.pdf

Lussier, J. P., S. H. Heil, J. A. Mongeon, G. J. Badger, and S. T. Higgins. 2006. A meta-analysis of voucher-based reinforcement therapy for substance use disorders. *Addiction* 101(2): 192–203.

Marlatt, A., and D. Donovan. 1995. *Relapse Prevention.* New York: The Guilford Press.

Marlatt, G. A., and J. A. Gordon. 1985. *Relapse Prevention.* New York: The Guilford Press.

McKay, M., M. Davis, P. Fanning. 2007. *Thoughts and Feeling: Taking Control of Your Moods and Your Life.* Oakland CA: New Harbinger Publications.

Monti, P. M., D. H. Rohsenow, S. M. Colby, and D. B. Abrams. Coping with Social Skills. In Hester and Miller (1989), *Handbook of Alcoholism Treatment Approaches: Effective Alternatives.* (2nd ed.). Needham Heights, MA: Simon and Schuster.

New York Office of Alcohol and Substance Abuse Services (OASAS). 2011. 2011 Interim Report. Albany, New York: OASAS. Retrieved 8 November 2011 from http://www.oasas. state.ny.us/pio/commissioner/documents/5YPIntReport2011.pdf

Pavlov I. 1927. *Conditioning Reflex.* London, Oxford University Press.

Prendergast, M., D. Podus, J. Finnery, L. Greenwell, and J. Roll. 2006. Contingency management for treatment of substance use disorders: A meta-analysis. *Addiction. 101*(11): 1546–1560.

Prochaska, J. O., and C. C. DiClemente. 1982. Stages and process of self-change in smoking: Towards an integrative model of change. *Psychotherapy* 20: 161–173.

Prochaska, J. O., J. C. Norcross, and C. C. DiClemente. 1994. *Changing for Good.* New York: William Morrow.

SAMHSA. 2002. Anger Management for Substance Abuse and Mental Health Clients. Washington, DC: Substance Abuse and Mental Health Administration. Retrieved 8 November 2011 from http://www.kap.samhsa.gov/products/manuals/pdfs/anger1.pdf

SAMHSA. 2006. Consensus Statement Defines Mental Health Recovery. SAMHSA News March-April 2006 vol 14 No. 2 Washington, DC: Substance Abuse and Mental Health Administration. Retrieved 8 November 2011 from http://www .samhsa.gov/SAMHSA_News/VolumeXIV_2/article4.htm

SAMHSA. 2011. Recovery Defined—A Unified Working Definition and Set of Principles. Retrieved 8 November 2011 from http://blog.samhsa.gov/2011/05/20/recovery-defined-a-unified-working-definition-and-set-of-principles/

Schutte, K. K., R. H. Moose, and P. L. Brennan. 2006. Predictors of untreated remission from late-life drinking problems. *Journal of Studies on Alcohol 67*(3): 354–362.

Seligman, M. 1972. Failure to escape traumatic shock. *Journal of Experimental Psychology* 74: 1–9.

Seligman, M., and M. E. P. Maier. 1967. *Biological Boundaries of Learning.* New York: Appleton-Century-Crofts.

Skinner, B. F. 1971. *Beyond freedom and Dignity.* Indianapolis, IN: Hackett Publishing.

Stall, R., and P. Biernacki. 1986. Spontaneous remission from the problematic use of substances. An inclusive model driven from the comparative analysis of alcohol, opiate, tobacco, food/obesity studies. *The International Journal of Addictions.* 21: 1–23.

Vaillant, G. E. 1995. *The Natural History of Alcoholism Revisited.* Cambridge, Massachusetts: Harvard University Press.

Velicer, W. F., J. O. Prochaska, J. Fava, G. Norman, and C. A. Reading. 1998. Smoking cessation and stress management: Applications from the transtheoretical model of behavioral change. *Homeostatis* 38: 216–233.

Waldorf, D., and P. Biernacki. 1977. Natural recovery from opiate addiction: A review of the incidence literature. *Journal of Drug Issues* 11:61–74.

Waldorf, D., and P. Biernacki. 1981. The natural recovery from opiate addiction: Some preliminary findings. *Journal of Drug Issues* 9: 61–76.

Waldorf, D., C. Reinarman, and S. Murphy. 1991. *Cocaine changes: The experience of using and quitting.* Philadephia, PA: Temple Press.

Walters, G. D. 2000. Spontaneous remission from alcohol, tobacco, and other drug abuse: Seeking quantitative answers to qualitative questions. *Am J Drug Alcohol Abuse* 26(3): 443–460.

Washton, A., and D. Boundy. 1989. *Willpower's Not Enough: Recovering from Addictions of Every Kind.* New York: Harper Collins Publishing.

Weisner, C., and R. Room. 1978. Financing and ideology in alcohol treatment. *Bulletin on Narcotics* 6.1.

White, W. L. 2009. Executive Summary: Recovery management and recovery-oriented systems of care: Scientific rationale and promising practices. *Counselor* 10(1): 24–32.

White, W. L. 2007. Addiction recovery: Its definition and conceptual boundaries. *J Subst Abuse Treat* 33: 229–242.

White, W. L. 2006. *Sponsor, Recovery Coach, Addiction Counselor: The Importance of Role Clarity and Role Integrity.* Philadelphia,

PA: Philadelphia Department of Behavioral Health and Mental Retardation Services. Retrieved 8 November 2011 from http://www.facesandvoicesofrecovery.org/pdf/White/2006-05-16_White_Sponsor_Essay.pdf

White, W. L. 2005. *Recovery Management: What If We Really Believed that Addiction Was a Chronic Disorder.* Great Lakes Addiction Technology Transfer Center. Retrieved 8 November 2011 from http://www.nattc.org/learn/topics/rosc/docs/RecoveryManagement.pdf

White, W. L. 2004. Recovery coaching: A lost function of addiction counseling? *Counselor Magazine* 5(6): 20–22.

White, W. L. 2000a. *Recovery Management and Recovery-Oriented Systems of Care: Scientific Rationale and Promising Practices.* Retrieved 8 November 2011 from http://www.attcnetwork.org/userfiles/file/GreatLakes/mng993-DLD1.pdf

White, W. L. 2000b. *Toward a New Recovery Movement: Historical Reflections on Recovery, Treatment, and Advocacy.* Paper prepared for the Center for Substance Abuse Treatment, SAMSHSA. Retrieved 8 November 2011 from http://www.atforum.com/SiteRoot/pages/addiction_resources/Recovery%20Movmnt.pdf

White, W. L., and W. Cloud. 2008. Recovery Capital: A Primer for Addictions Professionals Counselor Magazine November 6, 2008. Retrieved November 25, 2011 from http://www.counselormagazine.com/columns-mainmenu-55/27-treatment-strategies-or-protocols/816-recovery-capital-a-primer-for-addiction-professionals

White, B. 2002. *The Red Road to Wellbriety in the Native American Way.* Colorado Springs, CO: White Bison, Inc.

Winick, J. C. 1962. Maturing Out of Narcotic Addiction. *Bulletin on Narcotics* 6:1.

5

Group Treatment

Objectives

By the end of this chapter, students will be able to:

1. Describe at least three benefits of group treatment.
2. List at least four differences between interpersonal groups and other types of groups such as self-help groups.
3. Describe process versus content issues in group.
4. List four or more process behaviors to observe in group.
5. List four or more patterns to observe in group.
6. List four or more self-oriented roles played by members in group.

7. List four or more facilitated roles played by members of a group.
8. List three or more ways leaders can choose to intervene in the group process.

Introduction

Just about any gathering of clients is liable to be called a "group" or "group therapy." In this chapter the term *group treatment* applies to interactive groups that have an observable group process and in which the clients' talking to each other is the major activity, directly or indirectly facilitating personal growth and recovery from addiction. A variety of didactic and educational groups also can have important roles in addictions treatment, but in such settings interaction among members is not a central or defining characteristic.

Most alcohol and drug treatment occurs in group settings, which are well suited to the needs of recovering addicts. Groups break down isolation and encourage relatedness, social reemergence, and the identity of the "recovering addict." They provide hope, motivation, peer pressure, and support on recovery issues. Tension, shame, and guilt are reduced greatly when members bring out concealed feelings, thoughts, and behaviors, which often are shared by others in the group. Clients can form attachments and loyalties to something larger than the one-to-one, sometimes overdependent, counseling relationship, thus forming a counterbalance to the user/abuser milieu. Groups allow observation of real behavior patterns and replaying of roles, and they allow reflection on them. They are tremendously cost effective and "are also great fun" (Blume 1985, p. 75).

Groups work well at the individual, intrapsychic level because they activate so many therapeutic forces. At the small group/microsocietal level they teach social skills and facilitate interpersonal bonding. Groups also help bond clients to the treatment program itself, its values and norms, and to a culture of recovery and responsibility.

Although addictions groups are specialized among the group therapies in their focus on recovery issues such as denial and relapse prevention, they also touch on many of the emotional, behavioral, and cognitive issues found in all group modalities (Frank 1985). Group counseling methods are as diverse as those of individual counseling. Groups vary tremendously in focus, content, intensity, client characteristics, stage of treatment, format, and philosophy. Emotions may be screamed or politely discussed; behavioral changes may be harshly mandated or merely suggested; clients may interact freely or be discouraged from "cross-talk." The way in which a group is conducted is often based on a hallowed tradition within the agency milieu. Some addictions professionals believe that rigidly following tradition may clash with the individual needs of clients and research-based treatment design.

Interpersonal (Interactive) Versus Other Kinds of Groups

Psychoeducational (*didactic*) groups educate clients new to and ambivalent about recovery from chemical abuse, dependency, and relapse issues. They provide a low-intensity introduction to being in groups. The group leader is more of a teacher than a facilitator of group process, and he or she needs to have basic teaching skills (CSAT 2005, p. 14) so that he or she can deliver information in an organized, engaging, and culturally relevant manner. The group leader must manifest basic helper qualities such as caring, warmth, genuiness, and positive regard.

Groups modeled after Alcoholics Anonymous (AA) and Narcotics Anonymous (NA) are a "round-robin" of story-telling, perhaps with feedback. Members do not engage in "cross-talk" or bounce from member to member. (Format is described later in the chapter.) Spitz (2001) compared self-help (AA style) groups with interpersonal group therapy. Interpersonal groups differ from self-help groups in that they:

- Occur in a professional context with professional leadership
- Have members who are screened
- Emphasize group process
- Emphasize differences between members (self-help emphasizes similarities)
- Meet less frequently
- Are much more time limited, especially in the current managed-care climate, as opposed to the "lifelong fellowship" of AA and NA

This chapter pertains to interpersonal group treatment. For addicted people, who often have grown up in families with distorted communication patterns, chaotic organization, abandonment, and aggression, interpersonal group therapy based on the work of Yalom (1995) is a laboratory for learning, growth, and healing in the realm of relationships and for being part of healthy social systems.

According to the Interpersonal Group Therapy theory, the three levels of intervention in groups are the *intrapsychic* (what's going on in the "gut" of the individual client), the *interpersonal* (roles and relationships and interpersonal styles), and the *group as a whole* (how the group is functioning as a system; whether members are resisting, staying away from difficult topics, or scapegoating).

Carroll and Wiggins (1997, pp. 8–9) point out that while one sees a great deal of research on treatment efficacy, there is little evaluation of group treatment *per se.* This is partially due to the fact that it's hard to pull out the effect of the group from the other interventions that the client is exposed to, such as the quality of the case management, treatment planning, and individual counseling. It also is due to the fact that there is no standard set of outcomes, aside from sobriety.

Phases of Treatment and Placement in Groups

There are advantages to having a heterogeneous group in terms of time spent in treatment. Myers worked at an outpatient adolescent therapeutic community in which the long-term clients had positive attitudes and were familiar with treatment concepts and socialized (acculturated) "newbies" into the group/recovery culture. On the other hand, there is something to be said for placing clients into "levels" corresponding to time spent, readiness to change, or dominant issues of that phase/stage. In the early phase of treatment, clients are most ambivalent about ending chemical use, and they manifest resistance and adversarial relationships with authority (CSAT 2005, p. xix). In the middle phase of treatment, clients are more acculturated and have made gains that facilitators can point out. In the late phase of treatment, clients can more readily deal with conflict or deep emotion. Early stage patients might flee from displays of overwhelming emotion and intimacy.

As a general rule of thumb, putting someone with a severe personality disorder (such as severe borderline or antisocial personality disorder with poor impulse control) in a general population group can be a disaster (CSAT 2005, p. 39). Women who have suffered from trauma and abuse are served best in homogeneous groups.

Group Culture

Societies and groups have systems of behavior, values, and ideas that professionals refer to as their *culture.* The culture of a counseling group includes theme, content, group process, lore, format, and often a philosophy of human nature. A group's culture may derive from a particular tradition such as twelve-step, psychoanalytic, confrontational encounter group, and Gestalt psychology, or it may be a synthesis of styles. Agency and group culture is often summarized and transmitted in the form of slang, mottoes, and aphorisms. (Some examples: "When you think you're looking bad, you're looking good!" "You're as sick as your secrets." "It gets better." "Keep it simple." "Bad feelings get in the way of good feelings.") As happens in any culture, therapeutic culture engenders many concise descriptions of, among other things, the group dynamics and process. For example, protection from confrontation is described at Daytop Village

(New York) as "red-crossing" and at Integrity House (Newark, NJ) as "band-aiding."

Group cultures vary in the ways they map out personality dynamics. Models of the personality, although not always directly stated, are crucial influences on clinical approaches and should be recognized and critically evaluated. For example, anger is handled differently in different group cultures. The twelve-step model in a group setting may influence the identification of anger as a relapse trigger; members might then be encouraged to "turn it over to a higher power" or put it aside. In contrast, the therapeutic-community model, which also sees anger as a sign of potential relapse, recommends that such emotions be forcefully purged from the system in the group. Some clinicians (Brown and Yalom 1977, p. 452; Wallace 1985a, b) caution against pressuring clients to engage in extreme emotional outbursts in addictions groups because they are far too threatening and overwhelming and call for premature self-disclosure by clients.

Addictions agencies often have formal orientation to group rules and group culture. Group orientation facilitates the group process. For example, the almost universal rules of "No violence or threats of violence" and "Everyone stays in his or her seat except for a group exercise" reassure the members that this is a safe place where, unlike some family and community environments, expressions of opinion or anger will not meet with physical retaliation or abuse. Orientation and ground rules also provide structure and reassurance for the recently active alcoholic or addict who may retain some fear of losing self-control and physically acting out when angered. Other group norms that are commonly introduced in an orientation include the importance of regular attendance and punctuality, the rule against sexual contacts among group members, and strict confidentiality. While it is tempting to gossip, "Everything stays in this room."

ACTIVITY 5.1 Are you all together?

Sometimes it is difficult to assess "groupness." For instance, is a rock band a group? Is a baseball team? A family? The audience at a concert? Usually a group has some shared goals, some development of trust, norms of how to behave toward each other, some sense of leadership, and methods for making decisions. Probably most important of all is that members think of themselves as part of a group.

Form groups of six to eight and draw a picture of "a group" and of "a collection of people." How do your pictures differ? Small groups can post their pictures and describe them, differentiating the qualities of "group" and "collection of people."

PROCESS: Did all of the small groups come up with similar definitions? What processes took place in the small groups during the assigned task? Did some people push for completion, take over leadership, or bring up other topics?

Developing Awareness of the Group Process

Group process refers to all patterns and styles of interaction in the group. Content is what a group is discussing. It may be the problems or concerns of members or perhaps the tasks they are trying to accomplish. Although content should always be relevant to group objectives, even more important is the healing that goes on.

To help the group facilitate healthy behaviors, healing, and recovery from addiction, the counselor must be skilled in observing and evaluating the dynamics at work in the group.

First of all, counselors should think about how people present themselves. From these behaviors alone, none of which would be discernible in a transcription of the group, counselors can deduce the tone or atmosphere of the group (e.g., accepting, supportive, rejecting, tense or edgy, repressed, avoidant, overly polite) and the level of participation by each member. Behaviors to observe include:

- *Voice.* How do people sound? Listen to the voice qualities that members use.
- *Expression.* What are the facial expressions: smiles, frowns, raised eyebrows, sneers? If a person smiles, is it spontaneous, tight-lipped, fixed?
- *Posture.* What postures are adopted: bunched up, tipped back in chair, close or distant from the speaker or the next person in the circle?
- *Contribution.* Who talks a lot? Who seldom talks? Who talks only when probed?
- *Visual focus.* Where do people look when they talk? At others? At one person? At the leader? At the floor or ceiling? Out the window? Eyes closed?

Second, counselors should observe regular patterns of social interaction: how decisions are made and tasks are accomplished, agreements made and kept, roles developed and enacted. Patterns to observe include:

- *Influence.* Who influences whom in the group? How? What's their style of influence?
- *Rivalry and conflict.* Is there animosity or conflict between members? Is it open? Covert? Passive-aggressive? Aggressive? Constant or intermittent?

- *Level of participation:* Who takes part? Always the same people? How much? How often? Is participation encouraged or discouraged? How do members respond to nonparticipation by other members?
- *Decision making:* How are decisions made? Does one person dominate or take the lead? Does everyone have something to say or a chance to say it? Do decisions in the group come easily or with conflict?
- *Teamwork and productivity:* How are tasks accomplished, or not? Is the group following up on crises that have been mentioned? Are commitments being kept? Does everyone show up? Is everyone on time?
- *Roles:* What roles are developed? Why and how do people play parts such as "scapegoat" and "hero"? Who is "in trouble"? Examples of members who are in trouble include those who cannot get a turn to speak, are cut off before finished, are going to leave the group very upset, or are the target of derision or disrespect and cannot respond adequately.
- *Covert agreements:* Are there unspoken understandings such as taboo topics, nonconfrontation, and resistance to progress? Does this occur in subgroups or cliques, or on the part of the entire group?

Group process is a powerful tool; it can be healing and facilitate growth, or it can be devastating. Knowledge of group processes and continuous attention to process enable counselors to fulfill the ethical responsibility of promoting and safeguarding clients' welfare, emotional safety, and progress in recovery. The major role of an addictions group leader is not to give information, advice, or counseling but to facilitate the group process.

Group development is complex and slow and should not be rushed or mandated. Tension, conflict, resistance, and regression are expected; they provide important learning opportunities for the members. When members do not feel that they are being helped or feel stalemated in their attempts to progress, they may make the leader their scapegoat. Anger at the leader is a normal stage in group development, and the ability to express such feelings can be a growth experience for members (Ormont and Strean 1978; Stokes et al. 1980, pp. 124–125; Yalom 1975, pp. 306–311).

ACTIVITY (5.2) Process or content?

Decide whether each statement in the following group conversation is focused on process or content. Take about 10 minutes to read over the items and make notes where appropriate. Then discuss responses to the items.

> MARY: Let me tell you about my last slip.
> TOM: How does everyone feel about talking about this?
> JOHN: I don't like the word "slip." I prefer "relapse."
> MARY: It happened when I ran into my old girlfriend.
> SUSAN: I had a similar experience with my boyfriend.
> BILL: How does Terry feel about our discussion?
> TOM: I noticed Mary back off when you asked Terry to talk about it.
> MARY: He's always criticizing my decisions.
> TERRY: Tell us more about your reactions to Bill.
> SUSAN: I'd get a lot out of more discussion of resentment.

Intervening in the Group Process

It is important to realize that group process is always going on. The counselor or anyone designated as the leader or facilitator must decide when—if at all—to intervene in the group process. This decision depends on what the group leader sees as necessary to make the group interaction healthier and more productive, to encourage more interaction, remind the group of its goals and rules, and focus the group on process or recovery issues. Group leaders can choose to intervene in many ways and at various levels. They can choose between content (e.g., adding information to the discussion) or process (e.g., commenting on the silence, anger, or lack of involvement). They also can choose to address one, several, or all of the group members or encourage members to respond to one another.

Involving Marginal Members

Group membership is an important issue for each member. Members, particularly new members, are always struggling with whether they belong. To what extent they should or could share about themselves is a critical concern. Sharing of self is risky and requires trust of other group members and a belief that the benefits from the group outweigh the risks. Although new members of a group should not be forced to plunge directly into interaction, counselors must try to phase in their involvement. Waiting more than two group meetings sets a precedent that can dilute the group process below therapeutic levels. Moreover, marginalized members receive less help than they could, feel no investment in the group, and are in danger of leaving treatment or of relapse. Although they may not have articulated it, even to themselves, they feel extremely lonely and left out. In many cases, it is a relatively simple task for the counselor to help them initiate some contact with the group. One can, if no major pathology or other serious problem is suspected, gently force the issue. Subtle nudges include noting shared problems among members and asking the isolates to comment on their reactions to particular disclosures. At the very least, a counselor can note a group member's silence so that he or she does not feel invisible. Although many new members are overwhelmed by the self-disclosures and open exchange of emotions in group, it is important to identify other reasons for marginality and isolation. Possible reasons include fear of self-disclosure in a sensitive area such as sexual orientation, violence committed while intoxicated, or concomitant psychiatric diagnosis. These issues may be determined best in individual counseling. If an individual stays isolated and sees no way out of isolation and feeling unwanted, he or she will eventually leave unless compelled to stay.

Case in Point
Countering Isolation

At an agency that employed one of the authors, clients filled out confidential questionnaires asking with whom they preferred to associate. These connections were charted, and those who were not "on the chart" (called *sociometric isolates* by social psychologists) were rightly gauged as at risk of being "splittees" (individuals who leave treatment). Remedial interventions such as those discussed in this book were conducted to bring them into contact with other members.

Encouraging Peer Leadership in the Group

Counselors need to encourage a greater proportion of member-to-member interactions at the expense of leader-to-member interactions. This applies both to content (e.g., advice, confrontation, feedback) and to facilitation of group process.

If clients are still embedded in the drug culture, it may predominate over identification with a recovery program. Simply putting them into a room and expecting group therapy to occur is unrealistic, and in fact this may be asking for trouble. If clients have developed some measure of therapeutic alliance with counselors, the group is much less likely to go out of control. However, a large proportion of senior, committed clients is less often found in the current world of short-term and mandated treatment. The situation faced by the counselor whose client bragged of "skin-popping" (see the next Case in Point, "Peer Leadership") may be more typical. Luckily, the counselor in that situation was rescued by a senior staff member who developed a positive, healing group process by focusing on issues of common concern, such as teen parenting and parental abuse.

Case in Point

Peer Leadership

The importance of peer leadership and positive peer culture was made clear early in the career of one addictions counselor, who was trained at a branch of an adolescent intensive outpatient program where senior group members trained, confronted, and helped new members. The leader, in fact, had little to do. Interventions by peers were much more effective than interventions by authority figures. The following month the counselor was placed at a new branch where he and another staff member had to conduct a large group of teenagers who were not socialized to group culture and process or to drug-free norms and goals. They watched in horror as a member bragged to a receptive audience of having "graduated" from sniffing heroin to subcutaneous injection ("skin-popping").

It is important for counselors to examine whether they behave in ways that centralize the group around themselves, and, if so, why. For example, a counselor may fear that silences signal that the group is not functioning and will fail, or that time will be wasted, or that a point will be missed unless he or she makes it in the (theoretically) correct or most articulate way. A counselor may be afraid of losing control of the group or feel gratified by playing the role of revered leader, wise oracle, or healer. Of course, clinical or legal emergencies that require quick decisions by the staff override preferences for letting the group process develop at a natural rate.

Helping the Group Understand the Group Process

Group members are primed during orientation to focus on what is going on in the room. During orientation as well as during the first few group sessions, clients learn slogans and terms that describe group processes. In order to encourage the group's reflection on its process, the counselor must be aware of his or her own feelings in the group and how they reflect the prevailing atmosphere. The leader can and should comment on his or her observations of group processes, but it is more powerful for members to have and communicate these insights. The best facilitative interventions are those that encourage the group to observe itself and discuss the group process, which is often called a *here-and-now focus*. Such observations offer growth experiences for addicts; they provide insight as to how one actually behaves and how others react, and they reveal or highlight the consequences for one's identity, addiction, or recovery. Such a focus creates involvement, relevancy, and excitement. It is the basis for many group benefits listed in the introduction to this chapter.

The group leader has a heavy ethical burden. The group can unleash powerful forces such as memories of abuse, a need to share painful secrets, overwhelming emotions that can lead to desire to leave the program, or—worse—suicidal intent. Proper clinical supervision is needed to help the novice counselor deal with the potential "Pandora's box" situation.

Failure to prevent suicide is a big chunk of medical malpractice claims made against behavioral health systems. One-shot "sensitivity groups" held outside of an agency purview, where participants are not screened, and for which the participant is not protected by any follow-up, pose a big risk in terms of precipitating a psychiatric and/or suicidal crisis. Leaders need to protect individuals who don't wish to, or cannot, participate in cathartic and intense emotional outbursts. Rather than let emotions get totally out of control, the leader should limit conflict, step back to discuss what is going on, and try to determine where the powerful feelings are coming from (Yalom 1995, p. 350). Whereas "emotional contagion" is useful in groups, the domino effect of a crescendo of feelings can build to a level that can potentially terrify some clients, or at least create a climate of discomfort.

Developing Group Intimacy

An atmosphere of intimacy is necessary for individuals to feel trusting, which is a precondition for taking the risks involved in curative self-disclosure of information and emotion. Under ideal conditions, it happens this way: orientation, developing trust, calling members on violations of rules, nudges by the counselor, reminders, and so on. Unfortunately, most groups, especially addictions groups, operate under restraints. Groups are most often limited by financial issues, such as a member's number of group sessions or the reimbursable fee being limited by his or her insurance company. Therefore, structured ice-breaking activities can accelerate the process in the early stages of a group.

Activity 5.3 and others have been developed (Napier and Gershenfeld 1973; Stokes et al. 1980) and used successfully for decades to help a group move quickly to intimacy. Activity 5.4 was developed in the late 1960s at Daytop Village, Inc., to help addicts shed their street or "dope fiend" images, which were thought to impede recovery. It allows people to shed stereotyped perceptions of themselves, known as their *jackets* (a term based on the manila file folder of information that follows the person in the criminal-justice system). This type of sharing allows people to explore intimacy in a nonthreatening manner, lessens group defensiveness, and establishes an atmosphere of trust.

ACTIVITY 5.3 It made me who I am

Form pairs based on differences that you perceive in the other. First, discuss the criteria you chose to define "difference," and then discuss a pivotal or critical event in the formation of your personalities or lifestyles, regardless of whether it was positive or negative.

PROCESS:

- Was it hard to share the critical event with your partner?
- Did you quickly censure your choice of events and settle on an easy one?
- Do you feel closer to your partner now? If you do feel closer, how does that closeness or intimacy affect you?
- Does it make you feel vulnerable, embarrassed, or anxious to have disclosed personal information to your partner?

ACTIVITY (5.4) Blowing my image

"The Philosophy," by Richard Beauvais (1964), was read at the morning meeting of Daytop Village. Read "The Philosophy" or ask someone to read it aloud.

The Philosophy
We are here because there is no refuge, finally, from ourselves.
Until a person confronts himself in the eyes and hearts of others,
He is running.
Until he suffers them to share in his secrets,
He has no safety from them.
Here, together, a person can appear clearly to himself,
Not as the giant of his dreams, nor the dwarf of his fears,
But as a person, part of a whole with a share in its purposes.
Here, together, we can at last take root and grow,
Not alone anymore as in death, but alive in ourselves and others.

DISCUSS: What does "the dwarf of our fears" represent? Some answers might be that we are afraid that what we have to offer is insufficient or not good enough, that we can't measure up in the eyes of others. Some counselors humorously refer to an unrealistically poor self-image as *delusions of inferiority*.

Can low self-esteem, poor self-efficacy, or fear of being attacked make a person feel as if he or she needs to put up a mask, present a false image, or maintain a grandiose or tough exterior? Can this in turn make a person feel unknown, dishonest, or not liked for who he or she truly is? Do you think people can see through images to know what people really need?

What does "the giant of our dreams" represent? Here the giant symbolizes what we would like to be; it is a wish-fulfillment image.

PROCESS:

1. Each member receives feedback from the group on the image he or she presents to the world.
2. Each member then honestly recounts his or her self-image and secret, wish-fulfillment image.
3. Each member performs a simple task that changes his or her image in the eyes of others. For example, a person perceived as super serious tells a joke or does something silly, a "good guy" admits a nasty impulse, or a "tough guy" admits to vulnerability or fear.
4. Each member briefly explores how the self-disclosure and having his or her image blown made him or her feel. Others may offer brief reactions.

Keeping the Group on Task

Staying on the Issue

A goal in the development of a well-functioning group is that the group members themselves realize when the discussion has gone astray and point it out. Until the group can do this, however, the counselor needs to refocus the group on recovery issues. This is particularly a task in groups composed primarily of beginners, such as those in detox units.

Many groups emphasize feelings in the here and now. This helps the clients become aware of their emotions, identify them, differentiate them from thoughts and attitudes, learn to communicate them assertively and appropriately, feel comfortable with them, and learn to ventilate and share them rather than chemically anesthetize them. Feelings are hard work; they are also threatening. It is natural to drift into an easygoing discussion about sports, clothes, or even drugs. Counselors monitor this so that every moment of the group is used in a productive way, maximizing the gains each client can achieve. Effective group counselors do not stamp out all utterances referring to past events; however, they help to distinguish between war stories of addiction, which are not productive for interactive groups, and accounts that evoke emotion in the speaker and other members of the group.

Staying in Routine

The counselor has the task of gently assuring that the group format, to the extent that there is one, is followed. *Format* refers to the way the group's time is structured. There are an almost unlimited variety of formats, including the following examples:

- *Open discussion*: Members take random turns as they wish, without cross-talk, a format found in twelve-step fellowships.

- *Rigidly timed segments*: Each member has the same amount of uninterrupted time to speak.
- *Loosely timed segments*: The length of time each member speaks shifts from client to client according to the issues and emotions that arise.
- *Unstructured interaction.*

Within the overall group format, the individual client's turn in groups also may follow a predictable routine, as does the personal "story" or "drunkalogue" in AA. There are various approaches to how a client should use the time in a group. Aside from attempts to help a client focus on relevant issues, there may be some attempt to structure the turn taken by a client. For example, it may be considered important to ensure that the client gains insight into his or her behavior, thinking, and emotions, or that the client sees the connections among these areas. Years before formal schools of psychotherapy and counseling attempted such a broad synthesis, some addictions programs staffed by recovering addicts structured groups so as to "cover all the bases." In one such format, clients took their turns to be helped by focusing first on a specific problem, then on feelings related to the problem, then on positive behavioral changes they could attempt, and finally on identification and feedback from group members. This cycle could be repeated for each client who took a turn "on the hot seat."

In the format just described, the *problem* segment could address an issue raised by a client, or an observation by another group member of behavior seen as problematical, in a concerned inquiry or confrontation. The *feeling* segment could involve helping the client identify, evoke, communicate, and accept her or his emotions concerning the issue. It may entail:

- Simple questions such as, "How did you feel about that?"
- Focusing and clarifying questions
- Going around the room and telling everyone present the feeling, speaking to someone not present,[1] or speaking to a person playing the role of the absent subject[2]
- Venting an emotion by shouting or crying

The third segment of this format is commitment to a plan for behavioral change or experimentation broken down into specific behavioral steps, as well as contingency planning. These are written down so that the group can follow up on them in the next meeting. The commitment may be as simple as getting phone numbers of two group members and calling them during the week.

---

[1] This is the "empty chair" technique (Perls 1969).
[2] This activity has roots in psychodrama; some grounding in essentials of psychodrama would improve its effectiveness.

Identification and feedback come through supportive comments from others. Group behaviors in one segment may provide material for the next member's turn. There are two functions to such a segment:

1. In one study (Feeney and Dranger 1976), alcoholics rated identification with others as the most helpful element of group therapy. It is a tremendous relief for a client to realize that his or her problems and feelings are shared by many others, that others have "been there, done that," and that they can empathize with what the client is going through.

2. A "cooling-down" phase involves closure and summation of the segment. If the client is upset, an attempt is made to sooth ("patch up") him or her prior to the end of his or her segment. Cooling-off and closure segments are found in many group counseling approaches; they provide a transitional period from the vulnerability of deep emotion to the outside world.

In formatting the entire group meeting, time should be budgeted for possible crises, a cooling-down phase, and at least a moment for each member to be noticed and acknowledged.

The Cognitive Therapy Addictions Group format of Bruce Liese et al. (2002) is as follows:

1. *Facilitator introductions* (5 minutes). Introduce self, the group, the cognitive model

2. *Group member introductions* (20–40 minutes). Facilitator may relate problems to cognitive model

3. *Challenging thoughts and beliefs that lead to (trigger) addictive behaviors* (20–40 minutes). Examples are "I need some drinks before bed so I can sleep," "Just one drink won't hurt me," and "I'll stop tomorrow."

4. *Coping skills training* (10–20 minutes). These include developing healthy relationships, mood control, motivation and readiness to change, crisis management

5. *Goal setting and homework commitments.* These include envisioning the future, setting specific and achievable goals, identifying resources, committing to specific behavioral steps

6. *Closure.* Reflecting on what members have learned

Finally, formats of groups for specific stages of change and for identifying triggers for relapse, managing stress, effective communication and refusals, managing criticism, thoughts, cravings and urges, and developing an action plan, are presented in the group therapy Stages of Change manual developed by Velasquez et al. (2001).

Helping Group Members Explore Roles

Roles are patterns of behavior, sets of expectations, and parts played in a social system. As in physical systems (such as the solar system), the parts interact and resonate with each other. Members of addictions groups can benefit tremendously by reflecting on how their behavior in group replays, repeats, or transfers from another situation, past or present. The counselor needs the skill of facilitating this self-reflection. When counselors attempt to analyze a system of roles, they look for motives that the individual members of the group may have for each person to play an assigned part. The benefits accrued to one or more members may be obvious, indirect, or even based on false perceptions. However, the group leader should take care not to fall into glib formulae that interpret behavior in terms of simple transference from other roles. A group member's behavior may be a situational adaptation not typical of other settings.

....

Case in Point

Different Faces for Different Places

People play various roles. Someone can loom larger than life in one setting and then fade into meekness in another. One example is an assistant principal who is the terror of the classroom but is timid in the presence of peers at the faculty lunch table. Another example is the camp director whom all acclaim as "easy to work with and wonderful with the kids" but who has no time, energy, patience, or understanding for her husband and children.

Groups offer the possibility of learning to be accepted based on authentic feelings and reactions, not on some image someone thinks he or she needs to erect. This has a humanizing effect, lowers anxiety, and reduces the need to self-medicate with psychoactive substances.

Personal Roles Enacted in Groups

The role a member takes in a group has roots in his or her emotional history. The following roles are often cited as parts played in families, which can be transferred into other group settings. Again, it may be glib and deceptive to interpret all such behaviors as transferential of family issues or patterns. In the following sampling of roles typically found in addictions groups, it is important to note the variety of motivations that generate or maintain such behaviors.

The term *scapegoat* is perhaps the most common example of a group role. The name comes from the Biblical book of Leviticus and refers to the goat driven out into wilderness bearing the sins of the tribe. As originally described by Jackson and Bateson of the "Palo Alto group" in family therapy (Satir 1967, pp. 33–35), an individual brought into therapy as the identified patient may be the scapegoat in a dysfunctional family.[3] Both professional and folk psychotherapy systems have long recognized the advantages of scapegoating for group members, such as

- Deflecting attention from their own behaviors
- Forestalling possible attacks on themselves
- Creating a convenient, cathartic whipping-boy

People commonly chosen as scapegoats include different, weaker people or those who are new to the system. Although one would not expect an individual to seek out such a role, some might find it convenient to justify leaving the program in order to relapse. Orientation sessions and written rules for groups in various programs may include injunctions against scapegoating. Groups use many terms to identify destructive scapegoating behavior. In its most egregious forms, when a group "jumps on" a person and bombards him or her with criticism, it can be called "rat-packing," "rat-raging," or "piling on." There is also a more subtle holier-than-thou form of criticism, which serves to scapegoat other members. The latter is identified and thwarted by the slogan, "If you can spot it, you've got it."

The *leader*, *protector*, or *pseudotherapist* role involves taking responsibility for the problems of others. It also sets the individual apart from and above the ranks of the group members. There are many motivations behind adopting such a role. It might stem from:

- A recapitulation of the super-responsible or family hero role in the addictive or other type of dysfunctional family
- A fear of intimacy (i.e., a way of holding people at arm's length)
- A wish to avoid confrontation and direct the focus away from self
- A feeling of not being entitled to acceptance and attention as an ordinary group member, but only in this special, exalted position
- Faulty thinking such as, "If I'm not on top, I'm a flop"

Approaches by the facilitator to the member who consistently adopts this type of role should start with encouraging the member to take time for him- or herself, to ask for help with problems, and to make statements that include "I feel …" or "I need …" Once the member has gained that skill, the group can explore which motivation might apply in this case. Another type of approach is for the facilitator to encourage members to turn the tables on the "leaders," confront them, and strip them of their carefully constructed images.

The *provocative*, *hostile*, or *resentful* role may represent, to some extent, recapitulation of a scapegoat role in the family of origin. Other motives that bear exploration include:

---

[3] The group of researchers that has become well known as the Palo Alto group is officially the Western Behavioral Science Institute.

- A "counterdependent" defense, fear of intimacy, or vulnerability
- Testing of limits and quest for imposition of structure
- Wishing others to really prove their concern despite the unpleasantness
- Wishing to be ejected—an excuse for avoidance or relapse
- Lack of skill in better ways of getting attention

The group should not rise to the bait of the provocative member, but defuse the situation by asking what the provocateur really needs from the group or from specific members of the group. The group can help a hostile member understand that he or she is actually painting him- or herself into a corner of isolation.

The *class clown* or *joker* role may be generated by:

- Anxiety
- Fear of intimacy
- Boredom
- Fear of confrontation
- A need for attention, lack of skill in better methods of getting it
- Hostility, a wish to provoke
- Unrecognized attention-deficit hyperactivity disorder (ADHD)
- A need to compete with the leader

The class clown often attempts to involve others in his or her act and searches for an audience, sidekick, or straightman. Again, the group can defuse this role by asking the joker what he or she really needs or wants from the group or from specific members of the group and by encouraging statements that begin "I feel" or "I need." Finally, every attempt to provide a bit of humor need not be denounced as a pathological role!

The "weakest" group member, or the "sickest" one, may be pathologically dependent and may have come to this role through:

- The feeling that he or she is entitled to attention only if very sick or in crisis
- The need to regress, be babied, or get permission to not be responsible
- The fear of termination; if one gets healthy or grows up, one has to leave the group and be independent
- Hoping to find an enabler in the group to feed, promote, encourage, and justify weakness
- Identification with addicted parents in the family of origin, who modeled the sick behavior
- Hope that less will be expected of him or her in the group, which may come from fear that he or she can't do what is expected and can't measure up

Roles That Facilitate the Group's Work

Another approach to analyzing and categorizing roles in groups has to do with how members focus on facilitating the accomplishment of group tasks or on satisfying their own needs. Such an approach is less personal and clinical; rather it focuses on the needs of the group as a "living organism." This approach to categorizing roles was developed by early group dynamics theorists (Benne and Sheats 1948; Deutch 1953). It became the basis for human relations training (Nylen et al. 1967) and was later borrowed for group counselor training adapted for alcoholism counselors (Stokes et al. 1980, pp. 78–80).

Group facilitators or group maintainers typically engage in

- *Harmonizing* to reconcile differences and reduce tensions (usually associated with the placater or peacemaker role in an addictive family)
- *Gatekeeping* to keep communication channels open and facilitate communication by others
- *Compromising* to reconcile conflicts and help people admit errors

In contrast, self-oriented roles tend to interfere with the group's mutual efforts. These behaviors include:

- *Dominating* by monopolizing the group, not listening to others, and trying to make all the decisions
- *Withdrawing* and making no contributions, appearing apathetic or afraid or having no affect
- *Blocking*, usually by being aggressively critical, attacking others' opinions, and being hostile
- *Seeking recognition* and trying to be the center of attention, the entertainer, and by frequently straying off task and topic (perhaps related to the class clown)
- *People who monopolize the group*: "What do you want from the group now that you've said all this?" "How do you perceive the group members responding to you?" "Could you contribute to the group in 10 (15?) words or less?" (Carroll and Wiggins 1997, pp. 68–69). Member: "Carol's impossible to stop." Leader: "Is that right, Carol—are you really impossible to stop?" Leader: "My hunch is, Carol, that when you go on and on, you don't feel quite connected here; we need to find a way for you to share that will make you feel connected to others, and they to you … just using a lot of words isn't getting you what you need" (Vannicelli 1992, pp. 166–169).
- *Verbally aggressive/abusive member*: Provide a safe environment in which interactions can be processed and understood. "What was going on for people as John was talking just then?" "You have a

lot of feelings, and you express them very forthrightly. When you get upset, can you try communicating in a way that doesn't push people away? Let's try right now."(Vannicelli 1992, p. 165). In other words, maintain an empathetic attitude toward John.

- *The mandated, involuntary client who doesn't want to be there.* He/ she will show strong resistance to group goals. Vannicelli (2001, pp. 54–55) suggests incorporating resistance into treatment by inviting clients to discuss their anger at having been made to come and then praising their honesty.

It is more difficult to get members to appreciate the importance of focusing on tasks in groups than on emotions, behavior, and lives of the individual members. Obviously, tasks do not have the personal impact of, for example, realizing that one is being scapegoated or recapitulating a family role. Approaches to educating members on healthy approaches to the work of the group need to be reduced to basic questions such as, "What are we trying to do right now?" and "Is this helping?" Such questions encourage direct and assertive communication of needs and feelings and help to short-circuit manipulative or self-serving behaviors.

According to Carroll and Wiggins (1997, pp. 68–69), the dominator or monopolist is the most troublesome role for novice facilitators to change. The usual alternatives are letting the monopolist get his or her way or allowing resentment to build and boil over into angry confrontation. Asking the monopolist what he or she wants or needs from the group, or how he or she perceives the group's responses to him or her, is a better strategy.

ACTIVITY (5.5) How do I see this group?

Form a group of six to eight volunteers and play roles that facilitate the group's work (approximately 15 to 20 minutes). As observers, other members of the class identify the roles. Observe the levels of trust and self-disclosure, the levels of participation, the decision-making process, the levels of loyalty, and the sense of belonging. Then, six new volunteers form a group and play roles from the list of self-oriented or so-called negative roles. Again, the rest of the class can offer observations. Discuss what was different. Questions for discussions can include:

- What roles are being played or enacted here?
- What levels of trust or self-disclosure were displayed?
- What was the level of participation?
- What was the level of loyalty, sense of belonging?
- What was the decision-making process?

- How did other members react to blocking of the group process by a member? Did they adopt a unified reaction, did they overcome it, or did it lead to chaos?
- What feelings were evoked during the enactments by actors and observers?
- How might the group facilitate the adoption of productive roles for themselves and group members?

ACTIVITY **In my family …**

Use the same format as in Activity 5.5; however, use family-style roles. By drawing slips of paper, you can be assigned one of the broad roles such as scapegoat or clown. Other members or observers identify the role or defense being enacted.

Helping Group Members Translate What They Have Learned in Group into Life

Social skills learned in groups won't automatically translate into a repertoire of behaviors practiced on the outside. People are habituated to certain modes of interaction with others and will regress to the old norm when confronted, say, with family and friends. A process needs to be built in to check on this "translation" effect, which is often seen in a "homework" segment in groups and in the follow-ups in weeks to come.

Some people come to groups more engaged and outgoing, whereas others are more shy, reticent, and fearful. They may have a history of emotional or physical abuse, abandonment, or other attachment and trust issues. The danger is in letting those who take longer in mastering social skill sets feel like failures, become marginalized, or even be scapegoated. Positive feedback for our less gregarious brethren, and care to involve them from time to time, is a must.

Case in Point

Coming from a Different Place

In a high-energy encounter group for volunteers at an addictions program on Staten Island, New York, in which some recovering addicts participated, a young Scandinavian woman had difficulties convincing the other members that she was upset. Time and again they challenged her statements by observing that she "acted like she had no feelings," "acted like a zombie," and "seemed stoned." Finally, the psychotherapist who was facilitating the group stated that one would not expect the nonverbal cues of "upset" Scandinavians to be as dramatic, on average, as those of the Mediterranean, Latino, and Jewish people who formed a majority of the group members.

Defense Against Emotion

It is often difficult to be vulnerable, trusting, and emotionally open to a group of relative strangers. It is also hard work. Labeling a new member defensive may not be helpful. Participation in the group process and natural reverberations to the expressed emotions of others should gradually help the new member share his or her emotions. In responding to "defensiveness" there are two extremes to avoid. One is egregious time wasting and unspoken agreements not to discuss threatening or challenging topics. The other is pounding away at clients until they are exhausted, hate the group, or are traumatically and prematurely stripped of carefully constructed defenses. Spots of humor can provide a respite from the hard work of revealing emotions. The group format may include a built-in mechanism that moves toward and away from anxiety-provoking content (see the section "Staying in Routine" earlier in this chapter).

Groups help to build emotional literacy, which is the ability to identify, acknowledge, experience, and communicate emotions (Goleman 1995). A large proportion of group norms, mottoes, and exercises concern emotion; treatment groups tend to be charged with emotion. Yet individuals invest a lot of energy in defending against emotion, for a wide variety of reasons. In groups, defenses to avoid emotion can be grouped into three categories: blunting or negation of feeling, staying in a cognitive or informational channel, and playing a role that enables avoidance of emotion.

Blunting or negating feeling. A variety of mechanisms can be employed to blunt or negate threatening or painful feelings. It is important to distinguish such defenses from unfamiliarity with the vocabulary of emotion and from the blunting of affect that may be symptomatic of depressant abuse or schizophrenia. Emotions can be negated by

- Denying emotion
- Withdrawing and isolating
- Staying vague or confused
- Using program jargon and clichés

Staying in a cognitive or informational channel. By providing only cognitive and informational content, a group member can avoid his or her emotions. Varieties of this defense include

- Intellectualizing
- Barraging the group with data
- Not venturing beyond the ritualized AA drunkalogue or "story"
- Story-telling (war stories)

Story-telling (in some programs this is called telling "war stories") can be seen as the lack of client orientation away from the AA/NA model, where the "story" is the centerpiece of a member's utterances. On the other hand, it can be a sign of resistance. As Carroll and Wiggins noted, "Reporting events that occurred outside of the group is easier than relating to group members" (1997, p. 32). A third possibility is that the person is holding on to the old group culture out of fear of intimacy, although he or she knows the group norm is of interaction.

Playing a role. People can avoid their emotions by playing particular roles. This includes

- Being a joker or class clown
- Remaining belligerent
- Acting as pseudotherapist
- Being fragile, weak, or a victim
- Insisting on uniqueness
- Staying the outsider, perhaps underscored by behavior such as repeated lateness

Some treatment milieu have a "gangbusters" tradition of group treatment, which, as Motivational Interviewing theory states, can engender resistance, denial, and defensiveness. We think that it also results in false victories, tears, confessions, and breakthroughs, followed by flight and relapse as the client feels humiliated, devastated, or simply overwhelmed.

Formulating Treatment Plans for Group Members

Groups are shaped by the agency's preferences and traditions. Ideally, these can be reconciled with (to borrow corporate phraseology) a management-by-objectives approach; that is, start with basic recovery goals and formulate strategies based on individual treatment plans and contracts, stages of treatment, and client mix.

One of the major tasks in planning group treatment is to make sure that issues and individual clients' concerns are addressed in the group, including issues emerging in individual counseling that warrant group attention (making sure to observe confidentiality). Likewise, information, issues, and problems that emerge in the group need to be forwarded to individual counseling when necessary. Clearly, staff need to function as a treatment team. There are three canons of long-range treatment planning in groups:

1. Phase goals appropriate to each stage of treatment.
2. Anticipate feelings that are likely to be evoked at each stage.
3. Make sure the approach is congruent with or appropriate to the setting or modality (e.g., an intensive outpatient treatment program, a residential program, a halfway house).

One example of rather predictable feelings is "the terrible twos." This phrase refers to the second year of recovery. In recovery milieu, it is a humorous analogy to the difficulties parents often have when their "little angels" exhibit stubborn behavior or tantrums when they are two years old. In early recovery, the addict is often on a "pink cloud," having ascribed all problems to the former addiction. When problems (inevitably) reassert themselves and result in cognitive dissonance or some attempt to set the blame on some lingering aspect of addiction, the client must begin to face his or her disappointment that recovery is not nirvana. These issues can be brought out and shared in the group setting. Another example of predictable feelings is the approach of termination. When a member is preparing to leave the group, he or she may have anxieties that are manifested in regression, threat of relapse, or behavior that covers up needy feelings (such as a show of independence or denigration of the group or leader). In addition to monitoring the departing member, the counselor should observe the group's reactions to the impending departure of the member in order to determine whether the group is motivated to undermine growth, emphasize weakness or danger, or "break the wings" of the client.

Planning Formats

The formats for planning treatment for groups that appear in Figures 5.1, 5.2, and 5.3 are based on some of the most important sets of goals for addictions groups. It is not realistic to expect counselors to chart all of their group goals, strategies, and impediments, especially in a short-term treatment setting, nor to follow any chart very closely in an interactive, unpredictable group. However, counselors should be prepared with appropriate interventions at each stage of treatment and anticipate the potholes and bumps that inevitably crop up when traveling these paths.

Interventions should be keyed to readiness to change. The stage of change (i.e., precontemplative, contemplative, planning, action, maintenance) that has been noted in clients should be available in the most current psychosocial assessment. It would be inappropriate for the precontemplative client (often a mandated or involuntary client) to be involved in advanced issues such as exploration of early abuse. A valuable group therapy manual based on the stages of change model promulgated by Prochaska and DiClemente is the work by Velasquez et al. (2001). Most of the Motivational Interviewing strategies and techniques can be successfully

Figure 5.1 Plan 1 for group treatment.

Goals *(apply to early treatment)*
- *Manage uncomfortable physical and psychological states of early sobriety.*
- *Manage the desire to drink.*
- *Manage the anxiety and stress of being in an institutional setting, in a hospital unit, or in the group.*

Strategies
- *Establish group norms of sharing.*
- *Use role models by pointing to more senior clients who have moved beyond acute withdrawal.*
- *Provide information about withdrawal and abstinence.*

Trouble-Shooting Areas

Problems: *Denial of desire to drink, flight into health*

Resolution: *Identification given by others more experienced, sticking with first-stage issues, reiteration that feelings are normal and natural*

Figure 5.2 Plan 2 for group treatment.

Goals *(appropriate to later treatment)*
- *Develop the ability to engage in conflict and resolving conflict without withdrawing, drinking or drugging, or becoming violent.*
- *Related Objective: Learn to be angry in a socially appropriate way, without anxiety, guilt, or acting out.*

Strategies
- *Orient to the group norm: No violence or threats of violence. Stay in your seat. One person talks at a time.*
- *Orient to group culture, including the mottoes: Bad feelings get in the way of good feelings. You are entitled to all of your feelings. If you talk about it, you won't drink about it. It's not that you're not good enough, only you is good enough!*
- *Discuss old ways of dealing with resentments and triggers for violence.*
- *Orient to a simplified version of assertiveness concepts: It is not hostile or aggressive behavior, passive behavior, or indirectly hostile (passive-aggressive) behavior.*
- *Encourage "I" statements: "I need . . . ," "I feel . . ."*
- *Reward direct expressions of anger. Show the positive aftermath.*

Trouble-Shooting Areas

- *Fear of rejection*
- *Conflict defined as part of "old, bad" ways*
- *Passivity, depression, and learned helplessness*
- *The low-conflict style of Alcoholics Anonymous*
- *Fear of own feelings, panic at premature self-disclosure*
- *Denial of feelings*

translated into a group format (Mitchesson and Greller 2011). A five-session motivational interviewing-based group curriculum was developed by Ann Fields (2004), replete with handouts and worksheets, which the purchaser may use without violating copyright.

Impediments to Change

Regardless of the planning format, counselors must observe, assess, and monitor the enormous variety of impediments to changing behavior. These include habitual roles, process variables, and the mix of clients in the group.

Figure 5.3 Plan 3 for group treatment.

Goal *(appropriate throughout treatment)*
- *Stability and responsibility, which are the broad behavioral objectives*

Strategies
- *Use punctuality and attendance as group material.*
- *Explore reasons for difficulty in establishing responsible behavior patterns. Link to chemical intoxication, addictive lifestyle, and hopelessness.*
- *Discuss difference between being "dry" and real recovery. Use the AA concept of the dry drunk.*
- *Discuss behavioral problems and specific commitments made to group for follow-up.*
- *Prioritize goals and objectives, breaking down behavioral changes into simple, nonthreatening, concrete steps to be taken one at a time.*

Trouble-Shooting Areas

- *Explore the impediments to changing behavior-habitual roles, process variables, and client mix.*

Roles

Almost any of the roles adopted by group members can create impediments to behavioral change. For example, some may be afraid to relinquish a "sick" role that offers some comfort. Others may engage in "rescuing." Rescuing enables the avoidance of confrontation or other uncomfortable situations. Such "red-crossing" or "band-aiding" in drug rehabilitation programs is often a problem with new members who identify with people "on the hot seat" and become anxious when others are pressured. It also can be a form of "flag-waving" (i.e., signaling that the rescuer needs help), presentation of a nice-guy image in order to be liked, or the habitual reprise of codependent and enabling behavior of the addictive family. Crying, in particular, is certain to bring out rescuing behavior. It is good material for group discussion when it occurs. A useful tool is the therapeutic-community concept of responsible concern (similar to the tough-love concept), which is that rescuing is not helpful to the individual or to the group. In behavioral confrontation, counselors are always steering a course between scapegoating and rescuing.

Process

Aspects of group process that can impede behavioral change include mutually protective, tacit agreements among members not to "make waves" or reveal certain information ("pulling covers"). Some programs call these negative contracts. They often reflect a relationship outside of the group. Entire groups also can develop a tacit understanding to avoid uncomfortable or pressuring areas and topics. So-called higher-level groups of experienced members are prone to this. While it may appear that the group process is well developed and group affiliation and solidarity are optimal, it is important to examine whether, on a deeper level, the group is resting on its laurels and resisting the difficult, anxiety-provoking work necessary to progress further. Scapegoating and steamrolling of a weaker, newer, annoying, or different member is another example of a group contract.

At some old-style therapeutic communities, members link the two concepts: It is sometimes thought "red-crossers" were "hustling for a contract." In more familiar language, people may do favors such as rescuing and protecting others in the vague or explicit hope that this will be reciprocated. Assertiveness skills training (Lange and Jakubowski 1976, pp. 23–24) refers to this as the *hidden bargain*.[4]

Defenses

Any of the defenses may come into play, such as deluging the group with data; offering a ferocious, hostile image (one who will retaliate); and

---

[4] Assertiveness skills training is a long-established system of learning appropriate, nonthreatening, and effective approaches to dealing with conflict, potential conflict, and communication of negative emotion. See Lange and Jakubowski (1976) for training options for this area.

presenting a weak, fragile, and guilt-evoking image (which Al-Anon groups have aptly labeled "the poor me," or "throwing a pity party"). A seductive or flattering member also may succeed in soft-pedaling confrontation. Experienced group members may present a super-honest, super-confessing image. The counselor should consider whether this is a subtle form of resistance, especially when real and difficult behavioral changes should be on the agenda. Another defense is the raising of distracting information or side issues, sometimes called "throwing a bone." This phrase also can refer to presenting real information in a skewed way in order to have something to say. (See the Case in Point, "Throwing a Bone.") In such a case, the group's response could help the client overcome his or her timidity and reticence in interpersonal, dating, and sexual matters, or it could make him or her feel more inadequate and alone. Group process in a confrontational-style group can set up a self-fulfilling prophecy: When the group relishes pouncing upon defenses, participants may feel anxious and evasive and become more defensive. Much of the behavior that is called denial is simply a reaction to anxiety.

Case in Point

Throwing a Bone

At an addictions group in a young adult intensive outpatient clinic based on the therapeutic-community model, a young man who had problems initiating romantic relationships had not spoken in weeks and was prodded for an update. He sadly recounted a steamy encounter that culminated in frustrating rejection. Then a friend remembered that this incident had taken place two years earlier. It was revealed that he had not, in fact, been dating for some time and in anticipation of "flak" on this score was "throwing a bone" to the group. The group met the discovery with derision, ridicule, and gales of laughter.

Group Recording

Recording group process is more difficult than recording individual process. There are several participants and a multiplicity of relationships. Moreover, note-taking during group sessions is rarely allowed. Notations on the content of sessions and on the process taking place in the group are often a summary of what the counselor recalls with detailed descriptions of events that were particularly dramatic or as especially illustrative of the process. Like individual process recording, a group process recording can be laid out in two columns (content and process) or it can be written in alternative paragraphs for the same purpose.

ACTIVITY (5.7) How was group today?

*To practice recording the content and process of a group, you can use the
processes at work in a real treatment group or in a "fishbowl" group set
up in the classroom. In the latter situation, a circle of students observes
either a smaller group that is conducting a scripted role-play or a group
that is simply discussing their feelings in the here and now. Do not take
notes during the role-play. Later in the day, write your process recording
of the group. When the class meets next, compare the perceptions and
descriptions you wrote with those of your classmates. How do your descriptions of each component agree and disagree? What accounts for the differences in perception of group processes?*

References

Beauvais, R. 1965. "The Philosophy." Unpublished. Retrieved 16 January 2012 from http://www.daytop.org/philosophy.html

Benne, K. D., and P. Sheats. 1948. Functional roles and group members. *Journal of Social Issues* 4(2): 41–49.

Blume, S. 1985. "Group Psychotherapy in the Treatment of Alcoholism," in *Practical Approaches to Alcoholism Psychotherapy*. S. Zimberg, J. Wallace, and S. Blume, eds. New York: Plenum Press.

Brown, S., and I. D. Yalom. 1977. Interactional therapy with alcoholics. *Journal of Studies on Alcohol* 38(3): 426–456.

Carroll, M. R., and J. D. Wiggins. 1997. *Elements of Group Counseling*. Denver, CO: Love Publishing Company.

Carroll, M. R., and J. D. Wiggins. 1997. *Group Counseling: Back to the Basics*. Denver: Love Publishing.

Center for Substance Abuse Treatment (CSAT). 2005. *Substance Abuse Treatment: Group Therapy*. Treatment Improvement Protocol (TIP) Series 41. DHHS Publication No. (SMA) 05-3991. Rockville, MD: Substance Abuse and Mental Health Services Administration.

Deutch, M. 1953. "The Effects of Cooperation and Competition Upon Group Process," in *Group Dynamics*, 3rd ed. D. Cartwright and A. Zander, eds. New York: Harper and Row.

Feeney, D. J., and P. Dranger. 1976. Alcoholics view group therapy. *Journal of Studies on Alcohol* 37(5): 611–619.

Fields, A. 2004. *Curriculum-Based Motivation Group*. Vancouver, WA: Hollifield Associates.

Frank, D. J. 1985. "Therapeutic Components Shared by All Psychotherapies," in *Cognition and Psychotherapy*. M. Mahoney and A. Freeman, eds. New York: Plenum Press.

Goleman, D. 1995. *Emotional Intelligence*. New York: Bantam.

Lange, A. J., and P. Jakubowski. 1976. *Responsible Assertive Behavior: Cognitive/Behavioral Procedures for Trainers*. Champaign, IL: Research Press.

Liese, B. S., A. T. Beck, and K. Seaton. 2002. "The Cognitive Therapy Addictions Group," Chap. 3 in *The Group Therapy of Substance Abuse*. D. W. Brook and H. I. Spitz, eds. New York: The Haworth Medical Press.

Mitcheson, L., and Greller, B. 2011. "Motivation and change: The role of motivational interviewing in substance use groups," Chap. 2 in R. Hill and J. Harris, eds. *Principles and Practice of Group Work in Addictions* New York: Routledge.

Napier, R. W., and M. K. Gershenfeld. 1973. *Groups: Theory and Experience*. Boston: Houghton Mifflin.

Nylen, D., J. R. Mitchell, and A. Stout. 1967. *Handbook of Staff Development and Human Relations Training*. San Diego: University Associates.

Ormont, L., and H. S. Strean. 1978. *The Practice of Conjoint Therapy*. New York: Behavioral Sciences Press.

Perls, F. 1969. *Gestalt Therapy Verbatim*. Moab, UT: Real People Press.

Satir, V. 1967. *Conjoint Family Therapy*. Palo Alto, CA: Science and Behavior Books.

Spitz, H. I. 2001. Group psychotherapy of substance abuse in the era of managed mental health care. *International Journal of Group Psychotherapy* 51(1): 21–41.

Stokes, J. P., R. C. Tait, and L. P. Miller. 1980. *Group Skills for Alcoholism Counselors: GFTP Trainer Manual*. Rockville, MD: Dept. of Health and Human Services, National Institute of Alcohol Abuse and Alcoholism.

Vannicelli, M. 1992. *Removing the Roadblocks: Group Psychotherapy with Substance Abusers and Their Families*. New York: The Guilford Press.

Vannicelli, M. 2001. Leader dilemmas and countertransference considerations in group psychotherapy with substance abusers. *International Journal of Group Psychotherapy* 51(1): 42–62.

Velasquez, M. M., G. G. Maurer, C. Crouch et al. 2001. *Group Treatment for Substance Abuse: A Stages of Change Manual*. New York: The Guilford Press.

Vinogradov, S., and I. D. Yalom. 1989. *A Concise Guide to Group Psychotherapy*. Washington, DC: American Psychiatric Press.

Wallace, J. 1985a. "Working with the Preferred Defense Structure of the Recovering Alcoholic," chap. 2 in *Practical Approaches to Alcoholism Psychotherapy*. S. Zimberg, J. Wallace, and S. Blume, eds. New York: Plenum Press.

———. 1985b. "Critical Issues in Alcoholism Therapy," chap. 3 in *Practical Approaches to Alcoholism Psychotherapy*. S. Zimberg, J. Wallace, and S. Blume, eds. New York: Plenum Press.

Yalom, I. D. 1995. *The Theory and Practice of Group Psychotherapy*, 4th ed. New York: Basic Books.

Family

Objectives

At the end of this chapter, students will be able to:

1. Describe the three major elements of a social system.
2. Describe the roles of status, power, and authority in a family system.
3. Define the terms *enmeshment* and *disengagement* as used in family therapy.
4. Describe the dysfunctional patterns of communication found in addicted families.
5. Describe at least four irrational belief systems in addictive families.
6. Define and describe the concept of *codependency*.
7. Describe the roles often played by a codependent in an addicted family.

8. Write out an accurate genogram for a family.
9. Describe at least three traps counselors may fall into when working with family members.
10. Describe a minimum of four major sober living tasks of a family in recovery.

Family Treatment

Readers should be aware that family therapy is a separate field from addictions treatment, with its own professional organizations, vocabulary, and licensing requirements. Addictions agencies may conduct family interventions and family education, but be careful not to declare that they perform "family therapy" without properly credentialed staff in that area. Also note that third-party payers are increasingly unlikely to reimburse for both substance abuse and family treatment. (The inability of agencies to get payments for hours spent with families has become so severe, in fact, that a colleague suggested that this chapter be omitted from this text!)

Family treatment is rarely contraindicated, but agencies must take care that negative patterns such as controlling, bullying, and domineering are not imported in the treatment setting. Conversely, they must assure that what goes on in a family session will not trigger family violence once the members go home. One does not try to initiate treatment with a threatened, terrorized family member and their persecutor, but instead gets them into a domestic violence program (CSAT 2004, pp. 17–18).

Family Definitions

Although "family" may connote to some a Mom, Pop, Twins, and Baxter the basset hound configuration, that's just one, actually fairly rare type of family (the so-called *nuclear family*). Far more typical among the nations of the Earth, and even in the United States a hundred years ago, is the *extended family* involving either three generations in a household, an uncle or aunt, cousins, or all of the above. It is not within the scope of this text to begin to describe the incredible diversity of family and kinship systems, which may include first- or second-cousin marriage, blended families, and/or gay families. Counseling trainees can benefit from an introductory course in cultural anthropology and/or marriage and the family. Family and kinship are a major focus of cultural anthropology (McGoldrick et al. 2005).

The Family as a System

Families are social systems. Three general principles of systems are that:

- Each element (in this case, person) plays a part or role in the system.
- The elements of systems (here, persons) influence each other.
- Systems tend to strive for balance and to maintain the status quo.

Like group counseling, family counseling focuses on process. Unlike a group of strangers together in a room, however, a family has a long-established system of rules, traditions, rituals, and modes of communication. Every family member knows the rules and plays his or her role. A good metaphor for the difference between individual and family counseling is the choice of seat at a football game. You can sit up close and see individual plays or sit farther back in the bleachers and see the entire team play as a unit. In family counseling, the counselor focuses on the way the "team" plays as a unit rather than on each individual's actions.

ACTIVITY (**6.1**) **In my family …**

Form groups that correspond to your family's size (only child, two children, three to five children, and so on). Discuss the rules, taboos, and family rituals of your childhoods. Consider issues of drinking, sex, and secrets. Discuss who had power in the family, who drank or took drugs, who supported whom, how you were disciplined and by whom, who came into conflict with whom, and how conflict was handled. Were there family secrets, things kept within the family? What happened on special occasions like birthdays, holidays, and anniversaries? Share only what you wish to share!

To help a family with an addicted member, counselors need skills in assessing, understanding, and facilitating change in a number of areas (see Table 6.1).

Status, Power, and Authority

It is important to determine who has power and authority in the family. Observations of who makes decisions are necessary but not always sufficient. Who determines whether a referral will be implemented or aftercare recommendations followed? It may be the oldest child, an uncle, a grandparent, a grandaunt, or even someone not living in the continental United States. In some urban communities, teenagers involved in dealing drugs

Table 6.1 Topics of Concern for Addictive Families

Status, power, and authority
Elements of the system
Definitions of relationships
Conflict—hidden and open
Styles of communication
Family belief systems
Harm to nonaddicted family members
Expectations of treatment
Concepts of privacy and boundaries

acquire unusual power in the family. If there are two languages or cultures involved, the use of a child to translate for parents may transform the child into a "family hero" or "cultural broker" on whom the family depends for information and representation. Even a counselor's intervention can play a role in the family's power system. The counselor can play a part in reinforcing the status and power of individuals who are neglected or suppressed within the family constellation by looking to them for responses and comments and by encouraging and rewarding their participation.

Elements of the System

Referring to the roles played by and the interdependency of family members, Minuchin and Fishman (1981) use special terms to characterize family relationships. *Enmeshment* describes excessive or intrusive involvement where there is no personal space, autonomy, or sense of personal competence. The term *fused* is almost synonymous. Enmeshment may be a reaction to trauma or loss, a "circling of the wagons," or a coalescing against a perceived threat. Quite typical in the family with an addicted parent is a pattern of enmeshment between the nonusing spouse and the children (Edwards 1990, p. 17). Enmeshed and fused relationships go beyond mere coalitions or alliances; people intertwine to the point of losing their autonomy, a condition that is necessary for personal growth. Keeping up appearances in the family with an active addict or other disabled person can involve an adaptation where everything revolves around the addiction of another person. To be enmeshed is also to be *dependent*. Enmeshment, then, comes close to the popular if overused concept of *codependency*.

The opposite of enmeshment is *disengagement*, an abnormal lack of involvement, communication, loyalty, and sense of belonging (Minuchin 1974). Many family members disengage from a problematic, untrustworthy, or troublesome member (living at home or not). An addict may drift away into an addictive netherworld and become disengaged, or he or she may pop in and out of a family or other social system when he or she needs help or wants to resume a normal role. As we discussed in considering the supervisory relationship, in between the extremes of enmeshment and detachment is a healthy zone that nurtures but allows growth.

Al-Anon teaches that in a family where a member is actively addicted, to avoid codependency and maintain some autonomy and individual identity, a nonaddicted family member must learn to "lovingly detach" from the addict. When individuals or systems are destructive or prevent someone's personal growth, disengagement is a healthy response. This may range from someone refusing to let the other person's addiction be the center of his or her life (for example, refusing to lie for him, clean up her mess, or bail him out) to making it clear that a relationship is not possible as long as the addict is not making an investment in recovery.

The degree of disengagement from addiction varies considerably by ethnicity. Fitzpatrick's study of Puerto Rican addicts (1990) found that their families did not reject addicted members, or, if the addict was isolated from the family and later went into recovery, he or she could re-enter with relative ease (p. 119). However, the addict's family may have to put up with a great deal of exploitation (p. 120). This acceptance may not extend to the disgraced or degraded female crack cocaine addict, particularly the crack house habitué who exchanges sex for crack (Williams 1989).

Definitions of Relationships

An addictive family system often has its own definitions of the way families are supposed to be, such as what constitutes a "good child" or a "normal marriage." Families may hold sharply contrasting views of what constitutes "good" and "normal." A "good" child may be a passive or quiet child, one who waits hand and foot on the parents, or one who excels in sports or academics. For some families, "talking back" to parents is a sign of spunk, spirit, and intelligence; for others, it is a sign of disrespect. Cultural norms shape many of these definitions. For example, in the film *Lovers and Other Strangers*, a young man complains that he and his wife do not love each other anymore and are planning a divorce. In response, his father explains that romantic love is not necessary in a marriage, that he and the mother were "content" with each other. Not only do family patterns vary among ethnic groups, but also historical changes in all societies affect concepts of love and the family.

Conflict

There are innumerable sources of conflict, hidden or open, in a family, as well as various methods of resolution. Reactions to conflict are based both on norms of appropriate emotional expression and on the propriety of conflict. There may be interminable "cranky" verbal recrimination and accusations, "cut offs" of family members (McGoldrick 1982), or a fused and enmeshed but conflicted relationship. Conflict may take the form of verbal violence, physical violence, indirect sarcasm, nonverbal signals, or attempts to manipulate (by guilt, loyalty, or fear). Conflict may be expressed in the form of verbal battering by a man who resents his wife for earning more money than he does. Disowning a grown sister may be the result of a conflict arising from her upsetting the family system by seeking help and talking about family issues in therapy. If a teen is the focus of conflict, he or she might be "sent back" to his or her country of origin if it is feasible. This might be a combination of a "geographic cure" and a way to minimize conflict. It also functions to remove the "problem teen" from the family and from peer groups that may be perceived as negatively influencing him, and perhaps to transport him to a stricter environment to "straighten him out." A family that has migrated may experience *transgenerational stress*, when members of the family do not adhere to traditional norms of deference and respect.

Styles of Communication

Families have many methods and styles of communication, which vary on many axes and dimensions: the degree to which communication is direct or indirect; the attitude such as assertive, playful, passive, hostile, or passive-aggressive; the "channels" employed (words, voice qualities, gesture, posture, and facial expression); and the degree to which emotion is displayed or shared. Some families air important issues at the dinner table; some post notes on the refrigerator; others ignore issues until a crisis erupts. Certain family members may have "permission" to communicate emotion (e.g., only Dad can get angry). An example of cultural differences in family interactions is a scene in the film *Hannah and Her Sisters*, which presents an exaggerated, stereotypical portrayal of ethnic differences for the sake of humor. A split screen contrasts arguments and discussion of medical problems at the main character's urban Jewish family dinner and the reticent and "proper" behavior at dinner with his fiancée's family, which is of old mainline American stock.

Addiction superimposes dysfunctional patterns onto an existing cultural pattern. To cope with pain and anxiety, denial among family members is practiced, resulting in an emotional climate where, as described in detail by Claudia Black (1981, pp. 24–48), the unspoken rules are "Don't talk. Don't trust. Don't feel." Thus, there is noncommunication, incongruent communication (double messages), or destructive communication, and family secrets.

It is important to distinguish between cultural patterns and addictive patterns, or their interaction. One common clinical situation is that a wife demurs from confronting a husband or refuses to confirm what is evident to the counselor about the family's sorry state of affairs. This might be a manifestation of required family loyalty/secrecy found in their culture, the exaggeration of a tendency toward that behavior, or an addictive adaptation.

Family Belief System

The addictive family constructs an account of its functioning that family members believe and present to others. The addiction and codependency in the family are often denied, rationalized, excused, or blamed on others. Families in general think of their own behavioral patterns as the norm, a kind of micro-ethnocentrism. This is also true of the dysfunctional family: The abnormal is perceived as normal. Its thinking patterns are also typically helpless and hopeless. Table 6.2 shows some irrational statements

Table 6.2 Irrational Thoughts of Addictive Families

- The alcoholic's drinking or the drug abuser's using is the most important thing in family life.
- Use of alcohol or drugs is not the cause of our family's problems.
- Someone or something else caused the problems; the addict is not responsible.
- Keep the status quo at all costs.
- Everyone pitch in and enable the addict.
- Don't discuss what's going on with one another or with outsiders.
- Don't say what you feel.
- If we stop enabling, something terrible will happen.
- Things will get better when …

---

or internal dialogues, which may not be consciously realized. Some of the items are adapted from the "alcoholic family rules" summarized by Wegscheider (1989, pp. 80–84).

Harm to Nonaddicted Family Members

The addicted family is a host to all sorts of problems growing out of addiction and codependency. These problems affect all members of the family including the nonaddicted and extended family members. The harm—which may be short term, long term, or both—includes sexual dysfunction, marital paranoia, emotional and physical neglect, and nutritional problems. Family life is traumatic and inconsistent: After an outbreak of violence to which the children and other family members bear witness, there may be a brief "honeymoon period" where the perpetrator feels remorse, and then the nightmare resumes. Chaotic functioning and not knowing what trauma is about to occur generate a great deal of anxiety. Family alliances shift as the system frantically attempts to cope with addictive loss of control. Other aspects of trauma to children include witnessing sex, being molested themselves, and being witness to police intervention in the home. Another harmful effect on families is that out of isolation or preoccupation with the family itself, or a subsystem within it, an individual member often gets "stuck" in the normal process of development (Edwards 1990, p. 59; Sweet 1990).

Expectations of Treatment

Family members coming into recovery hold many myths and unrealistic expectations. Among many working-class and poor populations, for example, the concept of family therapy is alien. They expect individual addictions treatment to be short term, as in a detox unit. Family counseling, to the extent that this concept is accepted, is also expected to be very short term. The family may expect primarily concrete instructions and advice. They may believe that "everything will be OK now that he or she has stopped." They need orientation about the process of family therapy. They need to know that all of the family members will have to work hard to avoid enabling and to communicate honestly and directly, both in treatment and at home. (See the section "Sober Family Living Skills" later in this chapter.)

Privacy and Boundaries

Concepts of boundaries around the family vary greatly. Discussion of intimate relationships with people outside of the family and public expressions of anger or discord may not be permissible. Families act as units, putting up boundaries around themselves. Concepts of privacy vary among families as well as among groups in society to which families belong. Topics considered privileged information include annual income, sexual orientation of members, psychiatric or legal status, adoptions, even ethnicity. The degree to which privacy about a topic is an issue varies and is expressed by reactions ranging from discomfort to absolute secrecy. Further, information may not be shared even with individuals in the family, such as children and adolescents. Again, addictive dysfunction is superimposed on regular cultural norms: In the addictive family, there is a great discrepancy between what goes on "backstage" and what is presented "frontstage" in order to "keep up appearances." The family tends to encapsulate, putting up thick boundaries.

Orientation to the concept of family therapy can precede the attempt to elicit such self-disclosure. The need to use a child to translate, mentioned earlier, can make certain topics even more taboo, and in general may seem disrespectful. Counselors must find out about these customs and attitudes before treading into unknown territory.

Counselors need to gather information in the above areas in order to help family members develop self-understanding of their work together as a system and to help facilitate a healthier, recovery-oriented system. There is a wide variety of "normal" families, and the counselor may find that he or she must tread a line between respecting the cultural norms of families (and not alienating the clients) and encouraging changes out of the need to facilitate honest communication, individual autonomy, and growth. For example, a counselor may want to bring children into an intervention to confront destructive or enabling behavior on the part of adult family members, but that may conflict with norms of respect for elders.

Enabling, Codependency, and Roles in Families

Family systems tend to adjust themselves around a member's dysfunction. If this happens during caretaking for a cancer victim, at least it is beneficial for the sufferer. In the case of chemical abuse, however, it makes it easier to progress onward in addiction. In treatment of families with addicts, behavior that contributes to continuance and progression of chemical abuse is called *enabling*. It may include cleaning up the mess made by a drunk, cleaning up the drunk, bailing an addict out of jail, paying his or her debts, getting out of dinner invitations, calling in sick to the addict's boss, and so on. In its more subtle manifestations, it may be playing peacemaker when conflicts erupt as a result of the addict's behavior. The family often does not see how its "helping" is injurious. A closely related term in the addictions self-help vocabulary is codependency. *Codependency* refers not only to the enabling role played by a significant other or family member of an active addict, but also to the overinvolved investment in playing that role and in making the addict and/or addiction the center of his or her life, like a small satellite circling a planet. Prominent examples of such codependent roles are the rescuer, the martyred caretaker, and the eldest child who takes on parental functions.

The term *codependency* has struck a chord with those who came to believe that their lives were overly circumscribed and defined by the needs of others, and the concept has spread to encompass or explain a multitude of phenomena in society, although rarely grounded in clinical observation or research. In this text, we limit the use of codependency to those who adjust their lives around addiction and who receive gain or benefit to themselves or to the system as a whole, although this gain may seem very indirect and, in fact, be injurious in the long run.

Edwards (1990, pp. 196–197) remarks that he never ceases to be amazed at the "sincere and abysmal ignorance" he encounters in family members who, for example, greet the returning, newly dried-out member with a drink. Moreover, telling family members *not* to allow the drunk back into the house or scrape him or her up off the front lawn and clean him or her up may run smack dab up against family norms of loyalty and protectiveness that are almost sacred in its culture.

Stress and Trauma

Counselors must take care not to ascribe all enabling to a pathological codependency. Stress, trauma, conflict, and disabilities can lead to adaptations, which are imposed onto existing patterns of behavior.

Pain, difficulty, and special needs are posed by a variety of familial situations:

- Death
- Physical or mental disability or illness
- Absence of a parent
- An addicted family member
- Major life events such as migration, job change, and unemployment
- Addition of a family member such as a new baby, a sick grandparent, a newly migrated aunt

All of these situations can contribute to some extent to the development of abuse or addiction, which augments the existing dysfunction.

Family Roles

It is normal for families to assign all kinds of roles, often predicated on birth order. The birth-order effect was discussed in detail as early as 1931 by Alfred Adler. Often an eldest child, particularly in a family where there do not seem to be many achievements, goes on to relative success and is pointed to as a family hero. Often a youngest child is the beloved baby or mascot. The middle child may have no special part to play, being neither the first born nor the baby, and may become invisible and/or depressed, misbehave to get attention, and become the identified patient or the scapegoat (Adler 2010).

Whatever the combination of factors, trauma or increased stress may cause even more need for a hero, a mascot, or one less person to bother about. In addition, the family frequently needs someone to "take up the slack"; one person must then do more than necessary and usually take on more decision-making authority, often at the expense of his or her own needs. Salvador Minuchin (1974) describes a "parental child" who carries decision-making authority in a family whose parent is unavailable (absent or unable to function). Virginia Satir (1964) describes a similar concept, the "super-responsible one." All of these adaptations need to be seen against the backdrop of family relationships typical of the culture of which this family is a part.

Scapegoating

Families, like other groups, may actually need someone to draw fire, to be a tension-reducer, to take the blame. The "Palo Alto group" of family therapy systems researchers (Don Jackson, Jay Haley, Virginia Satir, and Gregory Bateson) as early as 1959 described the way the family often acts as a unit, the communication disturbances, and the process by which the family creates a *scapegoat*, often a child who is identified as the patient (Kolevzon and Green 1985; Satir 1964; Vogel and Bell 1960). In one respect, however, the Palo Alto group came to a conclusion that was not borne out by later medical research. They reasoned that scapegoating caused childhood psychiatric illness, which does not apply, for example, to childhood autism or schizophrenia, although such an ill individual may indeed be scapegoated for other problems. We know now, however, that schizophrenia and other brain diseases are not caused by poor parenting. A family with an addicted member often directs its anger and frustration at the weakest, most deviant, or problematic member. The hyperactive child may be scapegoated, even abused. The chemically dependent member of a family may become the scapegoat for problems not of his or her creation. By scapegoating, the family is telling itself (Edwards 1990, p. 31), "If he didn't use, we'd be fine."

Parental children, scapegoats, and other such roles are especially typical of enmeshed families, whose members are overinvolved with each other and underinvolved with their own identities and outside relationships. However, many inner-city family systems beset by addictions do not fit any sort of enmeshed pattern; at the extreme the caregiver is a burnt-out grandparent or there is a no-parent family, which some inner-city schools estimate to be the plight of one-half of their students.

Popular Views

In modern, popular writing on addiction in the family and on codependent roles of children that are carried into adulthood, all of these roles, described by family systems giants such as Adler, Minuchin, and Satir, are depicted as especially characteristic of *addicted* families (Wegscheider 1989). There is usually no citation of the earlier researchers and clinicians who observed these roles in *nonaddicted* families (Myers 2002, 2011). For example, the Palo Alto group's research was not focused on addicts and addictive families. Moreover, the cultural context that determines family roles is also overlooked, as if there were one type of addicted family that transcended culture. These popular writings are the basis of what might be called a folk model of addicted family roles, subscribed to by many within the adult children of alcoholics movement, and find their way into handouts for trainings for counselors and education of families of clients. Because such roles are so common, many individuals identify with them and ascribe a variety of ills to their being the offspring of a particular variety of addict. To be sure, many individuals suffer tremendously from the legacy of family addiction, and some have indeed been cast in one of these roles as a by-product of addiction in the family. The testimony of such stars as Suzanne Somers has been helpful to those who had not recognized their pain, compulsive behaviors, and the origin of their emotional baggage. Still, there is the real danger that a counselor may identify behavior as that of a role of an adult child of an alcoholic or a codependent when the behavior is actually grounded in mood disorders, birth order, cultural patterns, or acculturative stress.

Case in Point

Codependent or Mentally Ill?

A 32-year-old recovering addict who had an alcoholic parent enrolled at a community college. He functioned quite erratically, became a student activist, drifted into irritability, and then dropped out for the semester. He entered an expensive rehabilitation clinic for treatment of mood swings caused by "codependency issues." He was later diagnosed as suffering from bipolar disorder; the original interpretation was unhelpful and even dangerous.

Other Disorders

Merlene Miller (personal communication) commented to an addictions-studies newsgroup in 1998 that the chaos in addicted families is sometimes the result of family members who have attention-deficit hyperactivity disorder (ADHD), some of whom self-medicate. Because ADHD has a genetic component, there may be a parent and a child who both suffer from problems of hyperactivity, organization, staying on task, and losing and forgetting things, and who also may serve as role models for other children. Yet addiction specialists tend to look only at the substance abuse as the culprit for the chaos.

Cultural Patterns

A counselor who is familiar with a client's regular cultural patterns might be guilty of *ethnocentrism*, that is, looking through cultural blinders and evaluating another culture by the standards of one's cultural rules. For example, McGoldrick's description of the Irish family roles also sounds like the roles that have been described as typical of addicted families. She says that the typical Irish family (not necessarily alcoholic) as described by the mother, contains "My Denny, Poor Mary, and That Kathleen"—a family hero, lost child, and scapegoat (McGoldrick 1982). Scheper-Hughes (1979) provides many examples of the Irish family's "pattern of mythmaking whereby each family in the village seemed to have its successful, high-achieving (usually first-born) 'pet son' as well as its black-sheep alcoholic or its shy, incompetent (often last-born) bachelor son" (Scheper-Hughes 1979, p. 179). These patterns are rooted in both birth order and economics; they are not results of addictive family systems.

As another example, the partially assimilated Mexican American family "retains" and infantalizes the youngest child as a defense against assimilation that has claimed other children. This role is similar to the mascot described by Wegscheider and colleagues (Falicov and Karrer 1980).

Assessment of Addictive Family Roles

Actress Suzanne Somers describes her father's vacillation between the drunken, violent monster one night and a benign parent the following day. Living with such a wild inconsistency generates tremendous cognitive dissonance and anxiety, which necessitates the need for considerable denial to self and others. On a less catastrophic (nonetheless disruptive) level, the addicted member may simply drift in and out of people's lives. The binge-drinking or chronically relapsing addicted single parent may vacillate between a "normal" parental role and an infantalized childlike role (Edwards 1990, pp. 76–78).

When assessing a family's roles, counselors must take into consideration its community and culture. If counselors are not familiar with them, they should consult someone who is. It is wrong to assume that a role derives from an addictive or dysfunctional adaptation.

ACTIVITY (6.2) **Assessing the role of the spouse/significant other**

The left-hand column is a list of roles played by spouses or significant others of addicts. The right-hand column represents the thinking patterns or rationale for these behaviors, but shows them in random order. In the first part of this activity, please match up the roles with the thinking associated with each role. You may wish to photocopy the page to draw lines across the columns to match up the items. In the second part of this activity, students can discuss how any of these roles apply to a case in which they are involved. In addition, they should consider whether the spouse or significant other vacillates between two of these roles or is transitioning from one to another. They also should consider if and how this role deviates from the traditional role of spouse or significant other in their culture of origin.

Role	Thinking
Rescuer	"It wasn't that bad. He didn't really mean it."
Caretaker	"Don't drink more than one drink tonight."
Long-suffering martyr and saint	"I just don't feel well at all."
Overextended super-responsible one	"Love conquers all."
Chief enabler	"Poor me, I do it all myself for their sake."
Scapegoat	"You're ruining our lives!"
Hypochondriac, somaticizing	"The poor man, he needs my help."
Joiner in addiction	"We'd all be better off if she'd just give up the booze."
Placater or peacemaker	"I don't care. After that last fiasco, I'm not having any more to do with my family."
Blamer, conscience	"I love you, but I can't be with you until you start getting better."
Battler, limiter	"Let's get high and stay together."
Disengaged and hostile	"I'll take care of it."
Recovering from codependency, lovingly disengaged from addiction, and/or attempting to achieve referral into treatment	"I'm just trying to help."

ACTIVITY (6.3) Role of the active addict

Each student should consider the case of a current or formerly addicted person. A student volunteer or the instructor may offer a description to help jumpstart this discussion. Check one or more of the following descriptions if they apply to the addict. If the addict, as is often the case, cycles between two behavior patterns depending on his or her state of intoxication, it is important to indicate this. This can be done by drawing a two-headed arrow between the two roles.

_____ *Absent, disengaged*

_____ *Baby and/or sick one*

_____ *Kept out of sight, encapsulated in family*

_____ *Not encapsulated*

_____ *Scapegoat*

_____ *Good, depressed caretaker*

_____ *Good, depressed dependent*

_____ *Out of control, but not particularly threatening*

_____ *Out of control and threatening or abusive*

_____ *Attempting relapse*

_____ *Other* _____

ACTIVITY (6.4) Role of the children of addicts

Each student should consider a family with whom they are familiar, in which there is an actively addicted parent. A student volunteer or the instructor may help jump-start this activity by describing such a family. Indicate which children play which role, by birth order and gender. A simpler technique is to enter the children's names and ages next to their roles. You also can draw an arrow to indicate transition or growth from one role to another, or draw a double-headed arrow to indicate vacillation. The binging or relapsing parent, for example, may propel a child repeatedly into "pseudoparent to parent" status and back out again. An individual can play one or more of the following roles:

_____ *Pseudoparent to other children*

_____ *Pseudoparent to parent*

_____ *Pseudospouse to nonaddicted parent*

_____ *Family hero*

_____ *Scapegoat, rebel who acts out*

_____ *Scapegoated child (some are colicky, hyperactive, or have fetal alcohol syndrome)*

_____ *Invisible one*

_____ *Placater*

_____ *Co-abuser who joins the parent in abuse*

_____ *Battler with addiction who attempts to limit someone's use*

_____ *Codependent in recovery, lovingly detached*

_____ *Other _____*

ACTIVITY (6.5) **How do I describe this family?**

Solicit volunteers to play family members in a mini-drama, taking roles from the assessment schedules. Identify a situation or a theme for enactment. One approach to implementing this activity is to set up a situation such as, "Alcoholic dad shows up drunk at Christmas celebration" or "Dad is downstairs drunk and is about to crash the Christmas celebration." Have students act out the typical responses of children in their roles as listed above in either situation, and have other class members then guess which roles are being played.

Addiction or Cultural Norm?

Counselors must take care not to confuse codependency with normal cultural roles, ADHD, bipolar disorder, or birth-order roles. For example, in many African-American families, the so-called executive authority over younger children can be the normal role of an eldest daughter as part of a broader pattern of role flexibility (Brisbane 1985a; Brisbane and Womble 1985). Family addiction and codependency literature has patented this role, the family hero, as typical of the addictive family. Such a role may not flow from an addictive framework. When a counselor sees an older child playing a parental part in the family, he or she must be careful to determine, as much as possible, whether this is culturally routine behavior or indicative of a response to addiction in the family.

According to Brisbane (1985b), the African-American female family hero elaborates upon a normal second-mother role, one who is in charge and is preparing for her (assumed) adult role. Unfortunately, in the addicted family, the executive/parental child has no adequately functioning mother figure to emulate. The addicted or codependent mother can, perhaps, provide concrete needs, but she is less likely to be capable of fulfilling psychological needs. The African-American female family hero may not complain about her plight. She is proud of her tenacity and ability; alcoholism is but one more problem to cope with, not to correct (Brisbane and Womble 1985). She is likely to leave home early, via a job or marriage, although she continues to be a source of emotional support for younger siblings and may provide a refuge or safe place for them. These pseudoparents are themselves victimized by not having the opportunity for nurturance, play, and age-appropriate dependence.

Charting the Family

Discussions about the family often focus on examples from movies rather than the participants' own families. Part of this is due to the fact that film exaggerates stereotypes for the purposes of entertainment, which makes it easy to separate personalities and dynamics. But it is also true that it is hard to reflect on one's own patterns of relationships. Sometimes people need help conceptualizing patterns and structures, especially their own, yet it is important. Genograms and family maps help counselors and clients see the patterns in their behavior. Figure 6.1 shows the symbols used in family charts to indicate relationships.

Edwards points out that family charts (genograms and maps) are no more than working hypotheses, ones that may need correction or amplification, or that may change. He warns that counselors "must guard against elevating [them] to the status of a fact" (1990, p. 50). They are a model of the family, which counselors may embellish with meanings that are not there, based on countertransferential identification with some role or ethnocentric assumption.

Culturally competent family assessment also must identify the generations since immigration, if appropriate: bicultural behaviors of the family as manifested in their identity, language, health care, and other areas; transgenerational gaps, if any; and the economic and educational status of family members.

The Genogram

A genogram is a family tree that includes data on the relationships among family members across the span of several generations. It is an efficient way to assess a family by recording information and gaining an overview and summary of relationships that reveal patterns of functioning.

Figure 6.1 Symbols for family systems charts.

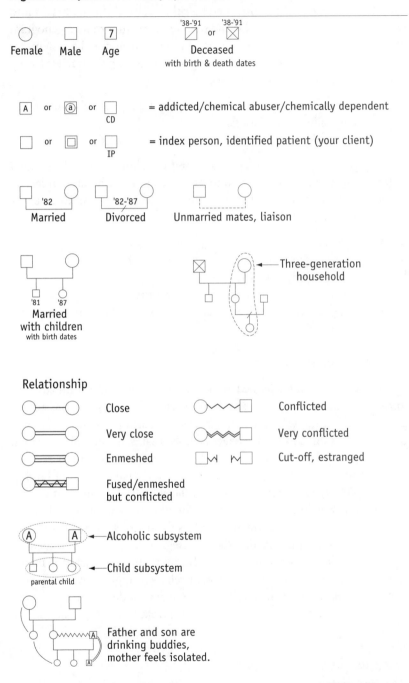

Note: The size of a symbol indicates a person's level of power and authority.

Genograms also generate new questions. It is useful not only to the counselor but also to the family members themselves, who are drawn into fascinating glimpses of their past and present. Very important, a genogram illustrates and underscores the nature of the family as a social system.

Many agencies use preprinted genogram charts with the nuclear family as the baseline. This has two drawbacks:

1. The traditional nuclear family is not the typical structure in many client populations.
2. It unduly focuses attention on the nuclear family.

The genogram should include all significant kin, informally adopted kin, stepkin, and persons referred to or treated as kin who are not legally or biologically related. To elicit information, counselors ask these kinds of questions (Garrison and Podell 1981; McGoldrick et al. 2008):

- Who raised you?
- Who was significant to you when you were growing up?
- Who is important to you?
- Have you gotten help from the community?
- Has anyone else ever lived with your family? Where are they now?
- On whom do you rely?
- To whom can you go for help?
- Who listens to you?

The nuclear family, defined as the normal family in the dominant culture of the United States, is out of the ordinary as families go, if one surveys cultures around the world. In more societies than not, the unit of family organization is some form of extended family; that is, it contains more than two generations or other relatives such as nieces, nephews, unmarried or widowed uncles or aunts, and so on. In fact, an extensive web of kinship alliances is found in a large proportion of societies. In the United States it is difficult to maintain common residence for all of these individuals because of the vicissitudes of employment as well as the size of apartments in cities.

While assessing the family, the counselor must take care to identify significant relatives who are not in the immediate household, in the vicinity, or in the same country. Absent relatives might play a large part in making decisions for the family, which may include encouragement of a referral into treatment or to an alternative, folk healing system.

....

Case in Point

Extended Families

One of the authors (PM) grew up in a largely Irish and Italian neighborhood where extended families continued to exist but were spread out over several blocks.

Many adult men worked on the nearby waterfront and congregated in the neighborhood bars after work. Their wives, wives' unmarried sisters, and mothers spent many daytime hours working together and visiting without having to walk more than a block or two. Later, while working in a tenant-organizing program in the 1960s on the Lower East Side of New York City, PM found members of extended Puerto Rican families occupying two or more apartments in the same or adjacent buildings. Members of the extended family walked in and out of any of the apartments as if they were contiguous. Babies and young children were watched by mothers, aunts, or grandmothers so that their mothers could work or complete high school.

The genogram can bring out powerful repetitive patterns within family lineages. One student, reporting on the book *Genograms and Family Assessment in 2002* (McGoldrick and Gerson 1985), read a genogram and accompanying text stating that the Kennedy family males had a pattern of taking risks, violent accidents, sexual impulsivity, and substance abuse. Students raised four more such incidents that had occurred in the Kennedy "clan" since the book had been published in 1985.

The Family Map

Mapping a family is simpler than constructing its genogram. It takes a few key family members and indicates their relationships. It may be an alternative or ancillary tool to the genogram of a large family system for which the number of lines necessary to indicate biological relations and the quality of relationships grow out of control. A family map is certainly quicker and easier to draw than a genogram. To create a family map, simply put down male and female symbols separated by a line to show who are the parents and who are the children, and do all of the relationship chart symbols between them. A square or circle can be bigger or smaller to show power and influence. Figures 6.2 and 6.3 are charts of Hanna's family that illustrate the case study.

Clinical Case: Hanna and Her Family

The patient is Hanna, a 15-year-old female referred to the clinic by the Student Assistance Program at her high school because of her truancy and alcohol abuse. Her parents, Robyn and Luis, were divorced in 1992. Robyn returned to live with her widowed mother, Hanna's grandmother, and Luis remarried a few years later. Hanna's genogram (Figure 6.2) and family map (Figure 6.3) identify two "strains" of problems in Hanna's heritage: depression and enmeshment on Robyn's side and disengaged and substance-abusing fathers on Luis's side.

Depression and Enmeshment

Hanna's grandmother and Robyn's mother was Ceil, whose father worked in another city while she grew up, leaving three teenaged daughters

Figure 6.2 Hanna's genogram.

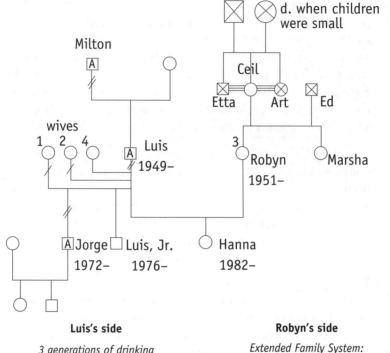

Luis's side	Robyn's side
3 generations of drinking and disengagement:	*Extended Family System:*
Milton, Luis, Jorge	Uncle Art lived with the family 1952–1966, until he died
	Ceil's husband, Ed, died 1969
	Widowed Aunt Etta lived with Ceil 1970–1981, until she died
	Robyn & Hanna move in with Ceil 1986
	Ceil died 1996

Figure 6.3 Hanna's family map.

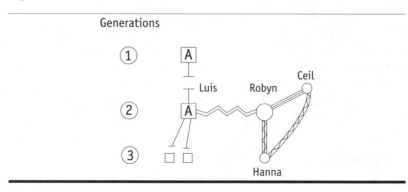

and three teenaged sons to fend for themselves. Ceil's mother, the functioning parent, died in 1929 at the start of the Great Depression when Ceil was 15. Many of the siblings continued to live together as young adults throughout the 1930s. Ceil married in 1940 and Art, an unmarried uncle, lived with the couple and their children until his death in 1968. Two other uncles (Ceil's brothers) were compulsive gamblers. When Ceil's husband died the following year, a widowed sister, Etta, moved in. The extended family household tradition encouraged enmeshment.

Ceil was described by her daughter Robyn as intelligent, but cynical, gloomy, and morose. She did Robyn's homework for her. When Robyn moved out, it was to an apartment above her mother's store, and her mother set up her utility accounts. Both Robyn and Marsha were diagnosed with dysthymic disorder, but in Robyn's case it was compounded with passivity and indecisiveness. She worked for many years at a clerical job that she despised.

Disengaged, Substance-Abusing Father

Hanna's father Luis, a Hispanic, had an alcoholic father who drifted in but mostly out of the family's lives. Luis's father did not attend his son's wedding, although he was living in the same city at the time and saw Luis shortly before as well as after the wedding. Luis, an intelligent man proficient in film technology, was a heroin addict for many years, including during his marriage to Robyn. He has two adult sons from a previous marriage, Jorge and Luis, Jr., who is religious and devoted to his father despite their infrequent meetings. Jorge is the third-generation alcoholic of this family. He calls Luis from time to time when drunk to curse him out and loudly berate him for his shortcomings as a father. Luis had financed his habit with the rent money and sale of Robyn's jewelry while she was pregnant. Robyn also endured occasional violent outbursts and bailed him out of jail when he was arrested for possession of drugs. Luis entered a methadone-maintenance program after the divorce from Robyn but augmented the synthetic narcotic with liberal amounts of beer. He married for a third time and, although technically skilled and stabilized on methadone, he did not seek employment but depended on his new wife's income.

The series of events that led to the referral of Hanna includes conflict with her grandmother, Ceil, who developed Alzheimer's disease and pestered Hanna. Robyn also was irritable and shouted at Ceil. Some of Hanna's anger seemed based on the neglect by Luis, her newly married father, who often failed to see her even on holidays. When Ceil died after years of decline, Robyn was devastated. Hanna found a bottle of vodka and got drunk at the funeral. In the following year, Hanna frequently exploded with rage at her mother and stayed out all night with her friends. She developed problems with lateness, truancy, and academics. Eventually, she started to "crash" at Luis's house, despite his neglect, which allowed her to escape from her conflicted, fused, yet combative, relationship with her mother. Robyn resented Hanna's new bond with her father, and she complained that she was left alone in the house. Hanna was referred by the student assistance counselor in her high school, after she had appeared in class twice with alcohol on her breath and had shown signs of marijuana intoxication after lunch period.

ACTIVITY (6.6) How do you relate?

Form pairs to serve as interviewer and interviewee, for the purposes of constructing a genogram. Make sure that each pair contains an individual who feels comfortable being the subject of a genogram. As a class, discuss such questions as, "What patterns of relationship were uncovered as a result of the genogram?" "What questions were helpful in eliciting information for the genogram?" "Were there times that the interviewee was uncomfortable, and if so, why?"

Treatment: Family sessions with Hanna and Robyn, using genogram and mapping techniques, followed by individual sessions with Hanna, helped her to identify the conflicted feelings she had about each parent. The genogram and map also helped her understand the guilt she had about their divorce and her relationship with her grandmother. All of this was a very confusing, painful, and emotional situation for a young person who had a familial predisposition to depression. The genogram showed her the pattern of relationships in the family and how people had a hard time building their autonomous identities. The charting gave a name and an identifiable design to nameless pain and confusion, enabling Hanna to talk about it rather than drink about it. Robyn was encouraged to go past the delayed developmental milestone of individuation and to develop extrafamilial relationships and activities.

Dunlap et al. (2004) provide a gripping ethnographic description of the intergenerational reproduction of violence and drug use in home and street life among distressed, victimized women in Central Harlem.

Family Intervention Skills

Vernon Johnson is the name most closely associated with the formal intervention. The term *intervention* is used in two ways in the human-services field: (1) as a general term to refer to any remark, technique, confrontation, or helping effort, and (2) to refer to a specialized technique of group confrontation by friends or loved ones to convince an addict to go into treatment. A group intervention can break through denial, at least for the time necessary to get the client into a chemical-free setting.

All addictions counselors have the opportunity to interact with their clients one on one and in group. Unfortunately, family counseling is not always on the agenda, due to agency priorities, lack of reimbursability for family sessions, or the short amount of time during which the agency treats the client. Moreover, the family may be dispersed, or members may be deceased, abroad, or alienated from the client to an extent that cannot be remedied during his or her association with the agency. All members of the family could benefit from even a brief exposure to the possibility of doing things differently. At the very least, counselors should be able to plant some seeds that will germinate when the family is able to listen. A treatment plan should include some family goals and objectives, but it has to be realistic in view of the limited time available for treatment. Lifelong patterns will not be reversed so easily, and counselors should not encourage clients to expect this to happen.

Family treatment has three governing principles:

1. Be aware of processes rather than focus on the topic or content under discussion or argument. What is going on between and among people? What is happening in the here and now?
2. Help the clients become aware of these processes and learn to recognize the roles and patterns in their family system.
3. Empower clients to change. In an addictive family, members must learn to disengage from codependent roles, build autonomy, and help get the addicted member into treatment.

The counselor facilitates awareness of the parts that each member plays in the family system, what everyone gets out of it, and if and how members communicate. The counseling skills are the same as some of those for individual and group counseling: listening, reflection, restatement, gentle probing, disputation, establishing a rapport, creating a safe place, and so on. The counselor attempts to facilitate change in the features of the system that thwart growth, individual autonomy, and recovery from addiction. Counselors should not simply give lectures and advice but encourage members to talk with each other and tell each other their feelings, bring silent members into the conversation, and eventually empower family members to take charge of this process themselves. The counselor needs to be aware of his or her feelings about different family members (possible countertransference) and how these affect the family. For example, counselors should be aware of a tendency to play favorites.

Earlier chapters contain discussions of counseling traps. One of the easiest traps to fall into is accepting the roles that the family communicates. Some examples are letting the invisible "lost child" hide out and be left out, going along with the notion that only the "identified patient" needs help, and letting the helpful, overextended, protective member avoid the necessity for change (e.g., avoid letting go of some of his or her tasks). One trap is arguing about labels early in treatment. It is a poor strategy to try to convert the family to a set of labels, such as "enabling" and "codependency," or, worse, tell these distraught people the family members are as sick as the addict themselves. If counselors provide educational materials about addiction as a family disease, and counselors facilitate honest self-reflection, the family's awareness will grow. Certainly counselors may have to probe or challenge family members by asking questions such as, "Do you think it helps Don face the consequences of his behavior when you bail him out of jail every time he is arrested for public intoxication?" Such a focused or specific question is different from "Do you see how you are an enabler?" The latter can be perceived as name-calling and damning by a person who has shown up to help the addict. The latter question is likely to elicit defensiveness and resistance rather than self-reflection and self-awareness.

The ways in which counselors help families can be broken down into five subprograms: family education, family self-understanding, personal growth, intervention skills, and sober family living skills.

Family Education

Families of addicts may know they are in pain, but they may not know "the nature of the beast" they are facing. Family education is actually the beginning of enlisting kin in the recovery process. Some of the basic elements of such a program include:

- *Basic knowledge of addictions.* This includes very basic psychopharmacology, addictive behaviors, and behavior patterns of addicts and their families and friends.
- *The nature of enabling and codependency.* Letting an addict face the consequences of his or her behavior—which might include embarrassment, loss of income, employment, or jail time—may actually save the addict's life. Keeping addicts from pain by bathing drunks and putting them to bed, mopping up a mess, making excuses, doing their jobs, or bailing them out enables them to continue and progress in addiction.

- *The nature of family systems.* The "family mobile," a moving sculpture of interdependent parts, is a concrete tool for showing a system and demonstrating that changing one part changes the system, which strives for balance.
- *The importance of direct, assertive, honest communication of needs and feelings.* These are the client's "I" statements.
- *The role of Al-Anon, Nar-Anon, and other supportive groups.* These provide hope, identification, positive role-models, and a surrogate family and support system to buffer stress and give strength.

Family Self-Understanding

Awareness is a critical first step to changing. Counselors need to help families come to self-awareness. For example, reasons for enabling that they need to identify may include guilt, shame, fear of hurting the addict, fear of losing the addict's love, misguided sense of loyalty, fear of humiliation, need to feel important or have a meaningful role as protector, and fear of change. This situation is delicate because it is a lot to ask people to "confess" motives they are not so proud of in front of their entire family. Some things are best discussed initially in individual sessions or in support groups without other family members present. The counselor must be sensitive to each person's status; some will be ready for self-divulgence before others. Counselors also have to help the family visualize other options and possibilities. What would actually happen if you didn't cover for her with her boss? If you revealed the situation to your child's guidance counselor?

To help families of addicts gain self-understanding, counselors facilitate:

- Understanding of enabling and codependent behaviors and other adaptations of the family to addiction; how "helping" hurts
- Identification of roles played in the family
- Understanding of the investment that each person has in his or her role
- Understanding of the investment others have in one member's staying in his or her role
- Understanding of alliances and subsystems
- Understanding of communication patterns in the family, or the lack of communication
- Understanding of how the family resists change
- Identification of self-statements, internal dialogue, and hidden assumptions

Individuation and Personal Growth

Nonaddicted family members contribute enormously to the family's recovery by focusing on their own individual growth into a healthier person.

Counselors facilitate and encourage this by supporting the nonaddicted individuals in learning the following skills:

- *Communicate using "I" statements.* When one person has something to say, he or she can learn to "say it straight." That means speaking for oneself without waffling or talking all around what he or she really wants to say. It also means keeping statements simple and concrete. While this kind of communication does depend on having a clear sense of self, it is also true that repeated practice of assertive "I" statements can contribute to self-empowerment and taking responsibility for self. Practice beginning statements with "I want," "I feel," "I need," "I don't like," or "I won't accept," rather than with "you," "they," or "we."

- *Acknowledge* feelings and needs—emotional, physical, mental, and spiritual. Acknowledge each person's right to have his or her own feelings and needs.

- *Set limits.* Don't let one member's addiction be the center of your life. Examples of setting limits are refusing to fight, refusing to cook at 11 P.M., and refusing to clean up spills caused by a drunken family member.

- *Practice doing things for yourself.* Examples include building relationships and support for yourself, joining a group, and taking a class.

- *Detach lovingly from the active addict.* People who find it impossible to stay in an ongoing relationship with an active addict while maintaining reasonable limits may have to go a step farther and detach from the addict. They should make it clear that they are still concerned with the addict but need to distance themselves for the time being.

- *Dispute negative self-statements* underpinning guilt when detaching from enmeshment, codependency, and enabling. "I got myself into this, so I'm stuck with it" can be countered with "I can't change the addict, but I can change myself and build a better life." Another example is, "He needs my help and protection or he'll die" can be countered with "My help is hurting him by keeping him from the consequences and reality of addiction; he'll die if I continue it."

- *Recognize abuse and losses* that may not be apparent (past and present), grieve them, and move forward. For example, taking care of a drunken mother and four younger children denied one woman a childhood.

- *Build personal responsibility.* Build self-awareness and learn to take care of yourself. Admit mistakes and make amends if possible.

Figure 6.4 provides a list of tips for when talking to family members.

Figure 6.4 Tips on talking to family members.

Learn active listening skills to communicate effectively. Make eye contact. If you think you know what your family member means, wants, or feels, briefly summarize it back to them and ask them if this is correct. Ask for more details or what they are feeling right now.

Validate your family members' feelings. Communicate that you understand their point of view, that it's OK for them to have their feelings, and that you care about them.

Use "I" statements and "I feel" statements. "When you _____, I feel _____." Empathic refusal. "I know you need me to help you move, but I have too much of my work to do."

Poor listening sends poor messages. When you don't seem to be listening, you are giving the message that you are not interested, that the other person is silly or foolish, and that their views are unimportant. Poor listening behaviors include:
- Self-summarizing: Constantly restating your position
- Cross-complaining: Answering a complaint with another complaint, instead of problem-solving
- Yes-butting: Sending the message that you don't want to change or meet the other's needs
- Character assassination: Attacking the whole person rather than pointing to some specific problem area
- Complaining rut: Constant complaints without suggestions for change or alternatives
- All or nothing statements: Saying "you always . . ." or "you never . . ."

Source: Adapted with additions from CSAT (Center for Substance Abuse Treatment). 1999. *Treatment for Stimulant Use Disorders* (p. 215). Treatment Improvement Protocol (TIP) Series 33, DHHS Publication No. (SMA) 99-3296, Rockville, MD: Center for Substance Abuse Treatment, Substance Abuse and Mental Health Services Administration. It is based on the active listening skills theory, such as found in a basic counseling course, and assertiveness training concepts.

Intervention Skills and Techniques

Johnson (1998) describes the steps in preparing a formal intervention:

1. *Gather the intervention team,* which consists of meaningful people who surround the chemically dependent person. They can be family, friends, or colleagues.

2. *Form and inform the intervention team.* Each person must be willing to risk his or her relationship with the addict, be knowledgeable about the nature of addiction, and be emotionally strong enough to perform as interveners. Part of this step may be addictions education for team members.

3. *Gather the data.* Each person writes a list of incidents or conditions related to the victim's drinking that illustrates his or her concerns. The counselor may need to guide the team to write concrete, first-hand incidents, not general gripes or statements. Johnson suggests using a video of the client while intoxicated (1989, p. 73). At this time, local treatment options must be explored. The intervention cannot proceed without this information because there will be a short window of opportunity to refer the addict to appropriate treatment.

4. *Rehearse the intervention.* Prepare an agenda and practice the scenario over and over, with someone designated as the client, and plan how to deal with the addict's likely or probable reactions during the intervention. Also think of realistic yet firm statements of future nonenabling stands by associates of the addict.

The tone of the intervention must be objective, unequivocal, nonjudgmental, and caring. It is *not* a therapeutic-community confrontation or "haircut." Significant others who cannot control their anger should be excluded and the reasons explained to them in an empathic, nonblaming manner.

Sober Family Living Skills

The rules of engagement change as the family moves from "wet" to "dry"; there is a different set of tasks and dilemmas. Presumably, the addict has been through treatment. Roles and rules are changing. Some of the areas that need to be addressed include the following.

Build Healthy Communication

Reestablish channels of communication and teach healthy communications skills that are assertive rather than passive, hostile, or aggressive. Assertiveness skills (sometimes known as *say-it-straight skills*) are important in all types of families. In the "wet" family they help people survive as individuals, set limits, and undermine the conspiracy of silence. In the "dry" family, they further and strengthen the recovery process and help to explore options for a new "family mobile."

Develop Sober Relationships

If a member of a couple was actively addicted when the two became involved and is now sober, it is almost as if they never were introduced.

If one of them has been addicted for a long time and gets clean and sober, it is like starting over. In couples therapy, one technique is to assign a "date" as homework. This provides the opportunity to fashion a relationship, to process the changes they're going through, and, if there are children, to allow some space and intimacy for themselves as a couple outside of the larger family system.

Stay In the Here and Now

Concentrate on family processes and feelings in the here and now, not content or details of arguments. Group therapy skills of staying in the here and now can be generalized successfully into work with the family systems. If a member can reflect on what he or she is feeling, and to what underlying issues these feelings pertain, he or she is less likely to pour it all into an argument over who was responsible for letting the toast burn.

Learn Appropriate Parenting Skills

Parents need to take back the responsibility and authority from whomever they gave it to, whoever took it from them, or whoever took over for them: parental child, grandparents, aunts, neighbors, teachers, and so on. They need to set boundaries, get help, distinguish themselves from their children, and distinguish their children from friends or other adults. Parents must support their children's growth through their understandable resistance, anger, built-up hostility, and fears. They must be patient as children develop trust of a parent who betrayed and abandoned them by not being a parent and being unavailable. Parents also must learn that children will test to see whether it is really safe to express their feelings. Parents should not respond to their children's challenges the same way they would to being challenged by another adult.

Children Learn or Relearn to be Children

They must relinquish pseudoparental or pseudospousal roles and acknowledge how that feels. They may have to grieve the loss of the old role with which they felt comfortable. They also may have to redefine relationships with siblings and learn to make friends with peers.

Adapt to the New Personality of a Recovering Member

Relating to the new personality of a recovering member is often very difficult for his or her family. Out from under a chemical haze, the sober member may be unexpectedly assertive, argumentative, irritable, demanding, or needy. People in recovery have to try out new ways of being and dealing with all of the other family members. Often, when the family resents the changes and wants to return to its old ways, someone will say, "We like you better drunk!" They may sabotage or undermine the real changes that go with recovery, or they may even go from blaming all problems on the addict for being an addict to blaming all problems on the addict for his new qualities in sobriety and recovery!

Adapt to the New Personality of the Recovering Codependents

The addict's codependents are developing a more assertive style, less controlled. Recovering codependents or enablers are discovering that they have feelings, opinions, and the right to express them. They may have a great deal of difficulty in doing so, and they may feel guilty the first few times. Another possibility is that their feelings, having been held in or repressed for a long time, are likely to be extreme and not expressed well when they are trying new methods of communication.

Adapt to a New Family Structure

Derail arguments about child rearing and finances: "I was used to doing the checkbook alone." "I can't believe you let him watch so much television." The counselor can help clients turn arguments into discussions about the possibilities of handling these things, helping them brainstorm new and different strategies, and saying, "Why not at least try it? The old ways were not working in healthy or satisfactory ways, were they?"

Adapt to New Activities and Relationships of Family Members

"All those damn meetings." "Some of your new friends sure look seedy." Loved ones of people in recovery have to deal with feelings about twelve-step or other support groups, fears of infidelity, unfamiliar beliefs and rituals, unavailability of the recovering member of AA/NA who is attending the recommended 90 meetings in 90 days, and resentment of the counselor, for example. "Now that you have your new friends, I suppose you don't need us anymore" or "I guess we're not good enough anymore" or "So now you just do everything she says?" Friends or extended relatives often interpret recovery-milieu involvements as dangerous or strange: "If she keeps going to those meetings, you're gonna lose her for sure. All those feminists giving her ideas. She'll leave you and take you for all you're worth—and you'll never see those kids again," or "She'll take off and leave you with the kids." More astute family members can be enlisted to educate the rest on the importance of growth, autonomy, and outside involvements of the recovering codependent.

Learn to Express Anger and Sexuality in Healthy Ways

Some clients have difficulties expressing anger or sexuality because in the past these were associated with alcohol, drugs, or violence. Some fear that the loss of control over feelings will precipitate a relapse. In fact, trying to control all of your feelings all of the time, or any form of obsessive perfectionism, is so exhausting and anxiety-producing that it could threaten a relapse.

Let Go

Once resentments, anger, and pain about the past have been acknowledged and ventilated, all family members (each in his or her own time) must let go of grudges and make direct amends to people they've hurt or offended. Even if drink or drugs were dominating when offenses were committed, an addict's acknowledging the hurt he or she has done clears the air and, even if it doesn't, helps relieve the offender of guilt.

Deal with the Emergence of Masked Problems

For example, some addicts never had sober sex. Others didn't think much about sex when they were using. Learning to come to terms with this as an adult can be terrifying. Therefore, although some experience sexual dysfunction while addicted, others experience it when clean and sober!

Continue Involvement in New Support Systems

Ongoing participation in fellowships (e.g., AA, Al-Anon, Nar-Anon, Gam-Anon, parenting classes, Al-A-Teen, Smart Recovery) offer a great deal of support as the family goes through the changes that come with sobriety.

Stop "Walking on Eggs" with the Recovering Member

Addicts who were very out of control during their addiction, or who've had several relapses, may have relatives who are afraid of antagonizing or upsetting them.

Build Trust

Having had good reasons to mistrust the recovering addict, the family finds it hard to shed the stigma and fear associated with addiction. On some level, kin may be saying to themselves, "We can never trust him or her again." The recovering addict may sense this mistrust and think, "They should recognize my recovery and treat me differently."

Abandon Unrealistic Expectations

Addicts and their families may think that the end of drinking/drugging means the end of problems when actually the journey has just begun. There are still problems with children, layoffs and downsizing, health problems, crime, pollution, and all of the emotional problems that people have who never had a drink or put a needle into their arms.

Counselors must be very patient while addictive family systems are changing. In working with couples especially, counselors have to stay in touch with their own countertransference, and they need to take care not to have an unstated, hidden agenda such as "saving the marriage" as a primary goal. Some counselors on some level may fear that if a couple separated, this would be a counseling failure; others have experienced their own or their parents' divorce and those feelings come up in treating couples who have children.

References

Adler, A. 1998. *What Life Could Mean to You.* Center City, MN: Hazelden.

Black, C. 1981. *It Will Never Happen to Me.* New York: Ballantine Books.

Brisbane, F. L. 1985a. "Understanding the Female Child Role of Family Hero in Black Alcoholic Families." *Bulletin of the New York State Chapter of the National Black Alcoholism Council, Inc.* 4(1 April): 47–53.

———. 1985b. A self-help model for working with Black women of alcoholic parents. *Alcoholism Treatment Quarterly* 2, (fall/winter): 47–53.

Brisbane, F. L., and M. Womble. 1985. Afterthought and recommendations. *Alcoholism Treatment Quarterly* 2, (fall/winter): 54–8.

CSAT. 2004. *Substance Abuse Treatment and Family Therapy.* Treatment Improvement Protocol Series 39, DHHS Publication No. (SMA) 04-3957, Rockville, MD: Center for Substance Abuse Treatment, Substance Abuse and Mental Health Services Administration.

——— 1999. *Treatment for Stimulant Use Disorders.* Treatment Improvement Protocol (TIP) Series 33, DHHS Publication No. (SMA) 99-3296, Rockville, MD: Center for Substance Abuse Treatment, Substance Abuse and Mental Health Services Administration.

Dunlap, E., G. Sturzenhofecker, B. Sanabria, and B. D. Johnson. 2004. Mothers and daughters: The intergenerational reproduction of violence and drug use in street and family life. *Journal of Ethnicity in Substance Abuse* 3(2): 1–23.

Edwards, J. T. 1990. *Treating Chemically Dependent Families.* Minneapolis: The Johnson Institute.

Falicov, C. J., and B. M. Karrer. 1980. "Cultural Variations in the Family Life Cycle: The Mexican American Family," in *The Family Life Cycle: A Framework for Family Therapy,* E. A. McGoldrick and M. McGoldrick, eds. New York: Gardner Press.

Fitzpatrick, J. 1990. "Drugs and Puerto Ricans in New York City," in *Drugs in Hispanic Communities,* R. Glick and J. Moore, eds. Rutgers, NJ: Rutgers University Press.

Garrison and Podell. 1981. Community support systems assessment for use in clinical interviews. *Schizophrenia Bulletin* 7(1): 101–108.

Johnson, V. 1998. *Intervention: How to Help Someone Who Doesn't Want Help.* Center City, MN: Hazelden Foundation.

Kolevzon, M. S., and R. G. Green. 1985. *Family Therapy Models.* New York: Springer.

McGoldrick, M. 1982. "Ethnicity and Family Therapy: An Overview," in *Ethnicity and Family Therapy*, M. McGoldrick, J. K. Pearce, and J. Giordano, eds. New York: Guilford Press.

McGoldrick, M., G. Gerson, and S. Petry. 2008. *Genograms: Assessment and Intervention.* New York, NY: W.W. Norton.

McGoldrick, M., and R. Gerson. 1985. *Genograms in Family Assessment.* New York, NY: W.W. Norton.

Minuchin, S. 1974. *Families and Family Therapy.* Cambridge, MA: Harvard University Press.

Minuchin, S., and N. D. Fishman. 1981. *Family Therapy Techniques.* Cambridge, MA: Harvard University Press.

Myers, P. L. 2002. Review of *Olivia Curtis Chemical Dependency: A Family Affair* by Olivia Curtis. *Journal of Teaching in the Addictions* 1(1): 91–94.

Myers, P. L. 2011. Problems of Scholarship in Family Addictions Writings. Presentation at National Conference on Additive Disorders 2011. September 20, 2011, San Diego, CA.

Satir, V. 1964. *Conjoint Family Therapy.* Palo Alto: Science and Behavior Books.

Scheper-Hughes, N. 1979. *Saints, Scholars, and Schizophrenics.* Berkeley: University of California Press.

Sweet, E. E. 1990. Unattained milestones in chemically dependent adolescents from dysfunctional families. *Journal of Adolescent Chemical Dependency* 1(2): 139–147.

Vogel, E. F., and N. B. Bell. 1960. "The Emotionally Disturbed Child as the Family Scapegoat," in *The Family*, N. W. Bell and E. F. Vogel, eds. New York: The Free Press.

Wegscheider, S. 1989. *Another Chance.* Palo Alto: Science and Behavior Books.

Williams, T. 1989. *The Cocaine Kids.* Reading, MA: Addison-Wesley.

Case Management: From Screening to Discharge

Objectives

At the end of this chapter, students will be able to:

1. Describe the seven steps in managing a case.
2. Define case management according to the International Certification Reciprocity Consortium (ICRC).
3. Define the purpose of screening and list at least one screening tool.
4. Describe the purpose of a biopsychosocial assessment.
5. List at least six major life areas to be assessed in a biopsychosocial assessment.
6. Describe the six dimensions of the American Society for Addiction Medicine (ASAM) Patient Placement Criteria 2 (PPC2-R).

7. List at least three variables to determining severity of dependency.
8. Write a treatment plan based on needs and resources developed in collaboration with the client.
9. Write a treatment objective using SMART (specific, measurable, attainable, realistic, and time limited) criteria.
10. Use the SOAP (subjective, objective, assessment, and plan) approach to write a progress note.

Introduction

The term *case management* is used by helping professionals to denote activities that bring the client through a service delivery system to a desired outcome. Beyond that very general definition, case management may refer to an aspect, task, or special emphasis in human and social services.

Many agencies view case management as an overarching model for the processing of addicted clients through the continuum of care from initial contact to closure, based on the specific treatment and recovery needs of each individual. Whatever the setting (e.g., inpatient, outpatient, halfway house) and whatever the intensity of services (e.g., 40 hours per week, 10 hours per week, 1 hour per week), the counselor assists the client through a series of stages from initial contact to final discharge. According to Ballew and Mink (1986), the counselor helps the client navigate through a set of stages that he or she identifies as engaging, assessing, planning, accessing resources, coordinating (others would add monitoring), and disengaging. Individual, family, and group counseling processes and relationships comprise the motor that drives the client through these stages.

The functions of case management include assessment, treatment/service planning, service coordination and system linkages, linking clients to services and resources monitoring, addressing problems other than addiction, and advocacy. All clients have case management needs, but these vary by severity, existence of co-occurring problems, and disorders. In working with clients, case managers must possess the same skills for empathy and engagement as in any counseling setting. When working with external systems, the case manager must learn considerable skills in mobilizing resources, bartering informally among service providers, pursuing informal networks, being knowledgeable about community systems, and being anticipatory, pragmatic, and flexible (CSAT 1998, pp. 13–14), all of which overlap with entrepreneurial, political, and/or fund-raising skills. Effective case management meets the goals of continuity of care, accessibility, accountability, and efficiency.

In other agencies, case management refers to a special emphasis on the coordinated and aggressive use of ancillary services to support all areas of individual life (e.g., housing, health care, mental health services, financial services), in contrast to counseling or treatment of addiction alone.

For example, Mejta and colleagues (1994) describe the Interventions Case Management Model. The underlying assumptions and philosophy of the model are that there are a "constellation of problems that encourage continued drug use and antisocial behavior" (p. 303) and there is a limited period of time to initiate action before the motivation to change dissipates. These two variables necessitate a proactive, coordinated, and decisive system of client management. The expression, *intensive case management services (ICMS)*, is used throughout the social services, including welfare-to-work projects, workers' compensation, addiction treatment, and mental-health delivery systems. It refers to a consortium of programs working to provide comprehensive, integrated, or "wrap-around" services. ICMS are seen as necessary to avoid fragmentation of care and to mobilize services for fragile and noncompliant populations such as chronic welfare recipients, the mentally ill, and the homeless. Consortia can range from small to large, regional systemwide efforts. In the addictions field, a prime example of the latter was the Target Cities Program, initiated by the federal Center for Substance Abuse Treatment in 1991 for several urban areas.[1] The funded cities used a Central Intake Unit to unify the various treatment providers of initial screening, assessment, and referral functions.

Addiction counselor certification boards affiliated with the International Certification Reciprocity Consortium limit the definition of *case management* to coordination of service activities only, excluding such functions as screening, assessment, and treatment planning. According to this definition, case management responsibilities of addictions counselors include planning and coordinating with clients in recovery as they access, link with, and use supportive services; client advocacy to secure resources; and education of clients to increase their awareness of community services. This definition is also found in the addiction counselor competency consensus document (CSAT 1997).

The Marriage of Case Management and Counseling

Human services professions often have drawn a distinction between counseling, which focuses on process (client self-awareness, self-reflection, and decision making), and case management, which focuses on outcome (e.g., goals, objectives, action steps, plans). In social welfare and offender services, the titles of case manager and caseworker may, in fact, denote individuals who perform duties outside of or not primarily pertaining to the counseling or clinical realms. These two important aspects of treatment, however,

---

[1]The Center for Substance Abuse Treatment (CSAT) operates as part of the Substance Abuse and Mental Health Services Administration (SAMHSA) in the U.S. Department of Health and Human Services (HHS).

depend on each other for successful treatment. Clients will not agree to a treatment contract, follow the plan effectively, if they don't see the need for the components of the plan as developed collaboratively with the counselor. This commitment can develop only within an empathic, supportive counseling relationship. Active listening and communication skills such as reflection of content and feeling are also necessary to identify problems that need to be addressed in the treatment plan. It is a revolutionary experience for a client to work with someone who actually seems interested in hearing about his or her feelings, problems, and thoughts, rather than dealing with the formal and impersonal bureaucratic routines to which he or she may have been accustomed. In short, all of the counseling skills identified in this text come into play when carrying out the various processing and management functions discussed in this chapter, and are crucial in their success.

Screening

All human services involve screening, which determines whether the client is eligible and appropriate for admission to an agency or needs referral to another agency to which he or she is eligible or appropriate for admission. Screening serves two major purposes:

1. It attests to the presence of a condition that may go unrecognized if not detected.
2. It provides data to decide whether a client is appropriate for a specific treatment program or vice versa.

In the first purpose of screening, social, health, and criminal justice workers determine if there is evidence for referral of a client to alcohol and/or drug treatment for further assessment. It is important that such screening take place because there is strong evidence that early intervention increases the success rate of treatment. Screening can have an active or passive connotation. That is, service delivery systems can attempt to screen large segments of the population in order to identify individuals with a particular condition. In many healthcare settings, this is known as *case finding*. Addictions units at a medical center can work with emergency room or general medical staff to seek out addicted patients, just as all patients can be screened for a disease such as tuberculosis.

The second purpose of screening relates to the initial process whereby it is determined that clients are appropriate for treatment or that they should be referred to other services. The counselor's recommendation depends on the client's clinical needs (such as health, living conditions, and severity of symptoms) and the capacity of an agency to provide such treatment. In order to provide such screening and recommendations, a counselor not only needs to know the client's symptoms and social and health problems but also must clearly understand his or her agency's eligibility requirements and scope of services as well as the eligibility requirements and capabilities of other treatment agencies in the region. It also means that the counselor has an ethical obligation to refer clients to the most appropriate treatment available. Awareness of and a willingness to refer to a broad range of health and social service agencies are necessary.

Engaging

In addition to gathering information and evaluating treatment options, the screening interview serves the following purposes:

- Establish as much rapport as possible during the first contact
- Establish the boundaries of clients and counselors
- Explore the client's expectations and desired outcomes of treatment
- Describe the program

Remember that the screening or intake worker is usually the first person a client sees and is, therefore, the representative of the agency and, indeed, of the entire concept and system of addictions treatment. The initial impression made on the highly ambivalent client may be crucial to accepting or delaying the first step on the road to recovery. When addictions screening of large populations in health or social services settings is the method of clients' entry to treatment, attention must be paid to the attitudes, motivations, and active listening skills of screening personnel who are not primarily trained as addictions counselors.

Screening Tools

It is useful for addictions counselors to be familiar with some of the screening tools that general and social service practitioners use. Although many clients abuse both alcohol and drugs, most screening tools are focused on either one or the other. Several instruments have been developed to detect alcohol problems, such as the CAGE mnemonic, the Brief Michigan Alcohol Screening Test (MAST), and the Alcohol Use Disorders Identification Test (AUDIT). The CAGE is the shortest and has been demonstrated to be valid (Ewing 1984). A physician, nurse, or social worker may integrate the CAGE questions into a medical interview. In a general interview, if clients indicate that they drink alcohol or have drunk in the past, the clinician can ask the following questions:

C = Have you ever thought you ought to **c**ut down on your drinking?

A = Have people **a**nnoyed you by criticizing your drinking?

G = Have you ever felt **g**uilty about your drinking?

E = Have you ever had an **e**ye-opener—a first drink—in the morning after a hangover?

Any positive response should be followed up with concerned interest. Two positive responses would indicate need for referral. Use of drugs and medications also should be investigated.

Kinney (1996) uses the mnemonics HALT and BUMP to list questions that can be helpful in gathering data to indicate alcohol or drug problems.

H = Do you usually use drugs and/or drinks to get **h**igh?

A = Do you sometimes drink or use drugs **a**lone?

L = Have you found yourself **l**ooking forward to drinking or using?

T = Have you noticed an increase in **t**olerance for alcohol or drugs?

B = Do you have memory lapses, **b**lackouts that occur during drinking?

U = Do you find yourself using drugs or drinking in **u**nplanned ways?

M = Do you drink or use when you feel anxious, stressed, or depressed, or for **m**edicinal reasons?

P = Do you work at **p**rotecting your supply, having drugs or alcohol available at all times?

A few positive responses to screening instruments are often taken as proof of addiction; however, they only indicate the need for further assessment. It is important that anyone who is doing screening realize that the results of screening are a preliminary indicator of a problem and not a diagnosis.

Figures 7.1 and 7.2 are examples of tools to screen for abuse of drugs and alcohol by adolescents and adults. (Details about specific screening tools are in CSAT 1991 and 1997.)

ACTIVITY 7.1   What do these people need?

Form groups of three. Assign each group a scenario and each person a role: client, counselor, or observer. Using the following scenarios, enact a screening interview to determine if the client needs a more in-depth assessment. As the counselor, you are working as an identification and referral counselor in a substance-abuse screening program. Using your listening and feedback skills, try to motivate the client to agree to further assessment. When playing the client, try to stay in character. Role-play each scenario for 10 minutes, allowing the observer 5 minutes to give observations. After all the role-plays are complete, process and discuss them in the large group for 15 to 30 minutes.

SCENARIO 1: The client is seeing this counselor as a result of a driving while intoxicated (DWI) arrest, her second. Following the first offense, she attended DWI School. To be without her automobile would be a serious inconvenience, so she is anxious to do whatever it takes to get her license back. Therefore, she is determined to be cooperative, but she is not convinced she has a problem.

Figure 7.1 Substance abuse screening instrument.

Please read carefully and circle the appropriate response.

Have you ever done something crazy while high and had to make excuses for your behavior later?	Yes No
Have you ever felt really burnt out for a day after using drugs?	Yes No
Have you ever gotten out of bed in the morning and really felt wasted?	Yes No
Did you ever get high in school?	Yes No
Have you gotten into a fight while you were high (including drinking)?	Yes No
Do you think about getting high a lot of the time?	Yes No
Have you ever thought about committing suicide when you were high?	Yes No
Have you run away from home, partly because of an argument over drug use?	Yes No
Did you ever try to stick to one drug after a bad experience mixing drugs?	Yes No
Have you gotten into a physical fight during a family argument over drugs?	Yes No
Have you ever been suspended because of something you did while high?	Yes No
Have you ever had a beer or some booze to get over a hangover?	Yes No
Do you usually keep a supply (of drugs) for emergencies, no matter how small?	Yes No
Have you ever smoked some pot to get over a hangover?	Yes No
Have you ever felt nervous or cranky after you stopped using for a while?	Yes No

Thank You for Your Cooperation.

ID#: _____ Age: _____ Gender _____ Race _____

Results: No. of yes answers: _____ No. of no answers: _____

Offense(s):_____

Comments:_____

Referred for further assessment? Yes _____ No _____

SCENARIO 2: The client has finally agreed to see a counselor, but only after an ultimatum from his wife that she would leave unless he seeks help. The precipitating problem is serious nightly quarrels that begin over dinner and end with the family in tears and his storming out of the house. He attributes the quarreling to the topic under discussion when the argument erupts (e.g., the children's grades, finances, the in-laws coming to visit) and his family's inability to listen to reason.

SCENARIO 3: A 65-year-old grandmother was referred by a visiting nurse. She was found in a stupor on her couch last week. Nearby were a bottle of pills (Darvon) and an empty bottle of sherry. She lives alone and sees her daughter about once a month. She has arthritis and is sometimes in pain. The nurse visits weekly and helps with some chores. The nurse insisted she come for help.

Figure 7.2 Short Michigan Alcohol Screening Test (SMART).

Screening Adults for Alcohol Abuse	Answer Yes or No
1. Do you feel that you are a normal drinker? (By "normal" we mean that you drink less than or as much as most other people.)	_____
2. Does your wife, husband, parent, or other near relative ever worry or complain about your drinking?	_____
3. Do you ever feel guilty about your drinking?	_____
4. Do friends or relatives think you are a normal drinker?	_____
5. Are you able to stop drinking when you want to?	_____
6. Have you ever attended a meeting of Alcoholics Anonymous?	_____
7. Has drinking ever created problems between you and your wife, husband, a parent, or other near relative?	_____
8. Have you ever gotten into trouble at work because of your drinking?	_____
9. Have you ever neglected your obligations, your family, or your work for two or more days in a row because you were drinking?	_____
10. Have you ever gone to anyone for help about your drinking?	_____
11. Have you ever been in a hospital because of drinking?	_____
12. Have you ever been arrested for driving under the influence of alcoholic beverages?	_____
13. Have you ever been arrested, even for a few hours, because of other drunken behavior?	_____

Assessment

Assessment is a broad term that encompasses a variety of critical knowledge and skills in addictions counseling. Assessment includes those activities, skills, and tools that facilitate the gathering of information throughout the case management and treatment process.

- It is designed to bring out clients' concerns, desires, fears, beliefs, values, and life experiences.
- It is a means to determine clients' needs, strengths, and resources and the impediments to successful treatment that might lay in misunderstanding, anxiety, perception, confusion, or denial.
- It uses tools and documents, each of which serve a specific purpose in the continuum of care, which may include a mental-health status exam, a suicidality assessment instrument, or a discharge summary. Client self-reporting is only one source of data. With the clients' informed consent, the counselor will seek information from family, employers, referring agencies, and past treatment agencies.

Although assessment may appear to be a separate stage of case management, it is in fact an ongoing process that informs treatment planning and the clinical use of individual, group, and family treatment. Initial assumptions about clients may be supported or need to be revised as more data become available and the client evinces change and movement into recovery. According to Hester and Miller (1995), there are six purposes for evaluation in addictions counseling (see Table 7.1).

Intake

The *intake* procedure is the point of formal admission to a treatment program. This assumes that initial assessment (e.g., through the screening process) has justified the step of admitting this client to this particular program. Also at this point, enough information should be available to prescribe the early critical components of treatment that are valuable and possible for this client. The intake procedures comprise a variety of documents and formalities, including those involving confidentiality. Some minimal orientation to treatment usually takes place at this point. If screening has been done externally (e.g., at a referring social-service agency), the intake process becomes the client's first exposure to the

Table 7.1 Purposes for Evaluation of Clients

Type	Purpose
Screening	To determine whether the client needs further evaluation
Diagnosis	To determine if criteria are met to make a clear diagnosis
Ongoing evaluation	To determine the nature and extent of the client's problems
Motivation	To determine the ways in which the client is ready and able to change
Treatment Planning	To determine appropriate interventions and needs for services
Follow-up	To determine what has changed and which aftercare services the client needs

Source: Hester, R. K., and R. M. Miller. eds. 1995. *Handbook of Alcoholism Treatment Approaches: Effective Alternatives,* 2nd ed. New York: Simon and Schuster.

treating agency and to treatment. Again, the intake person must pay attention to use of empathy, active listening skills, and other "human" aspects of this supposedly routine bureaucratic procedure.

Biopsychosocial Assessment

Biopsychosocial assessment provides a detailed overview of the social, biological, family, employment, and medical history of the client. It explores the critical issues in each major area of the client's life. It examines the client's functioning and negotiation of developmental problems that may have arisen in each of the areas. A thorough biopsychosocial assessment identifies the critical issues to be addressed in a treatment plan.

Components of Biopsychosocial Assessment

There is tremendous variation among the activities used to provide a comprehensive biopsychosocial assessment. The types of instrument employed vary in length, format, focus, detail, degree of specificity, and areas of knowledge to be elicited. Most biopsychosocial assessments address the following areas:

- *Childhood and adolescence,* including parental drug and alcohol use, loss of parent(s); relationships with parents, step parents, or other caregivers, social and cultural beliefs, and messages given in the family.

- *History of substance use and abuse,* including first use of alcohol and drugs, the patterns and changes, and the experiences that occurred under the influence of drugs, up until the present. This should include use of tobacco and over-the-counter medications.
- *Health problems and medical treatments* past and present, including those related to drug use or abuse, withdrawal, hospitalizations and the reasons for them (e.g., physical or mental, alcohol- or drug-related), HIV status, other sexually transmitted diseases (STDs) and infections, and medications.
- *Mental health history,* including previous evaluations and treatment summaries as well as the client's evaluation of whether previous treatments were helpful, and why or why not.
- *Family and social functioning,* including marriage(s), divorces, relationships with children, friends, and the impact of alcohol and drug use on these relationships. There are two categories of family: present family (spouse, children, and significant others) and family of origin (parent, other relatives, and significant others including peers or mentors who influenced the client's life). Is there a family history of alcohol or drug abuse or mental problems?
- *Employment, education, and recreation,* including past and present work and school problems and achievements, past and present ways client finds to relax and have fun, and the role of drugs and alcohol in these areas.
- *Sexual history,* including problems, sexual orientation, and the role of drugs and alcohol in this area.
- *Finances,* including income, sources of income, debts, changes in financial status, and the role of alcohol and drugs.
- *Legal issues,* including criminal history (probation, parole, having served time), incidence of DWIs, whether prior or present treatment is court stipulated, and the role of drugs and alcohol in a client's involvement in the criminal-justice system.

Assessment of Severity

The American Society for Addiction Medicine (ASAM) has six dimensions for determination of the severity of addictive disease, as shown in Figure 7.3 (ASAM 2001).

ACTIVITY 7.2 **What's the best way to ask?**

Break into groups of three to five. Choose one of the nine areas of biopsychosocial assessment outlined above. Develop assessment questions for that knowledge area. In doing so, consider the impact of each question on the client, the appropriate timing, and the effect on the development of empathy and a treatment alliance. For example, in the area of family and friends, you might ask, "Who was important to you as you grew up?" "Who could you turn to in your life?" "Who were you close to?" "Who did you have a problem or conflict with?" "Have you lost someone important to you?" "What are some good memories you have of your childhood/ teen years?"

Diagnosis

Diagnosis is a medical term that means "1. a. the art of identifying a disease from its signs and symptoms b. the decision reached by diagnosis. 2. a. concise description of a taxon" (*Merriam-Webster* 1993, p. 177). A diagnosis is also a categorization made after objective, standard diagnosing (diagnostic) activities. Diagnosis is done by matching clients' signs (observable objective data, such as is gathered in laboratory tests) and symptoms (information received from the patient) to established criteria that describe specific medical categories. A diagnosis of strep throat is made following a demonstration that *Streptococcus bacilli* are found in a patient's throat, by obtaining a sample on a cotton swab and growing it in a culture. Procedures to diagnose addictions, which are described variously as biological, psychological, and spiritual disorders, cannot be so simple and straightforward. Diagnosis should not be confused with a biopsychosocial assessment. It is only a part of such an assessment and does not give enough information to make important clinical decisions about clients. Diagnosis is performed usually by physicians or clinical psychologists. However, it is important that counselors be familiar with diagnostic criteria. The first reason is that physicians often rely on input from counselors and social workers to make diagnoses. Second, understanding signs and symptoms assists counselors in determining relevant data to explore in a clinical (biopsychosocial) assessment interview with clients. Third, and most important, being certain that a client has an addiction predicts reasonable therapeutic interventions that are necessary for counseling to be effective.

There are a number of diagnostic systems in behavioral health fields, but by far the most accepted and used system is the *Diagnostic and Statistical Manual of Mental Disorders, Fourth Edition, Text Revision (DSM-IV-TR)* published by the American Psychiatric Association (APA 2000). The *DSM-IV-TR* does not use the terms *addiction* or *alcoholism* but rather refers to *substance dependence*. Inclusion of a condition or syndrome in the *DSM-IV-TR* does not automatically imply mental illness. In fact, the *DSM-IV-TR* is designed to accommodate any kind of adjustment, emotional, or learning problem conceivable. In the arena

Figure 7.3 ASAM patient placement criteria for the treatment of substance-related disorders, risk rating in six dimensions.

	1	2	3	4
1 *Acute Intoxication/ Withdrawal Potential*	Mild to moderate intoxication interferes with daily functioning, but does not pose a danger to self or others. Minimal risk of severe withdrawal.	Intoxication may be severe, but responds to support; not posing a danger to self or others. Moderate risk of severe withdrawal.	Severe s/s of intoxication indicates an imminent danger to self or others. Risk of severe but manageable withdrawal; or withdrawal is worsening.	Incapacitated, with severe s/s. Severe withdrawal presents danger, as of seizures. Continued use poses an imminent threat to life (e.g., liver failure, GI bleed, or fetal death).
2 *Biomedical Conditions; Complications*	Adequate ability to cope with physical discomfort. Mild to moderate symptoms (such as mild to moderate pain) interfere with daily functioning.	Some difficulty tolerating physical problems. Acute, non-life-threatening medical symptoms are present. Serious biomedical problems are neglected.	Serious medical problems are neglected during outpatient treatment. Severe medical problems are present but stable. Poor ability to cope with physical problems.	The patient is incapacitated, with severe medical problems.
3 *Emotional, Behavioral or Cognitive Conditions; Complications*	There is a diagnosed mental disorder that requires intervention, but does not significantly interfere with tx. Relationships are being impaired but not endangered by substance abuse.	Persistent mental illness, with symptoms that distract from recovery efforts, but are not an immediate threat to safety and do not prevent independent functioning.	Severe psychiatric symptomatology, but sufficient control that does not require involuntary confinement. Impulses to harm self or others, but not dangerous in a 24-hr. setting.	Severe psychiatric symptomatology; requires involuntary confinement. Exhibits severe and acute life-threatening symptoms (e.g., dangerous or impulsive behavior or cognitive functioning) posing imminent danger to self and others.

	LOW	MODERATE	HIGH	SEVERE
4 *Readiness to Change*	Willing to enter treatment, but is ambivalent about the need for change. Or willing to change substance use, but believes it will not be difficult to do so.	Reluctant to agree to treatment. Able to articulate negative consequences of usage but has low commitment to change use. Only passively involved in tx.	Unaware of the need for change, minimal awareness of the need for treatment, and unwilling or only partially able to follow through with recommendations.	Not willing to explore change, knows very little about addiction, and is in denial of the illness and its implications. Unable to follow-through with recommendations.
5 *Relapse/ Continued Use/ Continued Problem Potential*	Minimal relapse potential, with some vulnerability, and has fair self-management and relapse-prevention skills.	Impaired recognition and understanding of substance use relapse issues, but is able to self-manage with prompting.	Little recognition and understanding of substance use relapse issues, and poor skills to interrupt addiction problems or to avoid or limit relapse.	No skills to cope with addiction problems or to prevent relapse. Continued addictive behavior places self and/or others in imminent danger.
6 *Recovery Environment*	Passive support or significant others are not interested in patient's addiction recovery, but is not too distracted by this and is able to cope.	The environment is not supportive of addiction recovery, but, with clinical structure, able to cope most of the time.	The environment is not supportive of addiction recovery and the patient finds coping difficult, even with clinical structure.	The environment is chronically hostile and toxic to recovery. The patient is unable to cope with the negative effects of this environment on recovery, and the environment may pose a threat to the patient's safety.

s/s: symptoms; tx: treatment

- **Rehab criteria** requires one "3" or "4" in Dimension 1, 2 or 3; and an additional "3" or "4" in Dimensions 1 through 6. For Dimension 1, risk rating of "3" or "4" within past 2 weeks.
- **Day Rehab** requires a risk rating of "1" or "0" in Dimension 1; a "2" or "3" in Dimension 2; a "2" or "3" in Dimension 3; and one "3" or "4" in Dimensions 4 through 6.
- **IOP criteria** requires a "0" or "1" in Dimensions 1 and 2; a "1" or "2" in Dimension 3; and one "3" or "4" in Dimensions 4 through 6.
- **Outpatient treatment** requires a risk rating of "0" or "1" in all Dimensions.

This document is a reference guide only and not an official publication of the American Society of Addiction Medicine, Inc.
Source: St. Peter's Behavioral Health Management. *Network News* 9: 21. Ballston Spa, NY.

of chemicals, one can be diagnosed merely as drunk or high (known as *substance intoxication*) for any of nine chemicals, or as following a pattern of substance *abuse*, or as *dependent* on any of nine chemicals, the dependency category being equivalent to many concepts of addiction. A client can have a diagnosis of marijuana abuse and alcohol dependence as well as any of a number of accompanying personality disorders, psychoses, and/or organic disorders that are related to chemical use, aging, and so on. The *DSM-IV-TR* describes *substance dependence* as a "maladaptive pattern of substance use, leading to clinically significant impairment or distress, as manifested by three (or more) of the following, occurring at any time in the same 12-month period" (197):

1. Tolerance, either as an increased amount needed to achieve the desired state or diminished effect with continued use of the same substance
2. Withdrawal, characterized either by standard withdrawal symptoms specific to the substance used or by taking a similar drug to relieve or avoid withdrawal symptoms
3. Increased amount and time using substances than user had intended
4. Persistent desire and/or failure to cut down on use
5. Great deal of time spent in obtaining and using a substance or recovering from the effects of the substance
6. Substance use interfering with or disrupting important social, occupational, or recreational activities
7. Substance use continuing despite knowledge of having a persistent or recurrent physical or psychological problem that is likely to be caused by or exacerbated by the substance

These criteria can be clustered into three major areas: (1) loss of control, a progressive inability to predict the consequences of the use of a substance, (2) compulsive use, involving a strong craving or the need to drink or use drugs, and (3) problems in which alcohol or drug use is implicated as a cause. Often the client does not perceive that these symptoms mean he or she is addicted or dependent or has any problems whatsoever. This phenomenon is often referred to as *denial*, which is not a conscious effort to distort the truth. It is normal to expect that clients will minimize, rationalize, or in some other way deny they have a substance-abuse problem.

Although the *DSM-IV-TR*, as well as any other diagnostic framework, establishes categories of severity, it is important to remember that addiction is a complex process that progresses from social or recreational use of substances to abuse to dependency. The amount of time that it takes an individual to progress through these stages depends on a number of variables:

- *Age of the user.* Adolescents who experiment with psychoactive substances tend to progress faster than adults into abuse and then into addiction.
- *The route of administration of the substance.* Individuals using drugs by snorting or injecting them tend to progress into abuse and addiction faster than those who use drugs that are drunk or eaten.
- *The purpose of use or expectation of the user.* The use of a substance to get high or "wasted" or to escape emotional pain lends itself to abuse and addiction more than when use of a substance is shaped by social and cultural norms.

Assessment of Readiness to Change

Three assessments of readiness to change can be incorporated into the formal assessment and/or treatment plan. These are the Importance Rules, Confidence Ruler, and Readiness Ruler. These rulers are shown and described in Chapter 3.

Treatment Plans

Like assessment, treatment planning is an ongoing process that begins with and builds on a core of information as treatment proceeds. On the basis of information gleaned from a sound assessment, a client and a counselor can collaborate to identify problems, goals, and objectives of treatment. Once this is done, they can determine priorities, the methods of treatment, and a schedule, which are all part of the initial treatment plan. A treatment plan provides a framework for logical decision making by a joint effort of counselor and client as well as reinforcement that clients are responsible for their recovery. In addition to input from the client and the counselor, the clinical supervisor and the agency's treatment philosophy influence treatment planning.

Some time and a considerable amount of paperwork are involved in writing and maintaining an effective treatment plan (Figure 7.4). Although counselors often avoid or resist doing paperwork, there are good reasons to document the treatment plan and treatment:

- *To give direction and focus to the counseling process.* Treatment plans provide the clients feedback on their progress and refocus them, if necessary. The documentation helps the counselor review the issues and progress with the client and supervisor.

Figure 7.4 Features of an individualized treatment/service plan.

This is "boilerplate" similar to standards such as are established by such entities as the Joint Commission for Accreditation of Health Care Organizations (JCAHO):

1. Based on a comprehensive assessment process and modified over time as warranted with receipt of new assessment information
2. Reflects participation from appropriate disciplines as warranted
3. Identifies the client's presenting needs and specifies the persons' strengths, resources, and limitations
4. Reflects a collaborative effort between clinicians and clients served
5. Consists of specific goals that pertain to the attainment, maintenance, and/or re-establishment of physical and emotional health, prioritized as to importance
6. Identifies specific objectives that relate directly to the treatment goals, action steps, and timelines for each activity
7. Includes criteria for ascertaining whether objectives have been met
8. Identifies each person responsible for implementing, coordinating, and monitoring the treatment plan or its components
9. Identifies readiness to change in the Prochaska/DiClemente model; i.e., precontemplative, contemplative, etc.
10. Identifies the services and/or settings necessary for meeting the client's needs and goals (counseling methods used, coordination of services needed, identification of resources), including current or anticipated gaps in services
11. Specifies the frequency of treatment contacts
12. Includes provisions for periodic re-evaluations and revisions, as warranted
13. Anticipates the date when treatment will be terminated, and plans for appropriate post-treatment supports and services, and re-entry tasks

- *To give tangible evidence of progress toward recovery.* Clients have an opportunity to see each step, no matter how small, of success and check it off the list. This increases the client's sense of self-efficacy and reinforces commitment to treatment.
- *To facilitate discussion of difficult issues that, if not addressed, would sabotage treatment.* Often in writing out and implementing the plan, such issues are identified and clarified and can be addressed effectively. Clients often leave treatment against professional advice because of failed expectations or concerns that were not identified or discussed.

- *To give a clear picture of the client's issues, history, progress, and current situation to all in-house members (present and future) of a treatment team.* In-house members might include a group leader, a family counselor, a supervisor, or anyone who needs to take over the case.

Treatment Planning Process

What do you think about treatment planning? Many students shudder at the mention of treatment planning.

- They think it's an awful lot of paperwork and means less time for seeing clients.
- They think it is done according to a set formula or routine, like a cookie-cutter approach.
- They think that it is often left to gather dust in the files once written.
- They worry about the additional tasks of writing progress notes that document progress, or lack of it, in meeting the goals of the plan.
- They think it cuts into the spontaneity of the counseling session.

But treatment planning *should* be:

- A dynamic means of engaging and motivating clients in setting realistic and clear goals and objectives to move in healthy and productive directions
- A way to provide hope for change
- A way of enabling clients to observe themselves change as they meet realistic objectives
- Since your written case is a legal document, a way to provide protection in court ordered cases

The treatment planning process can be seen as a series of thirteen steps or components.

1. *Identify issues.* The counselor uses the assessment results as a database. In addition, the counselor receives information from the client that helps to identify the primary concerns, problems, and issues.
2. *Identify needs.* After reviewing the client's case history, the counselor creates a list of the client's needs. Problems or obstacles identified by the client often can be reframed as needs (or "change areas"), which is less judgmental and more hopeful and motivating. Modern clinical practice frowns on pathologizing people and reducing them to a bundle of symptoms or problems.
   - Use nonstigmatizing language: Instead of "alcohol dependence" or "Charles is an addict," one could state, "Charles is experiencing increased tolerance for alcohol as evidenced

by the need for more alcohol to relax," or (more severe) "Charles' needs to drink to avoid acute abstinence syndrome symptoms as evidenced by having 'the shakes' in the morning." Instead of "Client is promiscuous" use "Client participates in unprotected sex four times a week." Instead of "Client is resistant to treatment" use "In past 12 months, client has dropped out of 3 treatment programs prior to completion." Instead of "Client is in denial" state the discrepancy as "Client reports two DWIs in past year but states that alcohol use is not problem" (Stilen et al. 2005, p. 212).

3. *List strengths and resources.* From the history and from what the counselor knows of the agencies and community resources, he or she develops a list of the client's strengths and a list of resources. It is important that the client review and internalize (own) these needs and resources (see DeJong and Miller 1995).

4. *Identify stage of readiness.* Use the Importance, Confidence, and Readiness Rulers to assess the client's readiness to change.

5. *Set long-term goals.* Having an understanding of the client's problems and needs, the counselor and client set long-term goals. Goals are broad, general outcomes that, when achieved, indicate treatment is complete. These could include being free of drugs and alcohol, having stable family relationships, returning to employment, having solid support systems such as twelve-step groups, and so on. Goals provide beacons, purpose, and direction to the treatment process.

6. *Write objectives.* Each need of the client should translate into an outcome objective. Outcome objectives must be specific, concrete, measurable, and relevant to the goals. *Specific* means that it is clear what the client will do, say, or demonstrate in the treatment process. *Concrete* means there is no confusion about what constitutes the desired behavior of the client. *Relevant* means that it should lead toward attaining the identified goals. "Marcia will learn to cope with strong feelings and conflicts without the use of alcohol" can have subgoals or short-term goals.

• Marcia will get on the waiting list of the Friendly Farms inpatient rehabilitation center. Target date: March 1.

• Marcia will find a home group and sponsor in Narcotics Anonymous. Target Date: April 15.

• Upon admission to Friendly Farms, Marcia will participate in individual, group, family, and didactic therapy sessions and review the treatment plan with her counselor every week.

An objective is a short-term step that the client will take towards moving towards the long-term treatment goal. Objectives should be:

- *Specific.* Use specific behavioral terms to indicate how functioning will be improved.
- *Measurable.* Objectives, interventions, and achievement are measurable via assessment scale or scores, client report, and/or mental status change.
- *Attainable.* During the active treatment phase, focus on improvements, not "cures."
- *Realistic.* Achievable goals given the clients' environment, supports, diagnosis, and level of functioning.
- *Time limited.* They have target dates.

These can be reduced to the acronym SMART (Stilen et al. 2005). They should be stated in the client's own language. They should focus on improvements rather than expect a "cure." They also can be developed collaboratively with clients by asking open-ended questions such as "what small things do you think you could do to work towards the goal?"

The counselor should be able to judge whether the client needs some suggestions, however. If the goal is " Hector will follow a plan to help him attain employability," there is a series of suggested knowledge and skills that would help to structure the treatment activity as well as reduce anxiety by boiling down the plan to steps that, in and of themselves, are not overwhelming.

- Assessment of skills and interests
- Learning how to read and understand the employment section of the newspaper
- Learning to use online sites such as Craigslist.org and Monster.com to identify jobs
- Learning résumé writing skills
- Learning how to produce an effective cover letter
- Learning interviewing skills such as how to be appropriately verbal and nonverbal and how to use your appearance to promote yourself effectively

7. *Prioritize.* Because there may be many, perhaps too many, objectives, it is important to prioritize them. Criteria can be weighted to establish priorities, for example: (a) How important is it to the client? The more valuable it is, the more likely the client will attempt to do what is necessary. (b) How realistic is it given the strengths and resources of the client? (c) What must be accomplished before the next thing can be done? Is there a logical order to the objectives? (d) How critical is it to the client's sobriety?

8. *List the steps.* The counselor develops with the client a set of steps that lead up to the objective. These are the activities that the client, the counselor, or significant others engage in to accomplish the objective. It is important to write concrete, specific, and doable activities to accomplish the objective. For example, simply to state that Jim S., a chronically unemployed male, "will become employed during February" misses the point. An effective list of steps might include, but not be limited to, writing a résumé, having the résumé prepared attractively and duplicated, completing a course of vocational rehabilitation, identifying a number of possible employers, acquiring clothing appropriate for a job interview, and so forth.[2]

9. *Interventions.* An intervention is what the program staff will do to assist a client in meeting an objective. We need to identify:

   - The theoretical approach that is the basis for our actions (e.g., rational-emotive behavior therapy, twelve-step facilitation)
   - The treatment services and modalities utilized (e.g., group counseling, personal and social skills development at facility A or B)
   - The treatment frequency/number of hours per week or month that the client will be seen for the identified treatment service

10. *Name the actors.* In each step toward the objective, it is critical to name the person who is responsible for carrying it out. It is important to give the client as much responsibility as possible. However, it is not always possible for the client to do every-thing. The counselor may have to make certain contacts or collect certain information. For example, if the client lost his driver's license, his wife may agree to take him to the clinic.

11. *Set deadlines.* It is not realistic to assume all deadlines will be met, but setting a deadline for each step and each objective allows an understanding between counselor and client of a reasonable timeline.

12. *Write a discharge summary.* When all objectives are met and they demonstrate that the client is ready for discharge, it is time to write a discharge plan. It summarizes what has been accom-plished in treatment and, most important, provides a plan for

---

[2]For a long-time addict, such an organized series of relatively simple, concrete steps might be nec-essary to form "straight" relationships. Such a list might be to make two phone calls to (potential) friends you met at a meeting; write down how you felt before, during, and after each call; tell people in group meeting a feeling you have about them (like them, annoyed or hurt by something they said).

the client to continue in recovery, indicating the steps he or she must take if there is a need for more help.

13. *Medication management.* This includes prescriptions, amounts, and compliance with medical regimen.

This process requires refinement depending on the specific treatment setting (residential, outpatient, detox) and mission of the program or agency in which the counselor works. Realistic goals and objectives vary. It is important to remember that a treatment plan is not set in concrete. It is a guiding document that needs to be renegotiated with the client when unexpected problems arise or objectives prove too difficult to meet.

The formulation of treatment goals takes into consideration the stage of treatment and recovery. Addictions counseling professionals are familiar with typical, common (almost invariable) issues of clients at each stage. For example, in very early treatment of a client who is barely post-detoxification, thought processes may still be confused, and motivation to stay sober and in treatment is threatened by uncomfortable and unfamiliar physical and psychological states. Overall treatment goals include alleviating anxiety and keeping the client focused on simple sobriety-maintenance steps and cognitions. Alcoholics Anonymous (not a treatment program) captures this in exhortations to novice members: "Don't drink, and go to meetings." "Stay away from people, places, and things connected to drinking/drugging." Objectives for the newly sober should be simple and concrete. Maintaining a drug-free state one day at a time is about all that one can reasonably put on the client's plate. When this treatment plan is successful, it reinforces the hopes for success in working with the counselor on future changes, personal growth, and challenges.

Because of the common pattern among clients in a given stage, some agencies follow a standard format for goals and objectives in early and middle treatment. Such a list can be helpful to prompt or remind counselors of items that may come into play, but treatment planning requires individualization of goals and objectives to correspond to the gender, culture, age, and characteristics of each client.

Affirmative Focus

In implementing the treatment plan, we must keep sight of the fact that clients may have experienced significant rejections and failures, and that underneath their bravado there is a sense of hopelessness, helplessness, and inadequacy. Therefore, it is important to build into the treatment plan all kinds of positive reinforcements, even when the improvements are small and incremental. Verbal recognition, award certificates for "member of the week," and graduation ceremonies are appreciated and keep up motivation.

Even the manner in which a relapse is dealt with can be framed in an affirmative way: "It's great that you were honest with us and returned to treatment; that was hard and showed your determination." This should be meant honestly, and not as "laying it on thick" with saccharine platitudes and phony smiles.

Monitoring Outcomes

It is important to monitor the attainment of outcomes. This can be overdone or underdone. A counselor can micromanage and over-track the attainment of outcomes, which disempowers the client, prevents the client from internalizing treatment/service goals, takes away from empathetic engagement, and burns out the counselor. On the other end of the continuum, there is laziness, neglect, and failing to track progress in reaching treatment/service goals. In the center is the zone of optimal engagement and effectiveness.

A client may quickly gain better self-management skills and a level of functioning once out from under the mind-clouding effects of psychoactive drugs. If behavioral objectives/outcomes were set up when the client was at a lower Global Assessment of Functioning (GAF) scale, ASAM Level of Severity, or other rating of functioning, it may have to be revised to avoid an overly complex treatment plan.

Relapse prevention continues to be a vital component of treatment planning throughout treatment, if not a lifelong concern. Planning should take into account not only the learning of coping mechanisms for high-risk situations and self-efficacy for a sober lifestyle, but also planning what to do if a relapse has begun (Chiazuzzi 1991; Gorski and Miller 1982; Marlatt and Gordon 1985).

ACTIVITY 7.3 What do we want to do here?

To practice writing treatment goals, write two treatment objectives you might have for a client. Then in groups of three or four members, pick three treatment objectives that best represent your ideas. Have each group report its objectives.

PROCESS:

- Whose objective is it? Would the client take ownership of it?
- When in the treatment process would it be appropriate to address the goal?
- How would you or the client know when the objective is accomplished?
- What would the client need to do to accomplish the objective, and what resources would he or she need?

ACTIVITY 7.4 Okay, how are we going to do this?

In small groups read the case of Lee C., and then complete the following steps 1 through 8.

CASE: LEE C.

Lee C. is a 25-year-old married male who is participating in an outpatient chemical dependency program. Lee is an electrician who had worked steadily until he was recently suspended from his job after a period of absenteeism and tardiness due to his drinking. Lee has been in treatment in the past and has maintained several periods of sobriety ranging from three to six months, with Alcoholics Anonymous participation. He often states that he drinks after arguments with his wife. They often fight about money and his running off to his mother's after they fight. He often drinks with his best friend and co-worker, Kim. Lee's wife does not permit him to live in the house when he is drinking, but his mother always allows him to stay with her. Lee recognizes he has "some kind of drinking problem" and wishes to stay sober because he is afraid of losing his wife and job. Following the steps, write a treatment plan for Lee C.

1. List Lee's strengths and resources.
2. List his needs.
3. Write a goal for Lee.
4. Write a problem statement for Lee.
5. Write an objective for him.
6. Write a set of steps to accomplish the objective.
7. Determine who will be responsible for each step.
8. Set a date for each step.

ACTIVITY 7.5 Are these good objectives?

Review and evaluate the following treatment objectives. Which objectives do you believe are satisfactory and complete? Rewrite objectives that are unsatisfactory or incomplete.

1. Mr. A will improve his self-esteem.
2. Mrs. B will work on her sobriety.
3. Mr. C will attend five AA meetings per week for the next six weeks.
4. Ms. D will start attending community college.
5. Mr. E will improve his social skills by the end of group therapy.
6. Mrs. F will participate by the third week of group by describing how her dependence on pills affected her.

7. Mr. G will participate in treatment.
8. The H family will learn to communicate more effectively through therapy by the end of the next month.

Progress Notes

The frequency of meetings between client and counselor depends on the context and the level of care (inpatient rehabilitation, intensive outpatient treatment, outpatient treatment), the intensity of help the client needs, and of course the limitations imposed by third-party payers and managed care organizations. There are important functions fulfilled by these meetings. First, the counselor checks with the client on the progress toward the objectives and goals of the plan. Second, regular individual, group, and family sessions are scheduled in order to work through problems and issues that the treatment plan has identified. And third, unforeseen crises that occur must be addressed in order for the plan to proceed. The plan must be renegotiated as circumstances and priorities change.

Each contact with a client requires documentation, whether it be a phone call, an individual meeting, or a group session. Continued accreditation of the agency as well as a positive evaluation of the employee often depends on careful documentation. Healthcare and social services settings use the term *chart notes* or *progress notes*, which are kept in official files of the agency. Most addictions counselors do not keep private notes on clients, unless they are in private practice. Counselors record the particulars of a meeting, either immediately after it or on the same day, while it is fresh in the counselor's mind (so time and intervening circumstances don't warp memories). The counselor can use these notes to refresh his or her mind just prior to the next meeting, which is especially helpful if the counselor has a huge caseload or there is a long time between meetings.

One well-known way of organizing progress notes is through SOAP, an acronym for Subjective, Objective, Assessment, and Plan. It is in a sense a "miniplan" around each significant client contact. The Subjective (S) focuses on the client's perception of the problem. The Objective (O) is the factual data the counselor obtains about the situation, for instance, laboratory or other tests, counselors' observations, records, and reports from reliable sources. The Assessment (A) is an analysis of the factual data and the client's perceptions of the immediate issues. The Plan (P) is a description of steps to take to solve the problems or work through the issues. For more detail and material on case recording, see Wilson (1976).

For example, using the case of Lee C., Lee agrees to avoid people who influence him to drink. Lee comes into a session to discuss this issue. The record of the meeting could look like this:

- **S**—Lee is concerned that his friend Kim will stop by on Friday and ask him to go out drinking. He is concerned that he will have difficulty saying no because he has not been able to do this in the past.
- **O**—According to the assessment and report from family members, Lee has demonstrated difficulty in asserting himself when pressured.
- **A**—Clearly Lee's sobriety is at risk if he goes out with his friend Kim. Lee needs a strategy to assert himself and explain that he cannot go out with Kim.
- **P**—In the counseling session, Lee practiced responses he could make to his friend Kim. In Thursday night's group, Lee will discuss these issues and practice his responses with the group and ask for group support.[3]

An alternative and newer form of organizing progress notes is the SOAIGP format (Kagle 1991). In this format,

S = *Supplemental,* new or revised information obtained from clients, kin, or peers

O = *Observations* from the counselor and those of other staff

A = *Activities* or tasks of treatment

I = *Impressions,* assessments, hypotheses, and so on

G = Current *goals*

P = Additional *plan* or action steps to be taken

Client information contained in agency documents such as treatment plans and progress notes are under confidentiality guidelines. The counseling field is beginning to grapple with the difficulties of ensuring confidentiality when information is filed and stored in a computerized management information system. Each agency should have guidelines for handling electronic files securely.

Resources and Services

Throughout the treatment process, the counselor must use his or her expertise to connect the client to the resources necessary to carry out the treatment plan. The counselor has this primary responsibility because he or she is the expert on the array of local health, educational, social, and economic resources that the client may use to address specific needs, in order to reach identified goals. This means that the counselor must

---

[3]Refusal skills that help Lee, which he can practice in a group setting, are "I statements," empathetic refusal, and limit setting ("I like you and I'd like to have some fun with you, but I really can't go out drinking"), which recognize the feelings and needs of both parties.

have a thorough understanding of the social services in the communities served by the agency. It is useful for counselors to visit and get to know local programs and develop personal contacts within each program. This facilitates referrals and ensures that a client will not be sent to an agency that cannot or will not be helpful.

It is helpful for the counselor to develop a personal directory of social and health services. This directory should contain all agencies in the continuum of care for treatment of alcoholism and other addictions. Directories are available through the United Way, local councils on alcoholism and addiction, and various state, county, and municipal agencies. They are good references to begin to develop a personal directory. The advantage of a personal directory is that it can be expanded with information the counselor learns about specific nuances of a program (e.g., which programs are most responsive to the cultural, ethnic, and personal needs of clients). Moreover, printed directories can become out of date in one year. To build a useful personal directory of resources, a counselor should include answers to the following questions:

- What are the eligibility requirements for the program?
- What services can a client expect from this agency? What is expected from the client?
- What is the cost of the service? Is it free? Is there a sliding fee scale? Does the program take insurance including Medicare and Medicaid?
- What is the protocol for referral?
- What is the culture, economic status, and ethnic makeup of the client population?
- Does the program provide services for needs such as disabilities (e.g., wheelchair access, deafness, blindness), foreign languages, babysitting, transportation, education, or job development skills?
- Who is the contact (name, telephone and fax numbers, email, and street addresses)?
- What are the hours of operation? Does the agency provide services during business hours only, or on weekends, evenings, and holidays?
- How long has the agency been operating? What is its track record? Who funds it?

The case of Mrs. Harris is an example of case management from intake to discharge. It illustrates the need to know the offerings of other resources and their contact people in order to coordinate all aspects and stages of a client's care.

"Mrs. Harris was referred by the Human Resources (HR) Department of an urban college to the in-house Employee Assistance Program (EAP).

The HR administrator had gathered information that documented decrements in Mrs. Harris's job performance, which warranted referral to the EAP. Mrs. Harris is a long-time, well-liked employee, and a recent widow who also was approaching retirement. Screening by the EAP administrator indicated the strong possibility of a late-onset alcohol abuse or dependency syndrome. Mrs. Harris's depression and grief were obvious, but she clearly did not feel comfortable to divulge information about drinking to someone who represented her employer. The EAP administrator thought that it would be useless and possibly insulting or threatening to confront Mrs. Harris strongly. Therefore, he decided to refer her to an outpatient alcoholism program in the community. The initial EAP screening impressions were borne out when Mrs. Harris acknowledged to the agency's intake counselor the degree to which she had been drinking. That intake counselor recommended to the referring EAP administrator that Mrs. Harris undergo a medical detoxification prior to further treatment. Because she was consuming more than a pint of whiskey per day, and considering her age, outpatient detoxification was not indicated because of the possibility of medical complications. There being no local detoxification facility, the EAP administrator contacted a medical center in a neighboring city and arranged Mrs. Harris's admission. At the same time, because of the waiting period for admission to inpatient rehabilitation, the EAP staff contacted the admissions department of an inpatient alcoholism rehabilitation program specializing in EAP referrals so that upon completion of a five-day detox stay, Mrs. Harris could be transported without a hiatus to the rehabilitation setting. The EAP also notified the HR department that Mrs. Harris would require a five-week medical leave.

After determining that Mrs. Harris's sister was a relative whom he trusted with information about her planned treatment, the EAP administrator worked with her to ensure a bag of clothes would be packed and that Mrs. Harris would be present the next day, at the time scheduled for the medical center van to pick her up from her sister's home and transport her to the detoxification unit. She detoxified from alcohol in four days, and was transported to the inpatient rehab setting. Following discharge, Mrs. Harris was cleared to return to work, and she had to attend the outpatient program for continuing care (*aftercare*). The EAP administrator monitored her aftercare via telephone and sent a monthly report to the HR department that Mrs. Harris was meeting the requirements of the EAP. None of the details of diagnosis and treatment went into Mrs. Harris's HR file, nor were they communicated to her supervisors. Mrs. Harris had become isolated from her church, an affiliation that she greatly valued. She was ashamed of her drinking and sought to avoid humiliation by a self-imposed ostracism. In discussions with the EAP staff and in treatment, her desire to find a way out of this situation emerged as a motivation for recovery, in addition to the formal requirements of the HR department for continued employment. Following treatment, she felt encouraged to forge anew her contacts with church and community. In this way, she also renewed a social support she needed to negotiate the stages of grief and loss of her husband. These steps successfully cemented her sobriety, which she maintained until retirement two years later, at which time contact with the EAP staff ended."

Impediments to Treatment

Some impediments to entering treatment are posed by caretaker roles, such as parent, breadwinner, household manager, and caretaker of ill or elderly parents. It is difficult to find time to attend an outpatient program, and it is seemingly impossible to find a way to enter intensive outpatient or inpatient rehabilitation. There are specialized programs for women and their children and for pregnant women. Components of such programs often include child care, compensatory special-education programs for children, screening for fetal alcohol syndrome, neonatal withdrawal units, parenting skills, vocational–educational rehabilitation, personal and social skills development, nutritional counseling and augmentation, and transportation. Some of these services are provided by social services agencies working with the addictions agency to provide integrated case management. Staff should be aware of them to make appropriate referrals.

Physical and Mental Abuse

Especially with women, it is necessary to assess whether the client has been or is being battered or sexually abused, usually by a relative or mate. Unfortunately, it is unlikely for women who are being abused to enter treatment. One of the elements of battered woman syndrome is that the dominating abusers isolate the woman from family and social relationships that might propel them in the direction of help. Moreover, the woman's sense of self is so low that she seldom thinks of getting help without outside encouragement. The tendency is to drink and drug more to numb out, escape, and get through the day. Of course, the abuser is highly threatened by the prospect of the woman entering treatment, and he usually forbids such thoughts. Often, an abused woman seeks or accepts help only when her children's lives and safety are at risk, and when children's protective services enter the picture. While rates vary by population and among studies, many agency directors state that at least half of the girls and women in treatment with their agencies have histories of physical, sexual, or emotional abuse. At the least, a battered client brings associated guilt, anger, or shame. Worse, a battered client may qualify for a diagnosis of post-traumatic stress disorder (PTSD). In one study of addicted women at Amity House, a long-term therapeutic community in Tucson, Arizona, 35 of 55 residents had been raped or molested before the age of 21, and an additional 15 after the age of 21 (Stevens and Gilder 1994). A valuable manual for screening, assessment, and case management of battered and abused women is available from the Center for Substance Abuse Treatment (1997).

Ethnicity and Social Class

The ethnic background and social class of clients also affect use and abuse of substances. Middle-class Caucasian women fit a bell curve of normal distribution in which moderate drinking is the modal or most typical pattern. In lower income African-American women, the distribution is flatter, with more nondrinkers and more heavy drinkers than moderate drinkers. Nondrinking is associated with women in middle age and has a high correlation to church affiliation (Cahalan, Cisin, and Crossley 1969).

Self-Assessment

Counselors usually make assessments of self-image, self-esteem, and self-efficacy from their general observations of a client's presentation, affect, body language, and oral reports. Psychosocial assessment of female addicts should rate self-efficacy and self-esteem because powerlessness, shame, and stigma are more often a major concern for female than for male substance abusers. Personal history may reveal depression, common in female alcoholics, as antecedent to alcoholism, secondary to it, or antecedent to but worsened by it.

Treatment planning for women addicts needs to address trauma, abuse, shame, and self-efficacy as issues in their own right and in relapse prevention. Many women recovering from alcoholism and other addictions report women's groups as a setting where such issues can be addressed and links shown, and where they can build a positive image and identity of recovering womanhood. In later stages of treatment, they need to construct models of a positive occupational and social role, interacting with recovering and nonrecovering individuals.

Criminal Offenses

As is well documented, the vast proportion of crime is alcohol and drug related, and treatment reduces recidivism (Lipton 1995). Treatment of criminal offenders must not be cursory and must include a meaningful, long-term relapse-prevention component. Even where treatment has occurred in prison, continuing care upon release is a priority. Offenders are especially at risk for relapse. They are the archetypal "hot-house" plant, coming from a "total institution" setting and flung into a chaotic, overstimulating environment with multiple requirements, stressors, decisions, and lack of support, as well as the task of being responsible for themselves (CSAT 1993, p. vii). They must look for jobs with little but jail time on their résumés and the stigma of "felon." They may have been involved in criminal activity and the criminal-justice system since adolescence, and never learned appropriate adult financial, occupational, and interpersonal skills. They need not so much rehabilitation as habilitation. Contrary to the common image of the offender as a hulking, snarling brute, the average offender who receives help from organizations such as The Fortune Society or Offender Aid and Restoration has a defeated, lost, and fragile quality. Such organizations generally provide or give a referral to vocational training, achievement of high school equivalency diplomas, addictions counseling, job-seeking skills, parenting skills, and child care for those attending program services. Many employ ex-offenders, which provides positive role-models for those who may feel destined to stay in the role of chronic recidivist.

Treatment and case management of an addicted offender require an integrated system. This involves the court, prison officials, probation and parole authorities, and the treatment network. Collaborative planning between criminal justice and treatment systems can make an effective joint effort to treat addicted offenders (CSAT 1995a). Drug courts, which are often the link between the systems, have been spreading from Florida to Texas, and north.

There are many points of contact between the criminal justice and addictions treatment systems. Offenders who are addicts are processed in a variety of ways, at the judge's discretion. Factors in disposal of a criminal case by the judge include the offense and its severity; criminal history of the offender; evaluation and the recommendations made by prosecutors, special court staff, or external social services agency; plea bargaining efforts by attorneys for the defendant; and the options available in the area, such as the following:

1. Pretrial hearing, with charges dropped or delayed contingent on entry into treatment for substance abuse
2. Presentencing plea bargaining, with placement in a diversion or treatment program
3. Probation to a treatment program
4. Treatment in prison
5. Serving of sentence in a halfway house, day-reporting center, or therapeutic community
6. Parole contingent on entry into treatment

Although a large proportion of clients has always entered treatment through mandated referrals from the criminal justice system, the proportion grew much larger in the United States during the late 1990s because state and federal funding for addictions treatment declined, as did the ability to seek reimbursement from managed-care entities and third-party payers. At the same time, criminal justice funds increased. Agencies began to scramble for government contracts to process offenders, and many either started new components for that purpose or shifted the overall focus of the agency. These system changes have implications for the development of addictions counselors. Many counselors who entered the profession as an extension of their own recovery have been dismayed that the offender population is less motivated to enter recovery than they had expected, and that their role in offender treatment amounts to noncharismatic case management or "babysitting" of clients. Although there are many excellent programs for addicted offenders, often adaptations of the therapeutic community model, some privatized correctional behavioral health services have not met clinical standards to which addictions professionals are accustomed.

Community Linkages

A referral network among community institutions is invaluable. Because many individuals turn to clergy in crises, informed clergy can recognize early addiction in individuals and signs of addiction in families even if it is not the addict who comes for help. Treatment can complement reintegration into the community via religious affiliation. Clergy can be an important bridge to treatment not only by referral but also by preliminary pastoral counseling and education and by supportive formal intervention by family members. As trusted and respected authorities in a community, clergy also can be very influential in an ongoing system that supports recovery. Optimally, treatment agencies should form a seamless network with clergy and pastoral care, with pastoral counseling training for clergy in addictions, family, and treatment issues. African-American clergy, in particular, are already a bulwark of help in both urban and rural communities (Sexton et al. 2006). Although *clergy* may be defined habitually to include only mainstream denominations, it should include alternative religions and healers such as the *espiritistas, santeros*, and *curanderos* among the Latino community. Addictions agencies can conduct training and educational efforts among clergy, or they can import trainers from their local councils on alcoholism and addiction to enable clergy and other influential community leaders to acquire skills in identifying and referring problem users.

An elementary task of any treatment agency is to establish a formal, ongoing, collaborative relationship with school administrators and counseling staff for timely intervention and referral of students. If the school has no drug counselor (Student Assistance Counselor or Coordinator), the agency could help the school establish this office, bring in other resources, or establish a satellite office at the school, depending on the needs and desires of the school.

The treatment agency also should establish formal and informal collaborative relationships with local employee assistance programs, child welfare agencies, Temporary Assistance for Needy Families (TANF) and food stamp offices, and other human and social services agencies, for the purpose of referral linkages and collaborative prevention efforts. It is outside the scope of this text to describe all of the new, science-based prevention strategies that can be implemented in communities where agencies exist.

It is critical to enlist the aid of community institutions in sending prevention and intervention messages. At the very least, agency literature can be made available on site. Again, a formal relationship with the school system is a <u>must</u> for treatment agencies. Regardless of how hard the addict and/or the addict's family has worked, maintaining sobriety is an uphill battle in a community that has no supporting role. Established institutions should consciously and actively give out messages that support, admire, and perhaps reward prevention and that encourage appropriate intervention and treatment. Counselors and agencies can—at the very least—provide literature to churches, stores, movie theaters, libraries, grocery stores, and other places where the public gathers. The literature, such as pamphlets or posters, will succinctly inform readers about signs of addiction and give a telephone number to call for further information.

References

APA (American Psychiatric Association). 2000. *Diagnostic and Statistical Manual of Mental Disorders*, 4th ed., text revision (DSM-IV-TR). Washington, DC: APA.

ASAM (American Society of Addiction Medicine). 2001. *Patient Placement Criteria for the Treatment of Substance-Related Disorders*, 2nd ed., revised (ASAM PPC2R). Chevy Chase, MD: American Society for Addiction Medicine.

Ballew J. A., and G. Mink. 1986. *Case Management in Social Work*, *2nd ed.* Springfield, MA: Charles Thompson.

Cahalan, D., I. H. Cisin, and H. M. Crossley. 1969. *American Drinking Practices*, Monograph no. 6. New Brunswick, NJ: Rutgers Center of Alcohol Studies.

Chiazuzzi, E. 1991. *Preventing Relapse in the Addictions: A Biopsychosocial Approach.* New York: Pergamon Press.

CSAT (Center for Substance Abuse Treatment). 1991. *Screening and Assessment for Alcohol and Other Drug Abuse in the Criminal Justice System.* Treatment Improvement Protocol, no. 7. Rockville, MD: Center for Substance Abuse Treatment, Substance Abuse and Mental Health Services Administration, U.S. Dept. of HHS.

———. 1993. *Relapse Prevention and the Substance-Abusing Criminal Offender*, Technical Assistance Publication no. 8. T. A. Gorski et al., eds. Rockville, MD: Center for Substance Abuse Treatment, Substance Abuse and Mental Health Services Administration, U.S. Dept. of HHS.

———. 1995a. *Planning for Alcohol and Other Drug Abuse Treatment for Adults in the Criminal Justice System.* G. Vigdal, ed. Technical Improvement Protocol, no. 17. Rockville, MD: Center for Substance Abuse Treatment, Substance Abuse and Mental Health Services Administration, U.S. Dept. of HHS.

———. 1997. *Substance Abuse Treatment and Domestic Violence.* Treatment Improvement Protocol Series no. 25. Rockville, MD: Center for Substance Abuse Treatment, Substance Abuse and Mental Health Services Administration, U.S. Dept. of HHS.

———. 1998. *Comprehensive Case Management for Substance Abuse Treatment.* Treatment Improvement Protocol Series 27. DHHS Publication No. (SMA) 02-3645. Rockville, MD: Center for

Substance Abuse Treatment, Substance Abuse and Mental Health Services Administration, U.S. Dept. of HHS. Retrieved 16 November 2011 from http://www.ncbi.nlm.nih.gov/books/bv.fcgi?rid=hstat5.part.22441

DeJong, P., and Miller, S. D. 1995. How to interview for client strengths. *Social Work* 40(6): 729–736.

Ewing, J. A. 1984. Detecting alcoholism: The CAGE Questionnaire. *Journal of the American Medical Association* 252: 1905–1907.

Gorski, T., and M. Miller. 1982. *Counseling for Relapse Prevention.* Independence, MO: Herald House/Independence Press.

Hester, R. K., and R. M. Miller. eds. 1995. *Handbook of Alcoholism Treatment Approaches: Effective Alternatives,* 2nd ed. New York: Simon and Schuster.

Kagle, J. D. 1991. *Social Work Records,* 2nd ed. Belmont, CA: Wadsworth.

Kinney, J. 1996. *Clinical Manual of Substance Abuse,* 2nd ed. St. Louis, MO: Mosby.

Lipton, D. S. 1995, November. The effectiveness of treatment for drug abusers under criminal justice supervision. *NIJ Research Report.* Washington, DC: U.S. Department of Justice, Office of Justice Programs.

Marlatt, G. A., and Gordon, J. R. 1985. *Relapse Prevention.* New York: Guilford Press.

Mejta, C. L. et al. 1994. "Approaches to Case Management with Substance-Abusing Populations," Chap. 21 in *Addictions: Concepts and Strategies for Treatment.* J. A. Lewis, ed. Gaithersburg, MD: Aspen.

Merriam-Webster's Medical Desk Dictionary. 1993. Springfield, MA: Merriam-Webster, Inc.

Sexton, R., R. Carlson, H. Siegal, C. Leukefeld, B. Booth. 2006. The role of African-American clergy in providing informal services to drug users in the rural south: Preliminary ethnographic findings. *Journal of Ethnicity in Substance Abuse* 5(1).

Stevens, S. J., and P. J. Gilder. 1994. "Therapeutic Communities: Substance Abuse Treatment of Women," in *Therapeutic Community: Advances in Research and Application,* F. M. Tims, G. DeLeon, and N. Jainchill, eds. NIDA Research Monograph series, no. 144. Rockville, MD: National Institute of Public Health, NIH, Public Health Service, US HHS.

Stilen, P., D. Carise, N. Roget, and A. Wendler. 2005. *S.M.A.R.T Treatment Planning utilizing the addiction severity index (ASI): Making required data collection useful.* Kansas City, MO: Mid-American Addiction Technology Transfer Center in residence at University of Missouri–Kansas City.

Wilson, S. J. 1976. *Recording: Guidelines for Social Workers.* New York: Free Press.

8

Ethics, Confidentiality, and Professional Responsibility

Objectives

At the end of this chapter, students will be able to:

1. Describe the importance of ethical decision making in addiction counseling.
2. Describe the need to utilize supervision in any ethical issue that they see arise.
3. Describe the value and purpose of both Federal Confidentiality Regulations and Health Insurance Portability and Accountability Act (HIPAA).
4. Explain to a client the meaning of informed consent.
5. List at least four exceptions to confidentiality when disclosure can be given.

6. List two conditions when there is a duty to warn.
7. Describe at least six principles that may be taken into consideration when an ethical dilemma arises in counseling.
8. Describe at least three ways to become involved in your own professional growth.
9. Provide at least three examples of how clients and counselors can cross boundaries and how these create ethical and legal problems.

Introduction

Ethical principles define and govern the right, good, and moral behaviors that are expected in proper professional relationships. Ethical standards are developed and maintained by associations and credentialing bodies of real estate brokers, lawyers, helping professionals, and others. They are motivated by a desire to protect clients, to avoid governmental interference and malpractice suits, and to develop public confidence in general and client confidence in particular.[1]

There is a compelling necessity for ethical standards in the counseling relationship. Counselors hold a great deal of power over clients; mechanisms are necessary to ensure that this power is not abused. The overall objectives of counseling ethics are to maintain client welfare as foremost, to do no harm (physical, emotional, or financial), and to maintain standards of responsibility, integrity, and accountability.

Although confidentiality is the area most regulated by legal statutes, not all critical areas of ethics are formulated into legal statutes. Professional conduct can be legal but not ethical!

Many addictions counselors, like their clients, participate in addiction recovery milieu. This and other relatively informal aspects of the addictions field blur boundaries and roles, creating possibilities for ethically compromising situations.

Ethical standards supersede all other considerations. All counseling actions and decisions must be considered from the standpoint of and be governed by these standards.

In the preparation of addictions counselors, specialized ethics training is the area most often cited as inadequate. Furthermore, internal agency discussion of ethical issues is sometimes muted out of shame, fear, confusion, or expediency; this can be summed up by the term *institutional denial*

---

[1] We are deeply indebted to William White, whose landmark book, *Critical Incidents* (White and Popovits 2004), has brilliantly outlined the areas of ethics training for addictions counselors. His "critical incident" method sets a standard for ethics training and has significantly influenced the format of this chapter.

(Myers 1990; White and Popovits 2004, p. i, 1). Counselors must bear in mind that institutional systems of the agency and broader society generate a climate and a range of options that bear on individual ethical choice.

ACTIVITY 8.1   Easier said than done

In a large or a small group, each person states one principle or guideline by which he or she lives (in the broadest sense, an ethics statement). Typical responses are "I never lie," "I never kill or hurt someone," and "Honesty is the most important to me."

DISCUSS: Consider the following questions and discuss your answers with each other.

- Do you subscribe to the statement "Thou shall not kill?" Have you killed an animal or put a pet to sleep?
- Do you believe it is wrong to steal? Have you copied an audio- or videotape or a CD instead of buying your own?
- Have you ever covered up for a friend's mistakes or lateness at work by lying to a supervisor?
- Have you ever been aware of mistreatment or neglect of a child but did not communicate this information to authorities, nor confronted the perpetrator?
- Have you taken an office item home from work or photocopied a personal item at the office?
- What other small or big actions reflect your ethics?

PROCESS: Can you identify connections among the ethics statements you made, your values and morality (preferences and judgments), group customs (traditional ways of doing things), and laws (standards set by legislative authority)? Are ethical choices absolute? For example, are there circumstances in which it would be permissible to plan to kill someone?

The mandatory orientation of a client that takes place during the intake process includes information about the agency's confidentiality guidelines and practices. The client receives a summary of regulations concerning confidentiality and signs the summary to attest that he or she has understood. The client and the agency each keep a copy of the signed form. At the same time, for the purposes of case management, the counselor may request that the client sign a Consent for Release of Information form that stipulates exactly what client information can be released and to whom. When information is divulged legally to a third party, that third party cannot release it to anyone. The two most common uses of the consent form are as follows:

- To allow continuity of care when different facilities are involved in the client's treatment (e.g., detoxification and rehabilitation units)
- To report a client's compliance to a referring agency (e.g., EAP administrator, parole officer)

Gray Areas

Activity 8.1 shows the impossibility of composing precise rules for human behavior. In ethical counseling, *knowledge* of guidelines must be supplemented by the *skills* of interpreting complex situations and of *applying* ethical standards to them. Also pertinent to ethical counseling are developing and maintaining awareness of the counselor's personal needs and feelings, evaluating how they color the counseling relationship, and ensuring that clients' interests are held foremost. Often, counseling situations occur in which there are competing ethical and/or other obligations. Moral dilemmas arise out of conflicts between two or more beliefs, values, laws, or standards. In resolving such dilemmas, it is useful to establish a hierarchy of ethical standards, that is, a list of ethical concerns rated according to which predominate or take precedence over others. Lowenberg and Dolgoff (1988) present such a hierarchy of ethical standards:

1. Protecting human life
2. Fostering independence and freedom
3. Fostering equality
4. Promoting a better quality of life
5. Protecting the right to privacy
6. Truthfulness
7. Abiding by rules and requirements

Standards vary in their attempts to be specific. Some are brief and sketchy; others go into great detail to cover every eventuality. For example, the American Counseling Association thought it important to stipulate that professionals engaging in intensive short-term training and counseling experiences ensure "that there is professional assistance available during and following the group experience" (ACA 1981, p. B17).

Supervision and Consultation

Consultation with supervisors or other professionals is necessary to ensure a continuing ethical relationship between counselors and their clients, especially in situations where there appears to be a conflict among ethical standards or between ethical and other considerations. Seeking appropriate consultation is considered an ethical necessity in most helping professions (NASW 1980, p. II8). Not to seek advice from others can be unrealistic, stubborn, unwise, and even unethical. One may need to speak to experienced peers or clinical supervisors or to call on the expertise of those trained in other helping professions such as psychiatry or neurology. Consultation should come sooner rather than later. Unfortunately, counselors are often compromised ethically and legally by pride and embarrassment.

Consultation with supervisors about ethical considerations, when carefully documented in clients' records, helps protect both the counselor and the agency in litigation and governmental audit. *Failure to consult* is a subcategory of negligence in malpractice law (Hogan 1978).

Guidelines for supervision of counselors in private practice vary considerably among the helping professions. Failure to provide adequate supervision is unethical and a basis for action under malpractice law (Hogan 1978). *Supervision* has both administrative and clinical dimensions. Although it would be ideal to separate these roles so that there is a space where counselors can feel safe airing their self-doubts, problems, and errors, in the real world the immediate supervisor serves both administrative and clinical functions. This reality challenges the supervisor's own ethics when he or she must weigh the factors of a situation that puts clinical and administrative concerns in conflict. Probably the most typical example of this conflict is that a client needs more personal attention and a longer stay in treatment, but the supervisor is charged with encouraging counselors to see as many clients as possible during a workday and to discharge them from treatment as quickly as possible.

Ethical supervision must be adequate and nonvindictive and facilitate growth. The supervisory process should be based at least in part on routine procedures and objective criteria for evaluation, a structure that helps to avoid, but cannot prevent all, personalistic or subjective processes. Some addictions treatment agencies hire graduates of the program as counselors. Objective evaluation may be compromised if supervision is assigned to a former primary counselor of this individual. The supervisor should share evaluative data with supervisees on a regular basis, and the supervisees need an opportunity to respond.

There is a continuum in supervisory relationships: At one extreme a clinical or administrative supervisor may micromanage the counselor and perhaps employ a punitive or parental style, preventing professional growth and self-sufficiency as well as generating tension between counselor and supervisor, and at the other extreme of the continuum, there may be a detached and/or lazy supervisory relationship, and/or the supervisor may attempt to be a "buddy." In between is the zone of effective supervision.

Case in Point

An Unacceptable Excuse

A clinician treating a very hyperactive preadolescent failed to diagnose attention-deficit hyperactivity disorder. She felt increasingly angry and frustrated, which compromised her ability to counsel the child. Instead of withdrawing from the case, she ended up in a physical struggle with the child, in which she administered a spank. When confronted by the parents, the clinician brought in a post hoc "consultation" with an eminent psychologist that justified the events that had transpired.

Documented consultation should not be used to excuse egregious violations of ethical standards, nor as part of an ongoing plan for expedient but unethical practice. Unfortunately, such misuses of consultation do occur with alarming frequency and are a violation of ethical standards.

Boundaries

Addictions treatment is unique because a large proportion of staff is also in recovery from that which they are treating. Boundaries are a theme in all realms of counseling but come to the forefront more often and more easily in the addictions field, because recovering counselors and clients share similar histories, issues, and even membership in self-help fellowships. Such an issue cuts to the core of the professional counselor–client relationship. With the best will in the world, failure to delineate and differentiate these identities destroys the professional identity and role and leads to any of a number of ethical compromises, violations, and manipulations. Regardless of the setting, but especially in addictions counseling, counselors are counselors—not bowling buddies, lovers, or business associates. Counselors cannot paint clients' houses, sleep with them, treat them to lunch, provide lodging, lend them money, or borrow money from them (not even $1 for a cup of coffee). The recovering counselor faces a continual strain in maintaining boundaries, but that eases in time.

Although there are some very strict standards about personal boundaries, there are also gray areas. For example, how much self-disclosure by counselors is appropriate or ethical? How about hugging, which is permitted and encouraged by many support and self-help groups? Touching a client with the appearance, implication, or suggestion of sexuality is clearly an ethical violation, but is it always wrong to hug or put an arm around a client? Obviously, this is an area where ethical standards vary (Pope and Vetter 1992, p. 401; Rhodes 1992, pp. 43–44).

Legal Issues

Confidentiality

A major legal and ethical obligation of addictions counselors is to maintain a zone of privacy around information revealed by clients, whether it be in written records (charts, memos, notes, messages, email, and electronic files) or verbal communications. The counseling relationship, like that of lawyer and client, or cleric and penitent, is *privileged*, legally covered with a code of silence. Federal laws protect clients' identities and records.[2] Quite extensive federal guidelines were published in July 1975 and came into effect August 1, 1975. They were amended in August 1986 and published in the *Federal Register*, vol. 52, no. 110, on June 9, 1987. Violations may bring fines ranging from $500 (first offense) to $5,000. State regulations vary, and the law of privilege, in recent years, has been strengthened in some states but threatened or eroded in others. Where there is a conflict between these statutes, federal guidelines prevail. Every counselor must be informed as to how specific state regulations interpret federal statutes (see "Professional Growth" later in this chapter).

The federal confidentiality regulations are known as Confidentiality of Alcohol and Drug Abuse Patient Records (42 CFR Part 2). In addition, in December 2000, the Department of Health and Human Services (HHS) issued a Privacy Rule ("Standards for Privacy of Individually Identifiable Health Information" pursuant to provisions of the Health Insurance Portability and Accountability Act of 1996—the infamous HIPAA regulations). HIPAA parallels 42 CFR Part 2 to a great extent. HIPAA applies to "covered entities," which are health plans and healthcare providers who transmit health information in electronic/computer-based forms, as for submission of claims, coordination of benefits, referral certification, and authorization. If you work in a small storefront operation, HIPAA may not apply to you at all. You probably have noticed a new setup at your pharmacy, where you are supposed to stand behind a line so you can't see who is signing for their medications (although we once heard a pharmacist call out, "your Thorazine [antipsychotic] is ready, Mrs. Cohen!"), or at a clinic where the sign-in sheet isn't there for all to see who is in attendance. This is HIPAA in action. If your agency is really getting with the program, you'll see the computer workstation log off automatically if you spend too much time in the bathroom, the passwords change at an alarming rate, and the workstation placed so that passersby can't glance over to get a quick glimpse of Mr. Johnson's diagnosis. If you are a "covered entity," all staff members are expected to be trained in the implementation of HIPAA so as to properly process "Protected Health Information" (PHI). Agencies have found it a pain in the neck to implement HIPAA, while acknowledging that there are a lot of valuable safeguards to clients in this electronic age. It's not enough that we practice all of these safeguards; we're expected to make sure that the program participants know about it. Agencies subject to both the old federal (42 CFR) and the new HIPAA regulations can combine them into a single notice. There are some new patient rights, such as the right to request restrictions in the uses and disclosures of PHI,

---

[2]Federal guidelines are set forth in Title 42, Part 2 of the *Code of Federal Regulations*, often referred to by their abbreviation, 42 CFR Part 2, and also in Title 42 Section 290dd: 3, US code.

and the right to access, amend, and receive an accounting of disclosure of PHI. Most large agencies will have compiled their own manual of regulations and forms, and have designated a privacy officer to oversee the whole affair, and we suggest a perusal of these manuals rather than trying to wade through the regulations in their original forms. CSAT (2004) has published a relatively short summary (a mere 34 pages) together with the text of the regulations, which can be ordered without charge from the National Clearinghouse on Alcohol and Drug Information (NCADI).

The governing principle is that all information communicated by clients in programs or individual treatment is privileged and confidential. This principle is based not only on the right to privacy, but also on the likelihood that clients will accept and succeed in treatment if they can be confident that information is protected. There are a few, clear exceptional circumstances in which information revealed by clients can be communicated to others.

Duty to Warn

When information reveals a clear danger to the client or others, such as suicidal or homicidal intent, a professional obligation called the *Duty to Warn*, in which you notify medical personnel or police, supersedes confidentiality. In addition, in most states it is a legal obligation to inform the police if any crime is threatened or committed against an agency's staff. Penalties for failure to warn vary from state to state. Individuals harmed by such failure often seek compensation by instituting lawsuits.

....

Case in Point

Duty to Warn: The Landmark Case

On October 27, 1969, Prosenjit Poddar killed Tatiana Tarasoff. Tatiana's father Vitaly Tarasoff sued, alleging that two months earlier Poddar had confided his intention to kill Tatiana to psychologist Dr. Lawrence Moore of the Cowell Memorial Hospital at the University of California at Berkeley. On Moore's request, the campus police briefly detained Poddar, but they released him when they concluded that he was rational. They further claimed that Dr. Harvey Powelson, Moore's superior, directed that no further action be taken to detain Poddar. Thus, the victim and her parents were not warned of her peril. The defendants included Dr. Moore, the psychologist who examined Poddar and decided that Poddar should be committed; Dr. Gold and Dr. Yandell, psychiatrists at Cowell Memorial Hospital who concurred in Moore's decision; and Dr. Powelson, chief of the Department of Psychiatry, who countermanded Moore's decision and directed that the staff take no action to confine Poddar.

Most counselors have heard of the famous Tarasoff case— *Tarasoff v. Regents of the University of California* 551 P.2d 334 (1976)—but few are aware that the supervisor as well as the treating psychologists were held liable in this landmark case. The supervisor has the same duty to protect a third party (Tatiana) as does the supervisee.

A later landmark case, *Jablonski v. United States* (1983, Ninth Circuit, U.S. Court of Appeals), found a therapist and their supervisor negligent for failing to accurately predict a homicide based on the psychological profile of their client.

Legal criteria for predicting dangerousness usually include:

- Past violent behavior
- Specific and/or detailed threats
- Repeated threats
- Violent thoughts
- History of irrational and unpredictable behavior

Supervisors must ensure that their supervisees understand and effectively implement mandates on warning a third party, and they must carefully document that they did so as well as document any warnings that did take place.

Duty to Protect an Individual at Risk of Suicide

A counselor would be liable if he or she:

- Failed to assess and diagnose the client
- "Abandoned" the client by abruptly terminating the client, failed to respond in an emergency, or did not have backup coverage when they were unavailable
- Assisted with the suicide, say, by encouraging the misuse of medications
- Through inaction contributed to a suicide

A supervisor would be liable if she or he failed to direct the counselor properly in this situation (Falvey and Bray 2001).

Duty to Report

Initial reports of child abuse and neglect are stipulated by the federal Child Abuse Prevention and Treatment Act of 1974, which denies federal grants to states that do not comply with reporting standards. The Duty to Report to child protective agencies in a region overrides or supersedes confidentiality rights.

The duties to warn and to report child abuse do not throw open agency files; they merely mandate the provision of specific information to the appropriate authorities. State regulations define what constitutes child abuse. Anyone who works with children is a *mandated reporter* of abuse, even abuse that the professional observes on the street or in the home of a friend or relative. However, there is considerable variation in how mistreatment of children is initially perceived, often influenced by the cultural background of the staff involved. In several instances, paraprofessional child-welfare workers in New York City overlooked what later was identified as serious physical abuse of children. In some agencies, a nondegreed counselor identifies abuse that is then "called in" by another staff member.

Case in Point
Eliza Fell Through the Cracks

The mother of six-year-old Eliza Izquierdo was a mentally ill crack cocaine addict who believed her child was possessed by evil spirits. Eliza was kept home from school, neglected, and abused. She died from beatings in November 1995. Warning signs had been missed or ignored by her school and her caseworker. Her death became a rallying point for social-service reform.

The Child Abuse and Protection Act also mandates confidentiality regarding specifics of child abuse cases, which has been frustrating to those seeking to root out negligence and neglect. Therefore, Congress amended it in 1992 to facilitate effective investigation and prevention of abuse. Specific implementing regulations were released in 1996 by the U.S. Department of Health and Human Services.

In New York, the Social Services Law has interpreted in even more stringent terms the stipulation of total secrecy. When child welfare authorities refused to testify in hearings on cases of severe child abuse that "fell through the cracks," legislators concluded that the state regulations functioned to protect bureaucratic bungling or inaction. After checking with federal regulators to verify they were in line with the 1996 regulations, New York enacted modifying legislation (Eliza's Law, see "Case in Point: Eliza Fell Through the Cracks") to permit more disclosure for investigative purposes.

Informed Consent

Informed consent means that the client has been educated as to the nature and form of disclosure. A client can give specific and written consent to the release of information. Every agency has a printed consent form that is explained carefully to every client (Figure 8.1). It is signed by the client and by the individual performing the intake procedure, and dated. The intake procedure, or the paperwork involved, may be implemented by an addictions counselor or a specialized intake worker. Blanket consent to release any or all information, or from or to any party, is acceptable in the Code of Federal Regulations (CFR). Written consent specifies the type of information that may be released, who is to release it and to whom,

Figure 8.1 Informed consent form.

Macedonia Memorial Medical Center Release of Confidential Information Consent Form

I, _____, a patient in the Addiction Services Unit at Macedonia Memorial Medical Center, hereby authorize the following disclosure of information from my treatment records/files:

I authorize Macedonia Memorial Medical Center to release information listed below to (name, title, organization to which disclosure is to be made):

_____

Purpose or need for disclosure (as specific as possible): _____

_____

Nature or extent of information to be disclosed (as limited as possible): _____

_____

This consent will terminate upon (date, event, or condition): _____

_____

I understand that my records are protected under federal regulations governing confidentiality of alcohol and drug abuse records, 42 CFR Part 2 and cannot be disclosed without my written authorization unless otherwise provided for in the regulations. I also understand that information disclosed in the party listed above may not be disclosed to a third party without a separate signed consent, and that I may revoke this consent at any time except as legally proscribed.

Signature of Patient: _____

Signature: ___ Parent ___ Guardian ___ Authorized Representative

_____

Signature of staff person: _____

Date: _____

and for what purpose. It should include a statement that consent can be withdrawn. A client can usually withdraw consent verbally as well as in writing, although the time frame within which this occurs varies by state. The release must be signed and dated.

Confidentiality is not limited to the time of treatment. It starts when the client applies or calls to apply, even if he or she does not make an appointment. Confidentiality responsibilities do not end when the client exits treatment, whether from completion, relapse, administrative discharge, or other

Figure 8.2 Prohibition of redisclosure.

> This information has been disclosed to you from records whose confidentiality is protected by federal law. Federal Regulation (42 CFR Part 2) prohibits you from making any further disclosure of it without the specific written consent of the person to whom it pertains, or as otherwise permitted by such regulations. A general authorization for the release of medical or other information is NOT sufficient for this purpose. The federal rules restrict any use of the information to criminally investigate or prosecute the patient.

circumstance, or if the client dies. The counselor and other staff must ensure that records are kept in such a manner that confidentiality will be preserved. The disposal of records presents the same expectation. "Dead" files cannot, for example, be taken in cartons to the street or left in unlocked cabinets in a storage room (ACA 1981, B2). They must be shredded or incinerated.

Disclosure and Redisclosure

Release of information with a client's informed consent binds the party to whom it is released not to release it to a third party (Figure 8.2). The information is bound by the confidentiality guidelines. Information disclosed by consent should be limited to that needed for case management, diagnosis, referral, and rehabilitation, and to process insurance claims or aid in the disposition of criminal proceedings.

The fact that clients are in treatment at a particular agency cannot be revealed without written consent of the client or a court order, regardless of who is inquiring. Relatives cannot simply call to speak with Joe or ask if Joe has arrived. Nor can staff always trust that a caller is who he or she claims to be.

Case in Point
I Can't Give You That Information

One of the authors called a large treatment facility to inform a staff member of a scholarship. The man who answered the phone gave a detailed and helpful account of the counselor's comings and goings, and how best to contact her. When he was asked, "Whom am I speaking with?" he responded, "I'm sorry, I can't give you that information, I'm a client."

Even when a counselor or other professional refers a client to treatment, once the client has completed intake at the treatment agency, staff are following correct practice if they no longer communicate information about that client to the referring party, unless the client has given consent for release of information.

Legally Incompetent Clients

If the client is incapable of understanding his or her rights and responsibilities, that client might be judged legally incompetent. Special consent provisions are made for legally incompetent persons and for minors; a legal guardian signs (or refuses to sign) consent form(s) (Figure 8.1). In the case of releasing information about a deceased client, consent forms are signed by the person who has the power of attorney. A medical diagnosis does not constitute legal incompetency: It is only a piece of the evidence presented in courtroom procedures to determine a person's "competency." It is the responsibility of the agency's administration to ensure that privileged information is not released unless appropriate forms have been presented to document such legal determination, according to federal and state statutes.

Clinical Discussion

Confidential information can be discussed for clinical and supervisory purposes. If such agency functions took place only in a strict chain of command, this would be quite clear. However, peer supervision, case conferences, and shift reports multiply the number of people who have access to confidential information. These factors, as well as the informal organization of the profession, make it difficult to define appropriate boundaries of secrecy. A baseline principle should be established that disclosure is on a need-to-know basis, as opposed to freely exchanging information with any and all personnel. Sharing of information cannot occur outside of a treatment unit in a larger institutional setting. For example, a nurse in detox cannot tell her friends on the maternity floor about her hallucinating patient. In addition to people involved in the client's care, the people who deal with billing and other record keeping may legally receive limited confidential information.

Any counselor or agency must establish clear guidelines for access to confidential records by secretarial workers and volunteers. If they must have access, they must fully understand and implement confidentiality guidelines. The CFRs apply to all support personnel, administrators, volunteers, interns, and so on.

ACTIVITY (8.2)   What's the right thing to do?

*Phil is a counselor in an intensive outpatient program where you work. He
has been employed in the field for three years and has been in recovery for
six years. You have been close to him for most of that time. A month ago,
Phil's son was killed in an automobile accident. In his grief, Phil went
out and got drunk. He immersed himself without delay in his recovery
fellowship as well as in short-term bereavement counseling, and he has
confided only to you about the situation. State regulations mandate that
counselors have at least two years uninterrupted "clean time." Phil is very
afraid that if the agency finds out about his relapse, he will lose his job.*

DISCUSS:

- How do you feel about this situation?
- What would you say to Phil?
- Can you consult someone about this to get advice on your position?
- What should or can you say to the agency administrators?
- When is withholding information a breach of honesty?
- If you fail to disclose Phil's relapse, do you think you'd lose your job?
- How can you reconcile, on one hand, the trust and confidence of a
  friend and, on the other, loyalty to the agency and safety of clients?
- What do you think would be the best thing to do for your friend?
- What would be the right thing to do? Does this conflict with what
  you think would be best for Phil?

Court-Ordered Disclosure

The pendulum has been swinging back and forth in recent years in
regards to legal use of client information. In some legal decisions, the need to
uncover evidence regarding criminal activity has superseded confidentiality
of the client–counselor relationship, while in other cases the opposite interpretation has been made. In the early 1990s the subpoena came to overrule
the client–counselor privilege and the anonymity of twelve-step fellowships.

An example of the latter is the 1994 Paul Cox case in New York.
Seven members of Alcoholics Anonymous testified under subpoena that
another member had told them of his emerging memories of killing a
Larchmont couple as they slept in their home, formerly lived in by the
Cox family, while in a drunken stupor. Cox was convicted of manslaughter
and sentenced to 16–54 years in prison. Many in AA were upset and angry
that information garnered from an AA group was allowed as evidence
(Hoffman 1994; Reed 1996).

In 1996 the U.S. Supreme Court ruled that federal courts must allow
psychotherapists and other mental health professionals to refuse to disclose

patients' records in judicial proceedings. This ruling created a new type of "evidentiary privilege" (Scarf 1996). *Privileged information* is information that remains within the confines of a professional relationship, such as between an individual and his or her minister, priest, lawyer, or psychotherapist. The term *evidentiary privilege* simply refers to the fact that by its "privileged" status, information cannot be used as evidence in court. The person holding that information cannot be forced to reveal it.

Medical Emergency

According to a SAMHSA publication on confidentiality (Lopez 2002, p. 5), "A federal, state and local court may authorize a program to make a disclosure of confidential patient identifying information. A court may issue such an order, however, only after following certain procedures and making certain determinations specified in the regulations. A subpoena, search warrant, or arrest warrant, even when it is signed by a judge, is not sufficient, by itself, to require or even permit a program to make such a disclosure." It further states that the court must give notice in writing with an opportunity to respond (unless it is prosecuting a patient). It must use a fictitious name in the process. It must have a "good cause" and cannot proceed if there is another source of the information. The information must be limited to the purpose of the order. Obviously, situations such as these must be handled through an attorney retained by the agency, who communicates only with the agency director or legal specialist.

Emergencies

Medical information usually shielded by confidentiality regulations may be released when necessary for evaluation and treatment of a medical emergency. For example, a diabetic woman may lose consciousness if her blood sugar is too high or too low. The fact of her diabetic status must be communicated without hesitation if the client has such an emergency. Another example is that of a man having great difficulty breathing or appearing to have some sort of heart attack. A counselor is obligated to inform paramedics or other medical personnel about the medications the man takes (Figure 8.3).

Statistical Aggregates

Information may be provided for statistical aggregates for research or audits, such as the percentage of clients who are entering treatment for the first, second, or third time (Figure 8.3). In releasing confidential information for these purposes, clients' names and other information that could identify clients cannot be released.

Qualified Service Organizations

The services of outside agencies such as laboratories and accounting firms are often required. Such agencies, known as *qualified service organizations,*

Figure 8.3 Client's rights to confidentiality.

ESSEX COUNTY COLLEGE STUDENT AFFAIRS AREA
Health Services Department
Office of the Substance Abuse Coordinator
877-3129

THIS PROGRAM IS REQUIRED TO COMMUNICATE TO EACH CLIENT
THAT FEDERAL LAW AND REGULATIONS PROTECT THE CONFIDENTIALITY
OF ALCOHOL AND DRUG ABUSE PATIENT RECORDS. A SUMMARY OF THE
LAW AND REGULATIONS MUST BE GIVEN TO EACH CLIENT.

YOUR SUMMARY OF THE LAW IS PROVIDED BELOW.

The confidentiality of alcohol and drug abuse patient records
maintained by this program is protected by federal law and regulations.
Generally, the program may not say to a person outside the program that a
person attends the program, or disclose any information identifying a client
as an alcohol or drug abuser *unless*

1. the client consents in writing.
2. the disclosure is allowed by a court order, or
3. the disclosure is made to medical personnel in a medical
emergency or to qualified personnel for research, audit, or program
evaluation.

Violation of the federal law and regulations by a program is a crime.
Suspected violations may be reported to appropriate authorities in
accordance with federal regulations.

Federal law and regulations do not protect any information about a
crime committed by a client, either at the program or against any person
who works for the program, or about any threat to commit such a crime.

Federal laws and regulations do not protect any information about
suspected child abuse or neglect from being reported under state law to
appropriate state or local authorities. (See 42 U.S.C. 290 dd-3 and 42 U.S.C.
290 ee-3 for federal laws and 42 CFR Part 2 for federal regulations.)

I HAVE RECEIVED A COPY OF THE ABOVE SUMMARY.

_____

(Client's signature)

Date: _____

Source: Victor B. Stolberg, MA, EdM

receive information that is necessary to perform their contracted functions.
They are governed by a signed Qualified Service Organization Agreement
(QSOA), under which they agree to abide by federal and local regulations
concerning confidentiality.

ACTIVITY 8.3   Should I tell?

Your 28-year-old male client was married but engaged in anonymous sexual encounters with men. His family and in-laws were very anti-gay. He contracted a sexually transmitted disease, and discontinued treatment. Then you read in the newspaper that he committed suicide. His grief-stricken father called you, requesting any information you have that would help the family understand why his son killed himself. They speculate over what they did or did not do that was responsible for his death. Your memories and notes clearly show that his suicide was related to factors over which they had no control. What do you do? Because the client is no longer alive, can it hurt to share information with the family?

DISCUSS:

- How should you respond to this family's wishes?
- Do you have an ethical responsibility to your client's family?
- Do you have to maintain this client's confidentiality even though he's dead? After all, you have information that would definitely lighten their grief.
- If the police investigate this unnatural death, what would you contribute to their fact finding?

Training

Where case information or material is used for training counselors, the identity of the client must be disguised. Individuals who participate in such training must be informed as to the need to maintain confidentiality. Unfortunately, participants in training who work at a local agency occasionally recognize a client and accidentally blurt out either the name or information that provides a substantial hint to the client's identity.

Pending Legislation

Counselors should be aware that specific state regulations that apply to minors, school-based programs, and other institutional settings might differ from those in effect for treatment agencies. These vary considerably from state to state, and litigation is pending concerning the role of parental consent and information that is provided to parents.

Finally, there is also considerable debate, as well as pending litigation, regarding the access of client information by managed-care entities. Many believe there already has been considerable rapid erosion of confidentiality by managed-care audits (Lewin 1996; Scarf 1996), which has resulted in harm to clients and decline of trust as to the privacy of the client–counselor relationship.

ACTIVITY (8.4) **Wearing two hats**

Two hats is a term for an individual who has dual roles. Employees of addictions agencies often talk about two-hat problems to denote the staffer who is in a recovery fellowship with clients.

Don is a recovering cocaine addict who works at Reality Lodge, a large long-term treatment program staffed largely by graduates of this therapeutic community. Don attends Narcotics Anonymous to maintain and strengthen his own recovery from addiction. At one meeting, a young woman named Cheryl makes a comment after the main speaker, in which she shares the difficulty she is having in staying drug-free. Cheryl happens to be a court-mandated client at the outpatient department of Reality Lodge, and Don knows that she has not shared these minor relapses with the staff.

As an NA member, Don would never carry that information outside of the meeting, but as a counselor he would notify his agency and then the court. Which hat decides what he does?

DISCUSS:

- What if Don calls the client on this and urges her to come clean herself? What if Cheryl tells him to mind his own business and warns Don not to break the confidentiality of NA?
- Should Don tell the agency staff what he heard at the NA meeting regarding this client's lack of sobriety? In weighing the anonymity of NA and the confidentiality of Don's agency, which carries more weight? What information can he share legally?
- What federal or state (use your state) regulations are relevant to Don's decision?
- Can you write a guideline for this type of situation to state clearly the agency's obligations? Shouldn't the agency tell counselors to leave a meeting where a client is present?
- What, if anything, should Don say to Cheryl?
- If Don remains silent, what are the implications for his interactions and relationships with his own supervisor and Cheryl's counselor?

Financial Ethics

In a national survey of "ethically troubling incidents" among psychologists, confidentiality-related problems were the largest category, followed by blurred, dual, or conflicting relationships. The category we are about to consider, the financial realm, ranked third (Pope and Vetter 1992).

Commissions or rebates (*kickbacks*) for referrals and fee-splitting are unethical and illegal. It is out of line for a counselor to seek or accept private fee arrangements with a client who is working with his or her agency. A counselor may not treat a client in an agency-run group and then see him or her "on the side" for a fee; nor can a counselor who has a position with an agency list that position on a brochure or print it in other literature (business card, stationery) to recruit clients to a private practice.

A counselor may not use client contacts to promote a personal commercial enterprise or that of a relative or friend. For example, a counselor who learns that his client needs a good lawyer cannot refer that client to his sister the attorney, even with all the goodwill and honesty possible. Or a counselor cannot help out her senior citizen client who has plumbing problems by getting him a good deal with her uncle in the septic tank business.

Borrowing money from a past or present client is a form of financial exploitation by the counselor who is using his or her position of power. It is unethical to accept gifts or tips from clients or their families (NAADAC 2004, Principle 7). For example, a counselor, even in a gesture of generosity, cannot lend money to a pregnant client for a taxi ride so she doesn't have to struggle with public transportation to get home. Or a counselor, while knowing the therapeutic value of a client's giving, cannot accept tickets to the ball game.

A counselor or other staff member should not regularly obtain meals from an agency's commissary designed for clients' meals, unless this is considered a convenience of employment, stipulated by contract or by-law, or at least approved by the governing board or other legal authority.

Regrettably, each of these practices occurs in the treatment community, usually involving some combination of (1) lack of clarity on the part of the treatment agency regarding ethical guidelines, (2) personal or recovery relationships between worker and administrators, leading to enabling of these behaviors, and (3) premature counseling role for an individual in early recovery. Such individuals may have unsolved problems such as compulsive gambling, overidentification with clients that leads to blurring of boundaries, overextension and burnout, or a need to compensate for low self-esteem by grandiose or narcissistic posturing.

Other financially unethical practices include:

- Data manipulated to indicate that more services are provided (such as calls of inquiry logged in as complete referrals) to justify continued funding levels or to boost reimbursement.
- In fundraising, concealing the actual use of funds for administrative purposes rather than for direct services, or concealing fees or percentage paid to fundraisers or to consultants who helped write a grant.

- In fundraising, portraying a "crisis" that threatens the existence of the agency and the loss of services to the deserving clientele.
- Solicitation of funds from former clients or client families who are subordinate in the power relationship and who are vulnerable and grateful. This also can lead to breach of confidentiality.
- In grant or other fiscal reporting, concealing use of funds for administrative purposes or for purposes that benefit administrative personnel, such as meals and travel not necessary for the operation of the facility.

The "Checkbook" Diagnosis

Counselors may recognize that a client needs treatment, yet policy guidelines or gatekeepers of their medical coverage exclude all but the most severely afflicted. Agencies may be tempted to provide a billable or *checkbook* diagnosis. This phenomenon, also called *diagnostic creep*, can be motivated by a desire to obtain help for suffering individuals or by the wish to fill available beds and keep reimbursement flowing to the agency coffers. The alternative is to deny care, refer elsewhere, or prematurely discharge clients whose problems are so severe that they might drain agency resources while bringing little reimbursement. Agencies that receive governmental support are often required by state regulations to set aside a certain proportion of treatment slots for "uncompensated care" or "charity care," that is, treatment of clients who have no medical coverage. Providing something other than an objective and proper diagnosis is unethical and if egregiously inaccurate could open an agency to fraud.

A related practice to diagnostic creep is to use an adolescent addictions unit as a catchall for adolescents with problems, such as giving chemical dependency diagnoses to one-time LSD users or without sufficient data. This is an unethical business practice. In addition, labels take on a life of their own: It is unfair, stigmatizing, and self-fulfilling to call teen drug experimentation an addiction.

This is but one example of *diagnostic slamming*, making the clients' diagnosis more severe or assessing the level of severity as more severe, in order to retain clients or garner a longer length of stay from third-party payers (White and Popovits 2004).

Representation of Services

Claims made for the helping process in general and for the process in addictions counseling in particular must be realistic. Addicts range from the vulnerable to the desperate, who have completely "hit bottom," or at the very least to those who live in chaos, disarray, and unhappiness. Counseling must not be presented as a miracle-working process or cash in on popular but unverified methods. It should not make claims other than the modest and realistic, addiction-specific, facilitation of recovery. A counselor or an agency should pay careful attention to how it represents itself, the services it offers, and the professional qualifications of employees.

Clients and prospective clients must understand the scope of treatment—what is and is not treated—methods of treatment, length and cost of treatment, and limitations of treatment. The client must be informed fully at the onset of counseling—if not before—about the purposes, goals, techniques, and procedures involved (ACA 1981, p. B8). The addictions counselor's core function of orientation is, then, prompted by an ethical standard. One corollary of this principle is that the client cannot be unknowingly or involuntarily the subject of any type of experiment (ACA 1981, pp. B15, D5, D6).

Neither addictions counselors nor agencies should claim or imply treatment for nonaddictive psychiatric disorders, related areas such as reduction of stress and anxiety, or solutions to problems of living. However, relapse prevention may draw upon techniques used in psychotherapies such as relaxation methods or assertiveness training for the specific purpose of reducing the risk of relapse (ACA 1981, p. A7).

Unethical marketing of services is quite common. This includes advertising every kind of specialized care where little is actually present. Examples include a general care unit that is promulgated as having a special women's program or a cocaine addiction program; patients being admitted to a "detoxification program," which is actually a general medical floor of a hospital with one part-time alcoholism counselor; and toll-free numbers that offer "free assessments," then tell all callers that they are addicts and refer them to their own programs or to those that have paid to be a designated agency. William White (White and Popovits 2004) chronicles many such examples.

Any representation of service must not engage in grandiose impression management that suggests, implicitly or explicitly, charismatic or other special qualities of the counselor (Vermont 1980, Principle 9). The guru pose should be avoided. Testimonials from satisfied customers are, in general, ethically inappropriate (Vermont 1980, Principle 9).

Claims made for counselors' credentials should be specific and not misleading or inflated (ACA 1981, A4). The basis for use of terms such as *clinician, therapist, certified,* and *licensed* must be clear. Some states have a tiered system that recognizes a minimal level of preparedness for the entry-level employee or addictions screening worker in a general social services setting as well as a professional counselor certification. It is unethical to represent the minimal credential as a board certification.

In-house job titles that are abbreviated after names (e.g., "John Smith, S.A.C." for an in-house title of Substance Abuse Counselor) must not be printed on agency stationery or business cards to imply certification or licensure. Some unethical misrepresentations include individuals employed in roles other than counseling at an agency who state or imply that they are counselors; volunteers who imply they are staff; aide positions that are represented as full counseling positions; and counseling roles that are represented as administrative (NAADAC 2004, Principle 4).

An "official seal" of twelve-step fellowship should not be claimed to attract clients. An agency should never give the impression that it is an "AA agency," or that many staff members are AA members. Alcoholics Anonymous would be the very first to object to this! Twelve-step fellowships neither recommend nor endorse agencies or organizations. Neither should personal membership in fellowships be used to enhance recruitment. Not only is this practice unethical, it leads to confusion about the roles of fellowship peers, sponsors, and counselors.

With the managed-care system, treatment options have come under severe limitations. Some managed-care entities have discouraged or even forbidden healthcare providers from talking freely with patients about their treatment options. Providers feel that such "gag rules" put blinders on patients, preventing them from intelligently participating in decisions that affect their lives and contradicting the principle of informed consent. For physician providers, it may even violate the Hippocratic Oath, which states, "First, do no harm." Gag rules on providers are being challenged in litigation in several states.

Competence

One of the key functions of ethical standards is to ensure that those entrusted to help are indeed reasonably ready and able to do so. Competency issues include counselor impairment, issues that cloud objectivity or distract from focus on the client's interest, and preparedness in a variety of knowledge and skills areas.

Impairment

Counselors are impaired if they suffer from conditions that cause measurable decrements in clinical performance or that compromise their counseling status. These include various psychiatric and neurological syndromes that render the counselor less than competent to perform counseling functions, as well as possible relapse into substance abuse. NAADAC Principle 4 (2004) states that professional impairment needs appropriate treatment, and the addictions counselor certification boards in many states stipulate that recovering counselors must abstain from addictive substances. In many states, relapses must be reported to the certification board and a two-year suspension imposed.

Lack of Preparedness

Lack of or inadequate training is a form of incompetence that jeopardizes clients' recovery. To put it even more strongly, because addictions are chronic, progressive, often fatal diseases, the incompetence of treatment staff can threaten the lives of clients. Various incompetent actions, such as "improper treatment, inadequate treatment, negligence in use of technique, inadequate diagnosis" (Hogan 1978), are the basis of many malpractice suits. However, competencies of addictions counselors have been a gray area. The definition of adequate preparedness has varied from state to state and from agency to agency. By the late 1990s, unified models of addiction counselor competency were becoming standard, as seen in the federally sponsored and published document, "Addiction Counseling Competencies: The Knowledge, Skills, and Attitudes of Professional Practice" (CSAT 2006), which has been endorsed by the major addictions counseling constituencies.

It is natural for grateful, recovering persons to wish to assume a counseling role and give back to the community what they have gained. In fact, the addictions field was founded and developed by recovering addicts in a self-help milieu, whose commitment, energy, and skills at engaging and motivating addicts are often the envy of "straight" staff. The certification process was not linked initially to professional training such as that required in nursing, social work, or psychology. The competence of nonprofessional or paraprofessional recovering counselors has been a great debate in the addictions field for over forty years (Krystal and Moore 1963; Lemere et al. 1964). However, few would claim now that personal recovery alone is sufficient preparation for the counseling role. Bissell and Royce (1994, p. 4) quote a halfway house director as saying, "Just because you had your appendix out doesn't qualify you to take out mine!"

The nondegreed addictions counselor faces disadvantages in completing paperwork, writing case presentations, and dealing with the certification process—topics that are taught in educational programs that lead to degrees. There are also questions regarding service to clients. For example, does lack of knowledge about psychiatric diagnoses or the *DSM-IV-TR* (*Diagnostic and Statistical Manual of Mental Disorders, Fourth Edition, Text Revision*) or the revised *DSM5* on the part of a counselor who interacts with possibly mentally ill chemical abusers constitute incompetence? Addictions counselors who have had no training in screening concurrent psychiatric diagnoses are increasingly rare. In the past, bipolar (manic-depressive) clients were occasionally mislabeled as *dry drunks* (a term used in recovery milieu to denote the disorganization, impulsivity, and mood swings that may be the aftereffects or consequences of long-term addiction). In 1990, a college intern, who had acquired basic knowledge of psychiatric symptoms from his coursework, observed a sober client seemingly in the throes of a manic state. His suggestion that a psychiatric consultation be obtained was rebuffed initially by naïve staff. He prevailed by petitioning the agency director; the consultation did confirm his suspicion of a mood disorder (Myers 1991). Failure to refer clients appropriately keeps them from proper treatment and jeopardizes their safety and lives.

On the other hand, addictions counselors bitterly note that other health-care providers, including supervisory medical personnel, often sorely lack first-hand knowledge of addictive disease, miss the diagnosis, and cannot see through denial and deception. In 1988 at a public hospital in Brooklyn, New York, new graduates of foreign medical schools routinely overdiagnosed paranoid schizophrenia among crack addicts in an inpatient psychiatric unit.

The responsibility for ensuring staff competency lies primarily with the agency. Some agency administrators are happy to use untrained, newly recovering individuals, sometimes graduates of their own programs. Their motives usually combine elements of naïveté and the opportunistic use of a cheap labor pool (Bissell and Royce 1994, pp. 5–6). To get a foot on the career ladder, many people might be glad to be so "exploited." Some argue that such hiring practices are not necessarily unethical, if the employer offers or requires a systematic and mandatory program of continuing education, professional growth, and certification. Unfortunately, such programs have often been absent. Hiring untrained individuals generates unsophisticated, clinically limited "hothouse plants" who cannot function occupationally outside of a certain type of recovery program, can hardly differentiate themselves from clients, are prone to ethical compromises or burnout, and have limited writing skills and unsophisticated clinical skills.

Lack of Responsibility

Irresponsible or careless behavior is incompetent and unethical. For example, a counselor's chronic lateness results in inadequate services, impairs the counseling relationship, and demonstrates a bad example to people who are emerging from the personal chaos of addiction. Poor record keeping, frequent interruptions of sessions to take phone calls, and failure to follow up in case management are ineffective and disrespectful practices that constitute unethical treatment.

It is no shame to recognize the limits of competence. A counselor may be very good at what he or she does, but should not feel impelled to tackle every skills area. Ability to identify one's limits of competency, as well as goals for further growth and training, is a clinical and ethical imperative, usually requiring some guidance and input from clinical supervisors. Not everyone can repair computers or perform brain surgery; why should any counselor who has not been trained as a family therapist feel compelled to assume the role of marriage counselor? Getting drawn into acting in areas outside of the scope of one's competency compromises ethical standards (ACA 1981, p. A7). Again, this also can harm clients and make the agency liable to lawsuits.

Many guidelines (NAADAC 2004, Principle 8) consider it a duty to report incompetence to certification authorities. Private practices, agencies, and hospitals should have guidelines for dealing with incompetence.

Professional Growth

Continued growth and ongoing education are tenets of ethics in most helping professions. No one would want a suicidal, bed-ridden, and biologically depressed relative treated by a psychiatrist who had never heard about Prozac, Zoloft, Paxil, or Effexor. Professional growth involves gaining the latest knowledge, strategies, and skills. It also means avoiding rote formulaic counseling, becoming stale, and burning out. There are myriad ways of broadening competency and upgrading knowledge and skills:

- Read addictions treatment journals in your specialty, which might include *Alcoholism Treatment Quarterly, Journal of Child and Adolescent Chemical Dependency, Employee Assistance Quarterly, Schizophrenia Bulletin*, and so on.
- Attend professional seminars. It is usually best to avoid the expensive lecture circuits and cruises for continuing education unit (CEU) credits that are advertised with glossy brochures and vague inspirational themes such as "Codependency in the Twenty-First Century."
- Attend agency networking events. Provider networks exist in many states or regions of states, but nonsupervisory staff are often unaware of their existence or are hesitant about asking to attend.
- Be active in The Association for Addiction Professionals (NAADAC), which has affiliate organizations in most states, and attend their regional and national conferences.
- Complete coursework in an addictions studies curriculum or in criminal justice or mental health curricula pertaining to special populations such as addicted offenders and mentally ill chemical abusers.
- Judiciously peruse Internet resources, including those of the Center for Substance Abuse Treatment (SAMHSA), National Clearinghouse on Alcohol and Drug Information (NCADI), and the Web resources on this text's website.

For professional growth, the areas of knowledge that counselors should pursue include:

- Biomedical knowledge and practice in regards to mentally ill chemical abusers.
- Multicultural awareness and sensitivity. The *DSM-IV-TR* addresses cultural sensitivity, both in diagnostic considerations for many long-recognized syndromes as well as in a special appendix of culture-bound syndromes. The American Psychological Association as well as the Addiction Counselor Competency document (CSAT 2006) consider cultural competency an ethical necessity.
- New medications such as antipsychotics, antidepressants, and drug antagonists, along with their therapeutic possibilities and side effects. Counselors also need to keep abreast of over-the-counter medications that addicts and abusers use to supplement or substitute for street drugs, including legal stimulants contained in appetite suppressants and decongestants and "herbal" or "natural" energy boosters.
- New laws and regulations concerning confidentiality, liability, professional duties, insurance, and emergency treatment. Addictions staff can be effective advocates for constructive legislation that favors parity for substance abuse and mental healthcare. Counselors should be aware of their professional association's stance on and analysis of upcoming legislation so they can be resources for information on how to vote on these important issues.
- Changes in the field such as the decline in inpatient rehabilitation in favor of intensive outpatient treatment, and new screening and assessment tools such as the Addiction Severity Index, American Society of Addiction Medicine Patient Placement Criteria, and others.

Nondiscrimination

Service cannot be denied to eligible clients because of their gender, race, ethnicity, nationality, sexual orientation, age, or physical characteristics. Neither can the quantity or quality of services vary according to any of these client characteristics. Note the word *eligible*. It is not discriminatory for an agency specializing in the treatment of addicted, pregnant women to refuse to treat a male, nor is it discriminatory for an agency to refuse to treat a child, where such specialized care is not within the scope of services provided by the agency.

Taking this a step further, some ethics guidelines state that a tendency to decline cases based on counselor bias and aversion to or anxiety about certain client types constitutes discrimination. Certainly indigent, home-less, and mentally ill chemical abusers tend to suffer from discrimination, which creates an army of unwanted clients and people who are not getting the help they need. There is a lack of training for health professionals in addictions intervention and referral skills; confrontation and intervention take more time and energy for these types of clients than may be avail-able to the professional with a large caseload. An old expression among physicians and nurses concerned with alcoholism is the *trash can syndrome*, an ironic reference to a derelict who was found out in back with the trash cans and subsequently treated for a host of ills directly or indirectly related to alcoholism, but never the alcoholism itself. Another expression for the undesirable or demented client is the *GOMER* ("Get Out of My Emergency Room").

Statutes of many states require agencies to accept and treat a number of indigent (nonpaying or charity care) clients. In such cases, it is discrimi-natory to set up a covert system whereby a referring agent must refer a certain number of paying clients for every nonpaying client.

Using the same logic, a caseload skewed toward types of clients from which the counselor derives the most personal satisfaction, or with whom he or she is most at ease, discriminates against others not in this category. This does not exclude an agency from assigning a counselor to work with a special population because he or she has the knowledge and skills required. For example, a Creole-speaking counselor may have a caseload primarily of Haitians.

It has become accepted among most helping professions that discrimi-nation and incompetence exist if a particular cultural or ethnic group is not being served because counselors lack cultural competency skills.

Objectivity

There is an incredibly wide range of opinion, theory, and belief in the addictions field, perhaps greater than in the treatment of nonaddictive disorders. The definition of addictions, beliefs as to the origin and course of addiction, and opinions as to how recovery is to be achieved inevitably vary among counselors and between counselor and client. While counselors need not hide their views, the counseling role is not to preach, lecture, convince, argue a position, or disparage the position of clients or other staff. Any of these stances disrespects the rights of others and is certainly a sidetrack from the counseling process. This is another gray area because, as Rhodes (1992, p. 43) remarks, clients may want help and guidance in an ethical exploration of their issues. The undersocialized client needs habilita-tion, and the sociopath requires treatment that includes development of a value system. A skilled, objective counselor can facilitate values clarification and development of an ethical system with clients without imposing his or her belief system or disparaging that of others.

ACTIVITY **Can't handle that God stuff**

Marcia, who comes from a Hasidic Jewish family and rebelled to marry a secular Jewish man, enters treatment under family pressure. She goes to a few AA meetings at the urging of her counselor, but feels she is being forced to go along with something she considers similar to her "repressive" family environment. "Another dogmatic in-group who only talk to themselves," is the way she puts it. She strongly declares her desire to recover from her alcoholism but does not want to be forced to go along with "the God thing."

DISCUSS:

- How would you approach Marcia?
- Are these religious issues or family issues?
- Would you address her issues about religion in a treatment plan? If so, how?
- Would forcing Marcia to attend AA meetings or denying her treatment be religious discrimination?
- Do you know anything about Hasidism?
- Would you need to know about Hasidism? Her family?
- Would it be ethical or appropriate to refer Marcia to another program or agency?

An Ethical Treatment System

It is important to identify systemic factors in ethical choices. The web of systemic influences (economic and regulatory systems, agency and societal cultures) reaches down to surround client and counselor, determining how policies and procedures are implemented in day-to-day counseling practice. An example is the screening function, which is supposedly an objective determination of appropriateness and eligibility for admission, but, distorted by market competition and managed-care constraints, stretches or even invents a diagnosis for mercenary or altruistic reasons. A more complex example is the apparent fact that a client cannot make sufficient progress in a particular setting. It is the ethical responsibility of the counselor and agency to terminate and/or transfer the client and to be knowledgeable about resources (NAADAC 2004). Or, within an agency, if a particular counselor is a bad match for the client, the client should be reassigned. All too often, however, clients are retained inappropriately. This situation may be caused by systemic factors such as the need to keep up client statistics as well as countertransference issues such as anxiety about appearing to be a failure, overinvolvement, and the need to play a rescuer role. Obviously, a great deal of honest, critical thinking is required to tease out the strands of influence. A climate of secrecy and denial, antithetical to a therapeutic environment, makes it unlikely that accurate assessment of agency practice or personal and professional growth will take place.

References

ACA (American Counseling Association). 1981. *Ethical Standards.* Alexandria, VA: Author.

Bissell, L., and J. E. Royce. 1994. *Ethics for Addiction Professionals,* 2nd ed. Center City, MN: Hazelden Foundation.

CSAT (Center for Substance Abuse Treatment). 2004. *The Confidentiality of Alcohol and Drug Abuse Patient Records Regulation and the HIPAA Privacy Rule—Implications for Alcohol and Substance Abuse Programs.* DHHS Publication no. SMA 05-4037, NCADI Publication No. PHD1083. Rockville, MD: Substance Abuse and Mental Health Services Administration, Center for Substance Abuse Treatment, U.S. Dept. of HHS.

————. 2006. *Addiction Counselor Competencies: The Knowledge, Skills, and Attitudes of Professional Practice, Revised Edition.* Technical Assistance Protocol Series 21. Rockville, MD: Substance Abuse and Mental Health Services Administration, U.S. Dept. of HHS.

Falvey, J. E., and T. E. Bray. 2001. *Managing Clinical Supervision: Ethical Practice and Legal Risk Management.* Pacific Grove, CA: Brooks-Cole.

Hoffman, J. 1994. "Faith in Confidentiality of Therapy Is Shaken." *New York Times,* 15 June, p. 1.

Hogan, D. B. 1978. *The Regulation of Psychotherapists, 3: A Review of Malpractice Suits in the United States.* Cambridge, MA: Ballinger.

Krystal, H., and R. A. Moore. 1963. Who is qualified to treat the alcoholic? A discussion. *Quarterly Journal of Studies on Alcohol* 24: 705–720.

Lemere, F. et al. 1964. Who is qualified to treat the alcoholic? Comment on the Krystal-Moore discussion. *Quarterly Journal of Studies on Alcohol* 25: 558–560.

Lewin, T. 1996. "Issues of Privacy Roil Arena of Psychotherapy." *New York Times,* 22 May, p.1/D20.

Lopez, F. 2002. Technical Assistance Publication 13 - Confidentiality of Patient Records for Alcohol and Other Drug Treatment. Rockville, MD: Center for Substance Abuse Treatment, Substance Abuse and Mental Health Services Administration, U.S. HHS.

Lowenberg, F., and R. Dolgoff. 1988. *Ethical Decisions for Social Work Practice,* 3rd ed. Itsaca, IL: Peacock.

Myers, P. 1990. Sources and configurations of institutional denial. *Employee Assistance Quarterly* 5(3): 43–54.

_____. 1991. "Cult and Cult-Like Pathways out of Adolescent Addiction," in *Special Problems in Adolescent Chemical Dependency*. E. E. Sweet, ed. New York: Haworth Press. (Orig. appeared in *Journal of Adolescent Chemical Dependency*, vol. 1 no. 4.)

NAADAC (The Association for Addiction Professionals). 2004. *Ethical Standards of Alcoholism and Drug Abuse Counselors*. Arlington, VA: Author.

NASW (National Association of Social Workers). 1980. *Code of Ethics of the National Association of Social Workers*. Silver Spring, MD: Author.

Pope, K. S., and V. A. Vetter. 1992. Ethical dilemmas encountered by members of the American Psychological Association. *American Psychologist* 47(3): 397–411.

Reed, T. J. 1996. The futile fifth step: Compulsory disclosure of confidential communications among Alcoholics Anonymous members. *Saint John's Law Review* (Fall 1996): 693–753.

Rhodes, M. L. 1992. Social work challenges: The boundaries of ethics. *Families in Society* 73(1): 40–47.

Scarf, M. 1996. "Keeping Secrets." *The New York Times Magazine*, 16 June.

Vermont Alcoholism Counselors Association, Inc. 1980. *Ethical Standards. Reprinted in Clinical Supervision: Skills for Substance Abuse Counselors*. D. J. Powell, ed. New York: Human Sciences Press.

White, W. L., and Popovits, R. M. 2004. *Critical Incidents*, 2nd ed. Bloomington, IL: Lighthouse Training Institute.

Co-Occurring Disorders

Objectives

At the end of this chapter, students will be able to:

1. Describe the extent of mental illness within the substance abuse population.
2. Explain the problems related to how clients' co-occurring disorders (COD) are often underserved.
3. List eight principles of Comprehensive Continuous Integrated System of Care (CCISC) of COD.
4. Describe the four quadrant model of categorizing severity of care for COD clients.
5. List at least eight of Mueser's twelve principles of care for COD clients.

6. Describe the unique aspects of the Wellness Recovery Action Plan (WRAP) approach.

7. List at least three psychiatric medications for treatment of mental illness in each category: antipsychotics, antidepressants, and antimanics.

8. List at least three *DSM-IV-TR* Axis I criteria for the diagnosis of schizophrenia.

9. List at least three *DSM-IV-TR* Axis I criteria for the diagnosis of major depression.

10. List at least three *DSM-IV-TR* Axis I criteria for the diagnosis of bipolar illness.

11. Describe at least five ways substance abuse and psychiatric symptoms can interact to cause diagnostic confusion and mislabeling.

12. List at least two *DSM-IV-TR* Axis II criteria for the diagnosis of antisocial personality disorder.

13. List at least two *DSM-IV-TR* Axis II criteria for the diagnosis of borderline personality disorder.

14. List at least two *DSM-IV-TR* Axis II criteria for the diagnosis of post-traumatic stress disorder.

15. List three major barriers to individuals with physical, cognitive, and sensory disabilities in receiving addiction treatment.

Introduction

One of the curiosities in the history of twentieth-century medicine was the separation of addiction and psychiatric disorders as fields of study and treatment. Contributing to this divide was that physicians found substance abusers difficult to treat, uncooperative, and unremunerative as well as the fact that addictions treatment began as an outgrowth of a grassroots self-help ideology. Those who qualified for diagnoses in both areas suffered from the division of thought and labor. Even today, training and education of mental health and addictions personnel often give short shrift to the other wing of the behavioral universe, although this situation is thankfully changing for the better.

The authors note emphatically that one chapter of a text cannot do justice to the development of all the knowledge and skills needed to provide services to individuals with severe mental illness and substance use disorders. Moreover, knowledge can swiftly go out of date as, for example, new medications are developed. Even the basic psychiatric reference work, the *Diagnostic and Statistical Manual of Mental Disorders*, fourth edition revised (*DSM-IV-TR*; APA 2000), will be replaced with a new edition,

the *DSM-5* in 2013 or 2014. Readers are advised to consult http://www
.dsm5.org to view the many proposed changes.

It is the norm, not the exception, that individuals with substance use
disorders have an additional mental health problem. According to surveys
done by the National Mental Health Association (2006), 52% of people
diagnosed with alcohol abuse or dependence also had a mental disorder
and 59% of those with other drug abuse problems also had a mental illness diagnosis. The National Alliance on Mental Illness (NAMI) (2011)
indicates similar prevalence data stating that 50% of individuals with
severe mental illness are affected by substance abuse and 37% of alcohol
abusers and 53% of drug users have a serious mental illness. Although
co-occurring disorder statistics and even treatment programs are usually
limited to those with so-called "severe mental illnesses," problems such as
obsessive-compulsive disorder, post-traumatic stress disorders, and panic
disorders can surely be severe, chronic, and debilitating, and many of these
individuals also have a substance use disorder. To confound our efforts at
coming up with an accurate picture, even individuals in substance abuse
treatment may have an undiagnosed, overlooked, or untreated psychiatric
problem, and those in mental health treatment are often unnoticed abusers
of psychoactive substances (Kivlahan et al. 1991).

The term *co-occurring disorder (COD)* to a large extent has replaced a
variety of acronyms to describe people with both psychiatric and chemical
use problems, which brought stigma to the labeled individual. In this
chapter CODs refer to such individuals. The old acronyms included:

- MICA = mentally ill chemical abuser
- MISA = mentally ill substance abuser
- MISU = mentally ill substance using
- CAMI = chemically abusing mentally ill
- SAMI = substance abusing mentally ill

The terms *dual disorder* and *dual diagnosis* are also seen as descriptors.

Among addicts with severe psychiatric disorders, there are higher
rates of suicide and suicidality, homelessness, legal and medical problems,
and longer and more frequent hospitalizations (Baker 1991). Because it
is uncommon for simultaneous and effective attention to be paid to all
of their many, varied, and complex needs (Cohen and Levy 1992), persons with CODs receive fewer services than other client populations in
proportion to their needs. Those who are diagnosed with CODs belong
to two stigmatized social categories. Until recently, they were underdiagnosed, undertreated, and often dumped from one system to another, or
discharged early from treatment as soon as they have been stabilized for
the moment. Their experience of treatment is less successful than that of

single-diagnosis clients. Until recently, when they did receive treatment for both psychiatric and addictive disorders, it was often sequential (first for one disorder, then the other) or parallel treatment (ping-pong style between units and services), rather than a single integrated model or facility.

In the 1990s the behavioral health field increasingly recognized and began to plan for integrated case management and treatment of COD clients (Baker 1991; Mueser et al. 1998). The degree to which treatment models are integrated, however, still varies greatly among states, counties, and municipalities. On the downside, cost-containment and managed-care trends tend to cause those with CODs to be released from the treatment system before sufficient time had elapsed to address or even properly assess their problems. Funding for inpatient treatment has been cut continuously since the 1960s without the provision of adequate community support systems. One and a quarter million mentally ill persons languish in prisons, and approximately one-half of prisoners have mental health problems. More disturbingly, these numbers quadrupled from 1998 to 2006 (Human Rights Watch 2006).

Integrated, Comprehensive Care Models

The Comprehensive Continuous Integrated System of Care (CCISC) model has been identified by SAMHSA as an exemplary practice (CSAT 2005) and has been implemented in an increasing number of states (Bachman and Duckworth 2003). As outlined by Kenneth Minkoff, a leader in integrative COD care (Minkoff and Cline 2004), the eight research- and consensus-derived principles that guide the implementation of the CCISC are:

1. Dual diagnosis is an expectation, not an exception.
2. The *four quadrant model* for categorizing persons with CODs according to high and low severity for CD (chemical dependency) and MH (mental health) are high-high (Quadrant IV), low MH-high CD (Quadrant III), high MH-low CD (Quadrant II), and low-low (Quadrant I). With high MH needs, integrated treatment takes place in the mental health system, but with relatively high chemical abuse problems it takes place within the addictions treatment system. (We add that the assigned quadrant can change in any direction as people improve or deteriorate in their psychiatric or substance using status ... the quadrants are best viewed as states, not traits!)
3. Empathic, hopeful, integrated treatment relationships are one of the most important contributors to treatment success in any setting.

4. Case management and care must be balanced with empathic detachment, expectation, contracting, consequences, and contingent learning for each client, and in each service setting.

5. When psychiatric and substance disorders coexist, both disorders should be considered primary, and integrated dual (or multiple) primary diagnosis-specific treatment is recommended.

6. Both mental illness and addiction can be treated within the philosophical framework of a "disease and recovery model" (25) with parallel phases of recovery (acute stabilization, motivational enhancement, active treatment, relapse prevention, and rehabilitation/recovery), in which interventions are not only diagnosis-specific but also specific to phase of recovery and stage of change.

7. There is no single correct intervention for COD; interventions must be individualized according to quadrant, diagnoses, level of functioning, external constraints or supports, and phase of recovery/stage of change.

8. Clinical outcomes for COD also must be individualized. Abstinence and full mental illness recovery are usually long-term goals, but short-term clinical outcomes must be individualized and may include reduction in symptoms or use of substances, increases in level of functioning, reduction in internal and external harm, and step-down in levels of care.[1]

Mueser and colleagues (2003, pp. 16–33) identify more principles of integrated treatment:

1. Shared decision-making among all stakeholders, including clients
2. The same clinicians providing both the mental health and the substance abuse treatment services
3. Residential support: safe, "dry" housing
4. Assertive community treatment, services delivered where clients are located
5. Vocational rehabilitation and supported employment
6. Family education
7. Social skills training
8. Stress management and coping skills training
9. Assertive case management, not waiting for clients to develop motivation and initiative, actively engaging reluctant individuals
10. Peer and self-help group involvement
11. Medication management and psychoeducational services concerning medications and medication side-effects
12. Alternative recreational activities

[1]Adapted from Minkoff and Cline (2004).

NASADAD (the National Association of State Alcohol and Drug Abuse Directors) is cooperating with the NASMHPD (National Association of State Mental Health Programs Directors) to foster collaborative, integrative treatment efforts.

Contingency management (CM) techniques are a useful component of COD treatment plans. CM is a system of positive and negative consequences that address specific target behaviors. It is based on simple behavioral conditioning familiar to students in Psych 101 as positive and negative reinforcement. Clinic attendance, medication adherence, and following simple behavioral prescriptions (such as personal hygiene) can be reinforced with cash, vouchers, prizes, retail items, and privileges such as flexibility in methadone dosing or passes. The system must be crystal clear and based on a behavioral contract with time limitations. The contract should be subject to review to keep it realistic and up to date (CSAT 2005, pp. 122–123).

As with all clients, treatment goals need to be broken down into clear and measurable outcomes, such as (Mueser and colleagues 2003, p. 79):

- Goal: Improved skills for making friends and meeting people. Objective: Client initiates at least three conversations per week including one in a new place.
- Goal: Developing alternative recreational activity.
- Objective: Client tries one new recreational activity per week and two old activities.

Wellness Recovery Action Plan

Mary Ellen Copeland (2002) developed a down to earth, concrete, and easy to follow set of tools and actions to facilitate recovery from CODs. This includes:

- Good medical care for physical problems
- Self-advocacy skills
- Medication management habits for clients
- Relaxation exercises
- A clear, posted crisis plan that involves
  - Monitoring for crisis triggers
  - Monitoring the level of stimulation in the environment and making sure it is not too high or too low
  - Links to support individuals
  - Instructions to caregivers
  - A suicide prevention plan
- Post-crisis planning
- Ongoing peer support

More details along with guidelines for copyrighted use of handouts are available at http://www.mentalhealthrecovery.com/wrap/wellness-recovery.php. Concise descriptions of specific programs that utilize the Wellness Recovery Action Plan (WRAP) perspective are at http://www.mentalhealthrecovery.com/wrap/program-descriptions.php.

Myriads of Dual Diagnoses

Given the range and severity both of addictive and psychiatric phenomena, there are a near-infinite variety of combined syndromes. In terms of the primacy of addiction or psychiatric illness, they range from those who suffer primarily from psychiatric disorders and who "self-medicate" with alcohol or illegal drugs, through complex cases in which psychiatric and addictive symptoms are hard to tease apart, to addicts whose chemical use causes organic brain syndromes such as stimulant psychoses, alcoholic hallucinosis, or psychotic conditions associated with the use of hallucinogens.

It is almost always the case that unless the chemical-dependency counselor is also credentialed in psychiatric social work, psychiatric nursing, or psychology, he or she is expressly denied the role of diagnosing a client. Nevertheless, because the counselor must treat the chemical abuse and dependency of persons suffering from other psychiatric conditions, he or she must be aware of behavior that suggests a serious psychiatric disorder in order to alert the agency to the necessity of psychiatric consultation.

Issues of Medication

Because the counselor may be counseling clients who are taking medications prescribed for psychiatric conditions, he or she must be familiar with the categories and names of commonly prescribed medications. It is important to distinguish antipsychotic, antimanic, or antidepressant medications from drugs of abuse. Although some "garbage head" abusers or experimenting teenagers might take a Prozac or a Haldol, drugs in these categories are rarely abused. Some recovering persons distrust psychiatric medications for a variety of reasons: they have been misdiagnosed as psychotic and misprescribed these medications; they have been given major tranquilizers as a behavioral control strategy (e.g., in prison); they have a drug-free philosophy; or the medications have undesirable side effects. Yet these drugs are frequently lifesavers, and they permit the social integration of the severely disabled.

A complete and up-to-date guide to psychotherapeutic medications may be downloaded for free from the Mid America Addiction Technology Transfer Center (ATTC 2011).

Diagnostic Issues

Clients arrive for treatment with any of a number of prior diagnoses, usually according to the categorization system in the *DSM-IV-TR* (APA 2000).

The *DSM-IV-TR* is a multicommittee attempt at comprehensive categorization or taxonomy of mental disorders. It is a guide to systematic diagnosis and classification of clients. It does not pretend to substitute for, nor does it espouse a theory of, mental disorders. It does not explain why someone is schizophrenic, or kleptomaniac, or attention-deficited. The categories are not "basic" underlying conditions, but terms found useful over the years that have some discrete validity about them in that they describe recurring clusters of symptoms. Some diagnoses may be symptoms of others, or they may be ideal types rarely found in nature. Some are more discrete than others: The disorganized schizophrenic or the bipolar mood disorder are fairly clear biologically based brain disorders, almost as obvious as strep throat or a broken leg. Why someone is a "pathological gambler" or an "avoidant personality" is less clear and perhaps reflective of some deeper, as yet unfathomed syndrome or imbalance. As we go to press with this edition, task forces are still struggling with these issues (see http://www.dsm5.org).

Misdiagnosis can occur in psychiatry even without the complicating factors of addiction. In a survey of bipolar members of a national support organization for depressive and manic-depressive patients (Lish et al. 1994), three-quarters of respondents stated it had taken an average of eight years to get a correct diagnosis. The similarities of psychiatric and addictive phenomena outlined in Table 9.1, the fragmentation of the behavioral health fields, and the spotty interaction of COD clients with the healthcare system make it all but inevitable that COD clients will be underdiagnosed and misdiagnosed. To establish a valid psychiatric diagnosis, the symptoms must manifest long after intoxication has abated.

Alcohol and other drug abuse (AODA) and psychiatric symptoms (PS) can interact in the following ways:

1. AODA may prompt the emergence or re-emergence of PS.
2. AODA may worsen pre-existing PS.
3. AODA may ameliorate, dampen, hide, mask, or disguise PS.
4. AODA may mimic PS.

Table 9.1 Similarities of Addictive and Psychiatric Phenomena

Drug Syndromes	can be confused with	Psychiatric Syndromes
High dosage amphetamines		Paranoid schizophrenia
Chronic cocaine use		Paranoid schizophrenia
Cocaine withdrawal		Major depression
PCP overdose		Schizophrenia
Cocaine intoxication		Mania

5. Cessation of AODA following development of tolerance or dependence results in a withdrawal syndrome that may mimic psychiatric symptoms.

6. PS must be distinguished from denial, resistance, and lack of motivation associated with AODA.

7. PS increases the risk of AODA.

8. Side effects of antipsychotic medications (i.e., sedation, involuntary physical movements) may be mistaken for symptoms of either PS or AODA.

9. Relative primacy and severity of PS and AODA symptoms may wax and wane, diminish, or re-emerge. Case management functions such as screening, assessment, and treatment planning are ongoing with COD clients.

For example, one cannot take as evidence of psychosis the paranoia of an active crack addict, the hallucinations of an active lysergic acid diethylamide (LSD) or phencyclidine (PCP) user, or the fevered imaginings of a client in the throes of delirium tremens. In 1987 such misdiagnoses resulted in an inpatient psychiatric unit in Brooklyn, New York, being filled with more "paranoid schizophrenics" than might be found in the state of Texas. This was due to the newness of crack cocaine, which was epidemic at the time, and the unfamiliarity with the symptoms of acute cocaine intoxication and abuse by psychiatric staff who had been trained abroad.

A factor that confounds assessment is that in those with CODs, substance use may mask pathology, numb its sharpest points, exacerbate it, or simultaneously improve and worsen different symptoms. Depressants blunt the mania of the bipolar client but drive the depressed deeper down. Alcohol or marijuana is the drug of choice of some schizophrenics. Marijuana soothes anxieties and holds demons at bay, without the agitation of alcoholic hangovers and withdrawal; yet alcohol and marijuana make cognition and memory all the more fuzzy. Crack and "angel dust" (PCP) are the absolutely worst things for schizophrenic, paranoid, and violence-prone people. Within the COD treatment community, there is considerable controversy about how long to wait with a clean-and-sober client in order to determine whether his or her symptoms constitute a "real" psychiatric problem (Evans and Sullivan 1990, pp. 58–59). With today's short-term treatment limits, it may be next to impossible to make such a determination.

The COD client population presents several specific treatment problems:

- Instead of feeling better after detoxification, as the nonpsychiatric alcoholic does, the self-medicating COD client may feel the full force of his or her schizophrenia, PTSD, or other symptoms.

- A COD client may focus on psychiatric problems while in addictions treatment, but may explain his or her problems in terms of drugs while with the mental health professional. With such interchangeable or free-floating denial, both conditions may be denied (Doweiko 1997, p. 275).
- To the COD client, chemical use can be the means of coping with a devastating mental affliction. Chemicals seem to provide some sense of control, even though the underlying syndrome is not addressed or is worsened. Counselors must recognize and empathetically reflect these motives if a treatment alliance is to be made.
- Most categories of COD are quite fragile; traditional confrontational methods would not be appropriate (Evans and Sullivan 1990, p. 30).
- With high mental health needs, the COD client can be assumed to have major life problems such as criminal justice involvements, homelessness, and poor physical health. These must be addressed early in treatment, or the client will be overwhelmed and devastated by life problems that will preclude engagement in treatment. The COD client is also more likely than the standard substance abuse client to be involved in many systems yet fall through the cracks. Therefore comprehensive services which provide continuity of care are needed (CSAT 2005, pp. 39, 47).
- The COD client suffers from multiple stigmata, which he/she has likely internalized into a helpless, hopeless, and self-loathing persona. The client is also likely to be isolated and socially disengaged. The therapeutic relationship with the counselor, perhaps the only stable and/or healthy relationship the client has ever known, will be central to any measure of recovery.
- Treatment staff is pessimistic about the chances of a deteriorated and decompensated COD client to ever get better.

Schizophrenia

Schizophrenia is a biologically based brain disorder. Like cancer, it is not just one well-defined disease. Schizophrenia results from some combination of inherited neurological vulnerability, and any of a number of external risk factors, including some in utero (usually second-trimester) environmental stressors (Andreasen 1999).

Identical (monozygotic) twins have a concordance rate of 30% to 50% for schizophrenia. This shows that schizophrenia is in part based on an inherited predisposition or vulnerability. Starting in the late 1980s, structural differences in the brains of schizophrenics were demonstrated. These observations also applied to twin studies. That is, where one identical twin is schizophrenic, there are significant differences in the brain structures of the two (Andreasen et al. 1990; Barta et al. 1990; Shenton et al. 1992; Suddath et al. 1990), and there are even subtle differences in fingerprints (Mellor 1992). Recently, the Salk Institute for Biological Studies (Brennand et al. 2011; Calloway 2011; Salk Institute 2011) grew stem cells of schizophrenics into neurons and found that they didn't connect normally, although the antipsychotic drug loxapine seemed to help reverse that effect. However, if schizophrenia was based totally on genetics, identical twins would always both be schizophrenic, or not. Family history is probably a necessary factor in a majority of cases, but it is not a sufficient explanation. A variety of pregnancy, delivery, and perinatal problems also have been implicated, which may include nutritional problems and viruses. A greater incidence of schizophrenia has been found in influenza epidemics, even among those without a family history of schizophrenia (O'Callaghan, Gibson, et al. 1991; O'Callaghan, Sham, et al. 1991). Schizophrenia, then, is a neurodevelopmental disorder with variations in etiology to the extent that genetics or environmental insults are involved.

Schizophrenia has an age of onset usually between 16 and 23 years. The major symptoms of schizophrenia include:

- *Delusions* (distortions of inferential thinking). One common set of delusions is those in which unrealistic associations are made between events in the world and the client. An example might be that a person seen on television is perceived to be talking to or about the schizophrenic client. Such delusions are called *ideas of reference.* They include but are not limited to paranoid persecutorial delusions.
- *Hallucinations* (major perceptual distortions), which are more likely to be auditory than visual in schizophrenic patients.
- *Disorganized speech, thought, and behavior.*
- *Flat affect* (restricted range and intensity of emotional expression); affect that is incongruous to the situation, and apathy or avolition.
- *Other neurocognitive deficits* such as difficulty in concentrating, sensory overload, and difficulty in sorting, integrating, organizing, and responding to sensations and information.

Schizophrenia is *not* caused by bad parenting, disordered family communication, or mothers who send double messages. Family members of schizophrenics have no more role in creating this disease than they do in cases of multiple sclerosis or Alzheimer's disease among their relatives. Neither is it caused by the surfacing of unconscious and unbearable thoughts or feelings, the alienation of modern society, or traumatic losses. Finally, abuse of alcohol or other drugs can cause any number of emotional or mental problems, but not schizophrenia proper.

The treatment of schizophrenia involves antipsychotic medications (also known as neuroleptics or major tranquilizers), which can reduce greatly the severity of psychotic symptoms such as hallucinations and bizarre behavior. Medications do not cure this brain disease, and some have side effects such as tremors, twitching, and tics. Psychiatrists call such behaviors *extrapyramidal symptoms.*

In addition to medication, schizophrenic COD clients and their families require education on the nature of their conditions as well as supportive case management, which may include monitoring medications, supportive group apartment programs, day treatment programs, occupational training, and programs to train clients in activities of daily living. Formulating or carrying out a treatment plan with a disorganized addicted schizophrenic is obviously more difficult than with ordinary addicts.

Confrontive treatment and "tough-love" forms of intervention are not recommended for persons with serious mental illness (Loneck and Way 1997). The simple and concrete nature of twelve-step slogans and suggestions, and the nonconfrontive and nonjudgmental quality of Alcoholics Anonymous and Narcotics Anonymous, make these groups a congenial environment for many COD clients, as does motivational enhancement therapy. Supportive group therapy and topical groups that focus on medication or daily living skills are also useful components of a COD program. However, not all AA/NA members and groups are sophisticated as to the necessity for antipsychotic medications. In some areas, specialized "double-trouble" groups exist, such as Dual Diagnosis Anonymous and Dual Recovery groups. Meetings can be easily located via utilization of a search engine.

Asher and Gask (2010) published an interesting set of interviews with homeless, substance abusing schizophrenics to gain insight into their varied motives for using. A link to the complete manuscript is provided in the bibliography.

Mood Disorders

The two overall categories of mood disorders are depression and bipolar disorder (manic-depression), which manifest in unusual swings or fluctuations between extremes of mood. Depression must be differentiated from simple exhaustion, normal grief, thyroid disease, dementias, and the "crash" at the end of a stimulant "binge." Although depression itself is broken down into dysthymia (formerly neurotic depression), which is the relatively mild variety, and major depression, there is a continuum of pathology, the true nature of which may be masked or exaggerated when presented to a counseling professional. Depression is a complex

Table 9.2 Depressive Thinking Patterns

Dichotomous thinking such as "all-or-none" self-statements
Awfulizing or catastrophizing
Jumping to conclusions, especially negative extrapolations and expectations
"Should" or "must" statements, demandingness
Self-referential, guilty, codependent thinking
Feeling helpless, powerless
Believing that one cannot tolerate frustrations, anxieties, or pain
Overgeneralizing about failures

Source: Summarized from the work of Aaron Beck, Albert Ellis, and others.

phenomenon, and each depressed client probably suffers from a unique mix of etiological variables, which may include:

- Biochemical predisposition, which often has a genetic basis
- Biological stressors such as fatigue and pain
- Cognitive and behavioral factors such as lack of self-efficacy, learned helplessness, and problematic thinking patterns and beliefs (Table 9.2)
- Unresolved, impacted grief and anger
- Interpersonal factors such as lack of support systems and poor interpersonal skills, which lead to isolation
- Depressants such as alcohol, barbiturates, or benzodiazepines

Antidepressant medications are often successful in the alleviation of severe depression. These medications are not stimulants and may require several weeks to take effect. The client also may require trials of various antidepressants before the most efficacious drug is identified. The vast majority of individuals treated for severe depression is now prescribed medications belonging to the SSRI category (see Table 9.1). Varieties of talk therapy are also helpful in the resolution of emotional, cognitive, and behavioral aspects of depression.

Bipolar (manic-depressive) affective disorder is based on one or more biochemical vulnerabilities and can be triggered by trauma, substance abuse, fatigue, or stress. In the manic phase of the disorder, thoughts race and tend toward grandiosity, behavior is reckless, and energy is boundless. Sooner or later the patient "crashes" into a phase of depression. There are several subtypes of bipolar disorder with which the counselor should become acquainted. At least one-half of people with this disorder go on to substance abuse syndromes and are at great risk for suicidal attempts. The simple chemical lithium carbonate enables many to stabilize their mood swings, as do a number of medications first used as anticonvulsants.

Persons with co-occurring bipolar disorder and substance use disorders are at great danger for overdose and death. Singers Janis Joplin and Amy Winehouse are but two examples of persons who succumbed at an early age to this combination. Bipolar disorders together with stimulant abuse are tricky to diagnose accurately. While bipolar disorder is typically under-diagnosed or misdiagnosed in the general population, it can be overdiag-nosed among stimulant misusers (Goldberg et al. 2008)

Case in Point
Ups and Downs

Mr. K., an adjunct professor and counselor at a community college, burst into an office, perched on a desk, and began to demonstrate his karate techniques. He described his plans to enroll in medical as well as law school, and he described his activities as a director of motion pictures. Two weeks later, his demeanor was totally different: His speech was slowed, his affect dejected, and his gaze averted. Mr. K. was put on medical leave and suc-cessfully referred into psychiatric treatment. He was correctly diagnosed as having bipolar mood disorder. His mood was stabilized through a course of lithium carbonate, and he returned to work in three months. His medica-tion (lithium carbonate) is monitored carefully because it has a very narrow therapeutic index; that is, it has a small window between ineffective and toxic. He also attends a support group for people who have bipolar disorder.

Personality Disorders

Chemical abusers often have diagnoses that fit the category of personality disorders (formerly called character disorders). In the listing of diagnoses in the *DSM-IV-TR*, personality disorders are coded separately as Axis II, as if they are on a separate dimension. In view of spatial limitations, this discussion addresses only the most common personality disorders diagnosed among chemical abusers: antisocial personality disorder (ASPD) and border-line personality disorder (BPD). Readers are advised to study the proposed changes in the classification of personality disorders in the forthcoming *DSM-5*, which cut down the number of such disorders from ten to five and emphasizes personality disorders as states rather than permanent traits, as well as how individuals may vary in the degree to which they are, say, impul-sive or sociopathic, along dimensional scales (see http://www.dsm5.org).

Antisocial Personality Disorder

Antisocial personality disorder (ASPD; *DSM-IV-TR* 301.7), also referred to as *sociopathy*, may be diagnosed only in individuals who are at least 18 years old, who manifest a "pervasive pattern of disregard for and violations of the rights of others, as indicated by three or more of the following: unlawful behaviors, deceitfulness, impulsivity, irritability and aggressiveness, reckless disregard for safety, consistent irresponsibility, lack of remorse" (APA 2000, p. 706). Addict sociopathy is a complex phenomenon, and the diagnosis of addicts as sociopaths raises more issues than it settles (Gerstley et al. 1990). It is important to avoid describing social problems in psychiatric terms. Clients who grew up in addictive family environments probably lacked proper role-models and had inadequate or abusive parenting, and thus are insufficiently socialized or habilitated. Others turn to crime for lack of job skills or economic opportunity. Addicts especially may be incapable of sustaining regular employment and may turn to criminal behavior to raise funds for survival needs and drugs. Other addicts participate in fighting, vandalism, stealing, and unwanted sexual behavior while intoxicated, which also can appear as antisocial behavior.

A quarter century ago, addictions researcher Marc Schuckit differentiated sociopathy proper, which precedes alcoholism, from "secondary sociopathy" of the alcoholic (Schuckit 1973). The *DSM-IV-TR* offers guidelines on this issue of differential diagnosis, stating that the diagnosis of ASPD is not made unless signs were also present in childhood. It also states that the diagnosis may be misapplied to urban settings where "seemingly antisocial behavior may be part of a protective survival strategy" (647). However, if both substance abuse and antisocial behavior began in childhood, the client may be diagnosed as suffering from both a substance-related disorder and an antisocial personality disorder, "even though some antisocial acts may be a consequence of the substance-related disorder" (pp. 648–649). To complicate the picture, both sociopathy and substance abuse are linked to other disorders. It is mentioned, almost as an aside, that the likelihood of developing ASPD is increased when there is early onset of attention-deficit hyperactivity disorder (ADHD; p. 647). Many individuals who have ADHD and/or periodic depression find it difficult to attain or sustain employment and drift into extralegal or manipulative means of survival. Such individuals are also at risk for substance abuse disorders.

Counselors should pay attention to one of the trademark features of the true, early onset sociopath: "lack of remorse, as indicated by being indifferent to or rationalizing having hurt, mistreated, or stolen from another" (APA 2000, p. 706). People who have ADHD and/or are substance abusers who act in ways verging on the sociopathic are less likely than a true sociopath to be conscienceless about predation against members of their families. Crack addicts are portrayed in the media as engaging in horrific abuse and neglect of their own families, yet numerous recovering crack cocaine addicts are truly remorseful about the effects of their addictions on their families. Also, some professionals falsely assume that a client who has multiple convictions or who has been incarcerated for long periods of time is a hardened sociopath not amenable to treatment for personality disorder. Yet many clients, once freed from the matrix of extralegal economic systems, subcultures of drug abuse, and the prison environment, are rehabilitated in offender programs within a frame of time that suggests that their core personality traits are not those of a basic sociopath.

One with a true antisocial personality is difficult to engage in chemical dependency treatment. He or she is likely to feign insight and personal change to escape sanctions and mandates of the criminal justice system. Group treatment and therapeutic milieu (e.g., application of the therapeutic community model to addicted offenders) are more likely to address underlying sociopathy than is individual counseling.

Borderline Personality Disorder

In popular parlance, "borderline" often refers to being on the edge of insanity. But the client's borderline personality disorder (BPD) is not defined by a point on a continuum from normality to insanity or from neurosis to psychosis; her or his disorder is a separate entity entirely. Most BPD clients represent a "stable instability," a severe disturbance in personality development and integration with a distinct cluster of symptoms. The BPD client shows instability, rapid changes, and extremes in relationships, moods, attitudes, and behavior and decision making, including impulsive self-destructive, and destructive behaviors. Many authors and schools of thought have contended with the borderline personality; in the universe of possibilities, each major author has delimited a slightly, or more than slightly, different subset of the psychiatrically disordered (Stone 1986, p. 492).

According to the *DSM-IV-TR*, borderline personality disorder (301.83) is marked by a "pervasive pattern of interpersonal relationships, self-image, and affects, and marked impulsivity" (APA 2000, p. 650). Clients with borderline personality disorders are intense and unstable. They also have sudden, dramatic, or impulsive shifts in occupational or educational goals. Clients with BPD often engage in impulsive, dangerous behaviors in the areas of sexuality, substance abuse, and suicidality. Persons with BPD and chemical abuse vary tremendously along the Global Assessment of Functioning (GAF) scale (O'Connell 1988), ranging from those with stable jobs and relationships to those who are severely self-destructive and who have psychotic episodes, often triggered by substance abuse, that require hospitalizations. Although severe BPD can be associated with self-harm, it is an error to assume that most teenagers who exhibit "cutting" behavior are diagnosable as being true BPDs.

According to the neopsychoanalytic object-relations theorist Otto Kernberg (1975), the client with BPD "splits" contradictory ego states:

He or she may seem to like and idealize someone one day, but hate and devalue the same person the next day. To make this work, the client also uses the mechanism of denial, manifesting an "emotional amnesia" about the preceding attitude or feeling. The client may switch from the "all-good" evaluation to the "all-bad" one when an individual cannot meet all of his or her considerable needs.

Many modern psychiatric authorities agree that BPD has no single origin (Gabbard 1995). Some researchers (Akiskal et al. 1986) have concluded that the preponderance of biologically based problems among borderline diagnoses (affective disorders, attention deficit, substance abuse) warrant removing it from the realm of "personality" problems and the *DSM-IV-TR* Axis II. Still, despite its origins, it describes a type or level of personality functioning familiar to many clinicians.

There are a variety of possibilities to consider when confronted with a diagnosis of borderline personality disorder. The borderline personality can be an adaptation to any combination of mood disorder, ADHD, or chemical dependency. Chemical dependency (CD) can appear as a borderline personality disorder. Alcoholic mood swings, alcoholic amnesia, "blackouts," impulsive behavior while intoxicated, and massive use of denial and confabulation to construct an account of this chaotic, out-of-control situation can present a clinical picture not unlike that described as BPD. At the very least, BPD can contribute to chemical abuse and dependency as a result of the need to self-medicate, relax, and numb pain.

Many problems of clients with BPD may be symptoms of mood disorders. People who are depressed may manifest extreme irritability and flashes of hostility, coloring of thought, rationalizing, or confabulating. Clients may also receive a diagnosis of major depression or dysthymia on Axis I and a diagnosis of BPD on Axis II, and be intricately bound up with chemical use and abuse as well.

Chemical abuse can be a "keystone" in the archway of borderline personality. Sobriety can afford the opportunity to grow and heal. Indeed, to avoid relapse, clients and counselors must address previously masked, powerful emotions, painful anxieties, and conflicts.

Post-Traumatic Stress Disorder

For more than a century, it has been observed that severe trauma (e.g., a train wreck, a wartime massacre, rape, child neglect, spousal abuse) can take its toll in ways that persist long after the event (Young 1995). The combined result has been named post-traumatic stress disorder (PTSD). The major symptom clusters of PTSD involve re-experiencing the trauma (sometimes called *flashbacks*), persistent arousal (e.g., insomnia, rage, hypervigilance, startle response), and numbing, avoidance, and detachment (APA

2000, pp. 467–468). In addition to experiential causes, a neurobiological basis for PTSD has been described (Krystal et al. 1991; van der Kolk 1991).

Many major theoretical writings on PTSD do not delve into its connections with abuse of alcohol or other drugs. Nevertheless, the two conditions often coexist; sufferers of both have the need to calm or numb themselves (Bremner et al. 1996). Some treatment programs that do deal with both conditions switch addicted PTSD clients from their drugs of choice to legal, prescribed medications such as the benzodiazepines (if these are not already their drug of choice), then wean them off medications as anxiety abates in treatment. Although the classic PTSD client is a veteran, many other populations suffer. For example, a large proportion of addicted prostitutes suffer from PTSD, being victims of rape and violence perpetrated by clients as well as pimps. Judith Herman (1992) thinks that PTSD underlies many other conditions, such as the borderline personality. Others (Young 1995) caution against overdiagnosing the disorder.

Given the large proportion of women in addictions treatment who have experienced trauma and abuse, formal trauma training of staff should supplement standard addictions credentialing (Harris and Fallot 2001). Treatment inevitably will bring out repressed feelings and memories of trauma, and it is best to create a therapeutic environment that doesn't suddenly flood the client with overwhelming affects, which can cause premature termination.

Attention-Deficit Hyperactivity Disorder

Attention-deficit hyperactivity disorder (ADHD) is a genetically based neurological disability. Although it is thought of as a childhood learning disability, it affects many aspects of functioning and often persists in some form into adulthood. ADHD is marked by inattention, disorganization, distractibility, impulsivity, and inability to concentrate, sustain, and follow through on efforts. There also may be motor hyperactivity and "fidgetiness" (APA 2000, pp. 92–93), which are really less of a disability than the other features. Although ADHD varies in its severity, it often results in impaired educational and career efforts (Kelly and Raimundo 1995; Wender 1986). This, together with the relationship problems and social rejection experienced by many ADHD sufferers, may result in depression and self-esteem and self-efficacy problems—typical risk factors for chemical abuse (Biederman et al. 1995; Horner and Scheibe 1997). Added to this is the need to damp down (i.e., self-medicate) "high-strung," frustration-intolerant, hot-tempered, anxious, and sometimes insomniac temperamental qualities.

A majority of clients with ADHD report some, even significant, help from medications, including (paradoxically) stimulants such as Ritalin (methylphenidate) and antidepressants such as Norpramin (desipramine).

Support groups are often beneficial. Clients with ADHD badly need to learn about their condition in order to reduce guilt and shame, learn drug-free coping strategies, and educate their families, teachers, and peers.

The client with ADHD often has a history of chaotic and unstable relationships, which were based on impulsivity and mood swings. In addition, having experienced pervasive relationship failures, even including childhood scapegoating, rejection, and abuse, the ADHD client may be tremendously ambivalent about relationships. This is reminiscent of the borderline personality discussed earlier, which makes diagnosis challenging. When the individual is also a chemical abuser, it may be difficult indeed to untangle the skein of behaviors.

There is tremendous variation in approaches to diagnosis of ADHD. In some areas it appears that ADHD is underdiagnosed, yet parent groups in some parts of the United States claim that ADHD is overdiagnosed and that stimulant medications are overprescribed. Addictions educators occasionally encounter bright, recovering students with undiagnosed ADHD or other learning disabilities.

COD clients can and do recover. Psychotropics can stabilize the client's mental health issues, and the tools of addictions counseling can aid the recovery from chemical dependency. In our teaching venues, we have had the pleasure of having graduates of COD programs who were assuming counseling roles. To be sure, these were individuals whose mental health issues were those of mood disorders, not pervasive sociopathy or severe disorganized schizophrenia. Some downloadable resources on co-occurring disorders from the Substance Abuse and Mental Health Services Administration are available at http://store.samhsa.gov/product/SMA08-4367 and http://www.samhsa.gov/co-occurring.

Disabilities and Addiction

Imagine:

- Being deaf but assigned to a treatment program where no one uses or interprets American Sign Language
- Being rejected from a residential treatment program because they can't accommodate your wheelchair or provide you with assistance getting into bed
- Being blind and in a treatment program where there are no Braille or audio materials for you to learn about addiction or participate in treatment planning

Estimates of how many Americans have a disability depend on the varying definitions of disability. One estimate by the U.S. Census (1997) is that one in five have some form of disability, and one in ten have a severe disability. This includes a wide range of citizens whose physical, sensory, or cognitive impairments limit one or more major life activities. Physical disabilities include, but are not limited to, spinal cord injury, cerebral palsy, multiple sclerosis, amputation, spina bifida, and arthritis. Sensory disabilities include being deaf, hard of hearing, blind, or visually impaired. Cognitive disabilities are associated with mental retardation and fetal alcohol syndrome as well as traumatic brain injury or stroke.

The disabled have a much higher prevalence of addiction than the general population (CSAT 1998). Many studies indicate that 20% or more of persons qualifying for state vocational rehabilitation services systems have symptoms of a DSM-IV-TR substance-dependence diagnosis (Buss and Cramer 1989). In a review of the literature, Amos Sales (2005) indicated that individuals with a disability are more likely to have a substance abuse problem yet are less likely to get treatment. There are several reasons for the higher prevalence: disabilities as a result of an accident involving drug and alcohol use, such as spinal cord injury or traumatic brain injuries. These accidents may well have been a consequence of substance abuse that goes undetected. People with disabilities often have more access to drugs that they may become dependent on. People with disabilities may suffer isolation and discrimination, feel stigmatized, and be under- or unemployed. People with disabilities often experience periods of depression, anger, guilt, grief, social isolation, and physical pain that they may self-medicate with alcohol or other drugs (CPNJ 1998).

People with CODs and substance abuse problems often do not receive adequate access to and accommodation for substance abuse treatment. There are at least three major reasons for this:

1. *Barriers that the addiction treatment system creates for people with disabilities.* Barriers can be physical, communication, and/or attitudinal. Physical barriers may be stairs, small doorways, or lack of handicapped bathrooms. Communication barriers include failure to provide interpreter service or other communication assistance devices necessary for people who are deaf, hard of hearing, or blind. Attitudinal barriers are the result of stereotyping and misguided beliefs about people with disabilities: Some staff assume that people with disabilities don't use or abuse alcohol and drugs. Others chalk up a client's inability to meet treatment protocols to lack of motivation or unwillingness to invest in treatment. Some also fear that a person with a disability will make others in treatment uncomfortable, or they think that serving a person with a disability is too expensive or will cause extreme programmatic changes. It is true that

some accommodations and some investment in time and funds are necessary, but they are generally more reasonable and less extreme than is often believed (CPNJ 1998).

2. *Family, friends, and disability service providers often fail to intervene with a person who is abusing drugs and/or alcohol.* They may believe the person is already stigmatized with their disability; service providers may not understand the progressive nature of addiction and the potential harm it can do to family, friends, or clients; or some may assume that the use is acceptable and reasonable given the life circumstances of the client. Disability service providers may feel uncomfortable in intervening with their clients and lack awareness of the services available for prevention, intervention, and treatment.

3. *Failure to complete treatment.* There are many people with "hidden" disabilities who become treatment failures because the disability goes unrecognized and appropriate accommodations in treatment methods are not made. A client may be cognitively impaired and fail to comprehend the materials used in treatment, or a person may have a visual or hearing problem that requires that he or she be close to the front of the room or utilize devices designed to enhance his or her visual or auditory acuity. There are many such examples in which increased awareness and willingness to address these impairments would improve treatment outcomes.

What can be done to improve the access and completion of appropriate treatment for addicted clients with disabilities?

- There must be greater advocacy for clients with disabilities.
- Addiction treatment programs must work toward becoming compliant with the Americans with Disabilities Act (for a description of the American Disabilities Act and the agencies and programs that need to be in compliance, see http://www.ada.gov/pubs/ada.htm).
- Addiction treatment administrators need to develop policies and procedures that contain statements of nondiscrimination, describe methods of accommodation, and promote significant training for their staff.
- Addiction treatment professionals need to increase their sensitivity and awareness to the specific needs of and resources for clients with disabilities.
- Disability service providers need to increase their awareness of signs and symptoms of substance abuse, effective intervention methods, and addiction treatment resources.

ACTIVITY (9.1) **Identifying disability issues and barriers**

CASE STUDY: JOHN

Background information: John is a 35-year-old married male. At age 17, John had a job delivering propane tanks. One day he did not carefully attach a tank to the truck, and the resultant explosion tossed John up into the air, causing him to land on his back, which resulted in a spinal cord injury that paralyzed him from the waist down. John received a large monetary settlement for his accident and bought himself a house. He married at 26. John knows he should be getting new skills to make a living and get a new job, but has been discouraged and demoralized. He has been spending down the settlement money with drugs and partying.

Substance Abuse History: There is no history of substance abuse in John's family. John began drinking at the age of 12 and was drinking regularly by the age of 15. He was a star athlete in high school and was drinking and doing drugs when there were no games scheduled. Because John did not abuse drugs during sports, the school did not recognize his problem. After the accident, John became bitter and angry. In spite of friends bringing drugs during his stint in physical rehab, no one in the rehabilitation facility addressed his drug and alcohol use with him. He resisted rehabilitation and "with nothing to do," increased his drug and alcohol use.

Present Situation: John's parents were originally supportive of his lifestyle but now realize that he needs help. At the insistence of his parents and his wife, he has come to an outpatient mental health and drug abuse clinic for help. You are the clinician he will be seeing.

QUESTIONS:
- What are treatment issues that need to be explored with John?
- What might be the barriers to John getting the help he needs?
- What can be done to ensure access and accommodation for treatment services for John?
- What are John's long-term needs, and what resources and/or agencies can be mobilized to meet them?

CASE STUDY: SHARON

Background information: Sharon is a 29-year-old single female born with a hearing deficit, a result of her mother's bout with rubella during her pregnancy with Sharon. When Sharon was 7 years old, her parents separated. Her father continued to maintain contact with her and her brother. Sharon recalls her mother being abusive verbally, physically, and emotionally.

However, Sharon also claims her mother taught her to speak at 18 months. She learned limited sign language at age 7, developed lip reading skills, and learned American Sign Language in college. Sharon describes herself as being very isolated and lonely in childhood. She is angry at her parents for not providing her with specialized services for the hard of hearing during her youth.

At age 20 Sharon went to Vocational Rehabilitation Agency and was trained in medical record keeping. Although she completed her training, Sharon could not function on the job due to drug abuse. She was frequently late or absent and eventually stopped working.

Substance Abuse History: Sharon began to drink during her senior year in high school. She continued drinking and began smoking marijuana every day, recalling that she only felt comfortable when she was high and did not have to deal with her feelings.

Present Situation: Sharon recently got drunk and attempted suicide. Upon discharge from a psychiatric unit where she was treated for this attempt, she was sent to a substance abuse treatment center for her addiction. You are the counselor that will initially see her.

QUESTIONS:
- What treatment needs does Sharon have?
- What might be major barriers to Sharon receiving treatment?
- What can be done to ensure access and accommodation of treatment for Sharon?
- To what long-term services and programs should Sharon be referred?

References

Akiskal, H. S., S. E. Chen, G. C. Davis, et al. 1986. "Borderline: An Adjective in Search of a Noun," in *Essential Papers on Borderline Disorders*, M. H. Stone, ed. New York: New York University Press.

Amico, J., and J. Neisen. 1997. Sharing the secret: The need for gay-specific treatment. *The Counselor* 5(3): 12–15.

Andreasen, N. C. 1999. Understanding the causes of schizophrenia. *New England Journal of Medicine* 340(8; 25 February): 645–647.

Andreasen, N. C., V. W. Swayze II, M. Flaum, W. R. Yates, and A. S. McChesney. 1990. Ventricular enlargement in schizophrenia evaluated with computer tomographic scanning: Effects of gender, age, and stage of illness. *Archives of General Psychiatry* 47(11): 1008–1015.

APA (American Psychiatric Association). 2000. *Diagnostic and Statistical Manual of Mental Disorders,* 4th ed., text revision. (DSM-IV-TR). Washington, DC: Author.

Asher, C., and L. Gask. 2010. Reasons for illicit drug use in people with schizophrenia: Qualitative study. *BMC Psychiatry* 10: 94. Retrieved 19 November 2011 from http://www.biomedcentral .com/1471-244X/10/94

ATTC. 2011. Psychotherapeutic medications 2011: What every counselor needs to know. Kansas City, MO: Mid-America Addiction Technology Transfer Center. Retrieved on December 4 2011 at http://www.attcnetwork.org/userfiles/file/ MidAmerica/Psychmeds%202011_FINAL%20as%20of%203-1-11.pdf and at http://www.findrxinformation.org/pdf/ Psychomeds_2011.pdf

Bachman, S. S., and K. Duckworth. 2003. Consensus building for the development of service infrastructure for people with dual diagnoses. *Administration and Policy in Mental Health and Mental Health Services Research* 30(3): 255–266.

Baker, F. 1991. *Coordination of Alcohol, Drug Abuse, and Mental Health Services.* Center for Substance Abuse Treatment Technical Assistance Pub. 4, Rockville, MD: U.S. DHHS, Substance Abuse and Mental Health Services Administration.

Barta, P. E., G. D. Pearlson, R. E. Powers, S. S. Richards, and L. E. Tune. 1990. Auditory hallucinations and smaller superior temporal gyral volume in schizophrenia. *American Journal of Psychiatry* 147(11): 1457–1462.

Biederman, J. et al. 1995. The psychoactive substance use disorder in adults with attention deficit hyperactivity disorder: Effect of ADD and comorbidity. *American Journal of Psychiatry* 152: 1652–58.

Bremner, J. D., J. Douglas, S. M. Southwick, A. Darnell, and D. S. Charney. 1996. Chronic PTSD in Vietnam combat veterans: Course of illness and substance abuse. *American Journal of Psychiatry* 153(3): 369–375.

Brennand, K. J., A. Simone, J. Jou, C. Gelboin-Burkhart, N. Tran, S. Sangar, Y. Li, Y. Mu, G. Chen, D. Yu, S. McCarty, J. Sebat, and F. H. Gage. 2011. Modeling schizophrenia using human induced pluripotent stem. *Nature* 473: 221–225.

Buss, A., and C. Cramer. 1989. *Incidence of Alcohol Use by People with Disabilities. A Wisconsin Survey of Persons with Disability.* Madison, WI: Office for Persons with Disabilities, Department of Health and Social Services.

Calloway, E. 2011, April 13. Schizophrenia in a dish. *Nature News.* Retrieved 19 November 2011 from http://www.nature.com/news/2011/110413/full/news.2011.232.html

Center for Substance Abuse Treatment (CSAT). 1998. Substance Use Disorder Treatment for People with Physical and Cognitive Disabilities. Treatment Improvement Protocol Series 29. 1998. DHHS Publication No. (SMA) 98-3249. Rockville, MD: USHHS, PHS, SAMHSA, Center for Substance Abuse Treatment.

———. 2005. *Substance Abuse Treatment for Persons with Co-Occurring Disorders.* Treatment Improvement Protocol (TIP) Series 42. DHHS Publication No. (SMA) 05-3992. Rockville, MD: Center for Substance Abuse Treatment, Substance Abuse and Mental Health Services Administration.

Cohen, J., and S. J. Levy. 1992. *The Mentally Ill Chemical Abuser.* New York: Lexington Books.

Copeland, M. E. 2002. *Wellness Recovery Action Plan.* West Dummmerston, VT: Peach Press.

CPNJ (Cerebral Palsy of New Jersey). 1998. *Substance Abuse Prevention Program* (Roads2Recovery). Trenton, NJ: Author. http://www.cpofnj.org/services/subpre.htm

Doweiko, H. E. 1997. *Concepts of Chemical Dependency*, 3rd ed. Pacific Grove, CA: Brooks/Cole.

Evans, K., and M. Sullivan. 1990. *Dual Diagnosis: Counseling the Mentally Ill Substance Abuser*. New York: Guilford Press.

Gabbard, G. 1995. Researchers study causes and treatment of borderline personality disorder. *The Menninger Letter* 3(5): 1–2.

Gerstley, L. J., A. I. Alterman, A. T. McLellan, and G. E. Woody. 1990. Antisocial personality in patients with substance abuse disorders: A problematic diagnosis? *American Journal of Psychiatry* 147(2): 173–178.

Goldberg J. F., J. L. Garno, A. M. Callahan, D. L. Kearns, B. Kerner, and S. H. Ackerman. 2008. Overdiagnosis of bipolar disorder among substance use disorder inpatients with mood instability. *Journal of Clinical Psychiatry* 69(11): 1751–1757.

Harris, M., and R. D. Fallot. 2001. "Designing Trauma-Informed Addictions Services," in *Using Trauma Theory to Design Service Systems*. M. Harris and R. D. Fallot, eds. New Directions for Mental Health Services series no. 89. San Francisco: Jossey-Bass.

Herman, J. 1992. *Trauma and Recovery*. New York: Basic Books.

Horner, B. R., and K. E. Scheibe. 1997. Prevalence and implications of attention deficit hyperactivity disorder among adolescents in treatment for substance abuse. *Journal of the American Academy of Child and Adolescent Psychiatry* 36(1): 30–36.

Human Rights Watch. 2006. Number of Mentally Ill in Prisons Quadrupled. New York, NY: Human Rights Watch News. Retrieved December 4 2011 at http://www.hrw.org/news/2006/09/05/us-number-mentally-ill-prisons-quadrupled

Kelly, K., and P. Raimundo. 1995. *You Mean I'm Not Lazy, Stupid or Crazy? A Self-Help Book for Adults with Attention Deficit Disorder*. New York: Scribner.

Kernberg, O. 1975. *Borderline Conditions and Pathological Narcissism*. New York: Jason Aronson.

Kivlahan, D. R., J. R. Heiman, R. C. Wright, J. W. Mundt, and J. A. Shupe. 1991. Treatment cost and rehospitalization rate in schizophrenic outpatients with a history of substance abuse. *Hospital and Community Psychiatry* 42: 609–614.

Krystal, J. H., T. R. Kosten, B. D. Perry, et al. 1991. "Neurobiological Aspects of PTSD: Review of Clinical and Preclinical Studies," in *Essential Papers on Posttraumatic Stress Disorder.* M. J. Horowitz, ed. New York: New York University Press.

Lish, J. D., S. Dime-Meenan, and P. C. Whybrow. 1994. The national depressive and manic-depressive association survey of bipolar members. *Journal of Affective Disorders* 31(4): 281–294.

Loneck, B., and B. Way. 1997. A conceptual model of a thera-peutic process for clients with a dual diagnosis. *Alcoholism Treatment Quarterly* 15: 33–46.

Mellor, C. S. 1992. Dermatoglyphic evidence of fluctuating asymmetry in schizophrenia. *British Journal of Psychiatry* 60: 467–472.

Minkoff, K., and C. A. Cline. 2004. Changing the world: The design and implementation of comprehensive continuous integrated systems of care for individuals with co-occurring disorders. *Psychiatric Clinics of North America* 27(4): 727–743.

Mueser, K., R. E. Drake, and D. Noordsy. 1998. Integrated mental health and substance abuse treatment for severe psychiatric dis-orders. *Journal of Practical Psychiatry and Behavioral Health* 4: 129–139.

Mueser, K. T., D. L. Noordsy, R. E. Drake, and L. Fox. 2003. *Integrated Treatment for Dual Disorders: A Guide for Effective Practice.* New York: Guilford Press.

National Alliance on Mental Illness (NAMI). 2011. Dual Diagnosis and Integrated Treatment of Mental Illness and Substance Abuse Disorder. Retrieved December 3 2011 from http:www.nami.org/ Template.cfm?Section=By_Illness&template=Content Management? Cc

National Mental Health Association (NMHA). 2006. Alcohol, Drug Abuse, Addiction and Co-Occurring Disorders. Retrieved December 1 2006 from http://www.nmha.org/ substance/index

O'Callaghan, E., T. Gibson, H. A. Colohan, D. Walshe, P. Buckley, C. Larkin, and J. L. Waddington. 1991. Season of birth in schizophrenia: Evidence for confinement of an excess of winter births to patients without a family history of mental disorder. *British Journal of Psychiatry* 158: 764–769.

O'Callaghan, E., P. Sham, N. Takei, G. Glover, R. and M. Murray. 1991. Schizophrenia after prenatal exposure to 1957 A2 Influenza epidemic. *Lancet* 337(8752): 1248–1250.

O'Connell, D. F. 1988. Managing the borderline patient in addiction treatment settings. *Alcoholism Treatment Quarterly* 5(1/2): 61–71.

Sales, A. 2005. "Substance Abuse and Disability," in *Substance Abuse and Counseling*. A. Sales, ed. Greensboro, NC: Caps Press.

Salk Institute. 2011, April 13. Salk Institute Press Release: Patients' own cells yield new insights into the biology of schizophrenia. Retrieved 19 November 2011 from http://www.salk.edu/news/ pressrelease_details.php?press_id=480

Schuckit, M. A. 1973. Alcohol and sociopathy: Diagnostic confusion. *Journal of Studies on Alcohol* 34: 157–164.

Shenton, M. E., R. Kikinis, F. A. Jolesz, et al. 1992. Abnormalities of the left temporal lobe and thought disorder in schizophrenia: A quantitative magnetic resonance imaging study. *New England Journal of Medicine* 327(9; 27 August): 604–612.

Stone, M. H. 1986. "The Borderline Syndrome: Evolution of the Term, Genetic Aspects, and Prognosis," in *Essential Papers on Borderline Disorders*. M. H. Stone, ed. New York: New York University Press.

Suddath, R. L., E. W. Christison, E. F. Torrey, M. F. Casanova, and D. R. Weinberger. 1990. Anatomical abnormalities in the brains of monozygotic twins discordant for schizophrenia. *New England Journal of Medicine* 322: 789–794.

U.S. Census. 1997, December. *Census Brief: Disabilities Affect One-Fifth of All Americans*. Washington, DC: U.S. Department of Commerce, Economics and Statistics Administration, Bureau of the Census. Retrieved 19 November 2011 from http://www.census.gov/prod/3/97pubs/ cenbr975.pdf

van der Kolk, B. A. 1991. "The Body Keeps the Score: Memory and the Evolving Psychobiology of Posttraumatic Stress,"

in Essential Papers on Posttraumatic Stress Disorder.
J. M. Horowitz, ed. New York: New York University Press.

Wender, P. H. 1986. *The Hyperactive Child, Adolescent, and Adult: Attention Deficit Disorder through the Lifespan.* New York: Oxford University Press.

Young, A. 1995. *The Harmony of Illusions.* Princeton, NJ: Princeton University Press.

10

Cultural and Other Special Populations

Objectives

At the end of this chapter, students will be able to:

1. Explain why being culturally competent is an ethical responsibility.
2. Describe the importance of assessing the client's cultural identity and his or her mental maps.
3. Provide at least two examples of how cultures evaluate and create myths about drugs.
4. Provide at least two examples of how cultures differ in their rules about drug use.
5. Explain how families label deviant behavior and its significance in counseling.

6. Describe how bicultural identity can create significant issues for both clients and counselors.
7. Describe at least two effects of acculturation stress on alcohol- and drug-abusing clients.
8. Describe issues specific to the development and treatment of substance use disorders of women.
9. Describe issues specific to the development and treatment of substance use disorders of adolescents.
10. Explain issues specific to the development and treatment of substance use disorders of elderly clients.
11. Name issues specific to the development and treatment of substance use disorders of gay, bisexual, lesbian, and transgendered clients.

Introduction

This chapter surveys the variation in beliefs and behavior regarding substance use and abuse among cultural groups, and discusses special considerations in providing counseling services. Counseling for different age-groups, genders, and sexual preference are discussed also.

Cultural Groups and Cultural Competence

In 1973 the American Psychological Association (APA) declared it unethical for clinical services to overlook the cultural backgrounds of their clients and for services to be denied or unavailable because staff lack "cultural competency." In setting standards for professional training in clinical psychology, the APA declared,

> the provision of professional services to persons of culturally diverse backgrounds not competent in understanding and providing professional services to such groups shall be considered unethical. It shall be equally unethical to deny such persons professional services because the present staff is inadequately prepared. It shall therefore be the obligation of all service agencies to employ competent persons or to provide continuing education for the present staff to meet the service needs of the culturally diverse population it serves (Korman 1973, p. 105).

To engage clients in treatment and understand their thoughts about drug use and expectations of treatment, counselors need information about the lifestyles of the groups to which clients belong. *Culture* is a learned, shared, changing map of reality and system of rules concerning behavior, ideas, communication, and values. Lifestyles of segments of society such as ethnic groups, age groups, social classes, and regions form subcultures. Culture shapes beliefs and behavior regarding chemical use, abuse, intoxication, problems, user roles, and curing. Being familiar with cultural patterns helps a counselor get to know clients. To this end, in 1999 several new treatment programs for new immigrants in New York City were designed to dovetail with gender and family patterns of the ethnic populations served. Korean clients, for example, were reported to be open to female counselors. Treatment for Russian teenagers was aided by involving grandparents, to whom the youth are more likely to listen than their parents (Sachs 1999).

Treatment providers need to be aware of barriers to treatment presented by family attitudes toward participation in substance abuse programs. Latina participants in a therapeutic community (Kail and Elbereth 2002, 2003) described how gender in cultural context presented several barriers to treatment: family members had no idea of what treatment entailed, and having a daughter in a drug program would be a big embarrassment. The female network of friends and relatives is expected to be "simpatia," with supportive and harmonious—not confrontational—social relationships. Being in a sex industry, a way of earning a living, also was a factor in keeping women "on the street" rather than in a recovery milieu.

Treatment and prevention programs may espouse values, definitions, and norms concerning alcohol and other drugs that are not congruent with those of the occupational or residential community. It is difficult to intervene in "cultures of drinking" in which the environment defines heavy use as normal and even expected. This is true not only of skid-row or economically marginal communities. The late Lakota anthropologist Beatrice Medicine (2007) stated that, "withdrawing from the world of drink on all Lakota reservations and social groups is a very painful process . . . with social isolation being the price one must pay for sobriety" (p. 120). Statements such as, "You're too good to drink with us?" and "You think you're white now" are used to pressure people whose grasp on sobriety is already tenuous.

Unfortunately, cultural competency skills have had trouble becoming part of standard practice in the human services; culture tends to remain a peripheral or exotic concern. Until the last decade or so, multicultural awareness, or rather cultural competency, has not been a major concern of the addictions field, where it is often felt that "a drug is a drug" and an "addict is an addict." This can result in overlooking key variables in engaging and treating addicts.

Research

Many studies of the cultural contexts of chemical abuse have investigated how and why beliefs and behaviors vary and how they shape addicts. However, due to the wide variety of subgroups and the constant cultural change that occurs, a comprehensive, clear map of chemical use among United States subgroups does not exist. Another problem is that ethnographers tend to study the most "pure" cultures in order to obtain neat, clear descriptions of rules and customs, while addictions counselors work among the least pure cultures—those that are constantly changing and are blended, disorganized, and often alienated from cultural roots. The client population varies from those who, for example, drink heavily within their standard cultural context to crack users whose ethnic affiliations are on the back burner. As a result of this lack of research, some assumptions about ethnic behaviors are based on observations made decades earlier. Rather than relying on old assumptions or informal observations of others, counselors must develop their own cultural competency.

Cultural Competence

Counselors are ethically mandated to build their awareness and knowledge of their clients' cultures. When hearing about cultural competency, some counselors are horrified at the prospect of having to learn all about Albanians, Bulgarians, Czechs, Danes, Ethiopians, Finns, and so on. This task is made even more impossible by a matrix of intra-group variation within many ethnicities according to social class, geography, gender, age, and generation of arrival. Training can highlight crucial issues but can't begin to address these vicissitudes of variation, and it can become quickly obsolete in a rapidly changing world. Because a counselor can't be a human encyclopedia, to be culturally competent he or she must learn the skills of a detective and have the eye of a cultural anthropologist to investigate and learn about cultural patterns in client communities. A counseling skill that must be developed is the ability to elicit information regarding mental maps and categories; value systems regarding alcohol and other drugs; concepts of normality and deviance; models of addiction, abuse, and curing in the client culture or subculture; and other symbolic and ceremonial importance of drug use (Myers and Stolberg 2003).

Culture Defines Drug Use

Cultural and subcultural baggage includes mental maps, charts, and categorizations of reality: colors, kinship categories, roles, and even chemicals. Consider the following actual interview:

PROFESSOR: Do you consider yourself a heavy drinker?
STUDENT: No, I only drink beer.
PROFESSOR: You were drunk when you came in here last week.
STUDENT: No, we only had a few beers.

This interview illustrates a mental map shared by many Americans, one that places beer almost outside the domain of alcoholic beverages, a step above soda. A prevention message aimed at modification of that mental map is, "When you drink a lot of beer, you drink a lot!" A beer has the same amount of alcohol as a shot of bourbon.

"I would never use drugs; I only drink" is the kind of statement made by a large proportion of Americans who put alcohol and drugs in different categories. Alcohol and other drug-abuse education counters this mapping by pointing out that alcohol is a drug. Similar to the way people do not consider beer alcohol, many people do not consider marijuana a drug. For example, Rita, a 22-year-old crack addict and prostitute, said while discussing her first "date" as a prostitute (Ratner 1992):

INTERVIEWER: Did you buy drugs with the money?
RITA: No, I wasn't using drugs yet—I bought reefer.

While placing a drug "off the map" may be simply naïve, it contributes to denying or defining away abuse and addiction. Treatment personnel need to be alert to the words clients use. Just as *drug* meant anything stronger than marijuana to Rita, the word *alcoholic* is sometimes used by alcoholics in reference to more severe alcoholics. Their definition agrees with an aphorism, "An alcoholic is anyone who drinks more than I do."

Culture Includes Evaluations of and Values Associated with Drugs

People put drugs into "good" and "bad" categories. Cultures weave *myths*, which are sometimes totally fallacious, or merely exaggerate or misinterpret some real effect. In the 1930s American college students acquired a "reverence for strong drink" (Room 1984) and considered heavy use romantic and adult. American culture in general evaluates beverages containing ethanol as sexy, mature, sophisticated, facilitating of socializing, and enhancing of status if a prestigious brand. In the 1930s and 1940s many people thought that marijuana was literally a "killer weed." In the exaggerated portrayal in the film *Reefer Madness*, marijuana resulted in homicidal psychoses and suicides, as if it were a large, combined dose of crack and angel dust.

Another example of cultural evaluations of drugs appeared in Gilbert's (1993) review of literature on Mexican-American drinking patterns, which revealed consistent findings that men conceive of alcohol as having many positive effects. Men had more positive expectations and fewer restrictions of use than women. This gender gap closed significantly in studies of Mexican Americans born in the United States.

Cultural Rules Tell Us When, Where, and How Much Drugs Can Be Taken

Many cultures, such as the traditional Italian, French, and Jewish cultures, permit moderate drinking within the family, especially at meals, but disapprove of "drunken" behaviors. Along with such commonalities, there are many differences among groups. Italians consider wine a food, while Orthodox Jews use wine for ritual. In one study of Scandinavian nations, drinking was considered absolutely separated from work. Where drinking was permitted, however, it was allowed to go on to the point of intoxication (Mäkelä 1986). In the United States there are a vast variety of subgroups: some heavy-drinking clients may live in a community where it is not considered excessive to drink with their friends out of paper bags or on the street in the morning. Other clients may belong to a "workplace culture of drinking," at a post office or construction site, for example. If a client's drinking is not much greater than that of his or her peers, to be "treated" for this behavior might seem as strange as going into rehab for eating birthday cake!

Culture Often Gives Ceremonial Meaning to the Use of Alcohol

In a variety of cultures, rituals involve the use of alcohol, hallucinogens, or stimulants to alter states of consciousness, for healing or spiritual purposes, or during a "time out" when normal rules are suspended. It is important to note that this behavior involves no social disruption and is culturally sanctioned. Hallucinogen use by practitioners of Native American religions and cannabis use by Rastafarians have met with legal sanctions.

Culture Defines "Problem Behavior" Associated with Chemical Use

A person's use of drugs is identified as a problem when it has negative effects on a cultural group or subgroup. Californians in one study emphasized drunken driving as a major problem, whereas Poles in Poland and Mexicans in Mexico focused on family disturbances and productivity (Österberg 1986, p. 13). Some U.S. campus cultural maps do not define drunken brawling on Spring Break as "problematical."

Culture Defines the Origin of Drug-Related Problems

When it is generally recognized that some problems are drug related, a cultural group looks for the cause. United States citizens define alcoholism as a disease far more than do the French Canadians or French (Babor et al. 1986). Some South Bronx Hispanics ascribe alcoholism to "spells," spirits, mal ojo (the evil eye), and *brujeria* (witchcraft) (Myers 1983). On the other hand, a group may ignore or bypass the entire addiction and attribute it directly to supernatural influence, ulcers, divorce, and car accidents that the counselor recognizes as alcoholism based. If a problem is traced back to a supernatural cause, a supernatural solution can be called upon. Thus, many seek the help of a folk healer (e.g., *espiritista, santero*).

Also, the client may be influenced by older members in the extended family who interpret the symptoms, make folk diagnoses, and suggest or plan action. These significant others are frequently less acculturated than the client, and they adhere to traditional belief systems.

Cultures Have Elements that Can Be Used to Encourage Healthier Choices

For example, although it is commonplace to cite Latino machismo as an incentive to drink, it is also macho to take care of your family. Many religious bodies that a client may wish to join or rejoin support healthy behaviors in individuals and families.

Culture Shapes Addictive Careers

For example, African Americans are diagnosed as alcoholic at an earlier mean age than Caucasians (James and Johnson 1996) and may progress into extremely heavy "gamma" alcoholism at an earlier age. Based on a Caucasian model, it would be unlikely to see a 35-year-old with alcoholic organic brain syndrome (AOBS). Clinicians working with such expectations could misdiagnose clients with AOBS as suffering from, say, schizophrenia.

Trends in drug use among various subgroups change continually, and addictions counselors should participate in inservice or other training to ensure that their knowledge of such patterns is not out of date.

Culture Shapes Personality and Psychiatric Symptoms, Responses of the Kin Network, and Diagnostic Decisions Based on Those Symptoms

There is a universal structure and chemistry in the human nervous system that is vulnerable to characteristic disorders. Major mood disorders (clinical or major depression and bipolar, or manic-depressive, illnesses) are related to abnormal neurotransmitter functioning at the synapse. Culture shapes the symptoms and manifestations of these diseases.

Psychiatric Labeling of a Client Begins with the Ways Deviance Is Assessed by His or Her Family and Peers

In one study, significantly more Irish families than Jewish families tolerated deviant thinking in a psychotic relative, while significantly more Jewish families than Irish families tolerated out-of-line verbal emotionality (Wylan and Mintz 1976).

Psychiatric Mislabeling of a Client Can Continue with Mental Health Professionals and Medical Institutions

Blacks with AOBS are misdiagnosed as schizophrenic (Bell et al. 1985). Minorities with bipolar disorder are misdiagnosed as schizophrenic

(Mukherjee et al. 1983). Hispanic women with dramatic emotional expression are commonly misdiagnosed as suffering from psychiatric or neurological syndromes (Myers 1983). As mentioned earlier, in the 1980s New York City psychiatric wards were filled with what should have struck clinical administrators as a disproportionate number of people diagnosed as "paranoid schizophrenics"; those patients were, in fact, suffering from crack paranoia. Currently, stimulant psychosis is recognized much more frequently by mental health professionals. Moreover, the crack epidemic has long since abated.

Ethnic Subgroups and Acculturation

Counselors must watch for statements that claim to describe the behavior of a cultural group as a whole. Any description of typical cultural behavior is only a description of the most common or most frequent behavior, the mode or center of the bell curve. For example, many Norwegians cry less than Italians do, but there are still some Italians who cry less than some Norwegians! With groups in the process of changing, there is an even greater range of variation. Counselors must take into account subgroups: rich and poor, urban and rural, male and female, and the degree to which groups have been absorbed. It would be a tremendous disservice, for example, to make statements about "Black" drinking patterns, which runs the gamut from middle-class cocktail lounges, to blue-collar wakes, to birthday parties, to the "bottle-gang" of the homeless and poor. African-American middle-class women drinkers are not so different from the Caucasian middle-class women drinkers, who are typically "moderate," with few nondrinkers and few heavy drinkers. Poorer African-American women in groups have a larger proportion of nondrinkers; but among those who do drink, there are more heavy than moderate drinkers. African-American men are more tolerant than women of heavy drinking. Breaking it down further, those being married, older, and church affiliated were associated with nonacceptance of heavy drinking (Gary and Gary 1985).

Gordon (1981) studied three Hispanic groups, all new to the United States and all blue-collar workers. Dominicans drank less after migration than before migration. They emphasized suave or sophisticated drinking and saw drunkenness as *indecente* (not respectable). Alcoholics were believed to be sick, perhaps from some tragic experience. Guatemalans drank more after migration than before migration; one-third of the males were often drunk and binged most weekends. Being drunk was glamorous and sentimentalized. They boasted of hangovers, even when they didn't have one. The Puerto Ricans broke down into three categories: middle-class American-style moderate drinkers; depressed, wife-abusing, alcoholic welfare recipients; and various sorts of polydrug abusers, including diffusion from mainland "druggie" youth culture (Gordon 1981). This represents only a fragment of the subcultural and acculturative spectrum.

Twenty-one years later, Michelle Shedlin and Sherry Deren (2002) conducted ethnographic research in the Dominican community of Washington Heights. They found that "getting ahead" for economic stability and family support were still important values. Moreover, "control and self-control . . . emerged as the most important attribute to be maintained in life . . . control of the family . . . future . . . behavior . . . resources . . . mind and body, are all seen as necessary for success and the respect of the family, of friends, and the community here and in the Dominican Republic" (78). What was intriguing in the terms of treatment was that these values persisted even among drug users. A common expression among drug users was, "I am trying to dominate/control the drug(s)." Crack use in particular was seen as loss of control, but even crack users evaluated themselves as relatively in or out of control in their use of that substance. Treatment providers working with clients totally immersed in addictive lifestyles can appeal to cultural values in their facilitation of clients' motivational and decisional balance.

Biculturalism

For years or even generations after immigration, people may straddle two worlds. The term *code-switching* usually applies to communicative behaviors such as speech or body language. For example, people change from English to their native language and back again during a conversation, a paragraph, even a sentence. The concept of code-switching deserves applicability beyond communication, and it can shed light on help-seeking and help-rejecting behaviors of clients in mental health and addictions treatment settings. This can be a function of an individual fluctuating between health resources of folk and "official" medical culture. The late Julio Martinez, who served as Director of the New York State Division of Addiction Services, recounted how he was brought to an *espiritista*, for both his heroin addiction and a bone infection that gave him a permanent limp, before he was recruited to a therapeutic community (personal communication to Peter Myers, 1980).

Bell and Evans (1981, pp. 20–22) point out that the addictions counselor, like the teacher or any other staff member in a helping or human services system, may not be aware of a bicultural identity because he or she only sees one "face" of the client. The seemingly successfully bicultural individual may, in fact, be adrift between the two cultures and flee from one to another when uncomfortable. In addition, if the "home" culture is the substance-abusing milieu and the counselor and/or treatment system is predominantly identified with the majority culture, this adds a motivational or cognitive disadvantage to the clean-and-sober road. Bell and Evans (1981, 28–29) further note that cultural identity has different "faces": how individuals see themselves, how they think others see them, and how they see themselves in relation to others.

Acculturative Stress

Families undergoing *acculturative stress* are at risk for development of chemical abuse and dependency. It is stressful and frustrating when individuals and families are no longer in their traditional culture but cannot successfully assimilate into the new culture. Some stress-inducing factors are denial of meaningful participation in the social structure, especially in a way that communicates a "loss of face"; reversal of power roles; lack of deference to elders; denial of culturally important roles such as breadwinner; isolation; lack of support systems; and communication or role patterns that result in not using support systems. Acculturation is uneven within the ethnic subculture: the poor, women, older persons, and city-dwelling families may be more immersed in traditional behavior patterns than economically stable men, youth, and rural families. This can lead to strain within the peer or family network (Avanzo, Frye, and Froman 1994).

Behavioral problems, including drug use, are linked in many studies not only to intergenerational differences due to different stages of acculturation, which accentuates family conflict, distance, and alienation, but also to inflexibility of parents to the traits of the new culture (Adrados 1993; Page 1990, 176; Rio et al. 1990, 211–212; Szapocznik and Kurtines 1989).

In the past decade, treatment and prevention programs have emphasized ethnic identity development as an essential component of a recovery program or sobriety culture. Ethnic revitalization movements with a temperance twist have a long history among Native Americans, beginning with the Seneca/Iriquois chief Handsome Lake whose mystical revelations in 1799 transformed not only his own alcoholism but also his depressed tribal culture (Wallace 1969). Among Native American populations of the present, such programs as the Red Road to Wellbriety (White Bison 2011), the Healing Forest model, the Talking Circle, and the Medicine Wheel (Coyhis 2000) have shown great promise in melding cultural/ethnic pride with a temperance and recovery message.

Other Dimensions of Cultural Competency

We've stressed cultural competency about beliefs and behavior pertaining to drug use. But client culture covers far more, and much of it is pertinent to our work:

- Kinship groups (nuclear versus extended family): kinship and peer networks; family structure, rules, and roles
- Community support systems, formal and informal: the bodega and barbershop, church, guys in the playground and on the stoop, gangs and cliques, other community institutions
- Social networks of substance users and their interface with the community
- Religious beliefs and behavior
- Beliefs and behavior on illness and curing; folk alternatives to U.S. medical systems; supernatural and natural theories of dysfunction, for example, Santería and espiritismo among Caribbean Latinos
- Attitudes towards deviance: stigma associated with addiction and co-occurring disorders, acceptance of active users and recovered users in the kin or peer group
- Language, dialects, and special terminology in use
- Body language (gesture, posture, facial expression) and use of space
- Economics; survival strategies, underground economy, structural unemployment
- Important ceremonial activities
- Music and folk art (including tattoos)
- Bicultural identity, degree of assimilation and acculturation, acculturative stress factors operating on the client and their family

Cultural competency in these areas informs many aspects of treatment. For example, case management practices are affected by a knowledgeable approach to the patterns of authority in the family that can facilitate referral into and successful completion of treatment. Cultural competency also demonstrates interest and engagement and in the building of a treatment alliance, most especially with a population that feels socially marginal, even segregated from the dominant culture.

Knowledge of music that is popular with a population is a quick and easy way to demonstrate some interest and bonding with the client culture. One of the authors so impressed staff when he identified music playing in an Arabic-run candy store (Farid Al-Atrache) that he was for years called "Farid" by the staff, who were amazed that an American would relate to their popular culture. Rural Mexicans now residing in the southwestern United States compose narrative ballads called *corridos* that concern celebrities and heroes, rebellion, and the adventures of bandits and smugglers. The Grammy and Latin Grammy winning group Los Tigres del Norte is comparable to the Beatles in popularity with Mexican youth. The *narcocorrido* is a version chronicling the adventures of drug smugglers

(Wald 2001). Clients may be encouraged to compose a corrido with a recovery message. With young Puerto Rican and Dominican clients, the musical genre is *reggaeton*. If you take the time to learn the arts associated with a culture, your clients may be amazed and feel more respected.

Age Groups

Childhood

Addiction is culturally defined as an adult enterprise. The vast majority of addictions agencies do not admit individuals aged twelve or younger. Nevertheless, children do smoke cigarettes and marijuana, drink, and engage in inhalant abuse. Experimentation or casual use progresses and solidifies into a pattern of abuse especially among neglected, abused, or isolated children and children suffering from undiagnosed and untreated learning or behavioral disabilities. The abuse of *inhalants*—vapors emitted by volatile substances such as solvents, glues, and correction fluids—is a special issue among counselors working with the child and preadolescent population. Inhalant abuse is common among hungry and homeless children in a variety of nations from Central America to southern Asia as well as among children in inner-city districts of North America. Inhalant abuse among children is often associated with a total lack of nurturing family structure. The use of many other substances, such as tobacco and alcohol, is motivated by a desire to augment status by appearing sophisticated and adult. Thus, their use can serve as a rite of passage. Admission to and participation in gangs are also often linked to drinking and drugging. When gang membership is seen as a logical self-protective strategy as well as a normative peer activity, prevention messages alone do not have much influence.

A general awareness of the typical developmental issues, conflicts, and stressors found in various age groups can facilitate assessment of critical issues facing clients.

Adolescence

Individuals from ages 13 to 20 are in a special risk period for use of alcohol and other drugs. Individual risk factors are compounded by the confluence of developmental conflicts and stressors that occur during adolescence and by the desire to try out symbols of adult freedom. It is imperative that developmental issues be assessed, especially conflicts in maturational tasks, independence, sex, romance, and intimacy (Filstead and Anderson 1983).

The clinical observations of Levine (1984) found adolescent substance abuse to be associated with a "developmental logjam" of unfaced dilemmas, which result in some combination of boredom, drift, malaise, inability to conceive of a future for themselves, social isolation, separation problems, meaninglessness, difficulty in achieving intimacy, and dissatisfaction with their own impulsive behaviors (pp. 28–38, 41). Attention-deficit hyperactivity disorder (ADHD) or other learning disabilities, depression, and family problems can aggravate this logjam (see the section "Attention-Deficit Hyperactivity Disorder" in Chapter 9). Taking risks, rebelling, and abusing substances are often linked to adolescents' attempts to resolve these conflicts. Initial assessment of these issues is difficult when clients find these topics painful and threatening, cannot articulate them, and are slow to trust a counselor who is associated with disliked authority structures.

In addition, addictions counselors need to learn the skill of diagnostically differentiating the youth who is experimenting or using as a rite of passage and the youth who is seriously abusing substances. On college campuses, the situation is complicated by an entrenched and ancient tradition of binge drinking. This practice remains fairly constant even as prevention programs make gains against use of cocaine and marijuana in college populations. Among high school and college-aged youth, heavy drinking is associated with a majority of driving fatalities, sexually transmitted diseases, academic failure, accidents, unwanted sexual encounters, violence, property damage, and insurance claims.

Adolescent Treatment

Treatment models simply copied from settings for adults are not appropriate to the developmental stage and needs of youth. This became glaringly obvious from studies in the 1990s that showed a woeful lack of abstinence among youth treated in many models (Liddle and Rowe 2006). For example, features of high-risk situations for teenagers are different than for adults. Unsupervised social situations where teens are "having fun" are risky, whereas for adults it is negative emotional states involving anger and interpersonal conflict. Secondly, youth have little motivation to abstain, because they don't have or can't visualize the negative consequences, unlike the adult who may face liver problems, loss of employment, and so forth (Brown and Ramo 2006).

Case-finding and appropriate referrals are difficult due to institutional denial, participation of adult role-models in heavy drinking, campus tradition, and encapsulated subcultures of abuse in fraternity settings. Counselors must consider an appropriate level of care in referring an adolescent: Experimentation or casual use does not warrant referral into an intensive rehabilitation program. It is understandably difficult to convince students or their parents to accept an inpatient referral during the academic year. There is no shortage of role-models of recovery for adults in addictions treatment, nor of subcultures of recovery (e.g., AA, NA, therapeutic communities, Smart Recovery). In the treatment of adolescents, however, one dilemma is the dearth of a recovery subculture. Even individual role-models are relatively scarce, because adolescent substance abusers either mature out of addiction or, following treatment, tend to get on with their lives rather than remain in a self-help milieu. Substance-abusing adolescents are often in environments in which users set the tone and in which successful clean-and-sober adult role-models are lacking. It is especially difficult for these young people to think through the consequences for their entire lives, leave the "using society" (which may comprise the majority of their family and friends), and stay clean and sober. Some treatment programs have a group of graduates who have "made it," whom clients can trust and identify with, and who can give them hope and pointers on how to get there.

Experimentation with or abuse of substances is seldom the only problematic area for adolescents. It is often part of a constellation of so-called acting-out behaviors. Other parts of the picture include depression, learning disabilities, suicidal ideation or gestures, truancy, driving while intoxicated (DWI) charges or convictions, history of family addictions, child abuse or molestation, vandalism, and petty (or not-so-petty) crimes. Counselors must beware of assumptions underlying assessment that lead to imagining a greater role for substance abuse in adolescents' problems than is actually the case. For example, the depressed, learning-disabled adolescent will not magically prosper when she stops using marijuana. Although depression and learning disabilities are worsened significantly and masked by chronic use of marijuana, eliminating the marijuana will not eliminate them as well. Failure to address such other issues jeopardizes recovery.

Adolescent treatment walks a fine line between treatment per se and prevention. Strategies need to capture their imaginations, excite them, and offer alternatives to using drugs. Programs that treat adolescents as a major component of their services need activities that:

- Are age-appropriate
- Are attractive
- Offer the opportunity to attain developmental milestones
- Help them identify and reach some maturational goals such as obtaining a high school equivalency degree and acquiring occupational skills
- Build a positive self-image
- Assess and build upon natural resiliency factors

These activities may be recreational, educational, vocational, artistic, journalistic, or athletic, depending on the needs of the client.

Some troubled and substance-abusing adolescents find an Outward Bound–type program helpful. Such programs are physically, socially, mentally, and emotionally challenging outdoor group adventures in a remote area (Gillis and Simpson 1992, 1994). However, because of costs, space availability, and the status of the client, Outward Bound is not appropriate to all adolescent addicts. Project Adventure incorporates many of the same features but with minimal travel requirement. Local variations came into existence in many states during the 1990s, but their growth has been stymied by limited funding. Special sports programs that incorporate therapeutic elements and antidrug messages also have been successful in creating an alternative to subcultures of abuse. These programs are sponsored by local government, social service agencies, the Police Athletic League, and community coalitions. An example is the Midnight Basketball Coalition program, which originated in 1986 in Atlanta, Georgia, and now exists in a dozen cities.

Motivational enhancement therapy (MET) and cognitive-behavioral therapy (CBT) have been adapted to adolescent treatment, one example being the combined MET/CBT approach in one iteration of the Cannabis Youth Treatment (CYT) project of CSAT. This approach delivers five individual MET sessions and three CBT group sessions within a six-week period and is known as MET/CBT5. The MET component seeks to help adolescents to tip the motivational decision sheet to the point that they see that the costs of use outweigh the benefits. The CBT component teaches coping skills so that they can initiate and sustain change effectively, specifically: refusal skills, establishing a supportive social network, coping with unanticipated high-risk situations, and making a plan for coping with slips. Another version of this treatment adds seven more CBT group sessions for a total time in treatment of 12 weeks. In the extra CBT sessions, adolescents learn to cope with interpersonal problems, bad feelings, depression, and craving without using. The group setting affords a laboratory to practice skills (Titus and Dennis 2006, p. 105–107). One can view this as facilitating developmental tasks, given that many adolescent abusers have feelings of being "stuck" in a developmental malaise. Taking CYT to a different system level, there is a version that includes parent education meetings, therapeutic home visits that examine family roles and routines, referral to self-help groups, and case management designed to facilitate treatment attendance (Titus and Dennis 2006, p. 107).

CYT research reports impediments to treatment and recovery that include:

- A large percentage of clients with co-occurring problems such as multisubstance abuse, depression and suicidality, ADHD, illegal activities, and alcohol/drugs in the home. Adolescent treatment needs to be integrated with co-occurring disorders treatment.

- Low recognition of substance abuse as a problem (20% out of 96% formally diagnosed with abuse or dependence; Titus and Dennis 2006, pp. 111–113)

CYT manuals (CSAT 2001a) are available online at http://store .samhsa.gov/home and http://kap.samhsa.gov/products/brochures/pdfs/ cytbrochure.pdf.

When treatment is provided in a therapeutic community setting, important modification must be made. Education needs to be a major focus of the stay, so the facility needs to be set up more as a school than as a "rehab" clinic (Jainchill 2006). Adolescents will be much less likely to tolerate harsh confrontational methods unless absolutely compelled to remain. As discussed later in this chapter, adolescents with ADHD tend to have a disastrous experience in residential therapeutic community settings that demand attention to detail such as turning out lights and making beds. ADHD teens can and should be expected to be responsible; it's just a rockier road if the community setting requires attention to detail, and errors are going to be made.

Links to resources for adolescent treatment are available at http:// www.chestnut.org/LI/APSS/SASATE/resources/.

The Middle-Aged and the Elderly

Middle-aged and elderly are categories that cannot be delineated precisely. However, late middle age is often defined as age 55+, and senior citizens (the elderly) are defined as 65+. Another pothole in the highway of life is late middle age and retirement, as it is not so much a logjam as too few logs to stand on. The empty nest and the losses of body image, friends, family, and occupational role bring grief, regret, disappointment, loneliness, and isolation. Counselors must teach and facilitate processing of losses and encourage new involvements and initiatives. Mrs. Harris was a widow approaching retirement whose drinking went from social to abusive after her husband's death. Her church peers were by-and-large teetotalers who disapproved of her drinking alcohol; her shame isolated her from the church, which she longed to rejoin. In assessment, it is important to differentiate between a late-onset alcoholic as in the case of Mrs. Harris and an addict who has simply aged along with his or her long-time addiction. The late-onset addict is less deteriorated and less antisocial and has fewer coexisting problems than the long-term addict.

Assessment of an elderly client must be informed by diagnostic issues typical of this age group. These issues include the differentiation among symptoms of alcohol or illicit drug use, use of prescription and over-the-counter drugs, and any combination thereof (Figure 10.1). This is compounded by the fact that the elderly frequently are over-medicated and often self-medicate. The bodies of the elderly do not detoxify substances quickly, which results in high levels of psychoactive substances lingering in the blood and brain. Medical care for the elderly is often compartmentalized. More than one physician may be involved in prescribing medications, and some seniors have difficulty keeping track of them. Possible overmedication or medication interactions are not always monitored adequately. Depression in the elderly can be generated or compounded by prescribed depressants and by alcohol use. Especially in this age group, it is important to determine whether problems with memory and cognition are results of alcohol and illegal drugs, incorrect use of prescriptions, or senile dementia.

Clinical concerns when treating the elderly that have been identified by SAMHSA (CSAT 2001b) include:

- Being sensitive to self-esteem needs, which are accentuated in clients who may feel depleted physically, socially, and emotionally. Counselors must avoid communicating a patronizing, dismissive, or impatient attitude. The term "substance abuse" should be avoided; refer directly to alcohol use and sedative use.
- Being sensitive to the possibility that perceptual acuity and speed may diminish with age. Avoid unnecessary background noise. Pause and give other cues when topics change.
- Being sensitive to cognitive needs, and have access to assessment data on cognitive impairments. Prevent ridicule if a client manifests a lack of understanding; keep explanations simple, and encourage clients to ask about words or concepts they don't understand.

Sexuality

Gender

Women are underrepresented in treatment in proportion to their numbers in the addict population, and programs addressing their special needs are also relatively few. According to the Centers for Disease Control (2007), 60% of women of child-bearing age drink, and, of those, one-third reported binge drinking (five drinks in a row in the last two weeks) compared to 43% of men; 23% of women reported any illicit drug use during the past year compared to 31% of males. When assessing a female client, it is important to explore relationships with significant others, support systems, impediments to treatment, and issues of abuse, shame, and stigma.

Figure 10.1 Screening senior citizens for substance abuse.

What are the risk factors for seniors?

Problems, pain, and anxieties

Retirees sometimes feel the loss of a meaningful part to play in society, feelings of worthlessness and obsolescence, loss of an occupational identity, the loss of friends on the job, loss of earned income, stress of living on a fixed income, and boredom.

Children "leave the nest," parents have passed away, and people may feel lonely. The illness and deaths of family and friends create loss and grief, which may be difficult to bear.

People may feel disappointed when life expectations don't pan out.

Physical pain and fatigue often accompany the aging process, as well as stress and loss of body functions and skills.

Chronic illnesses are accompanied by restricted activity, pain, stress, and fear.

Possible reactions

Depression

Denial

Repression or restriction of feelings

Withdrawal from others

Use of alcohol or other drugs to "numb" or deny feelings

Medication problems

Losing track of prescriptions

Forgetting how much was taken

Seeing several physicians who prescribe

Overprescription of sedatives

Other aspects of alcohol and other drug use

It is often hidden and private, not often in a bar or at a party.

It is often rapid in onset.

The effects are often worsened by use of prescribed medications and over-the-counter medications, which may contain sedating substances.

The effects of substance abuse may be hard to differentiate from memory and thinking problems of some elderly.

The effects are often compounded by decrease in liver function so that it becomes harder to eliminate substances from the body.

Older drinkers tend to attribute negative physical symptoms of drinking to aging.

Source: Courtesy of Essex County College Senior Alcohol and Drug Abuse Prevention Project, with support from the Newark Municipal Alliance.

The degree to which an addicted woman associates with a chemically abusing spouse or boyfriend is an important factor in her patterns of use. Hser and colleagues found that women tend to stay with addicted males, perhaps participating in the drug use, whereas nonusing mates are more likely to abandon addicted females. In addition, they found that the most important reason for first use and increase in use by women is an intimate relationship with a chemical abuser.

The degree of social support for entering treatment is significant. Women have much less support to enter treatment than do men. The variety of reasons include social stigma, the history of alcoholism as a men's disease, and denial of women's addictions. Counselors must remember the distinction between social support and support to enter treatment. All kinds of helping, sympathizing, and supporting of an addict can amount to enabling or buffering the addict against the consequences of addiction and keeping her or him away from treatment when that is an option. Alcoholism among women tends to be kept hidden in the house by both the drinker and her family. When questions are asked about a woman's functioning, answers are given in terms of fatigue, minor illness, or even depression. Men are more likely when drunk to get into public displays that eventually become noted in a police or hospital report. Statistics, therefore, tend to hide the proportion of women drinkers.

Lederer (1994, 264–266) has examined gender roles in denial from a feminist perspective. These issues may be summed up as follows:

- Women's thoughts and feelings are discounted by their spouses and others, which lowers their self-esteem and leads to denial of their perceptions of the family situation.
- Women are held responsible for the emotional well-being of the family, which leads women into self-blaming, enabling roles, and to denying situations that "must be," ipso facto, their fault.
- Women may go along with their husbands' denial because they have taken on executive authority in the family due to the addiction and dysfunctionality of their spouse. In sobriety, the husband might want his dominant role restored.

Gay, Bisexual, Lesbian, and Transgendered Clients

Chemical abuse among homosexuals can be linked to their social status as outcast, stigmatized, and deviant, which contributes to pain and isolation and can lead to substance abuse. For many decades, the "gay bar" was a secret gathering place, the only setting where homosexuals could interact, be open about their sexuality, safely explore possible relationships, and be themselves. Gay Pride marches beginning in the 1970s in New York

City featured many contingents that marched behind the banners of their bars. The gay bar scene has dwindled considerably over the past several decades. In San Francisco, the number of exclusively gay bars dropped from 178 to 33 (Thomas 2011).

While the old stigmatized, outcast status has changed a great deal in recent decades, it is still true that a majority of homosexuals have suffered some form of ostracism, discrimination, or family rejection. Clinicians with competency in the area of gay and lesbian alcohol and drug use agree that treatment must provide a framework for the client not only to acknowledge sexual orientation but also to explore unresolved sexual issues.

Shame interferes with sobriety, and counselors should create an environment that provides an opportunity to release shame and reclaim pride. It is not surprising that recovery and "coming out" often go hand in hand; a counselor's assessment should recognize that this wrenching period can be a time of increased risk of alcohol and other drug abuse. Addicted gays are an underserved population because of a spectrum of antigay attitudes in treatment agencies, ignorance of gay issues, or anxiety about gay issues. Considerable cultural change has occurred around stigma associated with sexual preference, as reflected in changes in same-sex marriage laws in several states.

Clients in the treatment facility are a microcosm of their culture, which, unfortunately, includes homophobia. One can imagine the stress and conflict of either concealing or acknowledging a homosexual orientation in group treatment. Yet it is far too glib simply to recommend referral to a facility that specializes in treating gays and lesbians. Given the fact that facilities specializing in treating homosexuals are few and far between, and that reimbursement may be difficult, counselors would generally limit such special referrals to those whose recovery seriously requires it. Gay and lesbian AA, NA, and Al-Anon groups are more accessible, especially in medium-sized and large cities.

Sexual preference plays a role in epidemiology. There has been an over-representation of crystal methamphetamine users in the gay community, which is also associated with sexual compulsivity, failure to utilize safe sex, and consequent raised risks of sexually transmitted diseases including HIV/AIDS (Braine et al. 2011; Marshall et al. 2011). The Gay Mens Health Crisis organization has a special prevention program targeting these concerns (GMHC 2011). A providers guide to working with lesbian, gay, bisexual, and transgendered clients is available for download at http://kap.samhsa.gov/products/manuals/pdfs/lgbt.pdf.

References

Adrados, J-L. 1993. "Acculturation: The Broader View," in *Drug Abuse among Minority Youth: Advances in Research and Methodology*. M. R. De La Rosa and J-L. Adrados, eds. NIDA Research Monograph 130. Rockville, MD: U.S. Dept. of HHS, Public Health Services.

Avanzo, C. E., V. Frye, and R. Froman. 1994. Culture, stress, and substance use in Cambodian refugee women. *Journal of Studies on Alcohol* 55: 420–426.

Babor, T. F. et al. 1986. "Concepts of Alcoholism among American, French-Canadian, and French Alcoholics," in *Alcohol and Culture: Comparative Perspectives from Europe and America*. T. F. Babor, ed. New York: Annals of the New York Academy of Sciences; 472.

Bell, C. C., J. P. Thompson, D. Lewis, et al. 1985. Misdiagnosis of alcohol-related organic brain syndromes: Implications for treatment. *Alcohol Treatment Quarterly* 2(fall/winter): 45–65.

Bell, P., and J. Evans. 1981. *Counseling the Black Client*. Center City, MN: Hazelden.

Braine, N., C. J. Acker, L. van Sluytman, et al. 2011. Drug use, community action, and public health: Gay men and crystal meth in NYC. *Substance Use & Misuse* 46: 368–380.

Brown, S. A., and D. E. Ramo. 2006. Clinical course of youth following treatment for alcohol and drug problems pp. 74–103, in Liddle, H. A., and C. L. Rowe eds, Adolescent Substance Abuse–Research and Clinical Advances. Cambridge, UK: Cambridge University Press.

Centers for Disease Control. 2007. Health, United States. Accessed on December 8 2011 from http://www.cdc.gov/nchs/data/hus/hus07.pdf

Coyhis, D. 2000. "Culturally Specific Addiction Recovery for Native Americans," in *Bridges to Recovery: Addiction, Family Therapy, and Multicultural Treatment*. J. Krestan, ed. New York: The Free Press.

CSAT. 2001a. *Cannabis Youth Treatment Series*. Rockville, MD: US Department of Health and Human Service, Substance Abuse and Mental Health Services Administration, Center for Substance Abuse Treatment. Accessed on December 8 2011 from http://kap.samhsa.gov/products/brochures/pdfs/cytbrochure.pdf

_____. 2001b. *Treatment Improvement Protocol (TIP) #26*. Substance Abuse Among Older Adults. Rockville, MD: U.S. Department of Health and Human Services.

Public Health Service, Substance Abuse and Mental Health Services Administration, Center for Substance Abuse Treatment.

Filstead, W. J., and C. Anderson. 1983. Clinical and conceptual issues in treatment of adolescent alcohol and substance misusers. *Child and Youth Services* 6: 1–2.

Gary, L. E., and R. B. Gary. 1985. Treatment needs of Black alcoholic women. *Alcohol Treatment Quarterly* 2(fall/winter): 97–113.

Gilbert, M. J. 1993. "Intracultural Variation in Alcohol-Related Cognitions among Mexican-Americans," in *Hispanic Substance Abuse.* R. S. Mayers, B. L. Kain, and T. D. Watts, eds. Springfield, IL: Charles C. Thomas.

Gillis, H. L., and C. Simpson. 1992. Project Choices: Adventure-based residential drug treatment for court referred youth. *Journal of Addictions and Offender Counseling,* 12: 12–27.

Gillis, H. L., and C. Simpson. 1994. Working with substance abusing adolescents through Project Adventure. *Addictions Looseleaf Notebook.* Aspen, CO: Love.

GMHC (Gay Mens Health Crisis). 2011. My Meth Life. Retrieved 20 November 2011 from http://mymethlife.org

Gordon, A. J. 1981. The cultural context of drinking and indigenous therapy for alcohol problems in three migrant Hispanic cultures. *Journal of Studies on Alcohol* suppl. 9: 217–240.

Jainchill, N. 2006. Adolescent therapeutic communities: Future directions for practice and research pp. 313–332, in Liddle, H. A. and Rowe C. L. eds. Adolescent Substance Abuse: Research and clinical advances. Cambridge, UK: Cambridge University Press.

James, W. H., and S. N. Johnson, eds. 1996. *Doin' Drugs: Patterns of African American Addiction.* Austin: University of Texas Press.

Kail, B. L., and M. Elbereth. 2002. Moving the Latina substance abuser towards treatment: The role of gender and culture. *Journal of Ethnicity in Substance Abuse* 1(3): 3–16.

———. 2003. Engaging and treating the substance-abusing Latina. *Journal of Ethnicity in Substance Abuse* 2(4): 19–30.

Korman, M. 1973. *Levels and Patterns of Professional Training in Psychology* (Recommendations of APA Vail Conference). Washington, DC: American Psychological Association.

Lederer, G. S. 1994. "The Use of Denial and Its Gender Implications in Alcoholic Marriages," in *Addictions: Concepts and Strategies for Treatment.* Gaithersburg, MD: Aspen.

Levine, H. 1984. *Radical Departures; Desperate Detours to Growing Up.* New York, Harcourt: Brace Jovanovich.

Liddle, C. L., and C. L. Rowe, eds. 2006. *Adolescent Substance Abuse–Research and Clinical Advances.* Cambridge, UK: Cambridge University Press.

Mäkelä, K. 1986. "Attitudes Towards Drinking and Drunkenness in Four Scandinavian Countries," in *Alcohol and Culture: Comparative Perspectives from Europe and America.* T. F. Babor, ed. Annals of the New York Academy of Sciences, vol. 472.

Marshall, B. D., E. Wood, J. A. Shoveller, et al. 2011. Pathways to HIV risk and vulnerability among lesbian, gay, bisexual, and transgendered methamphetamine users: a multi-cohort gender-based analysis. *BMC Public Health* 11: 20.

Medicine, B. 2007. *Drinking and Sobriety Among the Lakota Sioux.* Lanham, MD: Rowman and Littlefield.

Mukherjee, S. M., S. Shukla, J. Woodle, A. M. Rosen, and S. Olarte. 1983. Misdiagnosis of schizophrenia in bipolar patients: A multiethnic comparison. *American Journal of Psychiatry* 140: 1571–1574.

Myers, P. L. 1983. Cautionary notes on ethnic/psychiatric stereotypes. *Medical Tribune*, September 28.

Myers, P. L., and V. B. Stolberg. 2003. Ethnographic lessons on substance abuse and substance abusers. *Journal of Ethnicity in Substance Abuse* 2(2): 67–88.

Österberg, E. 1986. "Alcohol-Related Problems in Cross-National Perspective: Results of the ISACE Study," in *Alcohol and Culture: Comparative Perspectives from Europe and America.* T. F. Babor, ed. Annals of the New York Academy of Sciences, vol. 472.

Page, J. B. 1990. "Streetside Drug Use among Cuban Drug Users in Miami," in *Drugs in Hispanic Communities.* R. Glick and J. Moore, eds. New Brunswick, NJ: Rutgers University Press.

Ratner, M. 1992. *Crack Pipe as Pimp.* Lexington, MA: Lexington Books.

Rio, A., D. A. Santisteban, and J. Szapocznik. 1990. "Treatment Approaches for Hispanic Drug-Abusing Adolescents," in *Drugs in Hispanic Communities*, R. Glick and J. Moore, eds. New Brunswick, NJ: Rutgers University Press.

Room, R. 1984. 'A reverence for strong drink': The lost generation and the elevation of alcohol in American culture. *Journal of Studies on Alcohol* 45(6): 540–545.

Sachs, S. 1999, 16 June. "Treatment Rooted in Culture: Typing Drug and Alcohol Programs to Immigrants' Backgrounds." *New York Times*, B1, B10.

Shedlin, M. G., and S. Deren. 2002. Cultural factors influencing HIV risk behavior among Dominicans in New York City. *Journal of Ethnicity in Substance Abuse* 1(1): 71–95.

Szapocznik, J., and W. Kurtines. 1989. *Breakthrough in the Family Therapy of Drug Abusing and Behavior Problem Youth.* New York: Springer.

Thomas, J. 2011. The gay bar: Can it survive SLATE July 1, 2011. Retrieved December 8 2011 from http://www.slate.com/articles/life/the_gay_bar/2011/06/the_gay_bar.html

Titus, J. C., and M. L. Dennis. 2006. *Cannabis Youth Treatment Intervention: Preliminary findings and implications,* pp.104–126, in Liddle, H. A. and Rowe C. L. eds. Adolescent Substance Abuse: Research and Clinical Advances. Cambridge, UK: Cambridge University Press.

Wald, E. 2001. Narcocorrido. Retrieved 20 November 2011 from http://www.elijahwald.com/corrido.html

Wallace, A. F. C. 1969. *The Death and Rebirth of the Seneca.* New York: Knopf.

White Bison. 2011. *White Bison: Center for the Wellbriety movement.* Retrieved on December 4 2011 from http://www.whitebison.org/wellbriety_movement/index.html. *The Red Road to Wellbriety in the Native American Way.* Colorado Springs, CO: White Bison, Inc.

Wylan, L., and N. Mintz. 1976. Ethnic differences in family attitudes towards psychotic manifestations with implications for treatment programs. *International Journal of Social Psychiatry* 22(2): 86–95.

11

Thinking About Addiction Treatment

Objectives

By the end of this chapter, students will be able to:

1. List and explain a minimum of five fallacies of thinking often heard in the addictions field.
2. Explain the pros and cons of the disease model of addiction.
3. Explain the pros and cons of the harm reduction model.
4. Describe how attitudes often motivate and often bias behavior.

In this chapter, we consider critical thinking in terms of how people construct mental models of behavior, stigma and addiction, attitudes, and attitudes of recovering counselors.

Critical Thinking

Back in 1986, at an inservice planning session for a treatment provider consortium, a counselor suggested a training on Albert Ellis' Rational-Emotive Behavioral Therapy (REBT, or Smart Recovery) but was slapped down by an agency director who objected on the grounds that REBT was supposedly hostile to Alcoholics Anonymous. This was not only dogmatic thinking but acting to make sure that everyone else followed suit by excluding other possibilities from even becoming known, essentially stamping out heresy. Dogmatic thinking is detrimental to counseling and treatment of any behavioral health problem, prevents the adoption of helpful and innovative strategies, and is just plain stultifying (Myers 2002). Unfortunately, it has been common in addictions treatment. The opposite of dogmatic thinking is critical thinking.

Michael Taleff, a leader in addictions education, defines *critical thinking* as carefully weighing an idea or belief for its value and validity (Taleff 2006, p. 22). In addition to this definition, we offer this compilation of adjectives:

> Critical thinking means being rational, logical, independent, questioning, analytic, open, creative, curious, and skeptical.

Taleff found the lack of critical thinking in the addictions field to be so pervasive and debilitating to the effort of offering appropriate counseling and treatment that he wrote an entire text on critical thinking for addictions professionals (Taleff 2006, pp. 105–110). He has identified several fallacies in the thinking of professionals. In this enumeration, we have adapted his material and changed a few of the titles of the fallacies.

A. Fallacies that make you think they address the facts, but don't (presumption fallacies).

　1. *Settling a question by simply reaffirming your position (begging the question).* "It is a well-accepted fact that Primal Scream Therapy works best for addicts." "I know in my heart that Primal Scream Therapy towers over all other models of treatment."

　2. *Altering a definition rather than admitting other possibilities.* Saying, for example, that an alcoholic who returned to social drinking probably wasn't an alcoholic in the first place.

　3. *Either-or fallacy.* Assuming that there are only two possibilities when there may be many.

　4. *Slippery slope.* A presumed set of inevitable chain reactions. ("If we don't fight a war with the Zonians, then they will take over the next country, and then the next.") In prevention work, the authors have seen youngsters laugh at such predictions of disaster if they experiment with psychoactive substances. (The most extreme example of this fallacy was the 1940 movie *Reefer Madness*, which readers should badger their professor to play for the class.) Yet the entire disease model so standard in American addictions treatment was precisely the same. Using a career of deteriorated, "low-bottom" gamma alcoholics who had ended up, finally, in Alcoholics Anonymous, it postulated that alcoholism was a relentlessly chronic and progressive disease, excluding the majority of alcohol abusers who did not progress into serious alcoholism, not to mention the ones who got better on their own.

B. Classification Fallacies

   5. *Stereotyping/generalizing.* We are all taught of the dangers of stereotyping members of a particular ethnic group and its connection to prejudice and racism, or, more recently, the problems of stereotyping disabled persons. Yet even members of the counseling professions, whom we'd expect to be most discerning and sympathetic toward their clients, frequently are the most guilty of perpetuating the image of addicts as con artists who are manipulative, stubborn, and in denial. ("When do you know an addict is lying? When his lips are moving.") Children of alcoholics are labeled family heroes, lost children, scapegoats, and mascots. The hyperactive kid in the alcoholic family is assumed to be the scapegoat.

   6. *Imprecision/fuzzy categorizations,* such as codependent, enabler, and neurotic. *Insistence on using your pet classification system.* The client must admit *he/she is an addict (even a lifelong addict),* or has borderline personality disorder, or must see that he/she plays the scapegoat role in the addicted family. Rigid classification systems—and the belief in them—seem, in fact, to be the most important aspect of some treatment philosophies, which are in fact heavily invested ideologies.

   7. *Conspiratorial explanations of complex events.* For example, the CIA or the Freemasons put drugs in the neighborhood or spread AIDS.

   8. *Overdetermined thinking, making one factor paramount over all others.* One example is the old codependency movement of the 1980s, in which codependency was blamed for everything from manic-depression to communism. This is also called *reductionism*, because it reduces everything down to one factor, whether it be economics, sex, and so on.

9. *Ad hominem arguments.* Impugning the reputation of a person who is associated with a particular point of view, such as stating that "Charles Dederich, the founder of Synanon, was a paranoid megalomaniac. The program was a cult." (In fact, Synanon, the first residential therapeutic community for addicts, did develop into a cult-like organization, but that doesn't necessarily follow from observations about Chuck Dederich.) This line of reasoning is a fancy form of, "Don't listen to him, he's crazy." Finally, does the person who is described Dederich have any concrete knowledge about the individual?

10. *Mistaking correlation for causation.* "Global warming is correlated with the decline in pirates."

11. *If B follows A, then B is caused by A* (the *post hoc* argument). The full Latin phrase is "*post hoc, ergo propter hoc*," or "after this, therefore because of this." Heroin users first used marijuana and therefore marijuana use somehow predisposed heroin use. Actually, users first drank mother's milk, coffee, and diet soda!

Richard Paul and Linda Elder (2006), leaders in the critical thinking community, have identified five underlying assumptions of faulty thinking about issues:

1. It's true because I believe it (*egocentrism*).

2. It's true because we believe it (*sociocentrism*, blind faith in the group).

3. It's true because I want to believe it (*wish fulfillment*; believing what "feels good" and what supports my other beliefs, which doesn't make me have to admit I've been wrong).

4. It's true because I've always believed it (*self-validation*).

5. It's true because it is in my interest to believe it (*selfishness*).

When we encounter dogmatic or other faulty thinking about addiction and treatment, it is useful to identify the fallacy and the assumptions involved.

The psychologists Robert Fancher and Jerome Frank (1997) critically examined the modes of thought inherent in schools of American psychology, or, as they call them, *cultures of healing.* They stated that behavioral and cognitive psychology are based on underlying axioms such as:

Reality can't be the cause of pathology.
Problems are clearly and discretely definable.
Problems of life are easily manageable.
Simple operations suffice to institute major change.

They further examined the cognitive approach of Aaron Beck, a major influence on cognitive-behavioral therapy of addictions, as based on the hidden axiom that "changing one's life is as easy as changing one's mind, and changing one's mind is as easy as thinking empirically and logically" (Fancher and Frank 1997, p. 207). According to Beck, they state, the principal that thought is paramount in the psyche leads to the conclusion that profoundly negative views must be caused by cognitive distortion; in other words, they cannot be rational.

We introduce these arguments not to attack cognitive therapy but to get trainees to think about the underlying assumptions of their clinical practice and to think about schools of counseling and psychotherapy as systems of thought akin to ideologies or cultures. Fancher and Frank (1997) and William White (1996) have found it useful to think of therapy and treatment as conversion to a new perspective, a new culture to which the client forms an affiliation.

Taking a more sociological view of faulty, noncritical thinking in addictions, we can frame the problem as often being due to commitment to an ideology or dogma (Taleff 2006, pp. 29–30; Myers 2002). An *ideology* is a firmly held system of belief. It can be political, such as liberalism, neoconservatism, communism; religious; or therapeutic, such as Freudian psychoanalysis. An ideology that is set down in a strict set of rules for behaving or thinking can be fitted with the epithet of *dogma*. Viewing the client through the lens of this belief system causes us to distort information to fit the theory—even to the point of disregarding anything that fails to conform to our dominant hypothesis—thus leading to misdiagnosis and incorrect treatment. In other words, dogma kills!

ACTIVITY (11.1) Critical analysis of addictions writings

A critical issue in the addictions field, which is still bubbling and brewing, is the role of recovering counselors and recovery philosophies. Critically discuss and evaluate these two statements and their relationship to one another:

Well-known addictions researcher Rudolf Moos, writing in the journal *Psychology of Addictive Behaviors*, asked:

. . . does a 12-step philosophy provide a more coherent and sustainable belief system, and thus more goal congruence and clarity, than does a cognitive-behavioral orientation, which is based more on scientific evidence and technical expertise? Is it true that an ideology based only on empirical support cannot sustain service providers? (Moos 2003, p. 6)

Jimmy K., perhaps the best-known founder and leader of Narcotics Anonymous, in a speech made in 1973 to the twentieth anniversary World Conference of NA:

There are people all over this world dying of our disease. And believe it or not, we are truly the only people who can really help them. Let's never forget that you and I have been given, through illness, through suffering, and through disease, a talent for helping other human beings like ourselves. (Jimmy K., quoted in *The NA Way Magazine*, July 2003)

Traditional Models of Addiction

Models of Treatment and Recovery

How do counselors know what to do to facilitate personal growth and recovery? The traditions and philosophies of addictions treatment are based on beliefs, concepts, and values concerning addiction, recovery, and the human condition, some of which are unwritten or inexplicit. It is important to be aware of these concepts and the ways of organizing thinking about human problems.

The term *model* is used in science and philosophy to mean any representation or description of a phenomenon. Models identify:

- Parts or elements of what one is trying to describe, and their characteristics, whether atomic particles or family members.
- The interaction of these elements, and their places and roles in a system, structure, or process. How do members of a group communicate; why must they designate a scapegoat?
- Boundaries of systems. How does an addicted family or an organization build enclosing barriers?
- Changes that may occur in the system, whether evolution, adaptation, deterioration, or disintegration.

Although models are necessary, they have several pitfalls. A model is only a representation of a thing or process according to the builder's biases and thinking styles. It can easily oversimplify matters, leave out subtle connections, or include products of imagination. Fancher and Frank (1997) state that while counseling and psychotherapy certainly help people, it is seldom for the reasons stated, and that their theoretical underpinnings are pseudoscientific accounts of how therapists think they help.

People approach work with a preexisting model, and search for data to confirm it, tending to ignore contradictions. For example, if an addict resists a diagnosis, counselors will tend to attribute it to resistance and denial rather than fear of sanctions or stigmatization, cultural differences, or anger at a counselor's power over him or her (Taleff 1997).

As stated earlier, many models are part of elaborate systems of belief (*ideologies*) that have fierce adherents. An ideology can be interpreted in a dogmatic and rigid fashion, with hostility toward any different approach (Myers 1991). The addictions and psychotherapy fields have always been factionalized, polarized, and ideologized. In the addictions field, this is compounded by the fact that many people feel that their system of belief is necessary to save lives; anything else is a potential disaster. For example, many recovering alcoholics are horrified at approaches such as Moderation Management that countenance controlled drinking strategies. Yet the tendency to demonize differences goes far beyond personal experiences with alcohol and other drugs, and speaks to fears among the citizenry at large. Harm-reduction approaches, which include methadone maintenance, needle-exchange programs, and legalization of marijuana for medical purposes, are pilloried as pro-drug, and sympathizers are described as part of a conspiracy favoring drug use.

Models also can refer to a specific array of techniques or organization of services to achieve a certain goal, such as the MATRIX model for methamphetamine addiction. A term similar to model is *paradigm*, which carries the connotation of a pattern that governs behavior and thinking rather than a mere description.

Counselors must be skilled at thinking critically about models of addiction and recovery, and counseling and treatment, rather than parrot what they have read or heard. It is unethical and dangerous to staff treatment programs with individuals who are not trained to evaluate critically the models they employ in counseling and treatment.

The Disease Model

The twelve-step philosophy of Alcoholics Anonymous and Narcotics Anonymous is not classified easily. It has elements of psychology, medicine, and spiritual teachings, and is also associated with the so-called *disease model*. In fact, there are many models that describe addictive disease. Many authors have examined various models of addictive disease (Conrad and Schneider 1980; Tournier 1979), and it is not within the scope of this text to review the history of moral, medical, psychological, and other models of addiction (Thombs 1999).

As many AA members interpret it, the disease model states that addiction is a lifelong disease, which is held in abeyance "one day at a time" and over which addicts are powerless. This dictates the need for complete abstinence and continuous membership in a recovery fellowship to ensure sobriety through reinforcement, support, and "keeping the memory green." The principle is that addiction is a disease that progresses inevitably.

A Progressive Disease

The concept of alcoholism as a progressive disease was formulated within the professional world by Jellinek, who described stages of alcoholic disease (1960). For members of AA and for those who have entered treatment in terrible shape after many failed attempts at sobriety, this certainly seems to be the case. But research with problem drinkers indicates that it is a mistake to generalize from that sample. Many addicts remain functional, many fluctuate in their levels of functioning, and others experience natural recovery or mature out of use (Granfield and Cloud 1996; Vaillant 1983; Waldorf and Biernacki 1977; Winick 1962). Some workers in the addictions field have avoided or dismissed information about spontaneous or natural recovery for fear it might damage the rationale for treatment or tempt patients to "go it alone." To the contrary, research by Prochaska and DiClemente (1982; Prochaska et al. 1994) on recovery from tobacco addiction without formal treatment has provided tremendous help in improving addictions treatment.

Relapse

Some proponents of the disease-progression model point to the fact that some addicts who relapse after years of sobriety seem to move very quickly into a severe addicted state. They present this as evidence that the disease was progressing even during sobriety, which is hard to explain scientifically. Other people look to factors such as defeat, shame, guilt, and loss of social support to account for catastrophic relapse. Proponents of cognitive-behavioral treatment of addictions state that as part of the vicious cycle of relapse, the first use of alcohol (or other addictive substance) after a period of sobriety triggers thinking such as, "Since I broke my abstinence, I might as well go on a binge" or "I can't face my AA sponsor and buddies after all this clean time" (Wright et al. 1993, p. 125). The cognitive-behavioral model of the relapse process (Marlatt and Gordon 1985, p. 38) can be summarized as follows: Individuals in a high-risk situation, who have not learned an adequate coping response, and who have low self-efficacy and positive expectations about using the substance, "pick up the first drink" (or drug). This triggers the Abstinence Violation Effect. The step of initial use is seen by the client as evidence of personal failure with attending guilt, shame, and embarrassment. That peers and professionals may indirectly convey agreement with this self-assessment only reinforces this sense of failure. Many clinicians believe that the ideology of "once a drunk, always a drunk" contributes to the expectation that relapse is inevitable or likely and gives permission for a single drink to become a total, catastrophic relapse.

It would be a mistake to assume that members of AA or NA remain stuck in some "folk model." Many addictions counselors have blended twelve-step or therapeutic-community philosophies with professional research. For example, Marlatt and Gordon's relapse-prevention system (1985) promotes learning coping responses for high-risk situations, which increases self-efficacy about sobriety efforts, thus decreasing the probability of relapse. This is congruent with the twelve-step admonition to "stay away from people, places, and things" associated with drinking or drugging, and "HALT: Don't get too Hungry, Angry, Lonely, or Tired." Prochaska, Norcross, and DiClemente (1994) see relapse as a normal part of the process of spiraling upward through stages of change.

Some practices in traditional addiction treatment had a rationale when they originated, but that rationale may have been lost. For example, take the intense confrontations and emotionality found in the traditional residential therapeutic community (TC). The original populations in the earliest TCs were tough, "macho" street addicts. When clinicians observed progress being made with addicts at Synanon in 1962, they contrived the theory that addicts were "encapsulated" behind a fortress of defenses, withdrawn character structures reinforced by chemical anesthesia whose treatment required a sledgehammer approach. They also followed the old model of emotion as something almost tangible, stored in the system like water in clogged plumbing. ("If you don't express all that anger you're carrying around, you're going to get out and shoot dope again!") In Alcoholics Anonymous, by contrast, there is a concern that the recovering alcoholic not dwell on anger and resentments, as seen in slogans such as "Live and let live," "Take it easy," and "Turn it over." Some clients (and even some of our interns) lasted about ten minutes in the intense, cathartic atmosphere of the therapeutic community, whereas others flourished. The point is to be aware of the model of emotion, and of treatment, found in various agencies and modalities and how it differs from how ordinary men and women relate to emotion.

··

Case in Point

Comparison of Therapeutic Models

Self-help philosophies, such as those found in Alcoholics Anonymous (AA) and in therapeutic communities, have inspired millions to attain sobriety. Unfortunately, some individuals see only one treatment philosophy as the "correct" path to recovery. Dogmatism aside, other critics claim that AA, NA, and therapeutic communities are used in a coercive manner contrary to the spirit of voluntary recovery, religious freedom, and basic democratic rights. According to these critics, when used in an involuntary institutional context, such as mandated referral into a 12-step-based rehab program or a therapeutic-community program in a prison, they are transformed into a coercive, authoritarian program. According to Dr. David Halperin (1991), therapeutic communities present all of the qualities found in totalitarian systems, such as North Korean "brainwashing" as described by Robert J. Lifton (1989). Stanton Peele and others (Peele et al. 2000) find that thousands of Americans are coerced into a religious dogma when mandated to AA or AA-based programs. Charles Bufe (1998), who has a similar perspective, differentiates between the very democratic, almost anarchistic, "communal" AA fellowship and the hierarchical "institutional" AA of treatment programs, which he likens to a cult.

Question for discussion: Are AA and therapeutic communities coercive and undemocratic when compared to governmental or industrial institutions? Consider the following scenarios:

- Atheistic drunk driver forced to attend AA
- Atheistic employee mandated to enter AA-based rehab
- Inmate put through prison-based harsh, confrontational therapeutic community

Case in Point

"I'm Very, Very Angry!"

A counselor trainee in an outpatient adolescent therapeutic community "confronted" relatives and friends and cried voluminously about past painful events, to their consternation. The trainee's elderly mother even called up the agency and accused them of "making my son crazy."

Another participant in this program got in trouble at his day job when, not having heard about a new paperwork requirement pertaining to documenting hours, his paycheck was held up. He promptly and loudly confronted the firm's controller, and he was reprimanded as a result.

Question for discussion: How much anger needs to be expressed, and in what context? Will "getting out" anger in counseling solve problems? What will happen if we don't express anger?

Addictions Treatment Comes of Age

As French sociologist Émile Durkheim stated a century ago, "All preconceptions must be eradicated" (Durkheim 1964, p. 31). Counselors should not take psychological or addictions models on faith, without critically evaluating the assumptions that underlie them. Rigid adherence to any ideological model can lead to overlooking diagnoses that do not fit its narrow interpretation of behavior. For example, the manic-depressive, or bipolar, mood disorder of one individual was ascribed to unresolved codependency issues. Another was chalked up to a dry drunk. Severe attention-deficit hyperactivity disorder of adolescent TC residents resulted in such things as failing to turn off a light; the adolescents were thrown into the category "irresponsible behavior" and subjected to a severe verbal reprimand or "haircut" (Myers 1991, p. 131). Counselors need to examine and continually re-examine the philosophical bases of treatment interventions in order to determine what helps rather than rely on hallowed tradition or sacred ritual. Indeed, the popular concept of codependency has been tremendously useful to people whose lives revolved around the addiction of another, harming both in the process. Nevertheless, as mentioned earlier in this chapter, everything from communism to manic-depression has, at one time or another, been attributed to codependency. Counselors must remain mindful of the limits of explanatory models and the dangers of dogmatically cutting everything to a single form. Keep in mind the myth of the Procrustean Bed. King Procrustes cut down his guests or stretched them on the rack to fit a single-sized bed.

Gradually, much of the dogmatism and factionalism surrounding addictions treatment has abated. Several old-style, tough-love therapeutic communities advertise that they have incorporated cognitive-behavioral approaches, and there are even therapeutic communities with methadone clients (De Leon et al. 1993). The field is maturing and professionalizing, and, as in clinical psychology, addictions treatment is increasingly putting together what is best from all models. This includes the structure and love in the therapeutic community, the recovery charisma and emphasis on vigilance against relapse of AA and NA, and the strategies to avoid relapse and to bolster self-efficacy of cognitive-behavioral approaches. Regardless of the philosophical mix adopted, all treatment conducts assessment-based, collaborative planning and assigning clients to an intensity of treatment that matches the severity of addiction. Even methadone program administrators have found that the success of their efforts is related directly to enhancement with counseling and other services (Anglin et al. 1993; McLellan et al. 1988).

Attitudes

An *attitude* is a state of preparedness or a mind-set to make a particular response. It has cognitive, emotional, and behavioral components. Many attitudes involve evaluations of persons, groups, or institutions. For example, you may believe that your uncle is smart or well informed, you may feel affection for him, and you may be predisposed to act respectfully and interested in what he says. His coworkers might disagree; they might dislike him and act indifferent to him. As a result of prejudicial attitudes, some people are judged superior and enjoy the benefits, whereas others are judged inferior and suffer the effects of discrimination.

People are rarely aware of the complexity of attitudes that help govern their behavior. Attitudes are acquired from early experiences, parental and peer influence, media, education, and belief systems. They are often self-fulfilling prophecies because a counselor's approach to clients often leads them to act in ways that counselors expect. Moreover, people may ignore information that does not fit their preconceptions (Taleff 1997). Attitudes toward addicts and addiction are especially endowed with meanings, emotional attributes, and ideology—all of which combine to act as a lens coloring the way people think about them. The CSAT's consensus document itemizes attitudinal components that pertain to each dimension of counseling addicts.[1]

ACTIVITY 11.2 "When I first heard the word . . ."

Memories can give us clues to our unrecognized attitudes and to their sources.

LEADER: Relax, close your eyes, and take a few deep breaths. Let go of present concerns as you let out a deep breath. Remember as far back as you can to the first time you heard the word *alcoholic,* or *drunk,* or *addict.* Remember the situation as clearly as possible. Take a few minutes to do this.

LEADER: How old were you? Who was present? What was going on at the time? What was being said? Who was saying it? Most important, what were you feeling?

PROCESS: Return to the here and now and regather either in small groups or in one large group. Volunteers share their experiences. Note the variety of experiences. It might be useful to have someone write down the opinions and feelings.

DISCUSS: How do our early experiences color our views of alcoholics and drug addicts? In what ways do we stereotype? In what ways might our beliefs keep us from seeing a problem that does not fit our stereotype? Why might drug addicts and alcoholics feel stigmatized?

FOLLOW-UP: Think about your first encounter with an alcoholic or a drug-addicted client. What were your fears, concerns, expectations, and other feelings and thoughts? What happened and in what ways did your experiences and biases affect the encounter?

Aside from the beliefs and attitudes that counselors have, it is important to be aware of general, societal attitudes about drugs and alcohol. Attitudes differ by culture, but in general, American society provides very conflicting and inconsistent messages about the use of, the abuse of, and addiction to drugs.

---

[1] The 1998 addiction competency consensus document (CSAT 2006) is subtitled "Knowledge, Skills, and Attitudes of Professional Practice." This underscores the importance of attitudinal training to complement the knowledge and skills that are the traditional domains of addictions (and other) counselors.

ACTIVITY (11.3) Words can hurt

As a group, brainstorm (for 5 minutes) a list of synonyms for getting drunk. Have someone record responses on one-half of the board or paper. Next, brainstorm (for 5 minutes) to think of synonyms for a drunk. Have the recorder write all these responses on the remaining half of the board or paper.

PROCESS: What did you notice about the list of words? Usually the words about getting drunk—smashed, bombed, stoned, and so on—seem violent but exciting. The words associated with a drunk—a bum, a no-good, a lush, and so on—are usually derogatory.

DISCUSS: What messages do the media give about alcohol, tobacco, and over-the-counter drugs? What messages do the media give about alcoholics and drug addicts?

Another aspect of attitudes is the judgment of the social and behavioral characteristics of subgroups of alcoholics, drug abusers, and addicts. This is often related to personal value systems being applied to the behavior of stereotyped clients. When engaging clients in treatment, counselors need to identify their own reactions and biases to situations. The variety of these includes sexual and physical abuse, exploitation of others, criminal behavior, and sexual orientation.

ACTIVITY (11.4) Do I have attitudes?

Read the following description of the fictitious people and rank them from 1 to 10 on the basis of how strongly you feel about their negative characteristics. Number 1 would represent the character you feel has the most negative characteristics and number 10 would have the fewest negative characteristics. For example, one might rank a person who deliberately gives a child an apple in which she has hidden razor blades as number 1 and a person who cheats on his diet by having a candy bar as number 10.

1. Rita is a mother who uses diet pills, tranquilizers, and booze, but gets upset when her kids use drugs.
2. Mrs. Elling, a school counselor, tells the parents of a student who has confided in her about his involvement with drugs.
3. Stan is a good provider, but he gets drunk occasionally and beats his wife.
4. Jackson sells a mixture of Nestlé's Quik and saccharine as mescaline for $3 a hit.

5. Mariah obtains a large supply of "reds" (barbiturates) and passes them around at school.
6. Mohammed, a 22-year-old man, has been drinking heavily at a party and decides to drive his buddies home in his parents' car.
7. Police Officer Gaudette knows of a 9th-grade drinking party and decides not to investigate because "kids will be kids."
8. Lee, a 17-year-old, turns his 12-year-old brother on to drugs.
9. Eldon constantly argues with his wife and causes family problems because he drinks and cannot hold a job.
10. Janice is addicted to heroin and steals in order to support her habit.

PROCESS: After each of you has ranked all the people in the list, break into groups of four to six members. In your group, see if you can come up with a consensus ranking. Think about criteria you used to decide ranking. Discuss the values and attitudes that went into the ranking.

Categories of Attitudes

The addiction competency consensus document (CSAT 2006) lists attitudes in every subarea of each practice dimension. For example, there are nine subareas of the practice dimension of screening, each of which enumerates from one to four attitudes. The entire document names close to 300 attitudinal elements of counselor competency. We have categorized these elements for an overview of broad goals of attitudinal training in addiction counseling. Almost all of the attitudes in the CSAT document fall into the following categories:

- Respect for or sensitivity to clients' needs, perceptions, interests, rights, and input
- Collaborative work and rapport with clients
- Understanding of and respect for the importance or value of each practice dimension and subdimension
- Flexibility, which is demonstrated by being open to a variety of approaches
- Professionalism, including collaboration with colleagues, patience and perseverance, and recognition of personal biases and limitations

Stigma

Case in Point

It's a Matter of Attitude

A methadone-maintenance (MM) client was known to regale the staff with hilarious interpretations of the political sexual scandals of 1997 and 1998.

One day this client showed a different side; he gave a somber account of a close friend at an MM program who had cancer. He and his friend had visited a prestigious research and treatment center, which had initially offered the friend medical attention. When they saw from the voluminous charts that the patient was an addict being treated on MM, the admitting staff abruptly asked them to leave. The MM client then took in his friend and cared for him until his death.

The methadone-maintenance client described in the Case in Point had many wonderful qualities that may be at variance with how many readers view this population. We described the negative attitudes that many, even those in the field, hold with regard to methadone clients. Sociologist Erving Goffman wrote over forty years ago about the concept of stigma (Goffman 1963). *Stigma*, which is the Greek word for a mark, refers to something like an imaginary stain that sets you off from others. Society stigmatizes people who are different or deviant, discrediting and damaging their identity and reputation and often dehumanizing and isolating them; this discredited person faces a rejecting world. People who are obese, disabled, mentally ill, or of transgendered identity are stigmatized, perhaps subtly, but stigmatized nevertheless. A great deal of effort in the public health field has been devoted to de-stigmatize physical and—more recently—mental illnesses. "Respectable" gay and lesbian couples now appear in the *New York Times* marriage announcement sections, but transgendered identity is still taboo.

Case in Point
Wheelchair Stigma

The wife of one of the authors broke her ankle and leg and was in a wheelchair for six weeks as a result. The author and wife noted that people talked loudly to her as if she were hearing impaired, and often smiled condescendingly or nervously. It was as if they automatically attributed impaired cognition and perception to a person in the category of "disabled."

Addictions are a major stigma, and people with addictions who participate in methadone programs, or who have a co-occurring psychiatric disorder and/or HIV, may have multiple stigmas, creating a huge barrier to self-esteem, successful recovery, and re-entry into society. Clients' diagnostic stigmata also add to other stigmatizing attributes: poverty, race, and social marginality.

Stigma affects people with alcoholism in two ways: externally, through rejection by friends, family, relatives, neighbors and employers; and internally, through aggravated feelings of rejection, loneliness, and depression. (Cosco A. Williams, at a 2000 Stigma Reduction Forum in Washington, DC. Quoted in Landry and Robinson [2001])

Addictions counselors must strive to help people with addictions to overcome external and internal stigmas.

"One of our tasks as treatment professionals is to help shift clients away from their self-stigmatizing focus on their imagined worthlessness, and to open their perceptions to the sources of strength and hope that already live inside them, their strengths and resiliencies." Pamela Woll (2001, p. 51)

Many people are influenced, often unwittingly, by social stigma and are predisposed to dislike or distrust those in deviant, stigmatized categories. Helpers must also honestly confront their own stigmatizing attitudes toward people with addictions. When we discussed the preceding Case in Point in class, a good proportion of the class admitted they thought of methadone clients as unredeemed "junkies" and con artists; pretty much beyond help and certainly more likely to break into your car than to care lovingly for an ill friend. These attitudes will be communicated to clients, which of course is not conducive to a therapeutic situation where the counselor treats the client with a great deal of empathy and personal regard—the basic requirements for a successful counseling relationship. Moreover, failure to recognize these attitudes will lead to an expectation of failure in treatment.

Many stigma-promoting theories about addiction are prevalent in society at large: that addiction is primarily a moral problem, a freely chosen immoral/illegal behavior; sinful or a spiritual deficit; or the result of poor willpower. Even some clinical paradigms concerning addiction promote stigma, for example, the belief that addiction is or is caused by a character/personality disorder and/or an addictive personality (there is no such beast) (Landry and Robinson 2001, p. 9).

One of the things a helper can do is simply to foster the use of non-stigmatizing language. Don't define people by their disorder: don't say "you are an addict" but rather a "person with an addictive disorder." Avoid sensationalizing addiction, as in "afflicted with," "victim of," or "the scourge of" addiction (Landry and Robinson 2001, p. 13). Even the title of a program can promote stigma. In July 2006 a New York City newspaper published pictures of proud graduates in caps and gowns, from the Mentally Ill Chemical Abuser Program of a well-known behavioral health agency. A student remarked sarcastically, "That's screaming 'I'm crazy and a junkie and here's my diploma to prove it.'"

Recovery movements often turn stigma on its head, wearing the badge of recovery proudly. The early therapeutic-community member described himself as an "ex dope-fiend." Alcoholics Anonymous called themselves "drunks." In the last six years, various state and local recovery support groups have sprung up to create pride in recovery. The Substance Abuse and Mental Health Services Administration (SAMHSA, U.S. HHS) has made stigma reduction one of its prime focus areas.

Attitudes and the Recovering Counselor

The addictions counselor who is also in recovery brings attitudes that affect the ability to play an objective and professional counseling role. There are many avenues by which recovering individuals enter the counseling occupation. For example, a graduate of a therapeutic community may have been hired immediately as a counselor aide, or an individual recovering from personal or family addiction may have pursued a degree in addictions counseling. The emotional experience of recovery or codependency can exert a powerful influence on counseling attitudes, as the following examples show.

Sponsoring

The counselor who has been a member of a recovery fellowship and has sponsored new members finds it gratifying to "give back" some of what was offered to him or her by extrapolating this into the counseling role. Among addictions students enrolled in the Project for Addiction Counselor Training in Newark, New Jersey (sponsored in the early 1990s by the Federal Center for Substance Abuse Treatment), the majority had sponsored recovering addicts in the fellowships of AA and NA, and the number of individuals each student had sponsored ranged from two to five.

Twelve-Stepping

Reaching out and helping other addicts, or *twelve-stepping*, is a cornerstone of maintaining one's sobriety. If counseling is seen as an extension of twelve-stepping, then the counseling role is seen (although the counselor may not be aware of this) as a means for the counselor to maintain abstinence. When a client fails, does not make progress, or relapses, the counselor may perceive that as a threat to his or her own sobriety, which might result in fear, anxiety, or anger.

Sponsorship and twelve-stepping involve a level of intimacy that is helpful and healing, but it is inappropriate in a professional counseling relationship. A confusion of these roles can lead to unprofessional attitudes toward the counseling relationship.

....

Case in Point

The Start of Something Big

In 1935 William Griffith Wilson, a sporadically employed stockbroker, was traveling alone through Akron, Ohio. An alcoholic whose drinking had almost destroyed his life, he had finally stopped drinking but feared for his sobriety. He contacted Robert Smith, a physician whose practice was suffering as a result of his deteriorating alcoholic state. They talked for hours, and not only did Bill Wilson stay sober, but Dr. Bob put down the bottle as well. Alcoholics talking to alcoholics began Alcoholics Anonymous, and it remains a core feature of "the program." Step Twelve encourages carrying the message to other alcoholics and, as it did for Bill, reinforces sobriety. In times of stress and doubt, members are encouraged to go out and speak with suffering, active alcoholics. Service, sponsorship, twelve-stepping, and meetings are all therapeutic components of the fellowship of Alcoholics Anonymous and other self-help programs.

The Counseling Mystique

The experience of recovery can create a counseling mystique on the part of recovering individuals, leading to unrealistic expectations about the job (Lawson et al. 1984, p. 4). Frequently counselor trainees, aides, and new counselors "crash" from the charismatic experience of seeing someone come off the street and announce, "My name is Tom. I'm an addict and I haven't used in a week," to the realities of dealing with repetitive paperwork, bureaucracy, and other routines of social service agencies. Such an individual, especially if his or her training has not been through an accredited institution of higher education or an institution that has not had its addiction training program approved by an accrediting body, may not have "recognition of the value of accurate documentation" (one of the attitudes desired in Addiction Counselor Competency # 70; CSAT 2006, p. 93).

Limited Perspective

The counselor not trained in an approved academic setting is likely to suffer because their training was focused on only one traditional model. Such a counselor will not have the required attitude of "valuing of diverse concepts, models, and theories" (CSAT 2006, p. 9) or "acceptance of the validity of a variety of approaches and models and openness to new, evidence-based treatment approaches, including pharmacological interventions" (CSAT 2006, p. 15). This observation applies equally to any single-focus or dogmatic training model, whether derived from a recovery tradition or a school of clinical psychology such as psychoanalysis or behaviorism.

Case in Point

Crack Moms: Supersized Stigma

Thirty years ago, sociologist Stanley Cohen said that throughout American history stigmatized, deviant "outsiders" are demonized into "folk devils" (e.g., witches, alleged communists, Satanists, gays). Disliked characteristics of these individuals or groups are amplified out of proportion and sensationalized into a threat, creating a "moral panic" followed by a "moral crusade" to punish or contain them (Cohen 2002). Drugs have spurred many moral panics: The "dope fiend" hysteria of the 1920s and 1930s, whipped up by the Hearst papers and Federal Bureau of Narcotics chief Harry Anslinger, prominently featured marijuana users, who were later portrayed as homicidal maniacs in the 1940 cult classic *Reefer Madness*.

Crack, crack babies, and crack mothers were the subjects of a moral panic in the late 1980s to early 1990s (Goode and Ben-Yehuda 1994). Admittedly, any parent who is addicted to a powerful stimulant will likely make a terrible parent, but the crack cocaine-smoking mother of the latter 1980s was portrayed in the media as relentlessly and inevitably abusive, immoral, negligent, and lacking in basic human qualities such as parental instinct (Boyd 2004; Humphries 1999; Murphy and Rosenbaum 1999; Reinarman and Levine 1997). Even addictions trainees were given handouts such as the 1990 *New York Times* clipping retrieved by Peter Myers at a conference entitled "Instincts of Parenthood Become Part of Crack's Toll" (Hinds 1990). (Space precludes an elaborate account of the "crack baby" myth, which fits hand-in-glove with the "crack mom" myth, other than to mention that many of the medical and neurological problems of babies born to crack addicts were due to alcohol, tobacco, and heroin use and poor nutrition [Goode and Ben-Yehuda 1994, pp. 9–11]). The "moral crusade" that ensued from this panic consisted of new, draconian laws pertaining to crack cocaine and to being an addicted parent. Prosecution and jailing of crack mothers were way out of proportion to, say, heroin-addicted mothers, simply on the basis of this "folk devil," super-stigma status. Pregnant mothers in Michigan and South Carolina were charged with the felony of "delivering drugs to a minor" by virtue of their passing of cocaine via the placenta, even when they were successfully completing drug treatment programs! (Humphries 1999, pp. 83–94). We can contrast the attributes described by Hinds (1990) to this quote from a 32-year-old crack user (Shedlin and Deren 2002, pp. 312–313), which demonstrates a complex set of emotions and feelings that would create some optimism in an addictions counselor that this person might be helped to contemplate change:

"Having a baby made me happy . . . I always wanted to be a mother . . . When I see my son I feel badly. I don't know how to be a mother.

I'm sorry man . . . I can't help it . . . but he understands me. He doesn't put me down . . . no matter what I am, I am his mother."

Contemporary writers Susan Boyd (2004), Erich Goode and Nachman Ben-Yehuda (1994), Drew Humphries (1999), Shiegla Murphy and Marcia Rosenbaum (1999), and Craig Reinarman and Harry Levine (1997), link the crack mom panic to the cultural politics of race, class, and gender: 80% of the prosecuted women were African American or Latino (way out of proportion with drug users who are of color), very poor, and had violated their sacred roles as reproducers and caregivers, and thus were fair game to be scapegoated and punished. Early twentieth-century drug panics were also tied into outsider groups, such as racial minorities and immigrant groups, as evident from the famous "Yellow Peril" (Kinder 1992).

Many of the authors we have just cited are associated with the "harm reduction" and decriminalization perspective. Their work is rarely found in addiction training settings, and their views and conclusions are often in sharp contrast to those of the treatment community. Familiarity with this work is useful in honing critical thinking skills with regard to treatment, and as a valuable resource in combating stigma. There is a staggering impact for treatment: the women carry with them tremendous guilt, internalized stigma, and expectations of punishment; recovery and social re-entry seem a "mountain too high." Treatment personnel face hurdles in treating these clients with unconditional personal regard and empathy, and in conducting a positive asset/strengths search in assessment and treatment planning.

References

Anglin, M. et al. 1993. "Enhanced Methadone Maintenance Treatment: Limiting the Spread of HIV among High-Risk Los Angeles Narcotics Addicts," in *Innovative Approaches in the Treatment of Drug Abuse.* J. Inciardi et al., eds. Westport, CT: Greenwood Press.

Boyd, S. 2004. *From Witches to Crack Moms: Women, Drug Laws, and Policy.* Durham, NC: Carolina Academy Press.

Bufe, C. 1998. *Alcoholics Anonymous: Cult or Cure?* Tucson, AZ: See Sharp Press. Retrieved 21 November 2011 from http://www.morerevealed.com/library/coc/

Cohen, S. 2002. *Folk Devils and Moral Panics,* 3rd ed. New York: Routledge.

Conrad, P., and J. W. Schneider. 1980. "Alcoholism: Drunkenness, Inebriety, and the Disease Concept," Chap. 4 in *Deviance and Medicalization.* St. Louis: Mosby.

CSAT (Center for Substance Abuse Treatment). 2006. *Addiction Counselor Competencies: The Knowledge, Skills, and Attitudes of Professional Practice (Revised).* CSAT Technical Assistance Publication Series 21, Rockville, MD: Substance Abuse and Mental Health Administration.

De Leon, G., S. Sacks, and R. Hilton. 1993. "Passages: A Modified Therapeutic Community Day Treatment Model for Methadone Clients," in *Innovative Approaches in the Treatment of Drug Abuse.* J. Inciardi et al., eds. Westport, CT: Greenwood Press.

Durkheim, E. 1964 (orig. 1895). "The Rules of Sociological Method," Chap. 1 in *What Is a Social Fact?* S. Lukes, ed. New York: Free Press.

Fancher, R. T., and J. D. Frank. 1997. *Cultures of Healing: Correcting the Image of American Mental Health Care.* New York: W. H. Freeman & Company.

Goffman, E. 1963. *Stigma: Notes on the Management of Spoiled Identity.* Englewood Cliffs, NJ: Prentice-Hall, Inc.

Goode, E., and N. Ben-Yehuda. 1994. "The American Drug Panics of the 1980s," Chap. 12, in *Moral Panics: The Social Construction of Deviance.* Malden, MA: Blackwell Publishers.

Granfield, R., and W. Cloud. 1996. The elephant that no one sees: Natural recovery among middle class addicts. *Journal of Drug Issues* 26(1): 45–61.

Halperin, D. A. 1991. Residential treatment: The potential for cultic evolution. *Cultic Studies Journal* 8(1): 46–60.

Hinds, M. de C. "Instincts of Parenthood Became Part of Crack's Toll." *New York Times*, March 17, 1990, A1.

Humphries, D. 1999. *Crack Mothers: Pregnancy, Drugs, and the Media.* Columbus, OH: Ohio State University Press.

Jellinek, E. M. 1960. *The Disease Concept of Alcoholism.* New Brunswick, NJ: Hillhouse Press.

Kinder, D. C. 1992. "Shutting Out the Evil: Nativism and Narcotics Control in the United States," pp. 117–142, in *Drug Control Policy.* W. O. Walker, ed. University Park, PA: Pennsylvania State University Press.

Landry, M., and R. Robinson. 2001. *A Guide to Reducing Addiction-Related Stigma.* Silver Spring, MD: Danya International.

Lawson, G. W., D. C. Ellis, and P. C. Rivers. 1984. *Essentials of Chemical Dependency Counseling.* Gaithersburg, MD: Aspen.

Lifton, R. J. 1989. *Thought Reform and the Psychology of Totalism.* Chapel Hill, NC: University of North Carolina Press (originally published in 1961).

Marlatt, G. A., and J. R. Gordon. 1985. *Relapse Prevention.* New York: Guilford Press.

McLellan, A. T. et al. 1988. "Counselor Differences in Methadone Treatment," in *Proceedings of Committee on Problems of Drug Dependence.* L. S. Harris, ed. NIDA Research Monograph no. 81, DHHS pub. no. ADM 88-1564. Rockville, MD: National Institute on Drug Abuse.

Moos, R. H. 2003. Addictive disorders in context: Principles and puzzles of effective treatment and recovery. *Psychology of Addictive Behaviors* 17(1): 3–12.

Murphy, S., and M. Rosenbaum. 1999. *Pregnant Women on Drugs: Combating Stereotypes and Stigma.* New Brunswick, NJ: Rutgers University Press.

Myers, P. 1991. "Cult and Cult-Like Pathways out of Adolescent Addiction," in *Special Problems in Counseling the Chemically Dependent Adolescent.* E. Smith Sweet, ed. New York: Haworth Press (orig. appeared in *Journal of Adolescent Chemical Dependency* 1991; 1[4]: 115–137).

_____. 2002. Beware of the man of one book: Processing ideology in addictions education. *Journal of Teaching in the Addictions* 1(1): 69–90.

Paul, R., and L. Elder. 2006. *The Miniature Guide to Critical Thinking.* Dillon Beach, CA: The Foundation for Critical Thinking.

Peele, S., L. Bufe, and A. Brodsky. 2000. *Resisting 12-Step Coercion.* Tucson, AZ: See Sharp Press.

Prochaska, J. O., and C. C. DiClemente. 1982. Stages and process of self-change in smoking: Towards an integrative model of change. *Psychotherapy* 20: 161–173.

Prochaska, J. O., J. C. Norcross, and C. C. DiClemente. 1994. *Changing for Good.* New York: William Morrow.

Reinarman, C., and H. Levine. 1997. *Crack in America: Demon Drugs and Social Justice.* Berkeley, CA: University of California Press.

Shedlin, M. D., and S. Deren. 2002. Cultural factors influencing HIV risk behavior among Dominicans in New York City. *Journal of Ethnicity in Substance Abuse* 1(1): 71–95.

Taleff, M. J. 1997. *A Handbook to Assess and Treat Resistance in Chemical Dependency.* Dubuque, IA: Kendall-Hunt.

Taleff, M. J. 2006. *Critical Thinking for Addictions Professionals.* New York: Springer.

The NA Way Magazine. 2003. Van Nuys, CA: Narcotics Anonymous World Services. Retrieved 21 November 2011 from http://www.na.org/?ID=nawArchive

Thombs, D. 1999. *Introduction to Addictive Behaviors,* 2nd ed. New York: Guilford.

Tournier, R. 1979. Alcoholics Anonymous as treatment and as ideology. *Journal of Studies on Alcohol* 40: 130–239.

Vaillant, G. E. 1983. *The Natural History of Alcoholism: Causes, Patterns, and Paths to Recovery.* Cambridge: Harvard University Press.

Waldorf, D., and P. Biernacki. 1977. Natural recovery from opiate addiction: A review of the incidence literature. *Journal of Drug Issues* 9: 281–290.

White, W. L. 1996. *Pathways from the Culture of Addiction to the Culture of Recovery.* Center City, MN: Hazelden.

Winick, J. C. 1962. Maturing out of narcotic addiction. *Bulletin on Narcotics* 6: 1.

Woll, P. 2001. *Healing the Stigma of Addiction.* Chicago: Great Lakes Addiction Technology Transfer Center.

Wright, F. D. et al. 1993. "Theoretical Rationale," in *Behavioral Treatments for Drug Abuse and Dependence.* NIDA Research Monograph 137, NIH pub. no. 93-3684. Rockville, MD: National Institute on Drug Abuse.

Abused Drugs

Depressants

Ethanol (ethyl alcohol or ethanol or beverage alcohol)
Beer, wine, vodka, gin, bourbon, scotch

Opioids
Codeine
Trade names: Empirin with codeine, Fiorinal with codeine, Robitussin A-C
Tylenol with codeine
Street names: Captain Cody, Cody, schoolboy (with glutethimide—a hypnotic sedative), hits, doors & fours, loads, pancakes and syrup

Fentanyl
Trade names: Actiq, Duragesic, Sublimaze
Street names: Apache, China girl, China white, dance fever, friend, good-fella, jackpot, murder, 8, TNT, Tango and Cash

Heroin
Generic name: diacetylmorphine
Street names: brown sugar, dope, H, horse, junk, skag, skunk, smack, white horse

Morphine
Trade names: Roxanol, Duramorph
Street names: M, Miss Emma, monkey, white stuff

Opium
Generic names: laudanum, paregoric
Street names: big O, black stuff, block, gum, hop

Meperidine
Trade name: Demerol
Street name: Demmies

Hydromorphone
Commercial: Dilaudid
Street names: D, dillies, dust, footballs, juice

Oxycodone
Trade names: Oxycontin, oxycodone with acetaminophen: Percocet, Oxycet, Roxicet, Tylox
Street names: OC, Oxy, Ox, oxycotton, hillbilly heroin

Hydrocodone (with acetaminophen)
Commercial: Vicodin, Lortab, Lorcet, Hydrocet
Street name: Vikes

Methadone
Trade names: Symoron, Dolophine, Amidone, Methadose
Street names: Dollies, Fizzies, Meth

Sedative-Hypnotics
Barbiturates
Commercial: Amytal, Nembutal, Seconal, phenobarbital
Street names: barbs, reds, red birds, phennies, tooies, yellows, yellow jackets

Methaqualone
Trade names: Quaalude, Sopor, Parest
Street names: ludes, mandrex, quad, quay, disco biscuits

Gluthemide
Trade name: Doriden
Street name: Cibas
In combination with codeine: C & C, cibas and codeine, hits, loads, doors and fours

Benzodiazepines (BZDs; benzos)
Generic and trade names (in parentheses):
lorazepam (Ativan), triazolam (Halcion), chlordiazepoxide (Librium), diazepam (Valium), alprazolam (Xanax), clonazepam (Klonopin), clorazepate (Tranxene), oxazepam (Serax), flunitrazam (Rohypnol)
Street names: forget-me-pill, Mexican Valium, R2, Roche, roofies, roofinol, rope, rophies
Other Street names for BZDs: candy, downers, sleeping pills, tranks, benzos

Miscellaneous Depressants
GHB (gamma-hydroxybutyrate)
Street names: G, Georgia home boy, grievous, bodily harm, liquid ecstasy

Cannabinoids
Hashish
Street names: boom, chronic, gangster, hash, hash oil, hemp
Marijuana
Street names: blunt, dope, ganja, herb, joint, Mary Jane, pot, reefer, sinsemilla, weed

Dissociative Anesthetics
Ketamine
Trade Name: Ketalar SV
Street names: cat Valiums, K, Special K, vitamin K
PCP (Phencyclidine) and analogs
Street names: angel dust, boat, hog, love boat, peace pill

Hallucinogens
LSD (lysergic acid diethylamide-25)
Street names: acid, blotter, boomers, cubes, microdot, yellow sunshines
Mescaline
Street names: buttons, cactus, mesc, peyote
Psilocybin
Street names: magic mushroom, purple passion

Stimulants
Amphetamines
Trade names: Biphetamine, Dexedrine
Street names: bennies, black beauties, crosses, hearts, LA turnaround, speed, truck drivers, uppers
Cocaine: cocaine hydrochloride
Street names: blow, bump, C, candy, Charlie, coke, crack, flake, rock, snow, toot
Ephedrine (ma huang)
Trade Name: Herbal Ecstacy
MDA (methylenedioxyamphetamine)
Street Name: Ecstacy, Love Drug, Mellow drug of America.
MDMA (methylenedioxymethamphetamine)
Street names: 007s, 69s, Adam, B-bombs, Batmans, Bean, Dex, Diamonds, Lover's speed, Smurfs, Snackies
Methamphetamine
Trade Names: Desoxyn
Street names: chalk, crank, crystal, fire, glass, go, fast, ice, meth, speed
Methylphenidate
Trade Name: Ritalin
Street names: JIF, MPH, R-ball, Skippy, the smart drug, vitamin R
Nicotine
Street names: bidis, chew, cigars, cigarettes, smokeless tobacco, snuff, spit tobacco

Inhalants
Solvents
paint thinners, gasoline, glues
Gases
butane, propane, aerosol propellants, nitrous oxide
Nitrites
isoamyl, isobutyl, cyclohexyl
Street names: laughing gas, poppers, snappers, whippets

Other Compounds
Anabolic steroids
Commercial: Anadrol, Oxandrin, Durabolin, Depo-Testosterone, Equipoise
Street names: roids, juice

For a more comprehensive list, see http://www.tcada.state.tx.us/research/slang/terms.pdf
More information on these categories of drugs is also available at http://www.drugabuse.gov/

Q

R